An introduction to URBAN GEOGRAPHY

By the same author

Housing and Residential Structure (with Keith Bassett, RKP, 1980)

An Introduction to Political Geography (RKP, 1982)

Urban Data Sources (Butterworths, 1980)

Housing in Britain: The Postwar Experience (Methuen, 1982)

The Urban Arena (Macmillan, 1984)

The Human Geography of Contemporary Britain (co-editor with Andrew Kirby, Macmillan, 1984)

An introduction to URBAN GEOGRAPHY

John R. Short

Routledge
London and New York

First published 1984 by Routledge & Kegan Paul Ltd
Reprinted 1987
Reprinted by Routledge 1989
11 New Fetter Lane, London EC4P 4EE
29 West 35th Street, New York, NY 10001

Set in Press Roman 10/11 by Columns of Reading
and printed in Great Britain by
T.J. Press (Padstow) Ltd, Padstow, Cornwall.

British Library Cataloguing in Publication Data
Short, John R. (John Rennie), *1951-*
An introduction to urban geography.
1. Urban regions. Geographical aspects
I. Title
910′.091732

ISBN 0-415-04520-7

Library of Congress Cataloging in Publication Data

Short, John R.
An introduction to urban geography.
Bibliography: p.
Includes index.
1. Cities and towns. 2. Anthropo-geography.
I. Title.
GF125.S56 1984 307.7′6 83-21176

ISBN 0-415-04520-7

TO ADRIENNE
as a larger token of my love

Contents

Preface

This book is written for first- and second-year students at universities, colleges and polytechnics taking courses in urban geography. The book was written for many reasons, but it primarily arose from my dissatisfaction with existing texts which seemed to be both parochial in concern and limited in outlook. Too few textbooks seemed, at least to me, to combine an awareness of the urban picture outside of North America with an appreciation of the social context of urban living. The emphasis was on urban structure, often at the expense of social process. This book is an attempt to make students aware of the variety in the urban condition and to introduce them to some of the relationships operating between space and society.

The book draws upon some of my previous work. Those seeking a fuller discussion of the range of approaches to cities should consult *Housing and Residential Structure*, while those wishing a more explicit account of the core-periphery model constantly used in the text should read *An Introduction to Political Geography*. For students wishing, or more likely being forced, to undertake project work, *Urban Data Sources* aims to provide an introduction to some source material. The work presented here is thus in one sense a survey of past work. But by pointing to important areas it also hopefully points to future lines of enquiry. The aim of all textbook writers should be to generate enough interest so that their work is eventually surpassed.

In writing this book my greatest debt is to my colleagues at the Department of Geography, University of Reading, who have provided a tolerant and supportive atmosphere in which I was given time and institutional space to develop my ideas. Andrew Kirby, Sophie Bowlby, Dave Foot, Mike Breheny, John Whittow and Peter Hall have all given me material and ideas which I have incorporated in this text. In particular a number of colleagues gave me access to their slide collections. The generosity was much appreciated and the specific debts are mentioned in the acknowledgments section, where the bland list conceals the sincerity of my gratitude. A special thanks to Chris and Tony Holland. Chris typed most of the manuscript and Tony kindly gave me access to his excellent picture collection.

Acknowledgments

To illustrate the text I have used a number of photographs from my own and my colleagues' slide collections. For taking the time and effort, and for allowing me to use their prints, I am grateful to the following: Dr Erlet Cater (plates 4, 5, 16, 17, 23, 24, 29, 52); Dr Stephen Fleming (48); Brian Goodall (12, 28, 36, 37, 40, 45); Professor Peter Hall (7, 13, 20, 21, 22, 32, 33, 38, 39); Tony Holland (2, 3, 8, 19, 46); Andrew Millington (9); Dr Russell Thompson (15); and Dr John Whittow (6, 18, 49, 50, 51); plates 43 and 47 were taken from Jill Posener's *Spray It Loud,* Routledge & Kegan Paul, 1982.

I am also grateful for permission to reproduce figures from the following sources: figure 2.1, from Institute of British Geographers, *Transactions,* vol. 4:3, 1979; figure 2.5, from B. J. L. Berry, *The Human Consequences of Urbanization,* Macmillan, London and Basingstoke, and St Martin's Press Inc., 1973; figure 2.6, from B. J. L. Berry and Q. Gillard, *Changing Shapes of Metropolitan America: Commuting Patterns, Urban Fields and Decentralization Processes, 1960-1970,* copyright © 1977, Ballinger Publishing Company; figure 3.2, from P. Hill and R. H. T. Smith, The spatial and temporal synchronization of periodic markets, *Economic Geography,* vol. 48, no. 3, 1972; figure 3.5, from R. E. Dickinson, *City and Region,* Routledge & Kegan Paul, 1964; figure 3.6, from A. Lösch, *The Economics of Locations,* Gustav Fischer Verlag, 1954; figure 3.7, from R. E. Preston, The structures of central place systems, *Economic Geography,* vol. 42, no. 2, 1971; figures 3.8 and 3.9, from R. Bromley and R. D. F. Bromley, The analysis of bus services in Ecuador, *Geographical Journal,* vol. 145, part 3, 1979, by permission of the Royal Geographical Society; figures 3B and 3C from Brian J. L. Berry, *Geography of Market Centers and Retail Distribution,* copyright © 1967, reprinted by permission of Prentice-Hall, Inc., Englewood Cliffs, N.J.; figure 3.10, from A. R. Pred, *The Spatial Dynamics of US Urban Industrial Growth, 1800-1914,* MIT Press, 1966; figure 3I, Isodemographic map of North America, 1975-6 by Eastman, Nelson and Shields, by permission of the Cartographic Laboratory, Queen's University, Kingston, Canada; figure 3J, from D. R. Vining and A. Strauss, A demonstration that the current decentralization of population in the United States is a clean break with the past, *Environment and Planning* A, 9, 751-8; figure 3.16, from P. Hall and D. Hay, *Growth Centres in the European Urban System*, Heinemann, 1980; figures 4.3, 7G, 9.7 from J.R. Short, *Urban Data Sources,* Butterworth, 1980; figure 4.8, from P. Rimmer, The search for spatial regularities in Australian seaports, *Geografiske Annaler,* 1967, by permission of Professor Claeson; figure 4.10, from D. Barker, *Area,* vol. 9, no. 4, by permission of the Institute of British Geographers; figures 4.12 and 11.8, from D. N. Parkes and H. J. Thrift, *Times, Spaces and Places,* John Wiley & Sons Ltd, 1980; figure 4.13, from D. Janelle, Central place development in a shrinking network, *Professional Geographer* 20, 5-10, by permission of the Association of American Geographers; figure 5.2, from D. E. Keeble, Models of economic development, in R. J. Chorley and P. Haggett (eds), *Models in Geography,* Methuen, 1967; figure 5.3, from K. Warren, *North East England,* Oxford University Press, 1973; figure 6.2, from D. M. Smith, *Human Geography: a Welfare Approach,* Edward Arnold, 1977; figure 6.3, from OECD, *The Impact of the Newly Industrializing Countries,* 1979; figure 6.4, from M. Frost and N. Spence, Policy responses to urban and regional change in Britain, *Geographical Journal* vol. 147 (3), 1981; figure 6.5, from J. R. Short, Urban policy and British cities, *Journal of the American Planning Association,* vol. 48, no. 1, 1982; figure 7A, from E. W. Burgess, *The City,* University of Chicago Press, 1925; figure 7.2, from D. Harvey, The political economy of urbanization, in G. Gappert and H. M. Rose (eds), *The Social Economy of Cities, Urban Affairs Annual Review* 9, Sage Publications, 1975; figure 7.3, from Harold Wolman, Housing and housing policy in the U.S. and U.K., in L. S. Browne, *The Geography of Housing,* Edward Arnold, 1981; figure 7.4 is loosely based on a figure from R. Morril, The negro ghetto, *Geographical Review,* 55, 1965; figure 7.6, from Robert Murdie, Factorial ecology of metropolitan Toronto, *Research Paper 116,* Department of Geography, University of Chicago; figure 7.7, from J. Patrick, *A Glasgow Gang Observed,* Eyre Methuen, 1973; figure 8.2, from P. Hall, *Urban and Regional Planning,* 1975, by permission of A. D. Peters Ltd and Penguin Ltd; figure 8.3, from J. M. Thompson, *Great Cities and their Traffic,* Victor Gollancz Ltd, 1977; figures 8B-8F, from K. Jones and A. M. Kirby, Provision and wellbeing, *Environment and Planning,* by permission of Dr J. H. Ashby; figure 8G, from P. Hall, *Great Planning Disasters*, Weidenfeld & Nicolson, 1980, by permission of Weidenfeld & Nicolson Archives; figures 9.2 and 9.6, from D. Harvey, The urban process under capitalism, *International Journal of Urban and Regional Research* 2, 1, 1978, published by Edward Arnold; figure 9.3, from J. S. Adams, Residential structure of mid-western cities, *Annals of The Association of American Geographers*, 60, 1970; figure 9.5, from P. Ambrose, Who plans Brighton's housing crisis?, *Shelter Land Report* no. 1, 1976; figure 10.2, from R. Bennett, *The Geography of Public Finance,* Methuen & Co., 1980; figure 11.1, from K. Lynch, The Image of the City, MIT Press, 1960; figure 11.2, from P. Orleans, Differential cognition of urban residents, *Science, Engineering and the City,* no. 1498, by permission of the National Academy of Engineering Press, Washington, 1967; figure 11.3, by permission of Florence V. Thierfeldt; figure 11A, from James D. Harrison and William A. Howard, The role of meaning in the urban image, *Environment and Behaviour,* vol. 4, no. 4, copyright © 1972 Sage Publications Inc., with permission; figure 11.4, from D. Ley, *The Black Inner City as Frontier Outpost,* Association of American

Geographers, monograph series, no. 7, 1974; figure 11.5, from S. Weir, Red line districts, *Roof,* July 1976; figure 11.6, from BBC Audience Research Department, *What the People are Doing,* 1965; figure 12C, from F. Sandbach, *Environment, Ideology and Policy*, Basil Blackwell, Oxford, 1980.

Part 1

Setting the Scene

1 Introduction

DEFINING TERMS

The aim of this book is to introduce you to the field of study known as urban geography. There is no one accepted definition of urban geography. It is a shorthand notation for a set of concepts, techniques and theories applied to a particular area of reality we call urban. This introductory chapter affords us the opportunity to consider each of these two main elements in some detail.

Changing approaches

The body of theories which have been applied by geographers to urban areas has varied over time, indeed it varies by geographer. We can identify four distinct approaches:

1 **The ecological approach** grew out of the work of the Chicago-based sociologists in the early part of this century. The work of Burgess and Park was concerned with applying the princiiples of ecology to the urban area. Particular emphasis was placed on the study of specific neighbourhoods and on identifying the spatial patterns of urban social structure. The best-known example of this approach is the concentric model formulated by Burgess. The elaboration of the ecological principles outlined by the early workers has all but ceased as a major academic exercise. Most people no longer take the ecological principles as anything more than extended metaphors. Subsequent work in the ecological tradition has concentrated on identifying different sub-areas of the city. There has been a growing sophistication in the techniques used to identify the different fragments of the urban social mosaic. But much of the contemporary work on identifying residential neighbourhoods of the city owes a great deal to the early human ecologists and subsequent commentators.

2 **The neo-classical approach** takes its basic orientation from neo-classical economics which pictures the economy as a harmonious system in which firms seek to maximise profits and households maximise their net benefits (termed utility). The neo-classical approach seeks to understand how the distribution of different land uses in social groups comes about in the city with reference to profit maximisation on the part of firms and utility maximisation on the part of households. This approach focuses on the choices open to households and firms rather than the constraints. For this reason it has been criticised and many have argued that the neo-classical approach ignores too much of contemporary urban reality.

3 **The behavioural approach.** Discontent with the grand generalisation of the previous approaches has led to the emergence of an explicitly behavioural approach which stresses the behavioural basis to aggregate social processes and urban spatial patterns. This approach focuses on human perception of the city and individual decision-making in urban areas.

4 **The structuralist approach** is not one approach but a number of different strands. The broad emphasis is on treating cities and urban phenomena as part of the wider view of society. Individual decisions are seen to arise from an environment structured by broader-scale social and economic processes. Thus, in the structuralist approach, it is considered impossible to understand individual households' housing

decisions without reference to the structure and functioning of the housing market.

Within each of the broad approaches outlined there are variations. In the ecological approach there is a difference between the early workers who stressed ecological principles and the later work of urban social geographers who were and are much more aware of the individual decision-making processes which underlie aggregate spatial patterns and the social processes which structure the urban environment. In the structuralist approach we can identify the two strands (a) the institutional variant, which seeks to identify the main agents and institutions which shape the city, and (b) the more recent emergence of an explicitly marxist interpretation which seeks to draw out the connections between economic structure, social classes and the production and consumption of urban space. The four approaches outlined are broad terms which cover a variety and diversity of work.

These different approaches have sometimes been associated with different methods of analysis. The neo-classical approach, for example, has long used mathematical models while the behavioural approach has often been reliant on questionnaires. This methodological division has sometimes led to the erroneous belief that some methods are only consistent with certain approaches. This is incorrect. Just because your theoretical adversaries monopolise a certain method does not invalidate its wider use. This book is firmly based on the belief that in order to understand the complex urban world a variety of methods are needed. An understanding of the city is a difficult prize to attain, and one which is not won by any single line of attack.

This book aims to provide you with an indication of the range of approaches. Some of the chapters draw heavily on some approaches rather than others while the general flavour of the book is to show the ways in which elements of the behavioural and structural approaches can be combined in order to understand the city. Less emphasis is placed on the neo-classical approach, while the ecological approach is mentioned only at a number of key points.

The city

The field of enquiry of urban geography is urban areas, what we generally call towns and cities. The treatment of the urban has varied. Nineteenth- and early twentieth-century commentators, perhaps overwhelmed by the scale and pace of urbanisation, tended to view the city as an independent unit of enquiry. They thought it legitimate to append the adjective 'urban' to all manner of things. Habits still persist and we thus have 'urban' problems, 'urban' issues, 'urban' geography, 'urban' sociology and 'urban' studies. There were exceptions. Henry George, Thorstein Veblen, Frederick Engels and Karl Marx were amongst those who sought to relate an understanding of societies to an understanding of cities. This has also been the aim of much recent work in urban geography which sees the separation into the different disciplines and subsequent sub-disciplines as merely a convenient division of academic labour but not a reflection of the way society is structured. This book shares that belief. In this text the city will be identified as a useful object of analysis but not one independent from the nature of the wider society. A guiding principle of this book will be to integrate the study of cities and urbanism to a wider view of how society works. I will seek to show how wider social theories can be brought to bear on the analysis of the city and how an understanding of cities can enrich our view of society.

RECURRING THEMES

From the broad aim of seeking to show the relationships between urbanism and society flows a number of sub-themes. These reappear in slightly different forms throughout the exposition.

1 **The importance of cross-cultural comparisons and contrasts.** Most urban geography textbooks have a degree of parochialism which for geography textbooks is very disturbing. The rich diversity of world urbanism, the subtle nuances in the urban process in different societies and the noticeable differences of the city as lived experience in various countries seem to be reduced by most textbooks to either intellectual insignificance or to

the chauvinistic status of variations on a North American theme. The purpose of this book is thus twofold; to present an urban geography textbook which by virtue of its structure and exposition provides a fresh insight into that generator of economic, social and political change, the city, and which also allows cross-cultural contrasts to be made. Of course great care has to be taken in using a cross-cultural approach since it is all to easy to slip into a tourist-guide style which breathlessly surveys topics of local interest. The rich diversity of world urbanism cannot be covered in a book of this kind. However, by judicious selection of case studies it is hoped to highlight patterns of urbanisation in third-world countries and socialist countries. The main co-ordinates of the contemporary world order are a north-south dimension, to use the terminology of the Brandt report, although it is also termed core-periphery and an east-west dimension between centrally planned economies and capitalist economies. Most urban geography textbooks would thus seem to be concentrating on only one quadrant of these co-ordinates, the rich capitalist countries. But it is important to consider patterns of urban life in other societies in order to avoid the parochial view that cities of the world are merely variations on the basic theme found in Chicago. In most chapters, therefore, cross-cultural material will be presented at the appropriate points. The terms core and developed will be used interchangeably with reference to rich countries, such as USA and UK, while the terms periphery and third world will be used with reference to the poor countries of the world.

2 **Re-distributional consequences.** The city can be seen as an arena in which groups bargain, compete and come into conflict over scarce resources. It is important to make assessments of the outcomes. Thus a major element of this book will be to assess the re-distributional consequences of social processes and spatial patterns. We need to identify urban winners and urban losers. Often, the conflict expresses itself in the general form of a tension between equity considerations and those of efficiency. Efficiency can be measured in various ways: in capitalist countries profit maximisation is the general criterion while in centrally planned economies minimisation of costs is important. There is often a tension between the efficiency of individual firms or of public sector institutions and equity considerations. While it may be efficient for a firm to locate its manufacturing base in a suburban location, this denies job opportunities to central city residents unable to travel long distances to work. These considerations need to be borne in mind when looking at social processes and spatial structure.

3 **The role of government.** One of the most important actors in the urban scene is the government. Even in the capitalist countries the role of the government is large and it has been growing. An analysis of their role, form and function of government should thus play a central role in our analysis. In much of the geographical literature the study of public policy has been weak. But public policy impacts have a huge role in shaping urban areas. Although the role of the local government is examined in detail in chapter 10, throughout all of the book the role of the government is considered a key element in the analysis. The state is seen as an arena for struggle; in some instances the arena is held by one dominant group, but throughout most of the time, however, there are competing groups. The laws define the rules of the game while the legislation indicates the outcome of the struggles. The state's role is *regressive* when, as in the case of the urban renewal programmes of the 1960s and 1970s, public policy aids the rich and disadvantages the poor; *progressive* policies are those which re-distribute income from rich to poor.

Presented in this general form the major sub-themes of the book lack historical depth and explanatory width. In the subsequent pages life is breathed into these categories by analysis of actual events.

A NOTE TO THE READER

Each author when writing a book has a particular type of reader in mind and a broad aim in sight. Since I am no exception, readers may find it useful if I make the following points. My ideal reader is one who comes to this book with an enquiring mind eager to learn and unwilling to accept easy answers. When writing this book I did not assume that readers had taken any specific courses, although a general background in the social sciences as a whole is relevant. Through reading the book I hope the reader will become more interested in the work done and the work that needs to be done in this area. I hope I have presented enough food for thought and stimulated curiosity. Ultimately my ideal reader should end up dissatisfied with the book. All textbooks are only partial because they attempt to cover existing knowledge at one point in time, but reality is constantly changing. The book is a battle report not a victory salute. The campaign continues.

GUIDE TO FURTHER READING

There are a vast number of textbooks on urban geography. Amongst the general readers see:

Blowers, A., Brook, C., Dunleavy, P. and McDowell, L. (eds) (1982), *Urban Change and Conflict*, Harper & Row, New York.

Bourne, L.S. (ed.) (1982) (second edition), *Internal Structure of the City*, Oxford University Press, London.

Bourne, L.S. (ed.) (1978), *Systems of Cities*, Oxford University Press, London.

Brunn, S.D. and Wheeler, J.O. (eds) (1980), *The American Metropolitan System: Present and Future*, Edward Arnold, London.

Dear, M. and Scott, A.J. (1981), *Urbanisation and Urban Planning in Capitalist Society*, Methuen, London.

Knox, P.L. (1982), *Urban Social Geography*, Longmans, London.

Ley, D. (1983), *A Social Geography of The City*, Harper & Row, New York.

and the successive volumes of *Geography and The Urban Environment* edited by D.J. Herbert and R.J. Johnston, published by John Wiley.

General introductions to the different approaches in human and urban geography include:

Bassett, K.A. and Short, J.R. (1980), *Housing and Residential Structure: Alternative Approaches*, Routledge & Kegan Paul, London.

Gregory, D. (1978), *Ideology, Science and Human Geography*, Hutchinson, London.

Johnston, R.J. (1983) (second edition), *Geography and Geographers: Anglo-American Human Geography Since 1945*, Edward Arnold, London.

Johnston, R.J. (1983), *Philosophy and Human Geography*, Edward Arnold, London.

Different views of the city are discussed in:

Saunders, P. (1981), *Social Theory and the Urban Question*, Hutchinson, London.

Smith, M.P. (1980), *The City and Social Theory*, Basil Blackwell, Oxford.

Regular papers on urban geography appear in a variety of journals. The following is a sample of the range:

Environment and Planning A, (and D), Progress in Human Geography, International Journal of Urban and Regional Research, Economic Geography, Antipode, Urban Studies, Urban Geography, Urban Affairs Quarterly, Cities, Built Environment.

2 The Urban Transformation

'Towns are so many electric transformers. They increase tension, accelerate the rhythm of exchange and ceaselessly stir up men's lives.' (Braudel, 1973)

INTRODUCTION

Cities are transformers of historical change. They have been the scene and setting throughout human history of major social, economic and political change. In the subsequent pages we will look at the major points of rupture in the urban story. The tale will be selective. There are a number of books which look at the broad sweep of the city in history. The purpose of this chapter is more modest; it will be to concentrate on those key periods in which the city condensed and reflected changes in the organisation of society. The reflection of these changes on city form and function will be noted.

THE FIRST CITIES

The very first cities marked a change in human settlement. But before cities could arise, a number of preconditions had to be met. Since urbanisation involved the creation of non-agricultural occupations, there had to be a surplus of food in order to feed the population not directly involved in food production. The existence of a food surplus implied a degree of human control over the environment which allowed levels of agricultural productivity above subsistence levels. The first cities grew in the wake of the agricultural revolution of the neolithic period (8000-3500 BC) which saw domestication of animals, the development of cereal production and a growing sophistication in technology including irrigation techniques. The creation of surplus also meant a degree of control over the farmers in order to make them produce a surplus. The collection and distribution of surplus supposed a class of people who were able to exercise power over the food producers. The first cities were loci of power.

Trade was the life blood of the early cities. Trade was conducted over long and short distances and in both rare and mundane commodities. Trade kept the craftsmen going in raw materials and provided the goods which adorned the temples. The largest cities grew up along major trading routes and these routes emanated from the very first cities like the spokes from a hub of a wheel.

The very first urban settlements grew up in Mesopotamia between the two rivers Euphrates and Tigris (Mesopotamia is Greek for, 'between two rivers'). They emerged near the end of the neolithic period between 4000 BC and 3000 BC. The dates are necessarily hazy because we still do not have definite knowledge. Subsequent archaeological research may push back the date of the very first urban settlements. Paul Wheatley has identified seven areas of primary urbanisation: Mesopotamia, the Indus valley, the Nile valley, the north China plain, Mesoamerica, central Andes and, south west Nigeria. By primary Wheatley means that in these areas urbanisation was generated through internal forces rather than through secondary diffusion from other areas.

The exact form of cities in these different areas of urbanisation differs, but there are broad similarities. The form of the cities reflected their origins. Most of them were walled to keep out marauders and hostile neighbours; the early settlements were sites of communal defence. The city walls marked an important division between protected and unprotected sites. But protection had to be paid for. The walls also marked off an area of control. Within the city walls the population came under the direct control of the ruling elite. Within the walls there was a marked residential segregation. Grouped around the city centre was the ruling elite. Further away from the centre were the lower

THE PRE-INDUSTRIAL CITY

The urban historian Gideon Sjoberg makes a distinction between the form and characteristics of cities before and after the industrial revolution. The typical pre-industrial city, according to Sjoberg, has the following characteristics:

1 It is small, population less than 100,000 with a low population growth.
2 The city centre is the hub of governmental and religious activity.
3 There is a threefold class structure: (a) the elite who live in the centre, (b) a lower class of merchants and artisans situated around the centre, and (c) an outcaste group of slaves, and minority ethnic and religious groups, who live on the extremities of the city. There is a rigid class division reinforced by differences in location, speech, manners and dress.
4 There is minimum land use specialisation. Sites are multi-purpose, there is no separation between home and workplace.
5 Economic activity is regulated by the various guilds.

Sjoberg's model has provided the basis for much subsequent work.

References

Langton, J. (1975), Residential patterns in pre-industrial cities, *Transactions of Institute of British Geographers*, 65, 1-27.

Radford, J.P. (1979), Testing the model of the pre-industrial city: the case of ante-bellum Charleston, South Carolina, *Transactions of the Institute of British Geographers, New Series* 4, 392-410.

Sjoberg, G. (1960), *The Pre-Industrial City: Past and Present*, Free Press, Chicago.

Table 2.1 Areas of primary urban generation

Area	*Beginning of urban period*	*Cities*
Mesopotamia	4000-3500 BC	Lagash, Ur, Uruk
Egypt	3000 BC	Memphis, Thebes
Indus	3000-2250 BC	Mohenjo-dara, Harappa
China	2000 BC	Cheng-Chon, An-yang
Mesoamerica	1000 AD	Teotihuacán, Tenochtitlán
Central Andes	500 BC	Cuzco, Tihuanaco
S.W. Nigeria	1000 AD	Sagamu, Owo

Source: after Wheatley, 1971

class and outcastes (see Figure 2.1). The central area of the city was the site of the palace housing the apex of the social hierarchy and the granary, the community store house, and the temples. The religious places had special significance. The management of the surplus was partly based on force. But force is only a useful method of control in the short term. In the long term stronger bonds between the managed and the managers have to be formed. Religion in its various guises provided the justification for the status quo. Religion provided the cement binding the urban society and its rural

THE CITY AS SYMBOL

Urban centres, according to the historical geographer Paul Wheatley, grew up as ceremonial complexes. The complexes, which consisted of temples, shrines and palaces, developed in places where the ruling elite controlled the surplus of agricultural production necessary to maintain the urban population of priests, warriors, craftsmen and nobility. The first cities were the foci of power – power which was legitimised with reference to sacred appeal. To maintain the cohesion of these early societies more than just brute force was required. The existing social relations were seen to reflect a cosmic order, the chieftain or king was thus seen as being closer to the gods if not a god himself. Cities took on symbolic qualities as well as the more mundane role of an organising centre for managing and redirecting surplus. The cities contained the sacred space of worship; in Wheatley's words, 'they were symbols of cosmic, social and moral order'. The hierarchical society was reflected in the built form with sacred spaces and kingly residence as the apex of the social pyramid firmly centred at the heart of the city.

Through the ages the built form of cities has continued to reflect social relations. The early towns of the feudal period were dominated by the barons' castles and in the medieval period, when religion was a powerful force, huge cathedrals dominated the urban skyline.

The pattern continues. In advanced capitalist countries the business district constitutes the pivotal point of the city. Indeed we use the term *central* business district. The form of individual buildings takes on significance. The skyscraper has become as much a symbol of corporate virility as a place of work. It is not incidental that the largest building in Warsaw is the Soviet-built headquarters of the Polish Communist Party. The big corporation and the powerful state apparatus seek reflection of their status and power in the buildings which they occupy.

The city is more than just a collection of buildings. The built form is a non-verbal communication of symbols and images.

References

Leach, E. (1976), *Culture and Communication. The Logic by which Symbols are Connected*, Cambridge University Press.

Wheatley, P. (1971), *The Pivot of the Four Quarters: A Preliminary Enquiry Into the Origins and Character of the Ancient Chinese City*, Edinburgh University Press.

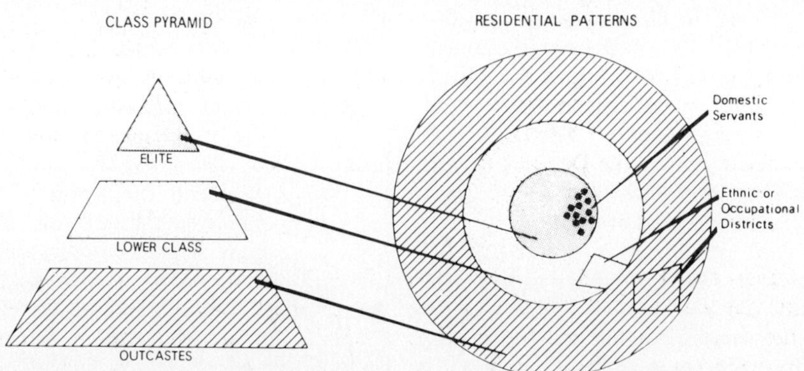

Figure 2.1 Relationship between class structure and the pre-industrial city
Source: after Sjoberg, 1960 and Radford, 1979

hinterland together. The temples took on symbolic importance. There were the buildings which gave substance to the ruling ideology. The temples dominated the urban landscape of the early cities towering above individuals and their dwellings (see Plate 2).

The early cities led a precarious existence. Susceptible to natural calamities of flood and silting of irrigation channels, they were beset by the man-made disasters of war and epidemics. Most of the very first cities fell to one or other of these disasters. Most of the very first cities are now eerie ghost towns echoing with the voices of distant conversations in bygone eras.

THE CLASSICAL CITY

The first cities, whose artifacts now are found in museums and galleries, are not immediately accessible to the contemporary observer. We squint at Egyptian hieroglyphics and only half understand Aztec cosmology. The first cities are important in human history but they fail to ignite more than our curiosity. The cities of classical Greece, in contrast, evoke admiration as well as wonder. Greek urban civilisation of the first millennium BC has been a cultural yardstick with which later civilisations have measured and modelled themselves. We still use the word barbarian (initially used with reference to someone who does not speak Greek) to refer to uncultured and unsophisticated people, and up until recently an education was considered lacking if the study of Greek was not included.

The Greek city state (the polis) emerged in what has been termed the Greek dark ages (1200-900 BC). Before this the eastern Mediterranean had seen the rise and fall of the Minoan culture centred on Knossos in Crete and then the Mycenean culture based in Peloponnese. The Myenean civilisation was destroyed by the Dorians, Greek-speaking tribes from the north west highlands of Greece, and seafaring migrants of the east.

The Greek dark ages officially end in 776 BC when the very first Olympic Games took place. The era opened with a number of small city states ruled by aristocrats. Although the city states were independent one from another – many of them refused to use a common calendar – they had a unity of language, culture and religion which allows us to speak of them as a whole.

Inside the city state there was an intense political struggle. The city state was originally ruled by an oligarchy of aristocrats, but the story over the next three centuries was one of more power being obtained by the mass of people. The Greek word for common people is demos, hence democracy. By the fifth century BC Athens had reached the zenith of democracy. Every Athenian citizen could sit on juries and hold public office. Public participation, involving the rotation of public offices, amongst citizens was encouraged. The urban historian, Lewis Mumford, sees the voice of the village in the Greek polis in that the more communal, reciprocative system of the village was transformed into urban democracy. To be sure, there was an undemocratic side. Women and slaves were not allowed to vote, many obstacles were placed on those attempting to gain citizenship, and politics was dominated by the rich who could afford the time. Nevertheless the idealised version of Greek democracy has continued to exercise its hold over the western imagination. When citizens of the USA, France or Britain set up town councils, they follow in the trail first set down by the ancient Greeks.

The rise and growth of the Greek polis went hand in hand with what the art historian E.H. Gombrich has termed the 'great awakening', to refer to the way in which artists and sculptures began to use their eyes in representing the human form. There is a world of difference between ancient Egyptian and classical Greek painting and sculpture. The latter appears to us more lifelike, more realistic, more accessible and ultimately more beautiful. In drama we see the development of the tragedy in the work of Aeschylus, Sophocles and Euripides; and the comedy in the work of Aristophanes and Menander. In science Anaximander in the sixth century is thought to have produced the first map of the known world, Pythagaros extended the world of mathematics, and Hippocrates emphasised the importance of hygiene to good health. In philosophy and ethics the writings of Plato, Aristotle, Diogenes and Epicurus still figure largely in western philosophical thought. Wedged between two dark ages, the great awakening is like a huge flame of human ingenuity, enterprise and intellectual endeavour.

The classical Greek experience was an explicitly

Plate 2 The history of the now ruined city of Ephesus (in Turkey) captures some of the urban experience of the classical period. It grew as a major trading centre in the sixth and fifth centuries BC

Plate 3 Alexander the Great captured the city in 333 BC. It came under Roman control in 133 BC, eventually becoming capital of Roman Asia. It was visited by St Paul, who wrote an epistle to the Christians in the city. It was sacked by the Goths in the third century AD and fell into decline

urban one. Questions of urban administration dominated political and philosophic debates. Both Plato and Aristotle, for example, spent considerable time discussing the ideal city, its form, size and administration. And when Greeks colonised abroad they established cities. For the Greeks civilisation was an urban affair. It is not accidental that not only do we get politics and policy from the Greek word 'polis', we also get politeness.

The form of the Greek city changed through time. The city states which emerged from the dark ages were small places with a population probably less than 20,000, with poor sanitation and no clear-cut plan. The cities were often built around sacred hills – an acropolis which provided religious significance – and good defensive positions. The houses grew up around the hill, producing a mazy pattern of unplanned streets winding around public and private buildings. As the years passed urban planning came to the fore in setting up new cities and in reconstructing those destroyed by natural calamities or barbaric enemies. Thus when Miletus was sacked by the Persians in 494 BC, a blank cheque was provided to the builders. The new town was constructed on the grid square principle, with standardised city blocks with a segregation of function, and an agora, a public open space, acting as a potential meeting point surrounded by symbolic buildings. There is an inverse correlation between the vibrancy of ancient Greek culture and the planning of cities. In the development of the polis from 700 BC up until 400 BC the culture was at its most vibrant and urban planning was weak. The greatest cultural advances were made in small, dirty, unsanitary, crowded, squalid cities. In later centuries streets were widened, garbage was disposed of and there was a regular iron pattern. Cultural advances, however, had declined.

The Romans were to extend the Greek urban tradition throughout the known world. As conquerers, the Romans established cities laid out on grid plans and built public open spaces and public buildings such as the forum and the baths. The Romans did more than take the former cities, they also accepted the notion of the city as a centre for culture. The terms city and civilisation have the same Latin root.

THE MERCHANT CITY

In that 900-year period between the end of the dark ages and the beginning of the industrial revolution, cities were an important scene in the transformation of society. In Europe they were the shell in which took place the change from the feudal to a capitalist society.

Towards the end of the first millennium AD western Europe was a feudal, rural society. The mass of people worked on the land and peasants had to give up some of their surplus produce and labour power to the local lord. The ideological cement came from Christianity which legitimised the rigidly hierarchical society. Religion was of supreme importance and something of its power can be seen in its towering cathedrals which even today dominate the urban scene.

Feudal Europe was a slow, small-scale society, and interaction was minimal. In this sea of rural feudalism towns sprang up as islands of trade and industry. There was both short-distance exchange in the basic commodities which grew as agricultural production increased, and long-distance trade in luxury goods such as spices, gold and silver, prompted by the whims of the rich and the concentrated buying power of the Catholic church. Trade increased from the tenth to the thirteenth centuries as did the towns. The growth of trade also saw the growth of the merchants as a class. After the aristocracy and the prelates they formed the third estate. They tended to be landless sons of peasants looking for a living in the interstitial areas of the rigid framework of feudalism. The lack of economic integration meant disparities in prices and in the supply and demand of commodities. Merchants connected suppliers and buyers, and by buying cheap and selling dear they could make a living and a profit. The merchants congregated in the towns. The feudal fortress gathered around its walls groups of dwellings, and the ecclesiastical towns provided the home for priests, prelates, deacons and acolytes kept alive by church tithes and wealthy endowments, but the merchant town became the centre of activity. The merchants congregated in space and in economic enterprise. Trade in the medieval period, especially long-distance trade, was a risky business. Merchants tended to band together in chartering one ship or a fleet of ships so that if anything went wrong the risk was spread widely. By the twelfth century the

Figure 2.2 Venice in 1500

nucleus of the old feudal towns were swamped by the aggressive merchant towns and cities where the market place and the rich merchants' houses were jostling with the dwellings of the aristocracy and the churches for attention in the urban landscape.

The growing towns attracted industry. An urban location assumed better supply and easier sale. The most important industry in the first merchant cities of Europe was the cloth trade, and Flanders and Florence, for example, had flourishing industries. The early industries were formed as associations of producers. The medieval guilds regulated entry into the professions and controlled the supply of the finished articles. In order to keep secrets of the trade the guilds could be ruthless. Glass manufacturers in Venice of the eleventh and twelfth centuries were not allowed to leave the city. Any workman who did was found guilty of treason, hunted down and killed.

Again, cities were an important part of culture. The cradle of the renaissance in Europe was the merchant cities of southern Europe. Florence and Venice were not only merchant cities but the centres for the reawakening of artistic pursuits. Trade and industry also meant the development of a money economy and the growth of banking. As trade moved beyond the simple exchange of commodities, there was a need for a universal medium of exchange, i.e. money. Thus with the development of trade came the growth of money and the introduction of finance capital. Even the terminology of contemporary financing owes much to the trading in the first merchant cities. The word bank comes from the Italian *banco*, the table on which the money-changers carried out their operations.

The first merchant cities of Europe – the most famous being the Hanseatic League towns in the north and Geneva, Venice, Milan and Florence in the south – stood apart from the surrounding rural areas. The cities were the site of trade, the accumulation of wealth and the spending of it in the opulent displays of buildings and art patronage. New classes were being formed. In Florence one could find the fabulously rich merchant family of the Medicis as well as the militant cloth workers. Although the merchant cities stood out from the rural areas, they were not entirely separate. Often the rich merchants would buy rural estates for investment and status purposes and sometimes the rural aristocrats would become involved in trade. The towns relied on the surrounding areas to supply food and the agricultural hinterland depended on the market of the towns. There was an economic symbiosis between town and country, but they lived in separate social worlds. In the towns the guilds ruled supreme. The feudal lord's power stopped at the city walls. Citizenship was often obtained by length of residence. In parts of Germany in the later middle ages men who escaped from the feudal lord could achieve freedom if they lived in the merchant city for a year and a day. Hence the Germany saying 'Stadtlust macht frei' – city air makes men free.

In the era of the merchant cities systems of cities developed, grew and declined according to the changing patterns of trade. The fate of individual cities hung on the threads of trade. As the world was being opened up by the merchants, new trade patterns were emerging, new cities were growing up and old cities denied the life-blood of trade were dying. Thus in the tenth and eleventh centuries Venice was the most important merchant city, London was a provincial backwater and Bristol was a huddle of huts. By the seventeenth and eighteenth centuries, however, Bristol was a major trading port with fine elegant terraces, London was a world city and on the other side of the Atlantic New York and Charleston were growing into major seaports, while Venice was a cultural and artistic centre but a commercial nobody. Cultural status lives longer than commercial virility. Old merchant cities have a tendency to become a bit snooty about their commercial past and patronising about their contemporary equivalents. New Yorkers think Houston is a bit gauche, while Londoners wonder if any life exists beyond the Watford Gap.

Within the merchant cities there was the development of trading and market areas and the development of distinct residential areas. The city in the merchant era was taking on a finer grain. With emphasis on profit and accumulation, the cities themselves became sources of investment. Urban land became an important commodity and land rent an important source of income. There was growing specialisation in urban land use due to the differences in rent-paying ability. The merchant city is a transitional category from rural feudalism to urban industrial capitalism. It grew up in a feudal context but it carried the seeds of a different society, a whole new order.

THE INDUSTRIAL CITY

In retrospect the merchant city was a preface to the industrial city which was an integral part of the industrial revolution. The great stirring of economic activity which took place at the tail end of the eighteenth century and flowered during the nineteenth century involved a tremendous concentration of people and capital. The factory system was the most characteristic form of this new industrialisation. By concentrating production in factories the owners reduced production costs and increased profits. Factories producing commodities were located close to centres of power, especially the coalfields.

Around the factories grew up dwellings and railway yards. The first cities of the industrial revolution were found in Britain, the first country to go through the transformation of the industrial revolution. The smoking factories arising from the urban landscape of Manchester in the first half of the nineteenth century became one of the new wonders of the world. Observers came from all over the globe. Their impressions were not favourable. The Frenchman Alexis de Tocqueville visiting Manchester in 1835 noted,

> from this foul drain the greatest stream of industry flows out to fertilize the whole world. From this filthy sewer pure gold flows. Here humanity attains its most complete development and its most brutish form, here civilization works its miracles and civilized man is turned back almost into a savage.

The American Colman also visited urban Britain and noted in 1845, 'every day that I live I thank heaven that I am not a poor man with a family in England.'

The urban centres of the industrial revolution were shock cities. The size of growth was alarming to comtemporary observers. In 1760 Manchester had a population of 17,000; by 1830 this had increased to 180,000 and to 303,382 in 1851. The industrial revolution was an urban-centred affair. And as industrialisation gathered pace so the cities grew. In 1801 70 per cent of the British population lived in places with a population less than 2,500. By 1851 over 40 per cent lived in cities with a population greater than 100,000. New cities grew up where there were green fields and major cities developed from tiny hamlets. The greatest growth was recorded in the coalfield areas.

The character of these new cities was radically different. The pace of growth stretched the existing infrastructure to its limits and beyond. In Glasgow, for example, the population increased in size five times between 1780 and 1830 but the urban fabric remained the same. The public services of sanitation, water supply, etc. were simply overwhelmed. Things were made worse by the prevailing ideology. The concepts of laissez-faire and free enterprise implied no state involvement. The factories were free to pollute the rivers and the builders were not constrained from building poorly lit, ill-ventilated slums. For the mass of people in the first two-thirds of the nineteenth century freedom meant the freedom to live in squalor. In the decade from 1831 to 1841 the death rate in the five largest British cities actually rose from 20 per thousand to 30 per thousand per annum. The new cities were dangerous places to live. The shock to the contemporary observers also came from the seeming breakdown of societal norms. The big cities were witnessing a breakdown of old social and family ties, and there were growing problems of drink, vice and social disorder. To the tidy Victorian mind the shock cities were both a blot on the landscape and a scene for social unrest. The historian E.J. Hobsbawm in examining the Victorian city has noted, 'the city was a volcano, to those rumblings the rich and powerful listened with fear, and whose eruptions they dreaded.'

The industrial cities had a distinct form. In the central areas were the factories and railway yards. Encircling this industrial and business core were the poor housing areas of the mass of workers. Here is Engels describing St Giles in London in 1844:

> the houses are occupied from cellar to garret, filthy within and without, and their appearance is such that no human being could possibly wish to live in them . . . The dwellings in the narrow courts and alleys between the streets, entered by covered passages between houses in which filth and tottering ruins surpass all description. Scarcely a window-pane can be found, the walls are crumbling, door posts and windowframes loose and broken . . . (Engels, 1973, p. 67)

Around the slums, which along with the factories and railway yards constituted the main elements in the industrial city, were the homes of the wealthier residents who sought to escape from the grime and the noise of the central area. A distinct class division was reflected in specially segregated quarters with little connection between them. The slums were hidden behind the main thoroughfares along which the wealthy residents travelled. The shops hid the grim reality of the industrial city. As a British government report in 1842 noted,

> the statements of the condition of considerable proportions of the labouring population of the

Figure 2.3 Two contrasting pictures of social conditions in London in the 1870s. A poor street trader and his family in the Houndsditch area of London's East End, and a fashionable croquet party. From *London. A Pilgrimage* by Gustave Doré (1833-83) and Blanchard Jerrold (1826-84), London, 1872

> towns into which the present enquiries have been carried have been received with surprise by persons of the wealthier classes living in the immediate vicinity, to whom the facts were as strange as if they related to foreigners or the natives of an unknown country.

The character of the industrial city evoked three general responses. First, there was the great refusal. Utopian socialists and anarchist groups sought to set up small, self-contained communities away from the cities. Many of the schemes rarely got off the drawing board and few were successful. But they proved influential and the British new town movement was a legacy of the early experiments. Contemporary hippy communes are part of a long tradition, a history of refusal.

Second, there was the socialist response in practice and in theory. In practice, the social historians John Foster (1974) and Gwyn Williams (1978) have vividly reconstructed the working-class response to the industrial revolution in different British cities. The industrial city also played a key role in marxist thought. For Marx and Engels the city encapsulated both the evils of capitalism – impoverishment, poor living conditions, naked exploitation – and the possibilities of socialist change. The industrial city brought together masses of workers where they could experience and guide their collective

strength. For Marx the city was pregnant with socialist consequences.

Third, there was the reformist response. For the reformers the evils of the industrial city were seen as solvable within the existing society. Throughout the nineteenth century, in Britain at least, it was being accepted that, in order to maintain the system, it was necessary for the state to become involved in laying down and enforcing minimum standards of public health, sanitation and housing. The origins of contemporary urban planning can be seen as a reformist response to the early industrial city.

THE CONTINUING TRANSFORMATION

World urbanisation

Since 1800 there has been a steady rise in the urban population. Figure 2.4 shows how the urban population has risen steadily both in absolute and relative terms from 1800 to 1950 and dramatically since 1950. More and more people live in towns and an increasing proportion live in the big cities. The number of cities with a population greater than 500,000 increased from 249 in 1960 to 485 in 1980. The urban transformation continues. The reasons vary across the globe. It is useful to disaggregate the world totals, and we can make a

THE CITY, CULTURE AND SOCIAL THEORY

The urban experience has been recorded and transmitted in culture and social theory. Raymond Williams has shown how the city juxtaposed with the notion of the countryside has been an enduring theme of literature from ancient times to the present day. There are two broad cultural images of the city. First, there is the city as evil and corrupt, a place of sharp practice, to be contrasted with the enduring virtues of the countryside. From Sodom and Gomorrah to Charles Dickens's *Coketown* and Fritz Lang's *Metropolis* to Boorman's *Midnight Cowboy* the city has been seen as something unnatural and unattractive. This tradition was boosted by the urbanisation experience of the industrial revolution and the alienating experience of contemporary big cities. Second, there is the city as a place of learning and tolerance to be contrasted with the ignorance, narrow-mindedness and bigotry of the rural dwellers. This image of the city is strengthened by contemporary perception of the classical period and the experience of the merchant city as an oasis of relative freedom. The writer Jonathan Raban presents the strongest case for the individual freedom afforded by contemporary cities.

The city has also been an enduring theme for social theorists. The British sociologist Peter Saunders highlights the importance and shape of the urban question in the work of Marx, Weber and Durkheim while the American sociologist Michael Smith looks at the city element in the work of Wirth, Freud, Simmes, Rozak and Sennett. Both writers make it clear that the urban question is part of wider social theories. Neither specifically 'urban' issues nor particular 'urban' problems can be abstracted from a consideration of the wider society.

References

Raban, J. (1974), *Soft City*, Hamish Hamilton, London.
Saunders, P. (1981), *Social Theory and the Urban Question*, Hutchinson, London.
Smith, M.P. (1980), *The City and Social Theory*, St Martin's Press, New York.
Williams, R. (1973), *The Country and the City*, Chatto & Windus, London.

rough twofold distinction between urbanisation in the core and the periphery.

Urbanisation in the core: Suburbanisation

In the core urbanisation went hand in hand with industrialisation. As the core economies have developed so cities have grown. Throughout the nineteenth and twentieth centuries urban expansion was part of industrial expansion and by 1960 almost two-thirds of the population of developed countries lived in urban places. The richest countries are now the most urbanised.

The form of urbanisation has differed in the twentieth century compared to previous periods. The suburbs are the most characteristic feature of urbanisation in the core in the twentieth century. Another significant feature has been the spread of urban influence. In the medieval period cities had a definite boundary. The city walls were the dividing line between an enclosed city and the countryside. In contemporary USA, by comparison, the city has spread all over the countryside. The two pictures of Detroit shown in Figure 2.5 give the feeling of an uncontrolled growth from 1900 to 1960. The process has continued. Figure 2.6 shows the continued increase in commuting fields of US cities from 1960 to 1970.

The low density spread of urban growth has been prompted by the construction industry, developers, federal governments seeking to boost aggregate demand in the economy and all aided by the growth of the automobile. In North America it has also been aided by lack of firm land-use controls and until recently cheap fuel. In other industrialised countries the spread is much less.

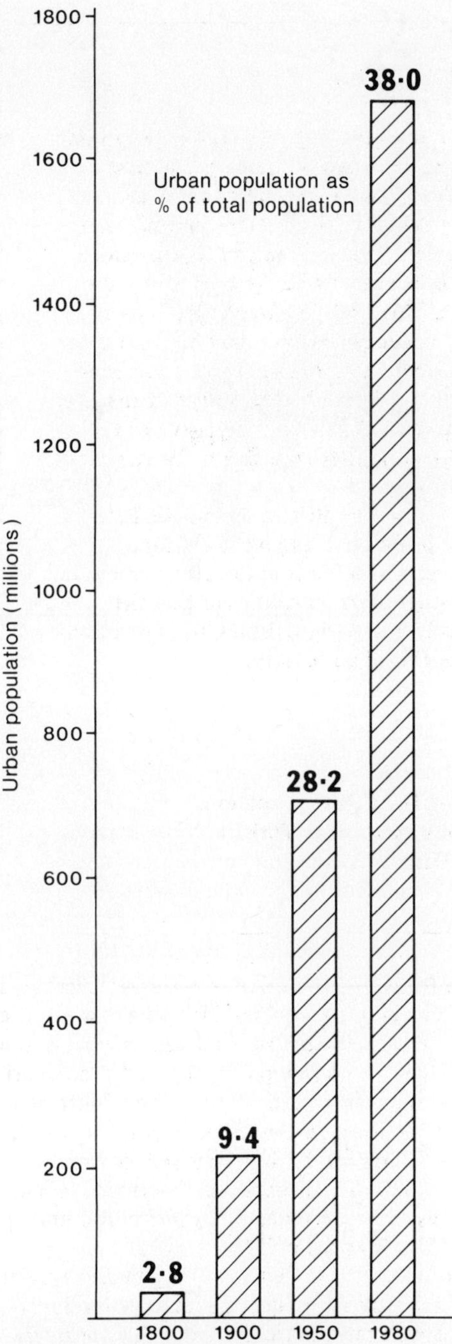

The 'urban' for 1800 and 1900 refer to places with a population greater than 5000. The figures for 1950 and 1980 refer to United Nations sources which accept the member countries' own definition of urban places

Figure 2.4

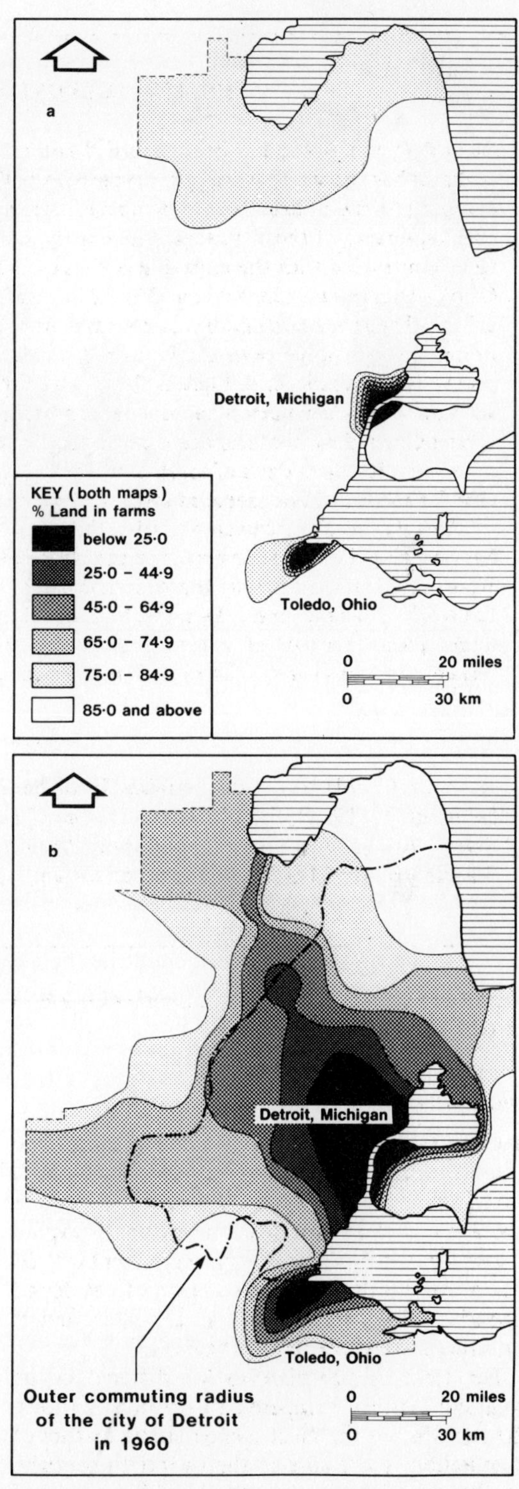

Figure 2.5 Urbanisation in Detroit (a) 1900, (b) 1960
Source: after Berry, 1973

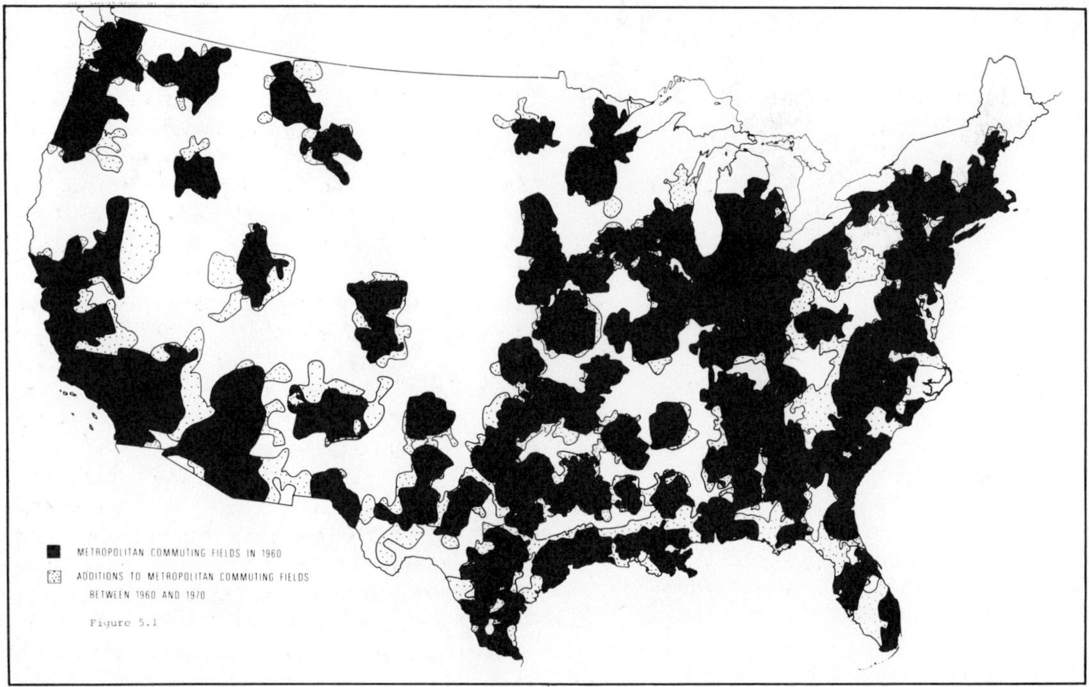

Figure 2.6 The urban spread
Source: Berry, B.J.L. and Gillard, Q. (1977), *Changing Shapes of Metropolitan America,* Ballinger, Cambridge, Mass.

THE POST-INDUSTRIAL CITY?

Cities are agglomerations. Their raison d'être is the need for people and activities to be concentrated in space. The incentive for growth in the industrial city was the economic benefits and profits to be gained by centralising production. Powerful agglomeration economies were at work.

In the advanced capitalist countries there have been two trends which may affect the future form of cities. The first is the move away from manufacturing to information processing. If the iron and steel industry, with its heavy material requirements, was the leading sector of the nineteenth century then the leading sector of the second half of the twentieth century is the microelectronics industry which requires less material inputs and is not so locationally tied. Small computer firms do not need to set up in towns and cities. Agglomeration economies are less important.

The second is the advance in telecommunications. People can talk via telephones, electronic mail can be delivered without a postal service and people can hold conferences in separate places if they have the audio-visual equipment. Face-to-face communication no longer implies physical proximity. The business sector no longer has an economic rationale for locating offices together in cities.

The net result of these two trends could be to make the city an anachronism; an exhibit in the built form museum to which future guides will point explaining to uncomprehending youngsters of the twenty-first century how the strange people of the twentieth century huddled together in huge masses called cities in order to conduct their business.

The post-industrial city may therefore be no city. People may be located across the surface of the earth in self-contained houses. But cities are more than sources of business interaction. They are places where quite literally people keep in touch. While the economic rationale may disappear, the social benefits of cities may still exercise some attraction in the years to follow.

In Great Britain, in contrast, land-use controls have been operated to avoid the sprawl of the suburbs. Nevertheless, despite the differences in degree the overall characteristics remain the same.

The modern urban area is large in extent and wide in spread. We may need to reassess our terms. For some places like Los Angeles or the commuting range of London the term 'city', with its image of easily identifiable dense urban settlements, perhaps needs to be dropped in favour of a term like urban region. The rural-urban distinction easily made at the edge of the merchant city and even the industrial city cannot be made in the modern city. There may be a definite centre, but the boundaries stretch to the furthest corners of the commuting range. The shadow of the city covers a wide area. The urban net is cast over most of the land. Can we then speak of urban and rural? Are these terms redolent of when distinctions could be made? The urban-rural division is collapsing into an urban-rural continuum with the terms city and country being appropriate only for the extreme ends.

Urbanisation in the periphery: The Swelling Cities

The most important feature of urbanisation in the periphery has been its recent tremendous growth. Starting from the comparatively low base, population in cities has increased dramatically in the post-war period. The growth has been caused by high birth rates and very high levels of rural to urban migration. Over two-thirds of the growth in third-world cities between 1950 and 1970 came from immigration. Over the period 1970 to 1975 this figure was 42 per cent. People moved from the countryside in search of the better life which many believe is found in the cities. The sheer scale of population increase in such a limited period has overwhelmed the existing public services which were already inadequate.

The third-world city is a place of high-density living, a degraded environment, high unemployment and under-employment. Although beset by huge problems, the cities are not without hope. While a third of the urban population is officially designated as unemployed and nine-tenths badly housed, inhabitants of third-world cities have fought back. There are two sectors of the economy in the periphery: the formal sector or upper circuit which is a system of exchange of commodities between institutions and firms involving fixed prices, high capital-to-labour ratio and an orientation towards export in world

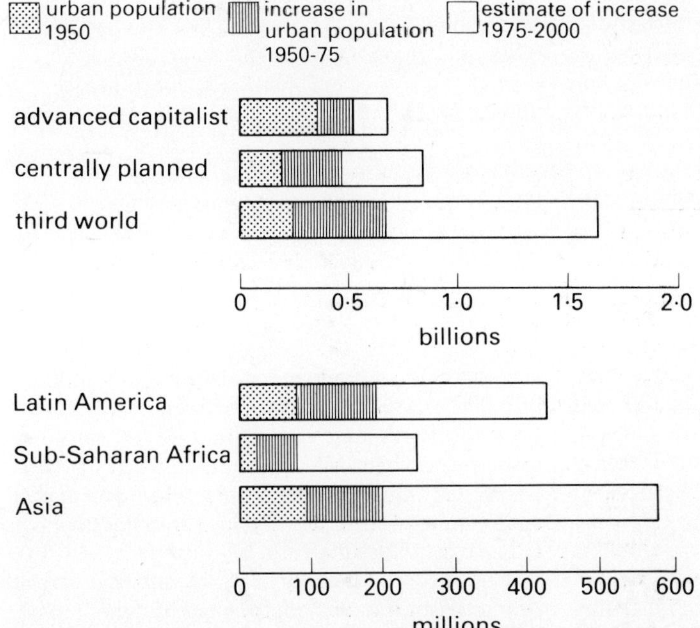

Figure 2.7 Patterns of urbanisation
Source: World Bank, 1980

WILL SUBURBS BECOME A THING OF THE PAST?

Two trends have been observed by studies of population distribution in the 1970s and 1980s. The first has been population growth in rural areas. The rural districts of Britain have reversed their long history of population decline. The trend follows the demographic pattern of the USA where the flight to the suburbs has been replaced by the flight to small towns and rural districts. The reasons behind the drift to the countryside are complex. Retirement migration and the growth of alternative lifestyles are only two of the reasons. More important, however, has been the development of small towns as economic growth points. Small towns have attracted footloose industries repelled by the high rates, expensive housing and urban problems of big cities. In the booming computer industry, for example, firms compete to attract the highly trained staff. The computer firms have found that staff are particularly attracted to small town locations in rural districts.

The second trend has been growth of population in selected central-city areas. Throughout the 1950s and especially the 1960s there was a steady loss of central-city population as comprehensive redevelopment and urban-renewal schemes replaced old housing with lower-density accommodation and people moved to the suburbs. The inner-city decline in population has been reversed in some cities as a consequence of the process of gentrification. This process involves the replacement of moderate to low-income households often in private renting with richer owner-occupiers. The process has been encouraged by property dealers and estate agents eager to enlarge their turnover and expand their profits. The gentrifiers are middle- to upper-income groups mainly in their late 20s, 30s or early 40s with few children and are typically employed in the design, advertising, media, education and publishing sectors. They have turned their back on the familiar route to the suburbs. These 'colonisers' of inner-city neighbourhoods provide the preconditions for further gentrification. By improving housing they make it easier for subsequent purchasers to get home purchase loans and as their well-organised articulate pressure groups are able to obtain better local services and improved education they make it increasingly attractive for other middle-class families. The move back to the cities has been pushed along by the rapid oil prices of the 1970s which have made cheap fuel and hence cheap travel a thing of the past. People are now aware of the cost of a separation between home and workplace. For these who work in the city, a central city location reduces the cost and time of travelling to work.

These trends suggest population increase in the rural areas and the central city districts. The result is the relative decline of the suburbs. This may be more than just a temporary pheno-

markets; and an informal sector involving owner-operators in traditional crafts, small trading and manufacturing activities involving little capital. The informal sector is a response to the inability of the formal sector to provide jobs, services or goods for the mass of the population. The same thing applies in housing. The weight of numbers and the inability of the market to provide decent cheap housing has meant appalling housing problems in most peripheral cities. In Calcutta, for example, out of a population of 8 million, 600,000 sleep out in the streets every night because they have nowhere else to go. The response has been the growth of self-help schemes, unplanned squatter settlements. The name varies throughout the world – favelas (Brazil); callampas (Chile); gecekundu (Turkey); bustees (Calcutta), barong-barongs (Philippines) – but the broad characteristics are approximately the same. Squatter settlements vary in levels of service and

menon. If we think about the suburbs – lower-density, single-family housing, predominantly residential areas located away from the centres of entertainment, shopping and employment – we can see a built form reflecting past demographic structures and former economic growth. Suburban housing implies a nuclear family with large inputs of family labour, typically female, to maintain the property. But now over a third of households are one-person households, people are having less children and overall the advertising agents' image of mum, dad, and the two kids is increasingly failing to capture the reality of contemporary household structure. Suburban housing, which makes up 40 per cent of the housing stock in USA and UK, is becoming more irrelevant to the housing needs of the population. Suburban housing can be seen as the product of the post-war economic boom. With rising real incomes during the 1950s and 1960s, rosy expectations, relatively cheap travel and low interest rates, people were willing to take on large mortgages. Many people over-committed themselves to buying the suburban house of their dreams. But with interest rates and in turn mortgage rates rising and transport costs tending the increase, fewer people are now willing to take on the burden of a mortgage for a suburban home. The costs of motoring have increased partly as fuel costs have risen but also because more married women are going out to work. Over 55 per cent of married women in Britain are now in employment. The average suburban household is now travelling more miles than ever just at the time when petrol prices are rising and the quality and cost of public transport are respectively decreasing and increasing. It is now more costly and more difficult to live in the suburbs.

The housing aim of the typical family in the 1960s was a house in the suburbs. This is changing. Some households can now find employment in sought-after rural districts. And in the inner cities there are the gentrifiers and the ethnic communities who for one reason or another have turned their back on the suburbs. For a considerable proportion of the population the suburban dream is either unobtainable or undesirable.

The growth of suburbs was based upon the number of conditions – economic growth, shared values, cheap and easy travel, and the nuclear family – which are now disappearing into recent history. As household size and form changes, the racial mix bubbles away, the economy falters, interest rates rise, and real incomes fall, people are looking for alternatives to the suburbs. If these changes are long term and large scale, this may lead to lack of demand for suburban housing and a rapid fall off in the house prices of suburban districts. Those who live in the suburbs may find it difficult to either sell their houses or recoup their investment. The suburban dream of the 1960s may become the headache of the 1980s and the urban dodo of the 1990s.

degrees of security of tenure. At one extreme there are the almost nomadic settlements where there is no legal right and poor accommodation while at the other there is the legal occupant with complete structures and modern utilities. The differences relate on the one hand to the length of residence, organisation and political know-how of the squatters themselves and on the other to the nature of the society in which they seek to find one of the most basic of human necessities. Squatter settlements are a response to the inability of the formal public and private housing markets to provide accommodation for the mass of the population.

The informal economy and the squatter settlements are both a sign of failure and a source of hope. They represent the failure of the society to provide jobs and homes, and the people's fight back.

Plates 4 & 5
Squatting (4) Darjeeling, India and (5) in hills overlooking Kowloon

GUIDE TO FURTHER READING

The classic book which summarises the changing position of the city is:

Mumford, L. (1961), *The City in History*, Secker & Warburg, London.

But see also:

Vance, James E. Jnr. (1977), *This Scene of Man: The Role and Structure of the City in the Geography of Western Civilisation*, Harper & Row, New York.

More specific works on the earliest cities include:

Adams, R.M.C. (1966), *The Evolution of Urban Society: Early Mesopotamia and Pre-Hispanic Mexico*, Aldine, Chicago.

Wheatley, P. (1971), *The Pivot of the Four Quarters: Preliminary Enquiry into the Origins and Character of the Ancient Chinese City*, Aldine, Chicago.

The classical city is discussed in:

de Ste Croix, E.E.M. (1982), *Class Struggle in The Ancient Greek World*, Duckworth, London.

Finley, M.I. (1966), *The Ancient Greeks,* Penguin, Harmondsworth.

Hammond, N.G.L. (1976), *The Classical Age of Greece*, Weidenfeld & Nicholson, London.

The best introductions to the emergence of the merchant city are:

Braudel, F. (1982), *The Wheels of Commerce: Civilization and Capitalism 15th-16th Century*, Collins, London.

Pirenne, H. (1936), *Economic and Social History of Medieval Europe,* Routledge & Kegan Paul, London.

The industrial cities, the centres of the industrial revolution, are described by:

Briggs, A. (1963), *Victorian Cities*, Odhams, New York.

Dyos, H.J. and Wolff, M. (eds) (1977), *The Victorian City: Images and Reality*, Routledge & Kegan Paul, London.

Engels, F. (1973 edition, first published in 1892), *The Condition of the Working Class in England*, Progress Publishers, Moscow.

Foster, J. (1974), *Class Struggle and The Industrial Revolution*, Methuen, London.

Hareven, T.K. and Langenbach, R. (1979), *Amoskeag. Life and Work in an American Factory – City in New England*, Methuen, London.

Joyce, P. (1982), *Work, Society and Politics*, Methuen, London.

Williams, G. (1978), *The Merthyr Rising*, Croom Helm, London.

General introductions to contemporary patterns of urbanisation include:

Abu-Lughod, J. and Hay, R. (eds) (1977), *Third World Urbanization*, Methuen, London.

Berry, B.J.L. (1973), *The Human Consequences of Urbanization*, Macmillan, London.

Friedmann, J. and Wulff, R. (1975), *The Urban Transition*, Edward Arnold, London.

Gilbert, A. and Gugler, J. (1982), *Cities, Poverty and Development*, Oxford University Press, London.

Wilsher, P. and Righter, R. (1975), *The Exploding Cities,* André Deutsch, London.

The changing attitudes to cities are discussed in:

Tuan, Yi-Fu (1974), *Topophilia, A Study of Environmental Perception, Attitudes and Values*, Prentice-Hall, New Jersey.

Part 2

The Urban System

Plates 6 and 7

3 Urban Systems and Economic Development

The aim of this chapter is to introduce to you the concept of *urban systems*. Urban places do not exist in isolation. There is a whole series of different types of relationships between separate towns and cities and we use the term urban system to indicate that the individual urban centres are linked to each other. In this chapter we will show the form and the character of these linkages with respect to economic development. The emphasis will be on urban systems in capitalist economies.

URBAN SYSTEMS IN AGRICULTURAL AREAS

Periodic markets

In the agricultural regions of the world the arrangement of towns and villages performs a number of functions. The most important is the provision of goods and services for residents and the population of the surrounding areas. In the poorest agricultural areas of the world people have very little income left after the main needs of shelter, clothing and food have been met. These conditions were found throughout the world prior to the industrial revolution and are still found in large areas of the third world. In these areas there is very little demand for the range of foods and services (e.g. grocery stores, record shops, doctors, etc.) which many of us now take for granted. Because of the weak demand, it is unprofitable for merchants and pedlars to set up business permanently in any one place as there is not enough local buying power to sustain the business over the long term. To keep their businesses going the merchants must travel. The result is a system of periodic markets in which markets are distributed in time as well as space.

A minimising distance

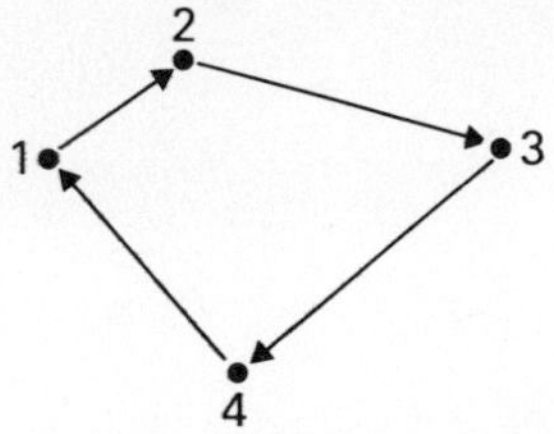

B maximising demand

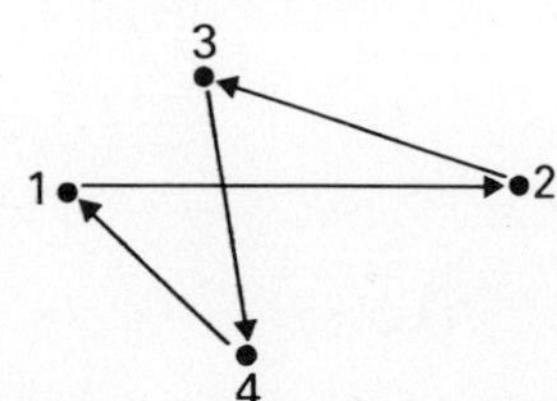

Numbers refer to days when market is open

Figure 3.1 Periodic market systems

Two features of the buying and selling process are important in shaping the form of periodic markets. The first involves the movement of the merchants and pedlars. Those specialising in the more expensive items will have to travel further afield than the merchants selling the cheaper, regularly bought goods. But for both types of seller the aim will be to reduce costs by minimising the distance travelled. Figure 3.1a shows the ideal pattern of markets arranged to minimise vendor travelling. There is a problem with this pattern. Because the markets are not 'moving' very far, the market area is not being efficiently covered. If two markets are close together there will be a degree of overlap in which both markets will be competing for the same consumer popula-

Plates 8 and 9
Periodic markets in Boston, Lincolnshire (8), and West Africa (9)

tion at approximately the same time. Thus, the second feature shaping periodic markets is the need to maximise demand, thus markets close together in distance must be spaced in time. Figure 3.1b represents the ideal pattern for maximising demand. Periodic market systems thus represent a compromise between the need to maximise demand and the desire to minimise distance. An actual pattern of period markets is shown in Figure 3.2. Same-day markets in this area of Northern Nigeria have a minimum separation of 10.6 miles and markets with meetings two days apart have an average spacing of 3.3 miles.

Periodic markets are found when demand density is low and vendors are mobile. If incomes rise or population density increases, then effective demand is raised. Demand may be so high that the travelling merchants do not need to move. The process is gradual. As demand increases, a number of vendors begin to stay put, they specialise in certain goods and open bigger premises. Eventually more and more merchants do the same until periodic markets are replaced by permanent ones. For some services the system of periodicity

know

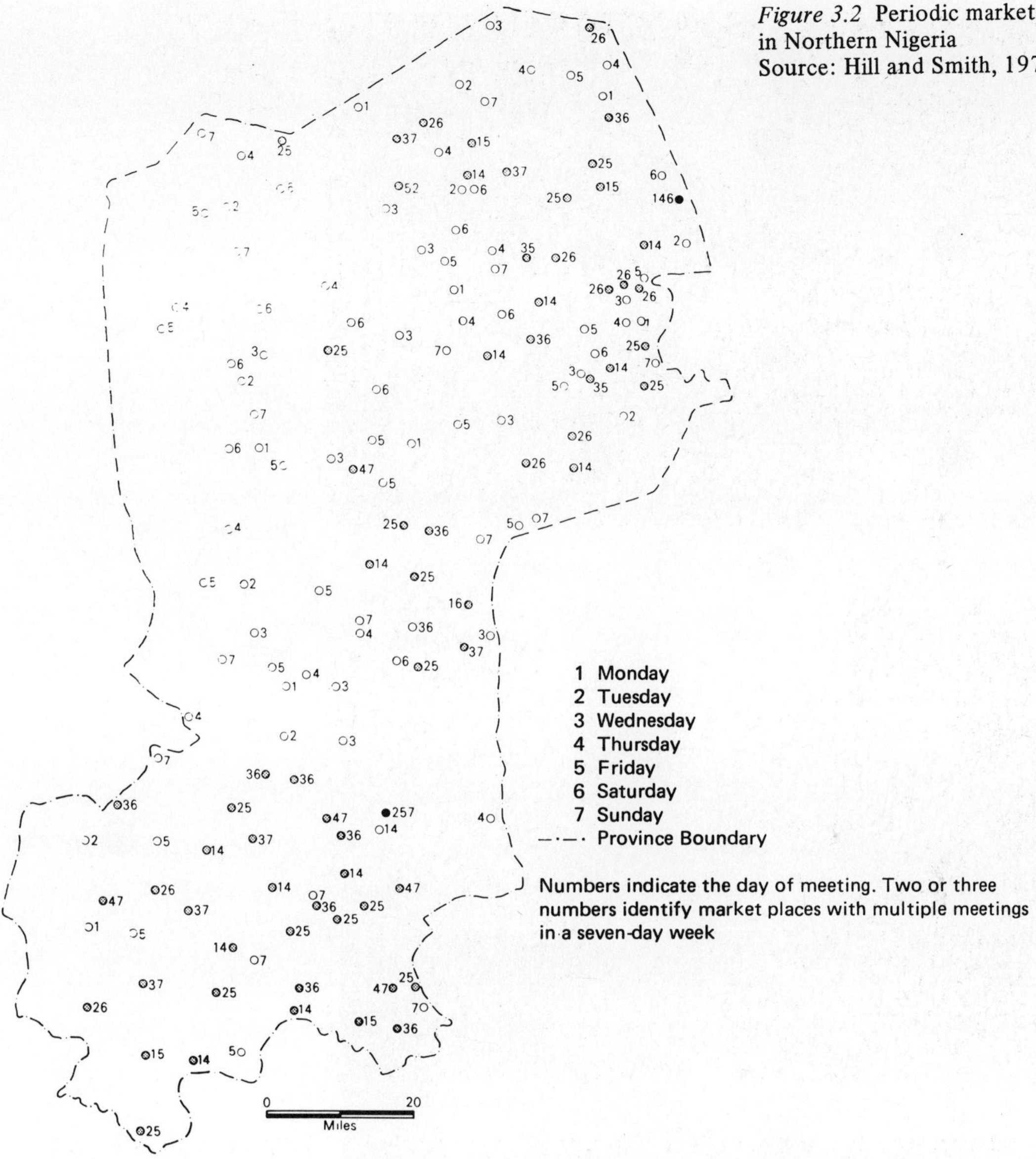

Figure 3.2 Periodic markets in Northern Nigeria
Source: Hill and Smith, 1972

remains: in small towns everywhere people still await the coming of the travelling circus with great expectation.

Fixed markets

In the richer agricultural regions of the world periodic markets have, very largely, been replaced by fixed markets. These are found in the towns and villages. The arrangement of these settlements has long been a source of fascination for social scientists. In 1919 the American sociologist Galpin studied rural communities in Wisconsin. He argued that, under ideal conditions, settlements with the same number and level of services would be spaced at regular intervals across the landscape and that the *complementary region* of each centre would take a circular form as suggested in Figure 3.3a. In

A. Galpin's model

Figure 3.3 Hypothetical settlement pattern

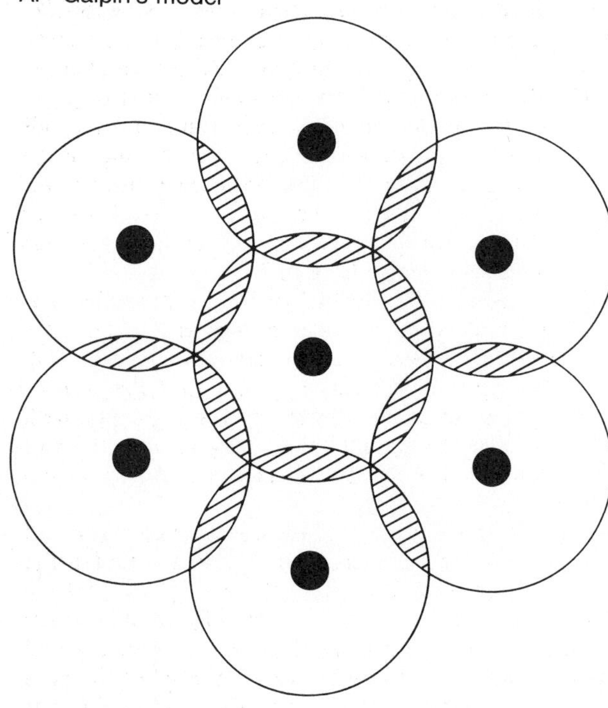

B. The derivation of hexagonal market areas

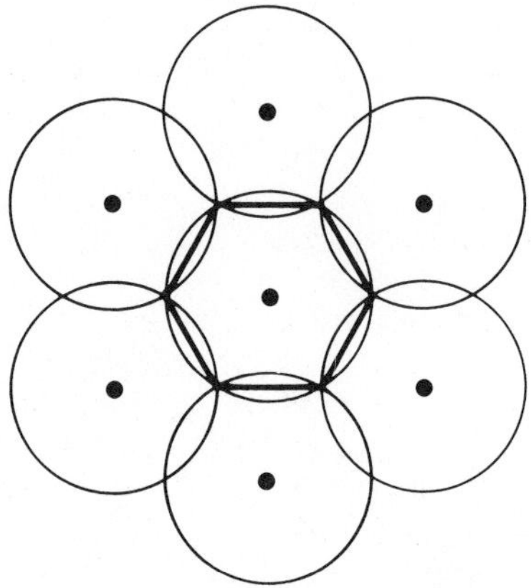

● market

Plate 10
Traders stay put: a shopping centre in Reading

England in the 1930s the geographer Dickinson studied the relationship between population size and number of different goods and services in the towns of the rich agricultural region of East Anglia. But perhaps the most important early study was by the German geographer Walter Christaller, first published in 1933 and translated into English in 1966. In his work on settlements in Southern Germany Christaller was concerned to answer the question 'What determines the number, size and distribution of towns?'

Central place theory

To answer this question he used a number of concepts which we now term *range* and *threshold*. Imagine, as Christaller did, a flat homogeneous plain with an even population distribution. The people on this plain require goods and services such as groceries, clothes, furniture, access to doctors, etc. These goods and services have two important characteristics. The first is *range*. The range of a good is the distance over which people are prepared to travel to purchase the good. Furniture has a larger range than milk because furniture is expensive and bought irregularly. People are thus willing to travel further to buy furniture than they are to buy milk. The *threshold* of a good is the minimum population necessary to support the continued supply of the good. Compare the case of a small grocery store and an expensive jeweller's shop. Since people regularly buy groceries, a grocery store only needs a relatively small local population to keep it in business. A jewellery shop, in contrast, needs a larger local population since expensive jewels are irregularly purchased. The jewellery store has a bigger threshold than a grocery store.

The goods and services with large thresholds and extensive ranges are termed higher-order goods and services. Lower-order goods and services have small thresholds and restricted ranges. We would expect to find the higher-order goods and services to be located in the larger towns where there are larger threshold populations.

On the imagined plain Christaller suggested that the urban places, which he termed central places, providing goods and services to the surrounding areas, would form a hierarchy. To service regular widespread demand a large number of widely distributed small places would provide lower-order goods and services. There would be a smaller number of larger centres providing both lower-order and higher-order goods and services. Successive steps of the hierarchy would consist of larger central places providing even higher-order goods and services. Because of the extensive range of the goods and services in the larger towns these towns would have large market areas. The exact form of the complementary regions used by Christaller was a hexagon. Why a hexagon?

If we look again at Figure 3.3a we can see that the circular complementary regions overlap. If we were to assume as Christaller did that people will only shop at the nearest centre, then the areas of overlap would be divided by a straight line with people on opposite sides going to the different centres. The resultant shape, as shown in Figure 3.3b, is a hexagon.

In his central place theory Christaller proposed a number of hexagonal structures. Under the *market optimising principle* he suggested that the structure of urban settlements would reflect consumer demand in that each consumer would be as close as possible to every level of the hierarchy. This arrangement would minimise the amount of travelling for the consumer. Notice that in Figure 3.4a each higher-order centre serves the equivalent of two lower-order centres plus itself. This is termed a k=3 system where k refers to the number of lower-order centres served by one higher-order centre. The pattern created by the market-optimising principle is responsive to demand but leads to an inefficient transportation network because routes which link the higher-order centres do not pass through the lower-order centres. Under the *traffic-optimising principle*, in contrast, the network is more efficient since routes which link higher-order centres pass through lower-order places (see Figure 3.4b).

Central places do not just provide private goods and services. They also perform a number of administrative functions such as schooling and the provision of various public goods such as art galleries, parks, libraries, etc. Under the *administration-optimising principle*, the settlement pattern is arranged so that each lower-order place is within the boundary of a larger-order centre as shown in Figure 3.4c. It is administratively inconvenient for lower-order centres to straddle the boundary of higher-order centres as is the case with the settlement pattern arranged

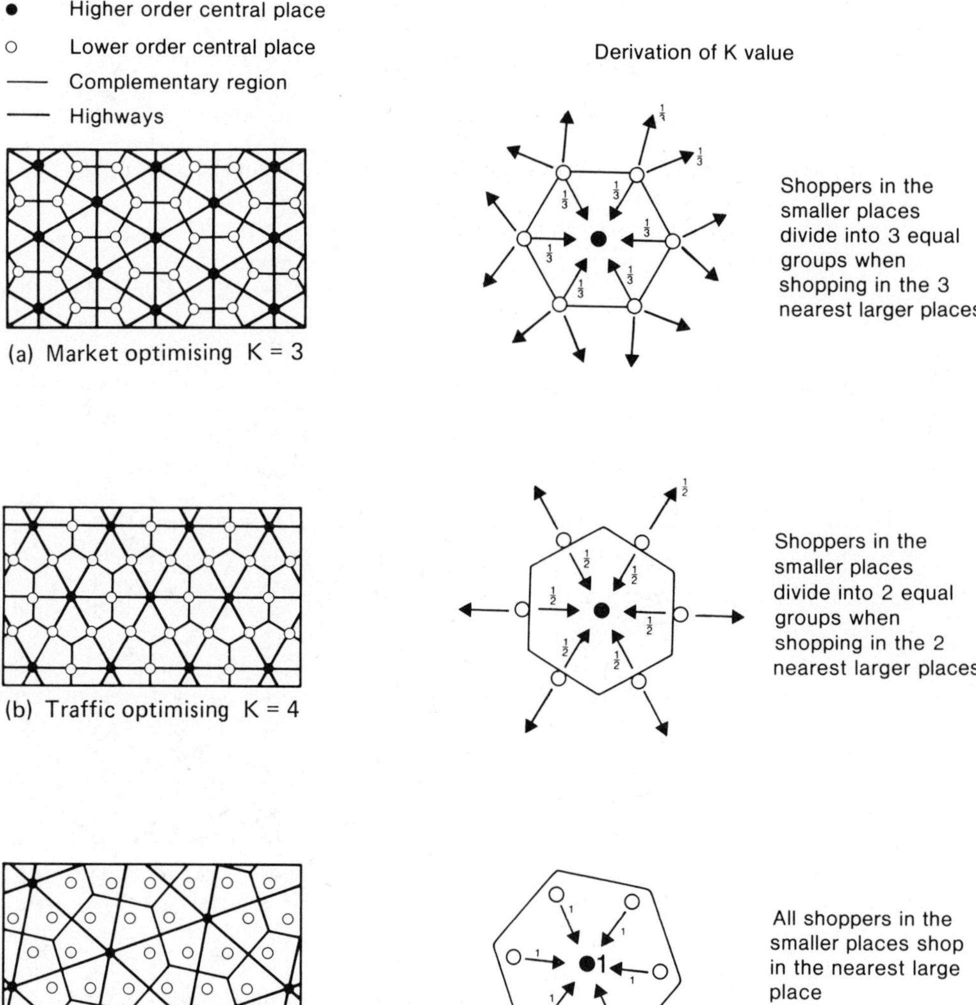

Figure 3.4 Different hexagonal structures

under the market-optimising and traffic-optimising principles.

In his work on southern Germany Christaller sought to discover how a real central place system compared with the theory. The first task was to find some yardstick which would allow towns to be classified into the various sub-divisions of lower order and higher order. He proposed a number of indices including giving a weight to each facility in a town (e.g. 10 for a grocery store, 30 for a jewellery shop and 50 for a hospital), adding up the weights and comparing the value for each town. Out of the many methods considered, Christaller decided to use telephone connections as a measure of centrality.

The results suggested a 7-level hierarchy as shown in Table 3.1 and Figure 3.5. The highest-order centres, those with the greatest centrality index, were Frankfurt, Nuremberg, Stuttgart, Strasbourg, Zurich and Munich. Christaller con-

MEASURES OF CENTRALITY

Christaller's centrality index

Centrality was operationally defined by Christaller as the number of telephones in a central place minus the place's population multiplied by the average density of telephones per population in the region. In mathematical terms,

$$C_t = T_t - E_t \frac{T_r}{E_r}$$

where, C_t centrality of town t
T_t number of telephones in the town
E_t population of town
T_r number of telephones in the region
E_r population of the region

In a town of 100,000 with 15,000 telephones situated in a region where there is a total of 25,000 telephones and 250,000 population, the centrality of that town, according to the Christaller centrality index, would be

$$Z_2 = 15{,}000 - 100{,}000 \frac{25{,}000}{250{,}000}$$

$$Z_2 = 5{,}000$$

Preston's centrality index

$$C_t = R + S - \alpha M_t F_t$$

Where C_t = centrality of town t
R = total sales in retail establishments ($)
S = total sales in selected services establishments ($)
α = average percentage of median family income spent on retail items and selected services
M_t = median family income in town t ($)
F_t = total number of families in town t

References

Christaller, W. (1966), *Central Places in Southern Germany* (translated by C.W. Baskins), Prentice-Hall, Englewood Cliffs, N.J.

Preston, R.E. (1971), The structure of central place systems, *Economic Geography*, 47, 136-55

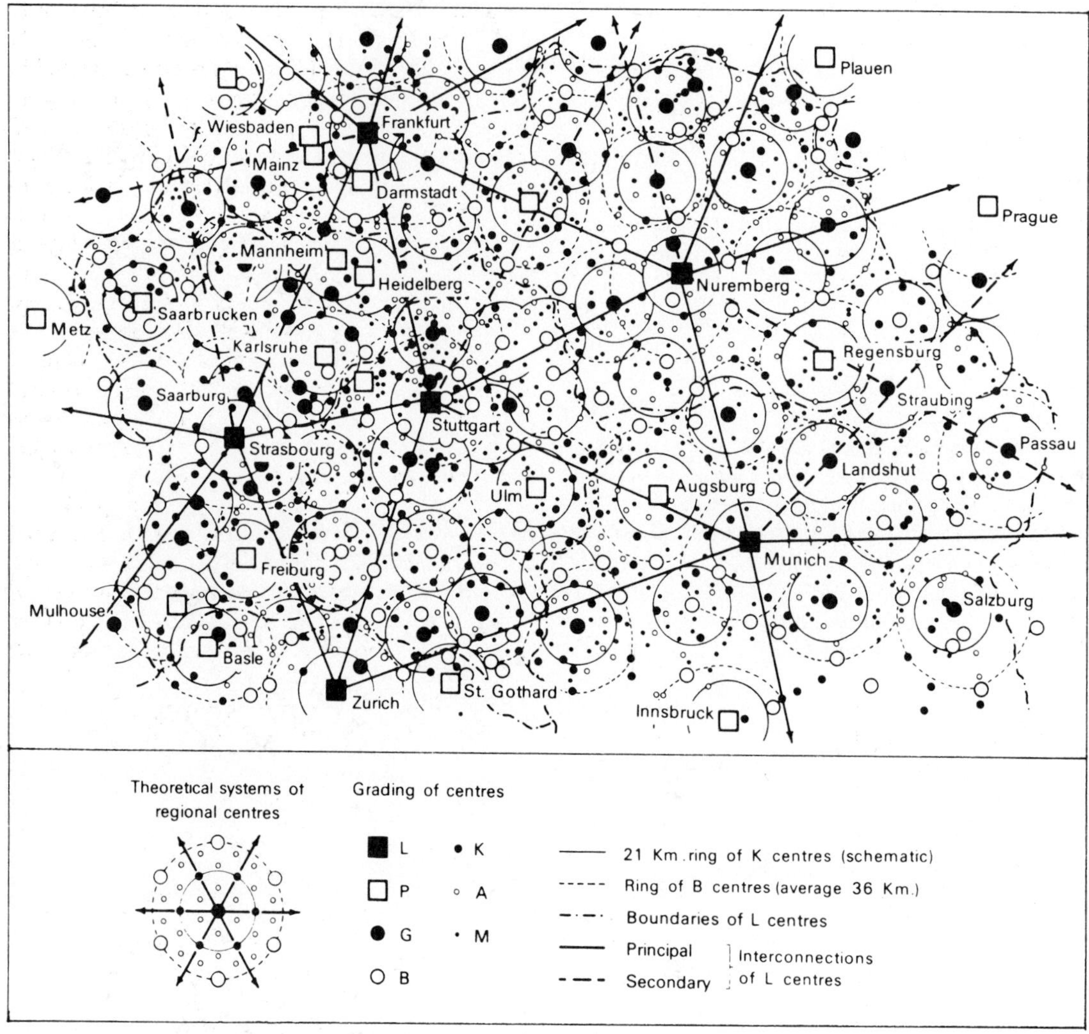

Figure 3.5 Distribution of central places in Southern Germany
Source: Dickinson, R.E. (1964), *City and Region*, Routledge & Kegan Paul, London

cluded that the central system in southern Germany was dominated by the market-optimising principle with the transport and administrative-optimising principles being of secondary importance. Deviations from the theoretical pattern were found to lie in the pattern of historical development: a number of towns were more central than their size suggested because they had been the site of city states or they had been the scene for industrial development. The physical landscape also played an important role in stretching and distorting the neat hexagonal pattern of the homogeneous plain. In some places the site characteristics, e.g. river crossings, promoted urban growth, while in others the rough terrain meant poor farming conditions which in turn meant dispersed populations and 'gaps' in the central place network in comparison to the pattern suggested by the theory.

Central place theory: subsequent work

Subsequent work on central place theory has

Table 3.1 Central places in southern Germany

Grade of town	*Population (approx.)*	*Centrality*
Landstadt(L)	500,000	1200 – 3000
Provinzstadt(P)	100,000	150 – 1200
Gaustadt(G)	30,000	30 – 150
Bezirkstadt(B)	10,000	12 – 30
Kreisstadt(K)	4,000	4 – 12
Amtsort(A)	2,000	2 – 4
Marktort(M)	1,000	0.5 – 2

Source: Christaller, 1966

taken two main directions. First, there has been a number of elaborations to the theory. The best known is the work of the German economist August Losch. Like Christaller, Losch used concepts similar to range and threshold. But, in contrast, Losch did not assume a fixed k network of k=3, k=4 and k=7. Rather than sharply demarcated thresholds and corresponding market areas Losch proposed a more flexible system in which different goods and services have differing thresholds, and different market areas. Figure 3.6 shows some of the different patterns suggested by Losch. The progression from a to i in this diagram reflects the progression of market areas for goods and services with successively higher thresholds. Figure 3.6(a) could be the market area for a grocery store while (i) could describe the market area for an expensive jeweller's store. For each good or service there is a different market area and Losch's model landscape is composed of the superimposition of the various hexagonal market areas.

The second direction of subsequent work on central place theory has been to take Christaller's techniques of research and apply them to other central place systems. Amongst the many empirical studies we will consider just two.

The first study is of the urban settlement pattern in the Pacific north west of the USA. The centrality of the 159 settlements was calculated by the researcher, Richard Preston (1971) using a formula which estimated the amount of consumption of goods and services in each town

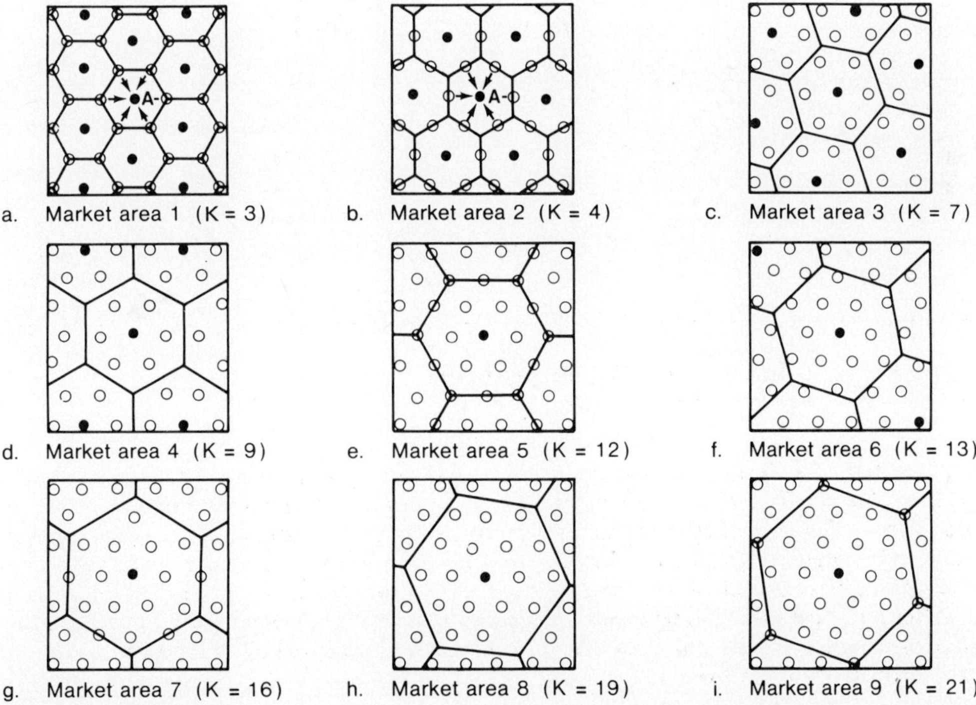

Figure 3.6 Market areas
Source: Lösch, 1954

greater than that consumed by the town's population. Preston's index gives an estimate of the consumption by out-of-towners and thus a measure of the town's centrality. The resulting values were then ranked. The results suggested a 5-level hierarchy. The first-order settlements were Seattle, Portland and Salt Lake City. The second order consisted of Spokane, Tacoma, Great Falls, Medford and Eugene while the towns of Salem, Everett, Bellvue, Yakima, Boise, Idaho Falls and Missoula made up the third. The fourth level consisted of 52 smaller towns and the base level of the settlement hierarchy contained 95 small towns and villages.

To calculate the complementary region of each centre Preston used two methods:

(1) Each town was allocated to the centre from which it received most Sunday newspapers.
(2) Each town was allocated to the centre whose companies provided the greatest number of branch plants and outlets in the town.

The first method produced the complementary regions of Seattle, Salt Lake City and Portland, while the second method distinguished between the complementary regions of the first, second and third order settlements. The composite map produced by these methods is shown in Figure 3.7. Notice how the centres of Everett and Bellvue do not have a separate sphere of influence; they have been 'swallowed up' by their big neighbour, Seattle. Apart from these two towns the diagram suggests a nesting relationship within which smaller settlements exert an independent influence within the overall sphere of influence of a big city.

The second case study is of an analysis of central places in Ecuador. Because the researchers, Ray and Rosemary Bromley, were faced with extra difficulties in obtaining data on retail trade, they decided to examine bus services. This had been a well-tried technique in early central place studies in Europe and North America but it had fallen out of favour as the motor car became the most important way of getting around. In poorer countries of the world, however, the technique is still valuable. In Ecuador buses are the most important means of passenger transport. On the basis of the number of services per week from the smaller settlements two 3-level settlement hierarchies were discovered centred respectively on the two main cities of Guayaquil and Quito. The system focused on Guayaquil is shown in Figure 3.8.

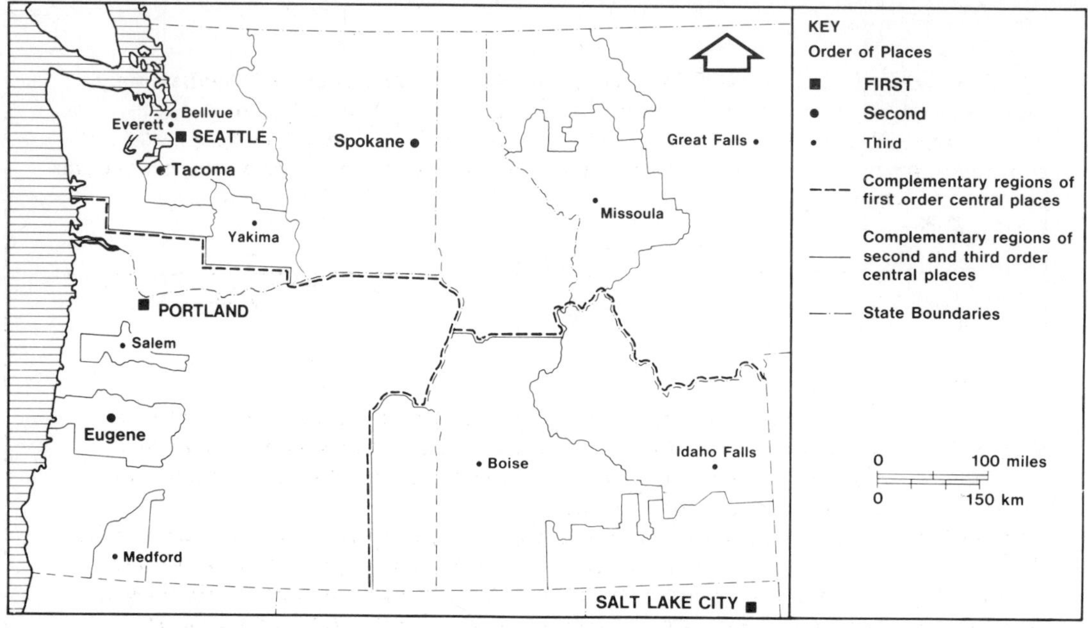

Figure 3.7 The urban hierarchy in the Pacific north west of the USA
Source: Preston, 1971

COMPLEMENTARY REGIONS

Each town or city exerts its influence over surrounding areas. People come from the surrounding area to the town for goods, services and jobs. The area over which the town exerts its influence has been termed complementary region, ülmland, hinterland and sphere of influence. We will use the term complementary region to refer to the area of general influence. The term market area is more generally used with respect to specific goods and services.

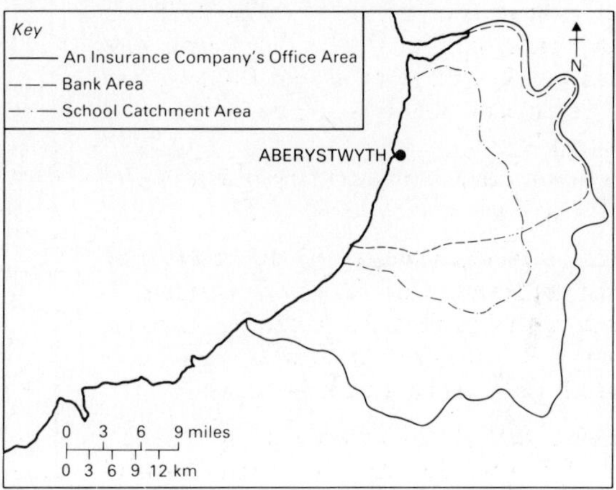

Figure 3A

Complementary regions can be measured in a variety of ways. Figure 3A shows how, for the Welsh university town of Aberystwyth, the complementary region varies according to the measure used.

The actual area of the complementary regions of a particular town can be compared with the area predicted by the Reilly model. Reilly argued that the boundary between the complementary regions of two towns could be predicted by the following formula

$$B_{ij} = \frac{D_{ij}}{1 + \sqrt{P_i/P_j}}$$

where B_{ij} is the predicted distance from town i to the boundary between its complementary region and that of town j. D_{ij} is the distance from town i to town j. P_i is the population of town i and P_j is the population of town j. The equation when applied to the following hypothetical situation suggests that shoppers will travel up to 5.85km to town j but people living beyond this point will travel to town i.

(a) 10 km

j (P_j = Population = 100) i (P_i = Population = 50)

$$B_j = \frac{D_{ij}}{1 + \sqrt{P_i/P_j}} = \frac{10}{1 + \sqrt{50/100}} = 5.85$$

(b) 5.85

i Boundary j

The Reilly model is a simple one. It uses straight-line distance and crude population totals. Elaborations to the model have involved more sensitive measure of distance, e.g. cost-time measures, and more sophisticated indicators of the pulling power of towns, e.g. number of shops, area of retail and service floorspace, etc.

The most general conclusion we can draw is that the larger the town the larger the complementary region. The larger the city the greater the likelihood of very specialised goods and services which will attract people from far and wide. The largest cities like New York, Paris, London and Rome attract people from all over the world. Their spheres of influence are international.

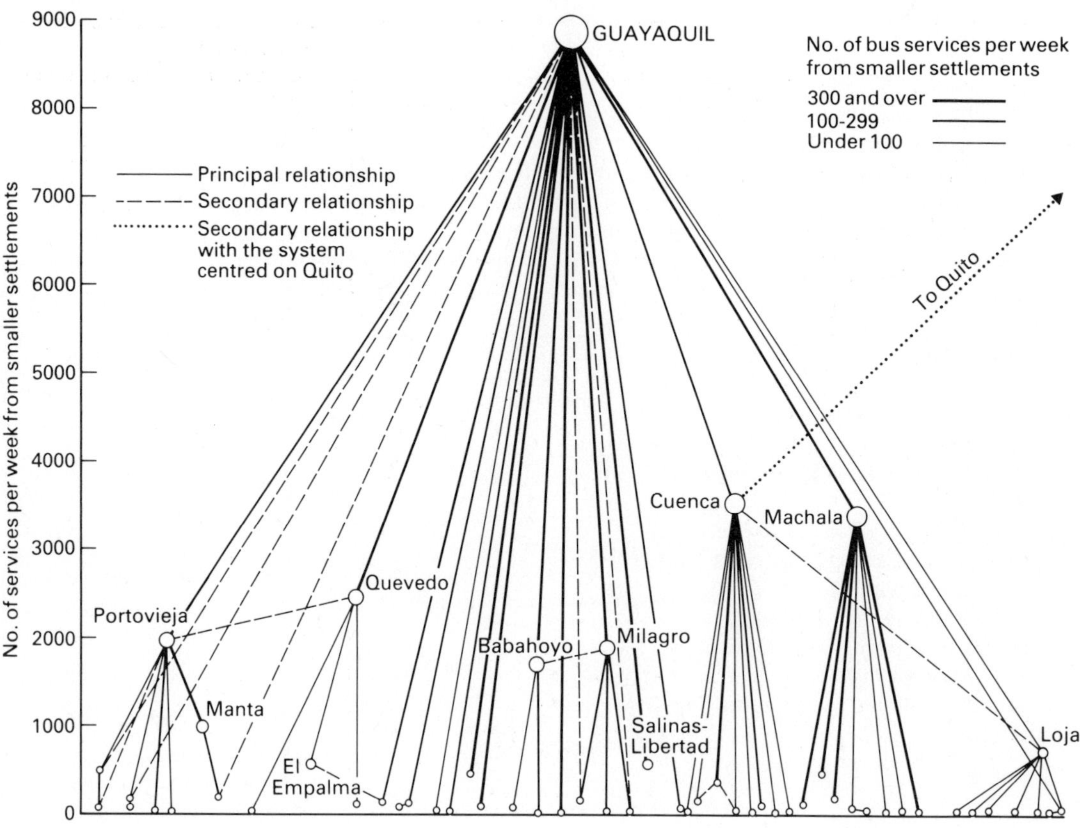

Figure 3.8 The functional structure of the system of centres focused on Guayaquil, 1975. Only the centres with over 500 services per week from smaller settlements are named
Source: Bromley and Bromley, 1979

To measure the complementary region of the major towns the two researchers assigned each place to the centre to which it had most bus services. The resulting picture is shown in Figure 3.9. The variation in the size of the complementary regions reflects variations in rural population density. Southern Ecuador has a smaller population and poorer roads than the central areas of the country.

Changes in the central place system

The size and centrality of settlements does not remain constant. The hierarchies and complementary regions depicted in the previous figures and tables represent snapshots at a point in time. They represent static pictures of constantly evolving scenes. Central place hierarchies change in response to a variety of factors. Three of the most important are (1) population density, (2) accessibility, and (3) retail distribution.

(1) The greater the population density the larger the number of settlements. If population density tends to increase in an area then, holding everything else equal, the central place system will tend to 'thicken' as settlements expand and new villages

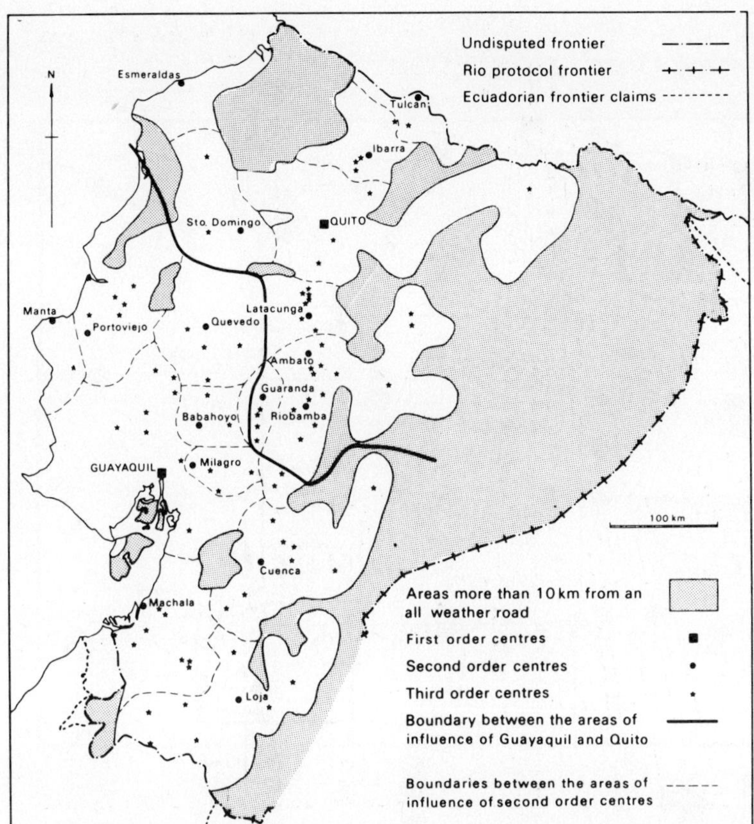

Figure 3.9 The urban hierarchy in Ecuador
Source: Bromley and Bromley, 1979

and towns are established. Conversely, if population falls, the system will tend to thin out.

(2) The system is also affected by changes in transportation. If accessibility is increased then people can move further afield. The range of goods is substantially increased and lower-order centres may be bypassed as shoppers can easily travel to the bigger places further away.

(3) Changes in retailing also have an important role to play. Throughout this century retailing in the core has become dominated by a smaller number of larger establishments. The small grocery store, for example, is being replaced by large chain stores and hypermarkets. More and more goods are sold through these large outlets which, because they have a large threshold, tend to be located in the larger, more accessible centres. Through time the provision of many goods and services has 'moved up' the hierarchy. This upward movement has been helped by improvements in transportation. The movement is not only upward; it also implies a movement away from the existing rural population. For those with easy access to cars this presents no problem, but research in the agricultural region of East Anglia, for example, has shown that those without access to cars – the

EVOLVING URBAN SYSTEMS

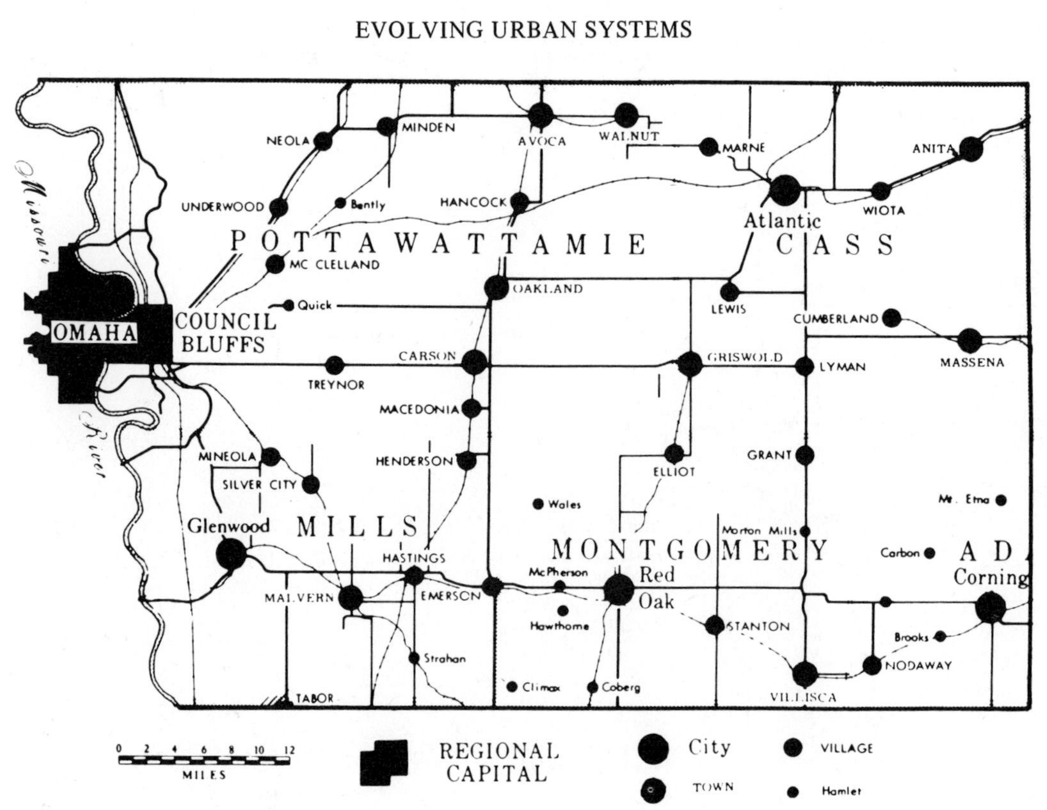

Figure 3B Status of market centres in south west Iowa in the summer of 1961
Source: Berry, 1967

Figure 3B represents the settlement hierarchy in south west Iowa at one point in time. It represents the product of past processes and the context for future developments. The nature of the evolving pattern is shown in the series of figures 3C (i-v). The figures represent the changing central place system through time. The location of the earliest stores reflected the settlement pattern of the pioneers. Pioneer farmers settled in the wooded areas of Iowa. The coming of the railroad changed this as farmers and traders sought locations close to the trade artery of the railways. With increasing population density the settlement pattern reached its peak in 1904. Thereafter there was thinning of the central place system as paved roads and easier access to automobiles allowed consumers to bypass the smaller centres. The population decreased due to farm mechanisations with the consequent shedding of farm labour. Large centres developed around highway intersections, railway connections or as county seats.

References

Berry, B.J.L. (1967), *Geography of Market Centres and Retail Distribution*, Prentice-Hall, Englewood Cliffs, N.J.

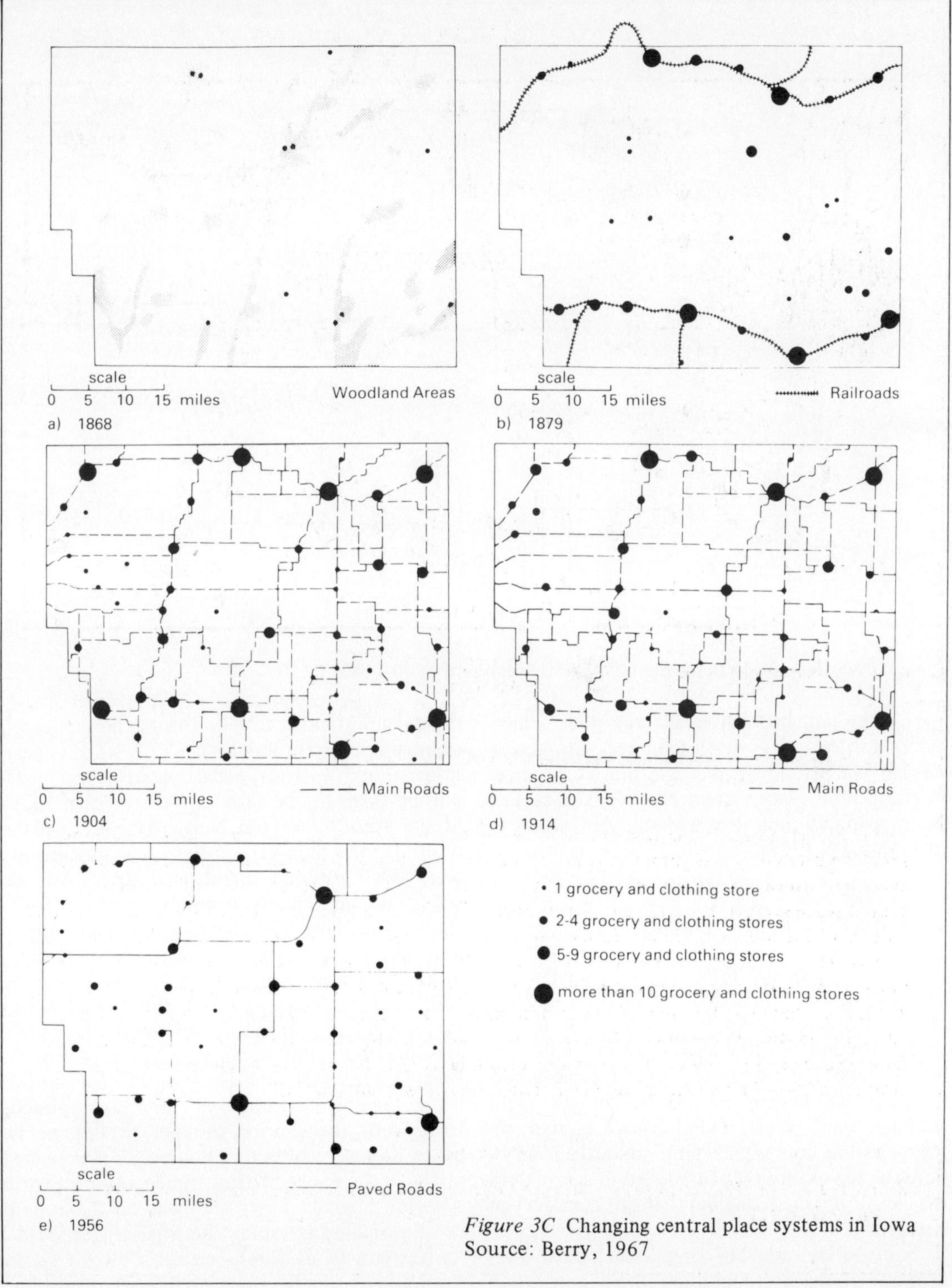

Figure 3C Changing central place systems in Iowa
Source: Berry, 1967

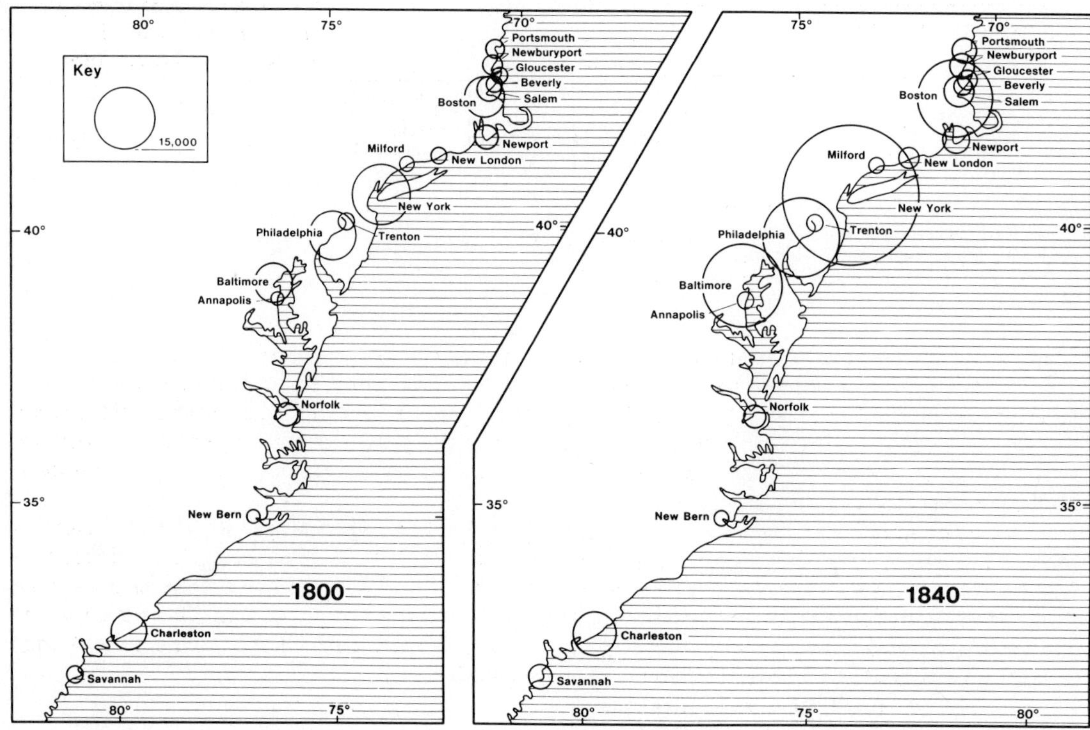

Figure 3.10 Urban growth on the US Atlantic seaboard 1800-1840

young, the old, housewives and the poor – have had a restriction placed on their access to goods, services and employment opportunities. Changes in the central place system have worked against those people in rural areas without ready access to cars (Moseley, 1979).

URBAN SYSTEMS AND TRADE

If central places did little more than serve the surrounding area, then they are unlikely to grow into large towns or cities. For growth to occur, the urban economy must be stimulated by more than the immediate demands for central place goods and services. Before industrialisation the main stimulus came from trade. Towns located on major trading routes grew larger than their neighbours as the expansion of trade led to a growth in the local urban economy. Let us consider an example.

Immediately prior to large-scale industrialisation one of the most important trading routes was the Atlantic trading system. During the eighteenth century the system was triangular, with European ships sailing to Africa, collecting slaves and transporting them to the sugar and cotton plantations of the West Indies and North America. On the return leg the ships carried sugar, cotton and rum from the Caribbean islands and south Atlantic states; fur and timber from the North Atlantic states. The slave trade became less important in the nineteenth century but the trade in commodities between North America and Europe continued to increase. Along the major trading routes a number of towns were established while existing settlements began to expand. In Britain, Bristol, Liverpool and Glasgow swelled in size while London developed an important entrepôt trade with the rest of Europe. In France, Le Havre, Rouen, Nantes and Bordeaux all expanded in the wake of the Atlantic trade. And in North America a whole series of towns on the eastern coast prospered as trading points (see Figure 3.10).

The growth of the mercantilist city, a settlement almost totally reliant on its trading position,

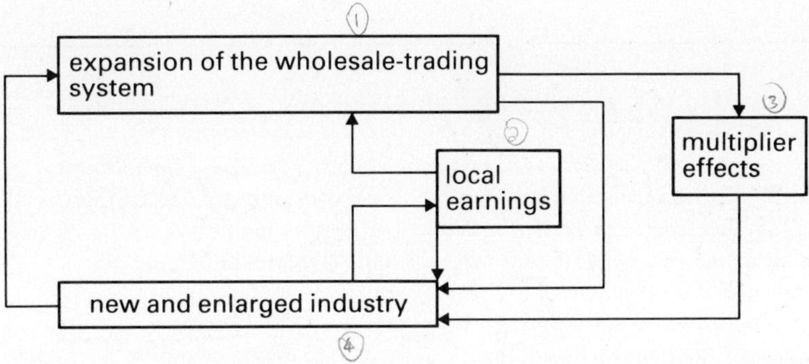

Figure 3.11 Growth mechanisms in mercantile cities
Source: after Pred, 1966

is dependent upon regular transfusions of trade. If the lifeblood of commerce dries up, then the city ceases to grow. There are a large number of cities whose relative decline reflects changes in trading patterns. Venice in Italy and Bruges in Belgium, for example, provide mute testimony to their former grandeur based on relict trading systems. The wealth and growth of Venice was based on the expansion of trade in the Mediterranean from the fourteenth to the sixteenth centuries while Bruges's riches were based upon the trading circuit of the Hanseatic League. The relative decline of these merchant cities reflects the change in the mode and direction of trade. A similar story can be told of the trading ports associated with the Atlantic trade system. In 1860 Charlestown in South Carolina was ranked twentieth in size of all US cities. By 1910 the city had fallen to seventy-seventh position.

Trade and the urban economy

How exactly does trade lead to urban growth? The American geographer Allan Pred has presented a model based on his analysis of US mercantile cities in the period 1800 to 1840. A simplified version of this model is shown in Figure 3.11.

The expansion of trade has a number of effects. Three of the most important are the multiplier effect, the expansion of local industry and the increase in local earnings. Take the case of a town shipping cotton. The collection and storage of the crop will involve improvements to transport routes and the construction of warehouses. There will therefore be important multiplier effects for the local transport and construction industries which will tend to take on more labour. The labour attracted to the wholesale-trading sector in addition to the extra labour associated with the multiplier effects on other sectors of the local economy will in total lead to a large increase in local earnings. The increase in consumer purchasing will attract the provision of more goods and services, and industries will be set up to meet consumer demand.

The effects act upon one another in a cumulative manner. The net result is for the local economy to grow and promote further expansion of trade which promotes more growth. The system is one of circular and cumulative increase in economic expansion.

Selective growth

Not all mercantile cities are equally affected by the process of circular and cumulative growth. Look again at Figure 3.10 and notice how some cities grew larger than others. New York and Boston more than doubled in size, but Savannah, Norfolk, Annapolis, Portsmouth and others scarcely increased their population at all. An examination of the map suggests that the process of circular and cumulative growth is a selective one; the process seems to be more pronounced in the larger cities. This is a general trend.

The urban economist Wilbur Thompson suggests that urban growth tends to occur in the larger cities because:

(1) Large towns have a diverse commercial and industrial base. Certain firms are tied to the city because of economic linkages with other sectors so they cannot relocate. The mix of industries ensures that growth will be maintained even if one industry or one sector declines.

(2) Big cities wield political muscle which is used to get federal and state aid and public works.

(3) The big city constitutes an important market in its own right.

MULTIPLIERS AND EXTERNALITIES

When a new trading complex, service unit or factory is established it has a number of effects on the surrounding environment. First, the new unit will affect the local economy by demanding goods and services, while the labour force employed will add to the purchasing power of the area. Existing businesses and shoppers will expand and new jobs and services will be created. This is the multiplier effect. Second, the new unit will also have an effect on the physical neighbourhood. These effects are known as externalities. There are two kinds. Positive externalities occur when the unit enhances the local surroundings, e.g. the construction of a new factory may involve the rehabilitation of derelict land and the creation of landscaped surroundings. Negative externalities involve damage to the local environment or disbenefits to the local population. A factory which pollutes the atmosphere with its smoke emissions, for example, imposes a negative externality on the local area.

URBAN RATCHET EFFECT

Thompson defines it thus,

> In sum, if the growth of an urban area persists long enough to raise the area to some critical size (a quarter of a million), structural characteristics, such as industrial diversification, political power, huge fixed investments, a rich local market, and a steady supply of industrial leadership may almost ensure its continued growth and fully ensure against absolute decline – may, in fact, effect irreversible aggregate growth. (Thompson, 1965, p. 24)

Notice how Thompson defines the critical level as a quarter of a million. Below this, he suggests, the ratchet effect may not work.

Reference

Thompson, W. (1965), *Preface to Urban Economics*, Johns Hopkins University Press, Baltimore.

(4) The big city is more likely to be the site for innovations in commerce or industry which provide the basis for subsequent growth.

Thompson's analysis suggests that big cities grow more than smaller cities and that large cities cannot contract as smaller towns and villages can. This is termed the *urban ratchet effect*.

In the case of the Atlantic ports, while all the towns were the scene of trade, the multiplier effects of the increase in the wholesale-trading system was experienced in New York and Boston.

URBAN SYSTEMS AND INDUSTRIAL GROWTH

With the onset of capitalist industrialisation the urban system was modified. There were two important changes.

First, the overall level of urbanisation increased. Industrialisation was associated with factory production which tended to take place in towns and cities. Industrialisation was also associated with mechanisation of farming. There was a shedding of labour in the rural areas and the creation of jobs in the towns and cities. As people moved to where they could get employment the net result was for the urban population to grow faster than the rural population. Consider the situation in the USA in the crucial period between 1860 and 1910. Over this period there was a 975 per cent increase in the level of manufacturing output. In 1860 the urban population constituted less than 20 per cent of the total US population. By 1910 this figure had increased to 45 per cent.

Second, the process of urban and economic growth was not evenly distributed across space. By way of initial advantage the existing large cities captured most of the economic growth but the pattern of growth in the smaller cities reflected *relative accessibility* and the pattern of *resource endowment*. These factors led to variations in profitability and, since capital was and is invested in the most profitable locations, the landscape of economic and urban growth mirrored the map of profitability levels. In the early stages of industrialisation the railways played an important role in changing the structure of relative accessibility. In the USA the railroads allowed the interior to be developed and were instrumental in the growth of Chicago, St Louis and Cincinnati. The early production processes were inefficient by modern standards. They required large inputs of raw materials. The materials were bulky and transport still rudimentary. Factory location was thus attracted to the sources of raw materials and power. The nineteenth century in both Europe and North America was characterised by the growth of towns and cities on sites close to important mineral deposits and sources of power. Particularly important were the growth of towns on the coalfields near iron-ore deposits. Urban growth in Pennsylvania and the North of England were examples of this process.

Industrialisation and the urban economy

The relationship between urban growth and industrial developments is similar to one between trade and urban growth. Again the outline model presented in Figure 3.12 is derived from the work of Allan Pred. When a new industry is located in a town or an existing industry expands its operations two things occur. The first is that the initial multiplier effects come into operation to stimulate the local economy. More jobs are created attracting more population and the population may go beyond the threshold for the introduction of other industries and services. For example, the town's population may increase to the extent that it will

A SIMPLE SEQUENCE OF INDUSTRIAL GROWTH AND POPULATION EXPANSION IN SMALL TOWNS

	Industry	*Community*
Growth	Firms locate on green field sites. Industry expands, employment grows and available land is filled up.	New population moves in. Housing supplied by landlords or employers.
Maturity	Local firms make profits and relatively high wages are paid. Growth of unions. Capital investors begin to seek more profitable locations.	Full employment and high wages make for buoyant housing market. Strong purchasing power means growth of retail and services provision. Stable community.
Decline	Profits made in local industry are invested elsewhere. Relocation of plants and decline of local industry.	More skilled workers move out. Remaining residents faced with declining services and restricted job opportunities.

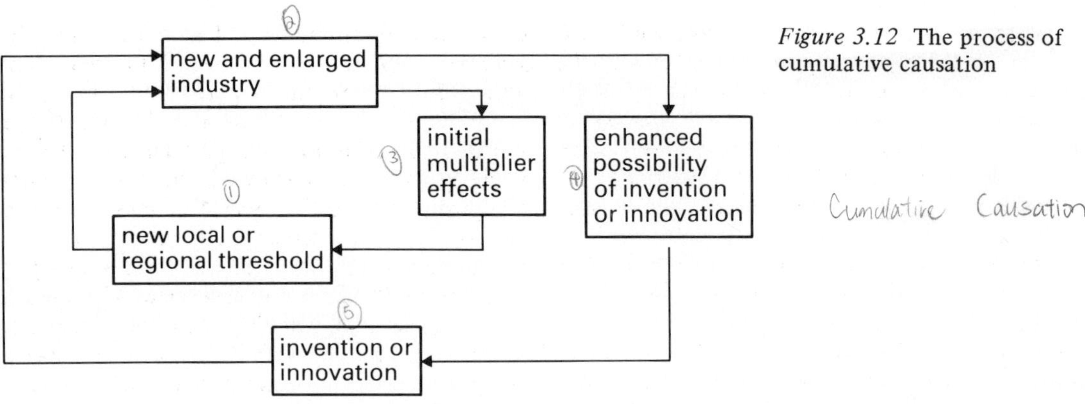

Figure 3.12 The process of cumulative causation

be able to support a daily newspaper or a major hospital which in turn creates jobs and new multiplier effects.

The second effect is less immediately apparent. Pred's model suggests that the increase in population and economic activity creates the climate for inventions and innovations. New jobs attract the more adventurous immigrants, the people with an eye to the main chance. The large booming city also provides the opportunities for cross-fertilisation of ideas. The net effect is for urban growth to promote invention and innovations which provide the platform for new and enlarged industry.

The big city

Growth is often concentrated in the existing large cities. They have many initial advantages; they are often the headquarters of the banks which lend money to industrialists; they have a large pool of labour, necessary infrastructure and a large consumer market. All these characteristics tend to attract industrial growth. Later, new industries will be attracted by this industrial base. It provides opportunities for economics of scale and linkage with other firms. The variety of firms and the diversity of the population in the largest cities create the conditions in which ideas develop into workable inventions. Sparks of genius occur in all places but in cities they are more likely to catch fire.

URBAN SYSTEMS AND PRESENT TRENDS IN MARKET ECONOMIES

ughout most of this century there have been three important changes in capitalist economies which have affected urban systems. The first concerns the nature of industrial organisation. There has been a general trend for industrial and commercial activities to be dominated by a smaller number of larger business enterprises. More and more business is controlled by the big companies, the largest are the huge multinationals whose interests cover a range of services, commercial enterprises and manufacturing sectors and whose operations span the globe. The rise of these big firms has been associated with large-scale production units. These units concentrate growth in selected points. The multiplier effects associated with plants may operate through the institutional channels of the company. If the company has widespread interests, then the multiplier effects need not affect the local economy. They will occur in the subsidiary and parent plants of the company wherever they are located.

Second, manufacturing processes have changed. With developments in transport and production techniques, industry is not so tied to raw material sources, pools of skilled labour or power supplies. Industries are more footloose in that they are not tied to specific locations. Compare a steel mill, the symbol of nineteenth-century industry, with a factory producing computer components. The steel mill used up huge quantities of iron-ore or scrap iron to produce massive quantities of steel. The most profitable location for the steel mill was either close to the raw materials or to the market so as to reduce transport costs. The components factory uses only a minuscule amount of raw materials by comparison. The materials can be brought to almost any part of the country while the finished goods can easily be distributed. In the high-level technology sector transport costs tend to constitute only a very small element of the final costs of the products. The growth industries of the twentieth century are less constrained by transport considerations. Levels of taxation, wage rates and unionisation, etc. are now the key variables influencing the location of manufacturing plants.

Third, there has been an enormous expansion in the tertiary and quaternary sectors of the economy, with a consequent rise in the number of white-collar office workers. The number of white-collar government workers has increased. And there have been changes in the private sector. Administrative functions have now become separated from the production processes. In the nineteenth century and the early part of this century the factory contained both the assembly line and the offices which administered the whole process of buying, making and selling. The administrative functions have expanded enormously, as have the research and development sectors. With developments in communication and the growth of the big multilocational company, these administrative and research and development sections have separated from the industrial plants. Office complexes and research and development sections are now important sectors of the economy in their own right.

A simple model

We can summarise these trends in a simple model of the modern business (see Figure 3.13); a model which sees the firm as composed of different levels with different locational requirements. The base of the enterprise is the routine assembly plant. The profitable location for these plants is where labour is cheap and taxes are low. In the United States the post-war years have seen the transfer to, and growth of these plants in, the southern states because taxes were lower and labour cheaper than in the traditional manufacturing areas of the north east. The lack of unions and the incentive packages offered by the state authorities have encouraged companies to set up their manufacturing base in the smaller towns and cities of the sunbelt. More recently these routine plants are setting up in the newly industrialising countries of the third world, e.g. Mexico, Brazil, South Korea.

The middle tier of a large company is composed of the more sophisticated production techniques and the research and development sections which require skilled labour and scientific workers. These complexes need to be located where taxes are low, and the environment is good enough to attract the key workers. These conditions are found in the suburban areas of selected states, e.g. New Hampshire, California, USA and Berkshire, UK.

The apex of the company hierarchy is the administrative headquarters. The administrative headquarters of major companies still tend to be located in the major cities, because metropolitan areas have a high level of specialised services which can service office complexes. A continuing attraction of a big-city location is the presence of the

	Location	Locational requirement	Changes
company headquarters	metropolitan areas	need for face-to-face contact close to business services close to government agencies	beginnings of suburbanisation: developments in telecommunications dispensing with need for physical proximity
research and development sections	suburban areas small cities	good environment to attract workers low taxes	movement to and growth in smaller towns in amenity-rich areas
routine assembly plants	small cities rural areas	cheap labour low taxes	growth in sunbelt and third world

Figure 3.13 A simple model of the modern business enterprise

URBAN SYSTEMS: EMPIRICAL REGULARITIES

The overall nature of urban systems in a particular region or country can be examined by plotting population size against rank on double logarithmic graph paper. Rank order refers to the position of a city with respect to the population sizes of the other cities. The largest city has a rank of 1, the next largest has a rank of 2 . . . and so on.

Three types of relationship between population size and rank are shown in Figure 3D.

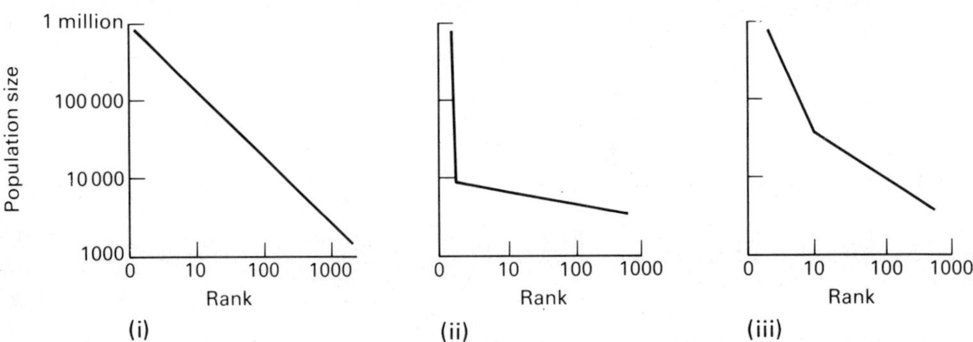

Figure 3D Three rank-size distributions

Figure 3D(i) is a *regular distribution* where there is a regular straight-line relationship between size and rank. It is expressed as the *rank-size rule*

$$P_n = \frac{P_1}{n}$$

where P_n is the population of the nth town and P_1 is the population of the largest cities. If the urban system exhibits a regular distribution then, if the largest city has a population of 50,000, the second ranked place should have a population of

$$P_2 = \frac{50{,}000}{2}$$

$$= 20{,}000$$

Figure 3D(ii) is a *primate distribution.* In this case the largest city, the primate city, dominates the urban system. This distribution is commonly found in the urban systems of third-world countries. Figure 3D(iii) is an intermediate distribution in which the larger cities dominate the urban systems.

By plotting population size and rank in this manner extra insights can be gained into the nature of the urban system. First, the relationship could be plotted over a number of years. as in Figure 3E. In this case notice how the lines for each years shift up the left-hand scale. This indicates growing urbanisation of the population.

Second, the position of individual cities can also be noted. This allows the identification

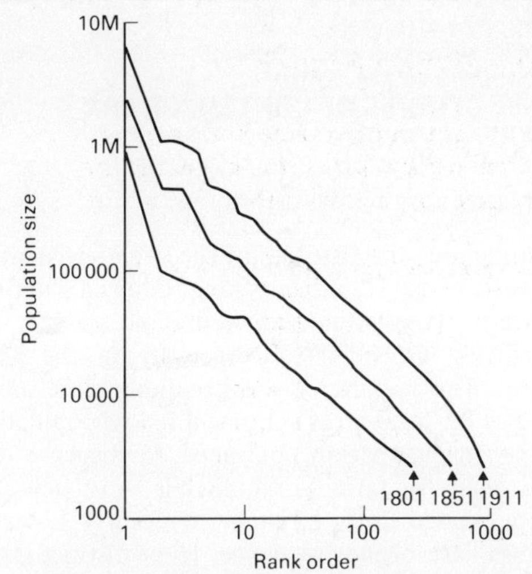

Figure 3E Rank-size relationship for towns in England and Wales, 1801, 1851 and 1911
Source: after B.T. Robson, 1973, *Urban Growth,* Methuen, London

of those cities which have remained relatively stable, those which have declined and those which have expanded. Figure 3F indicates the changing position of Los Angeles in the rank-size distribution over the 90-year period from 1860 to 1950.

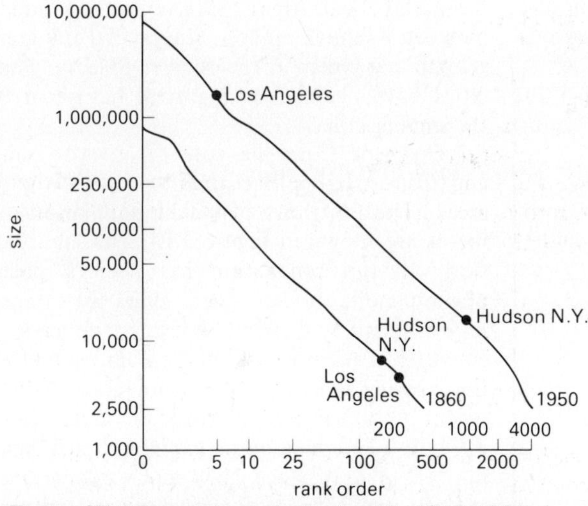

Figure 3F Changes in rank-size in US, 1860-1950
Source: after C.H. Madden, 1956 on some indications of stability in the growth of cities in the US, *Economic Development and Cultural Change* 4, 236-52

References

Madden, C.H. (1950), On some implications of stability in the growth of cities in the United States, *Economic Development and Cultural Change*, 4, 236-52.

Robson, B. (1973), *Urban Growth*, Methuen, London.

offices of other private companies and public agencies which tends to make face-to-face inter-organisation contact relatively easy. It is this contact which lubricates the wheels of business. Gradually, however, office complexes are beginning to move out from the metropolitan cores. This movement is stimulated by high taxes in the city centres and developments in telecommunications which allow easy communication at a distance.

Summary

The overall effects of these emerging trends in modern market economies are:

(1) Large cities are becoming more important, both relatively and absolutely, as a centre for white-collar administrative and services jobs.

(2) There has been a corresponding decline in the manufacturing sector in the big cities. New York is typical: over the period 1953 to 1973 the city lost 38 per cent of its manufacturing employment and increased its service employment by 49 per cent.

(3) New footloose industries are being established in the suburban areas of metropolitan regions and in the smaller cities and towns of selected regions where higher profits can be made and skilled labour be attracted.

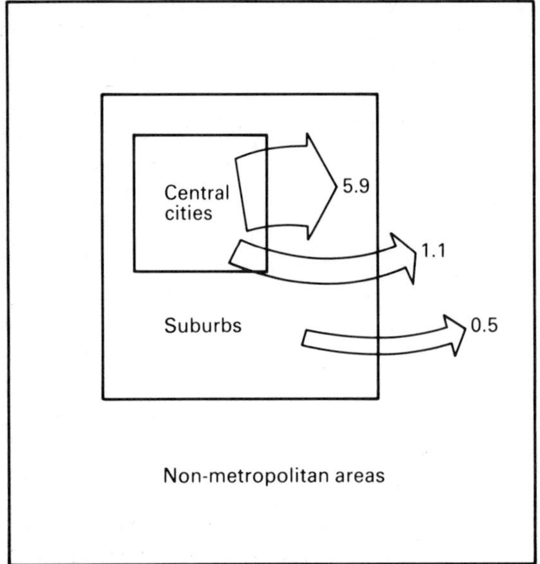

Figure 3.14 Outward movement: net population flows in millions, 1970-75
Source: US Census

CASE STUDIES OF CONTEMPORARY URBAN SYSTEMS

The USA

Throughout the first half of the twentieth century growth in the US urban system followed a definite pattern. Population and economic growth was occurring in the cities, especially in the larger cities. The population was becoming more urbanised as the rural areas continued to lose population. Farm mechanisation continued to dispense with the need for farm workers while most new jobs were created in the cities. More recently, however, things have begun to change. Three distinct trends in the contemporary US urban system can be noted. As a reflection of the economic changes we have just discussed, the movement of people and jobs has been:

(1) *Downward* from the larger metropolitan areas to the smaller cities. In the period 1960 to 1970 the greatest growth was in the Standard Metropolitan Statistical Areas (SMSAs) with populations between 1 and 2 million. Since 1970 the greatest growth has been in the smaller SMSAs. The big cities have declined and growth has occurred in the smaller cities.

(2) *Outward* from the core of cities to suburbs and from metropolitan areas to non-metropolitan areas. The net flows of recent population movements are shown in Figure 3.14. The suburbanisation of the population has been a post-war phenomenon. It has been aided by transport improvements, federal housing policies, the activities of the powerful house-building lobby and the growing affluence of the population. The more recent growth in non-metropolitan areas is a more difficult phenomenon to explain. It has become noticeable only since 1970 and explanations are still at the stage of tentative suggestions rather than fully confirmed statements. A number of suggestions have been put forward:

(a) Non-metropolitan growth simply represents an extension of commuting patterns beyond the present metropolitan boundaries. In some cases this is true. However, this does not explain the situation in those areas where commuting does not occur.

(b) In these cases non-metropolitan growth represents the movement of population to new growth centres. Typical places include special investment areas such as military bases and mining centres, college and university towns, retirement centres, tourist resorts and high amenity places. Retirement, recreation and education seem to be playing a crucial role in the growth of certain non-metropolitan areas. The growth centres of the 1970s and 1980s are amenity-rich locations which attract the more affluent households seeking a pleasant environment in which to live.

The net effect is for the US population to be dispersing outward from the central city to the suburbs and from the metropolitan areas to the non-metropolitan areas.

(3) *Outward* from the older industrial areas of the north east and midwest to the expanding sunbelt areas of the west and south. The major reason for this movement is the search for better jobs. The west and south are now important areas in the US economy for both the manufacturing and service sectors. Figure 3.15 highlights the differential growth patterns in the US space economy. Secondary reasons include the growth of amenity-rich centres in the sunbelt and the emerging trend of black counterstream migration to the south.

These aggregate figures need to be treated with some caution. The regional divisions mask large internal variation. Within the sunbelt, for example, growth has not been uniform throughout the region. Growth has been concentrated in certain states and in certain regions of certain states – e.g. Miami-Fort Lauderdale and Tampa-St Petersburg in Florida, Phoenix in Arizona, Houston and Dallas-Fort Worth in Texas.

The overall conclusion to draw concerning the US urban system is that the population is dispersing outwards from metropolitan cores to suburbs and non-metropolitan areas. Overlying this general trend is a marked regional shift in the population and employment of the country from the north and north east to the south and west; a

STANDARD METROPOLITAN STATISTICAL AREAS (SMSAs)

SMSAs are defined by the US Bureau of Census. They are defined to be functional urban regions. For an area to be designated an SMSA, there must be a central core city with a minimum population of 50,000. Contiguous counties are added to this core if they have 75 per cent or more of their total employment in non-agricultural sectors, 15 per cent or more of workers commuting to the central city and a population density of at least 150 persons per square mile. Boundaries are revised at each census when new SMSAs may be declared.

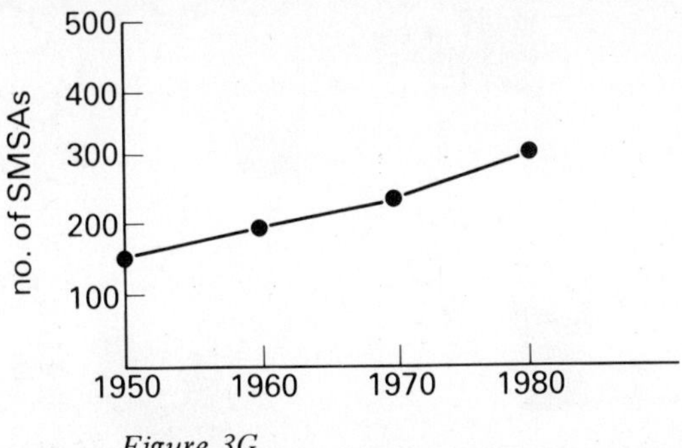

Figure 3G

Figure 3H illustrates the distribution of SMSAs in the USA. This map is based on area. We can change the perspective by mapping areas in relation to the population size. In Figure 3I, which covers all North America, the large SMSAs dominate the scene and the rural areas collapse into insignificance.

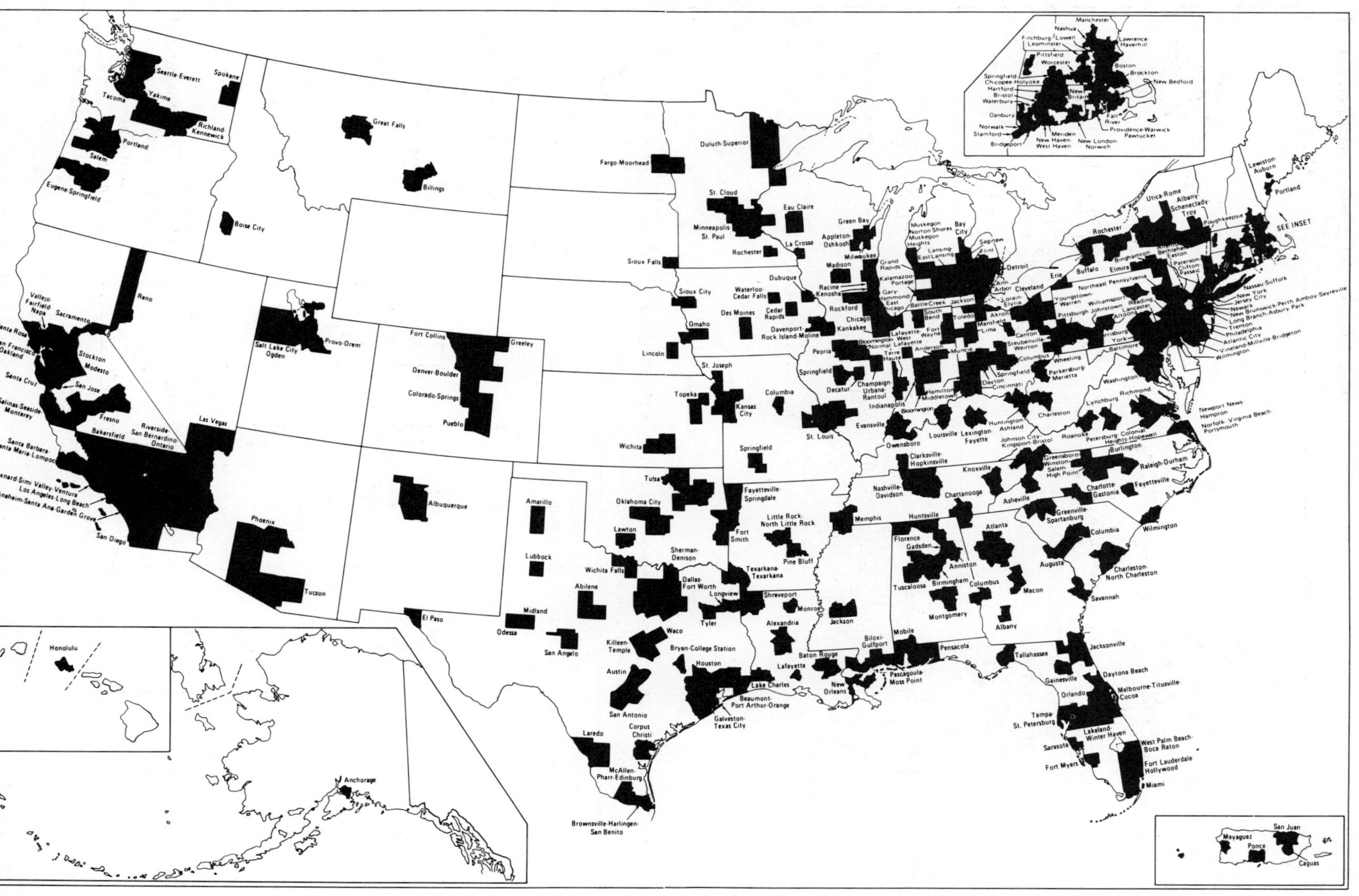

Figure 3H Standard Metropolitan Statistical Areas, 1976

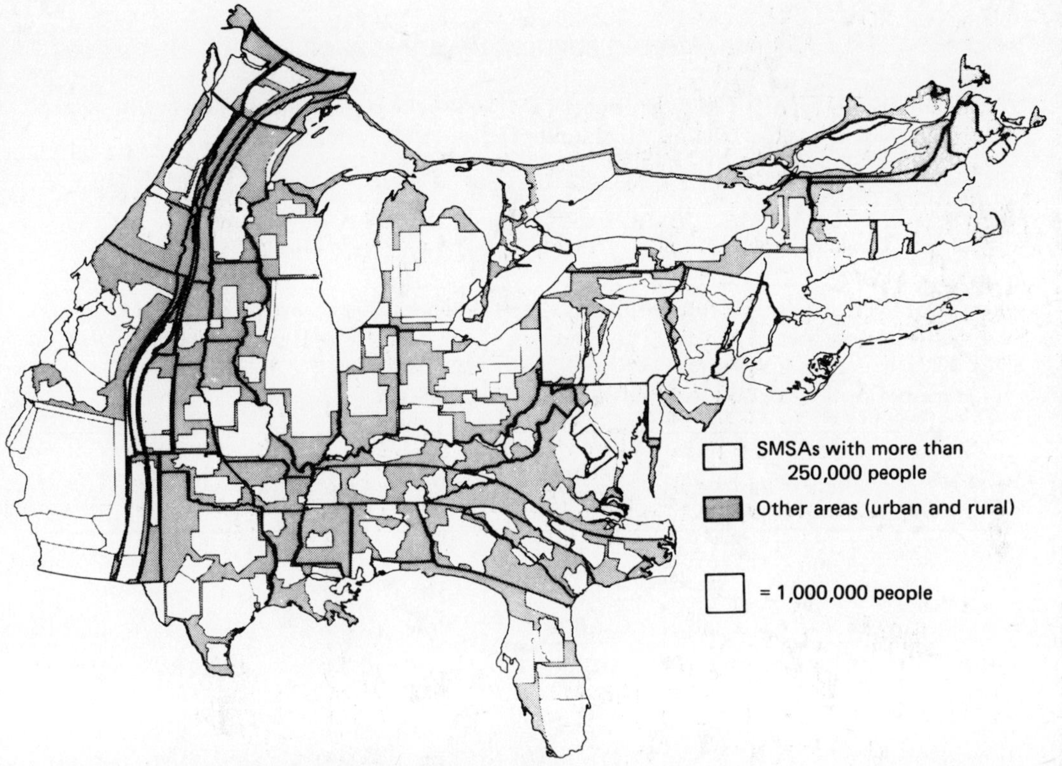

Figure 3I An isodemographic map of metropolitan North America
Source: Eastman, Nelson and Shields 1975-6

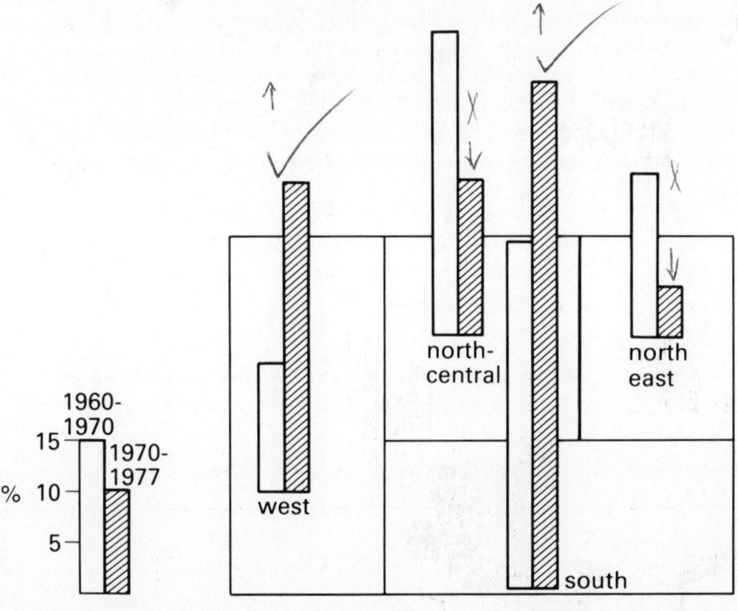

Figure 3.15 Regional growth rate as percent of total US growth in non-agricultural employment

MEASURING POPULATION DISPERSAL

To measure the degree of population dispersal we can use the Hoover index. This index, named after its originator, an economic historian, takes the following form,

$$H_t = \tfrac{1}{2}\sum_{i=1}^{k} (P_{it} - a_{it})\, 100$$

where H_t is the index at time t, P_{it} is the fraction of the nation's population in sub-area i in year t, a_{it} is surface area of sub-area i as a fraction of the nation's total surface area at time t and k is total number of sub-areas.

Let us see how it works. Assume three sub-areas in a nation – 1, 2 and 3.

Sub-areas	*Population*	P_{it}	*Surface Area (km)*	a_{it}	$P_{it} - a_{it}$	$(P_{it} - a_{it})\ 100$
1	25,000	0.5	4,000	0.4	0.1	10
2	10,000	0.2	4,000	0.4	–0.2	20
3	15,000	0.3	2,000	0.2	0.1	10
Nation (1+2+3)	50,000		10,000			$\Sigma\ (P_{it} - a_{it}) =$ 40

$H_t = \tfrac{1}{2} \times 40$

$H_t = 20$

If the population is uniform throughout the nation then all sub-areas will have similar population densities and $H_t = 0$. The larger the value of H_t, the closer it is to 100, the more concentrated the population is in particular areas. The closer the value is to 0 the less the population concentration. The H_t value is dependent upon the sub-areas used.

Two regional scientists, Vining and Strauss, working at the University of Pennsylvania, have used the Hoover index to measure population concentration in the USA. They calculated the index for different area units from 1950 to 1976.

The results shown in Figure 3J suggest that dispersal of the population has been occurring at all levels since 1970. They suggest that this represents a 'clean break' with past patterns.

References

Vining, D.R. Jnr and Strauss, A. (1977), A demonstration that the current deconcentration of population in the United States is a clean break with the past, *Environment and Planning A*, 9, 751-8.

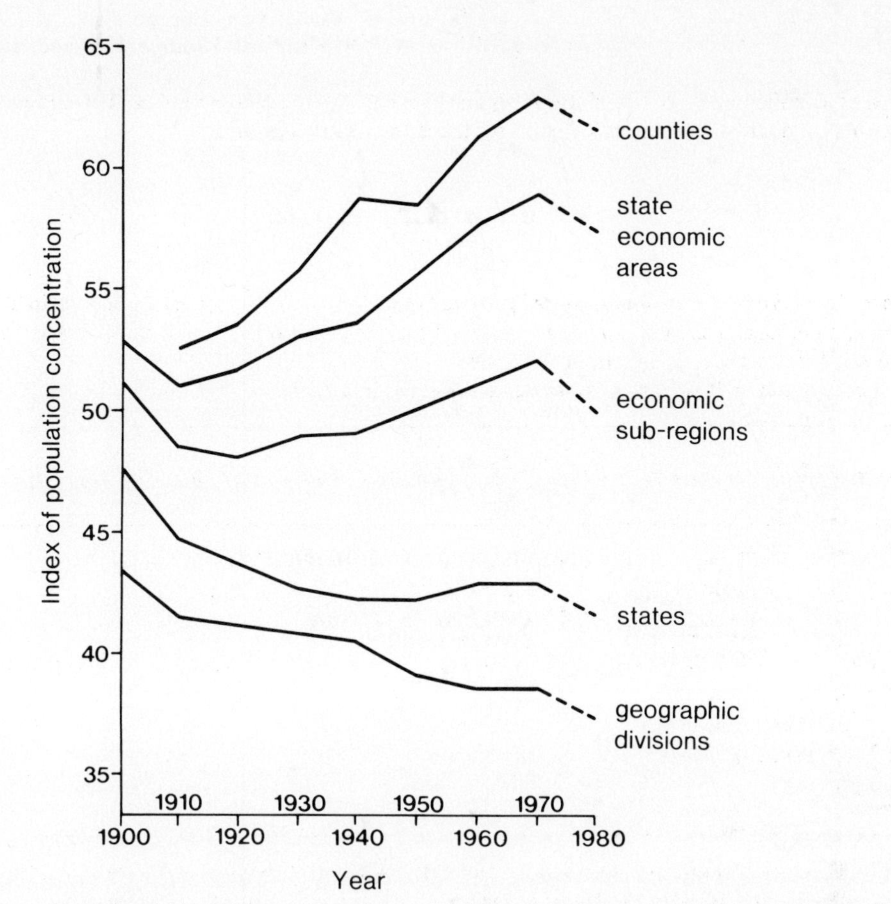

Figure 3J Indexes of population concentration for various systems of a real sub-division of the United States, 1900-74
Source: Vining & Strauss (1977)

shift in the centre of gravity from the frostbelt to the sunbelt. This regional dimension causes variations in the nature of urban growth and decline. The big city cores in the sunbelt are not declining to the same extent as the city cores in the frostbelt.

The case of Europe

Peter Hall and Dennis Hay, two British geographers working at the University of Reading, have examined the patterns of urban growth in Europe from 1950 to 1975. It was a vast undertaking since there was no comparable reference frame to the US SMSAs. For each of the countries of Europe they had to define metropolitan regions. The cores of these regions had to contain at least 20,000 jobs while the metropolitan rings, the suburban areas, were defined by the limits of commuting.

The metropolitan regions were the technical building blocks of the Hall and Hay study. From the analysis of these regions two broad conclusions were reached. First there was no simple pattern of population growth. The areas of greatest growth are shown in Figure 3.16. These areas, in which population growth exceeded 30 per cent in the

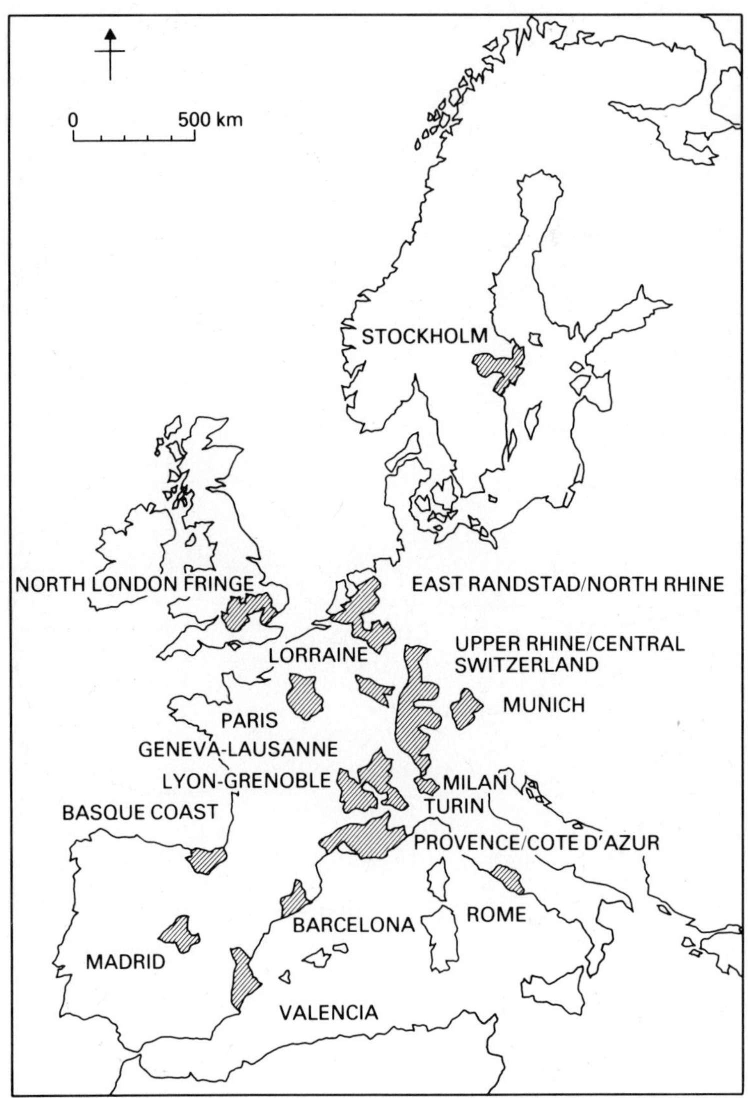

Figure 3.16 Growth zones in Europe
Source: Hall and Hay, 1980

period 1950 to 1975, took over 54 per cent of total European population growth in the twenty-five-year period. Growth occurred along the north-south axis of the Rhine and in selected centres in southern Europe. Outliers were found in the Stockholm region and the northern and western fringes of London. In comparison to the USA, economic and population growth is still occurring in the old industrial heartland; the Golden Triangle stretching from north Holland to Madrid and Rome. Second, there was no simple pattern of dispersal from the metropolitan cores as is occurring in the US case. A number of variations were noted:

(1) In Atlantic and northern Europe (Britain, Ireland, Sweden, Norway and Denmark) the pattern was one of declining cores and expanding suburbs. Non-metropolitan regions were continuing to lose population but the rate of loss was beginning to level off from 1970 onwards. Britain was typical (see Figure 3.17).

(2) In central and western Europe (Belgium, the

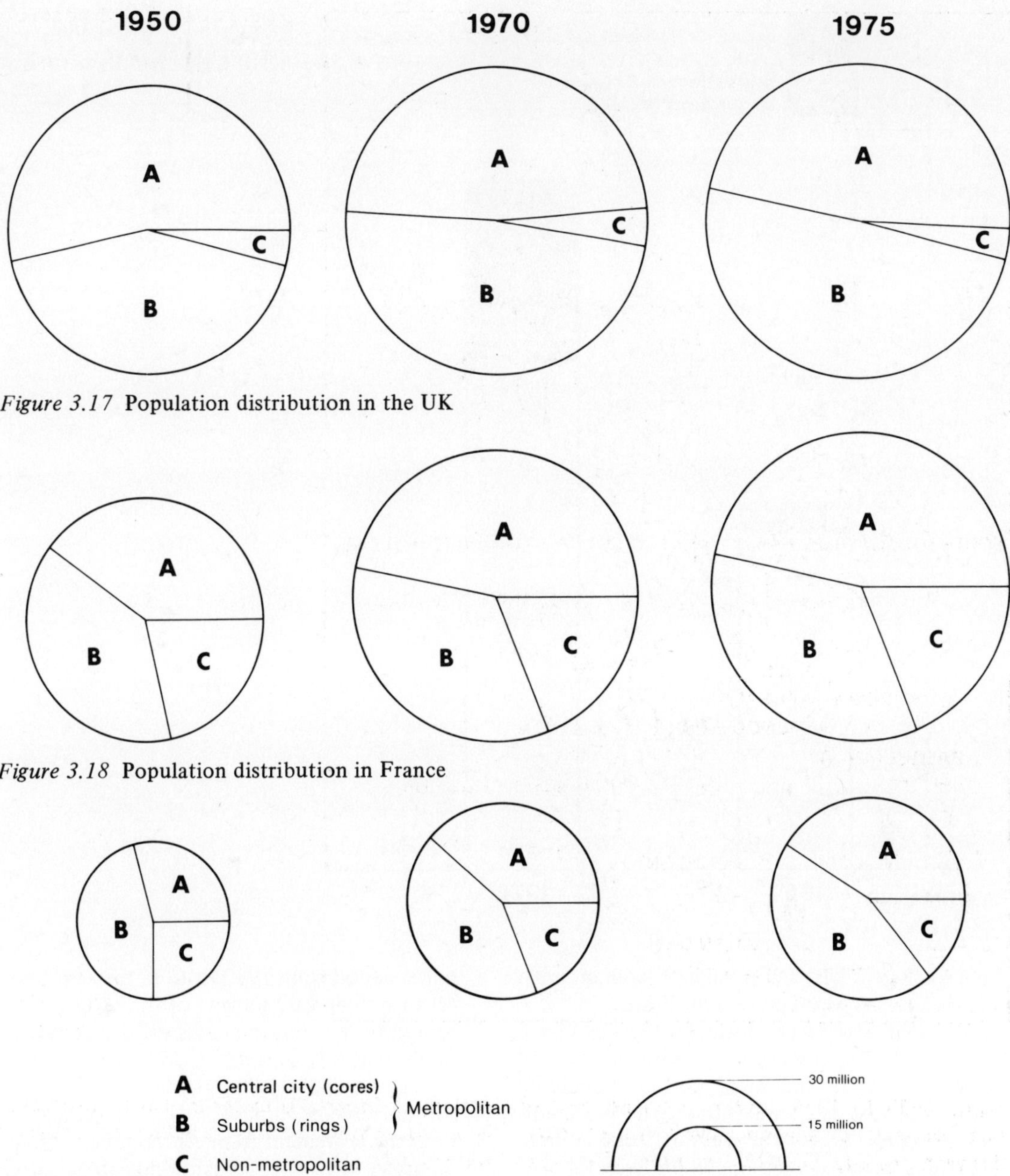

Figure 3.17 Population distribution in the UK

Figure 3.18 Population distribution in France

Figure 3.19 Population distribution in Spain

Netherlands, Luxemburg, France, West Germany, Switzerland and Austria) the general pattern was for a concentration of population in the metropolitan cores and a corresponding relative decline in the proportion of the population in the metropolitan rings and the non-metropolitan regions. The process underlying this pattern is one of continued rural-urban migration. Since 1970, however, the growth of the metropolitan core has not been as great as population growth in the

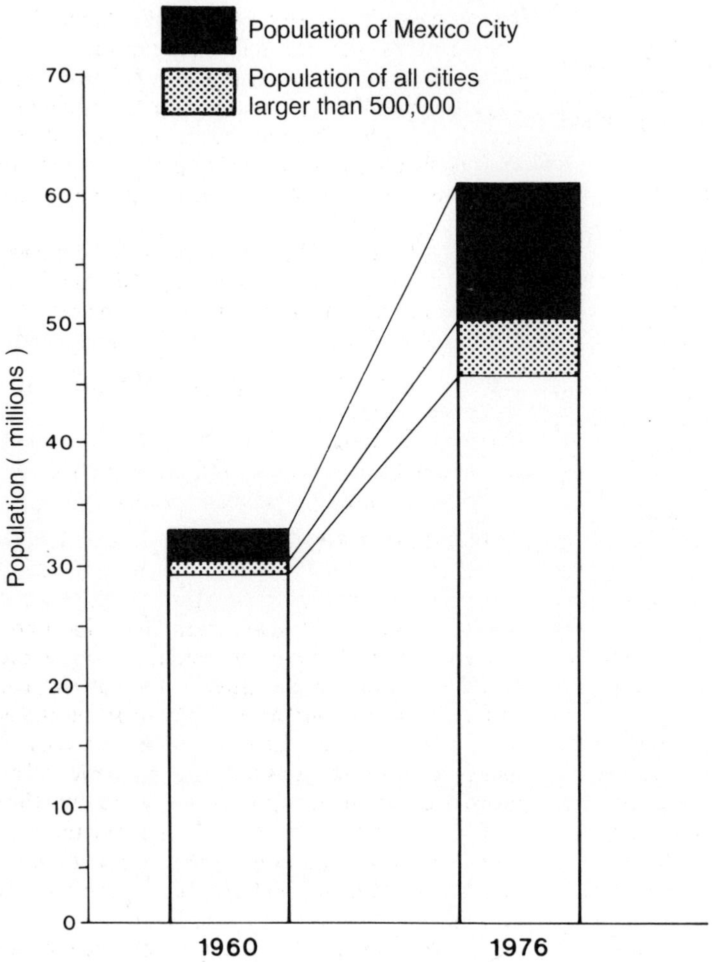

Figure 3.20 Population growth in Mexico

metropolitan rings and non-metropolitan areas. Figure 3.18 shows the picture for France.

(3) In southern Europe (Spain, Portugal and Italy) there was the complete opposite of the US experience. Over the same period, population became increasingly concentrated in the metropolitan cores as the process of rural-to-urban migration siphoned off population from the non-metropolitan areas. This trend has continued throughout the whole period. Since 1975, however, there is some evidence to suggest that suburbanisation is beginning to occur as the metropolitan rings increase their share of the population. The figures for Spain highlight these trends (Figure 3.19).

Hall and Hay summarise their results as follows:

> in the period from 1960 to 1975 the European urban system was failing to operate like the American. The tendency was still for population to move from rural to urban areas, not the reverse. The industrial heartland was still strong, and the remoter rural areas were still losing . . . Even the movement from central urban core to suburban ring was more tardy than in North America, with Atlantic Europe in the van and Southern Europe in the rear of the process. (Hall and Hay, 1980, p. 228)

The third world

Contemporary urban systems in third-world countries with market economies have exhibited two main trends in recent years:

(1) the enormous growth of urban populations;
(2) the increasing concentration of population and economic activity in the very largest cities.

These population characteristics are shown with respect to Mexico in Figure 3.20.

What has caused these patterns?

Third-world countries have experienced enormous growth of population. Over the two decades from 1960 to 1980 the population increase in third-world countries averaged 2.5 per cent per year. Comparable figures for the USA are 1.0 per cent, 0.3 per cent for the UK and 1.5 per cent for Canada. The population increase has been caused by the improvement in health facilities which has reduced child mortality and extended life expectancy. With fewer deaths and more births, the scene has been set for a population explosion. In Mexico the population has increased from 35 million in 1960 to over 62 million in 1976 and estimates by the World Bank suggest Mexico's population will reach 116 million by the year 2000.

Against this background of rising population there has been a greater relative increase in the urban population. There are two reasons for this. First, health facilities are better in the cities in comparison to the rural areas. Child mortality rates are lower in the city and population increase is thus proportionately greater. Second, there has been large-scale rural-to-urban migration. This form of population redistribution reflects the growing mechanisation and use of capital in the agricultural sector which reduces job opportunities in rural areas. Many people in the countryside are unable to find jobs. The only hope is to move to the cities where the prospect of jobs and better welfare facilities provides some ray of comfort in an otherwise bleak landscape. In third-world cities migrants from rural areas constitute between a half and three-quarters of the urban population increase.

The net result has been for the urban population to increase faster than the total population. In Mexico, for example, while the total population grew by 3.3 per cent per year in the period 1970 to 1977, the urban population grew by 4.6 per cent. Urban growth has not been uniform throughout the urban system. Growth has been concentrated in the very largest cities. Figure 3.20 demonstrates the enormous growth of Mexico City in relation to the total population. The experience of Mexico can be replicated throughout the third world. There are economic and political factors shaping this distinctive pattern, a pattern which is the opposite to that occurring in the developing world.

In the third world most industrial and commercial establishments tend to set up in the big cities because in comparison to the rest of the country there is:

(a) a better infrastructure of roads, railways, sewage, electricity, etc.;
(b) a bigger labour pool;
(c) better transport links with other parts of the country and with overseas markets.

In the third world there are not the counteracting forces pulling factories and offices to smaller towns or rural areas. The big cities stand out as the most profitable locations for local and foreign capital. Of course industrial complexes are found sometimes at the site of raw material and certain minerals. But apart from these resource-orientated industries all other economic activity tends to gravitate towards the big cities. The process of cumulative growth begins to function as the population drawn to the jobs in the city constitutes an important market for consumer-orientated industries and services. Growth tends to generate growth.

The big capital cities dominate the economic, social and political life of third-world countries. The web of political decisions, like the transport network, emanates from the primate city. Political power is firmly rooted in the big capital cities of Mexico City, Bogota, Cairo and Kampala. Power attracts business as the business community seeks to locate its activities and premises close to the centre of the political stage. The closer you are to the political action the more chance you have of influencing the outcome. The state plays an important role in the economic sphere. It makes major investment decisions. To be close to political power is to be close to economic power. There is also a definite urban bias to the development process. Development programmes in the third world tend to operate through state agencies. The political elite and the state bureaucracies are located in the capital city and development programme investments in welfare provision and infrastructure reflect this urban bias. This becomes a circular process as state investments make the big city more attractive for business and rural job-seekers. Even more people are attracted to the city. The greater the population concentrations in the city, especially of professional workers and politicians, the greater the urban bias of subsequent growth and investment. And so the process continues.

Multiplier effects in the era of multinationals

In Figure 3.12 the process of urban-industrial growth is portrayed as a process of cumulative causation in which the setting up or enlargement of an industry has important multiplier effects on the local economy. This model does not take into account patterns of ownership. In third-world countries multinational companies dominate the business scene as much as they do in the core. These multinationals are organised from the core. Their headquarters, control centres and shareholders tend to be in the developed world. In Mexico, 59 of the largest 100 companies are foreign-owned. The Senate Committee report which produced this figure noted that the Mexican subsidiaries were integrated into the workings of the parent company and profits and multiplier effects were being exported to the parent company in the developed world. Industrial growth in third-world cities may not stimulate growth in associated industries, as supplies, finance and services will be provided by firms in other countries. The city in the third world experiences the negative externalities of economic growth but not necessarily the multiplier effects.

Towards a general model

On the basis of comparing the different urban systems a simple model of urban system development can be developed (see Figure 3.21). Phase 1 is the period of initial industrialisation, when there is the establishment of factories in cities. There is large-scale rural-to-urban migration and the concentration of growth in the big cities. Phase 2 is associated with the suburbanisation of industry and population. Developments in manufacturing processes and transport allow industry to be more footloose and enable people to live further from their place of work. In this period the central city population begins to decrease while the suburban population increases. There is a continuing decline in the rural population. The final stage, phase 3, is associated with a much more dispersed population distribution. The negative externalities of the big cities and the attractions of small cities lead to a movement down the hierarchy of population and economic growth. Suburbanisation of jobs and people continues outwards into formerly rural areas and non-metropolitan growth occurs in selected retirement and tourist centres in amenity-rich areas.

This model reflects the experience of the US urban system. Phase 1 describes the initial period of industrialisation in the latter half of the nineteenth century and the early part of the twentieth. Phase 2 describes the urban experience until the late 1960s. And phase 3 is happening at the moment. The experience of the other countries can also be fitted into this schema. The countries of Atlantic and northern Europe are just beginning phase 3, the countries of central and western Europe are beginning phase 2 and the countries of southern Europe and the third world are still at phase 1. This model is a useful comparative yardstick on which to classify the current position of different national urban systems. However, we should be wary of seeing it as a deterministic historical sequence with all countries following in the wake of the USA. Reality is more complex. Other countries may not be able to replicate the US pattern. Consider the case of large-scale suburbanisation. In the USA this was predicated upon relatively cheap fuel which enabled commuters to travel large distances to their place of work from their place or residence. There are simply not enough oil resources in the world for all countries to have such large-scale private-car commuting as is apparent in US levels of suburbanisation. Moreover, other countries may not want to follow the path taken by the USA. There are cultural differences which play an important role. In central and southern Europe there is a tradition of high-density apartment dwelling for family households as well as single persons and childless couples. For the richer families this is combined with a rural residence. In these countries there is less desire for a suburban residence. The deconcentration of population from the urban cores may not occur on

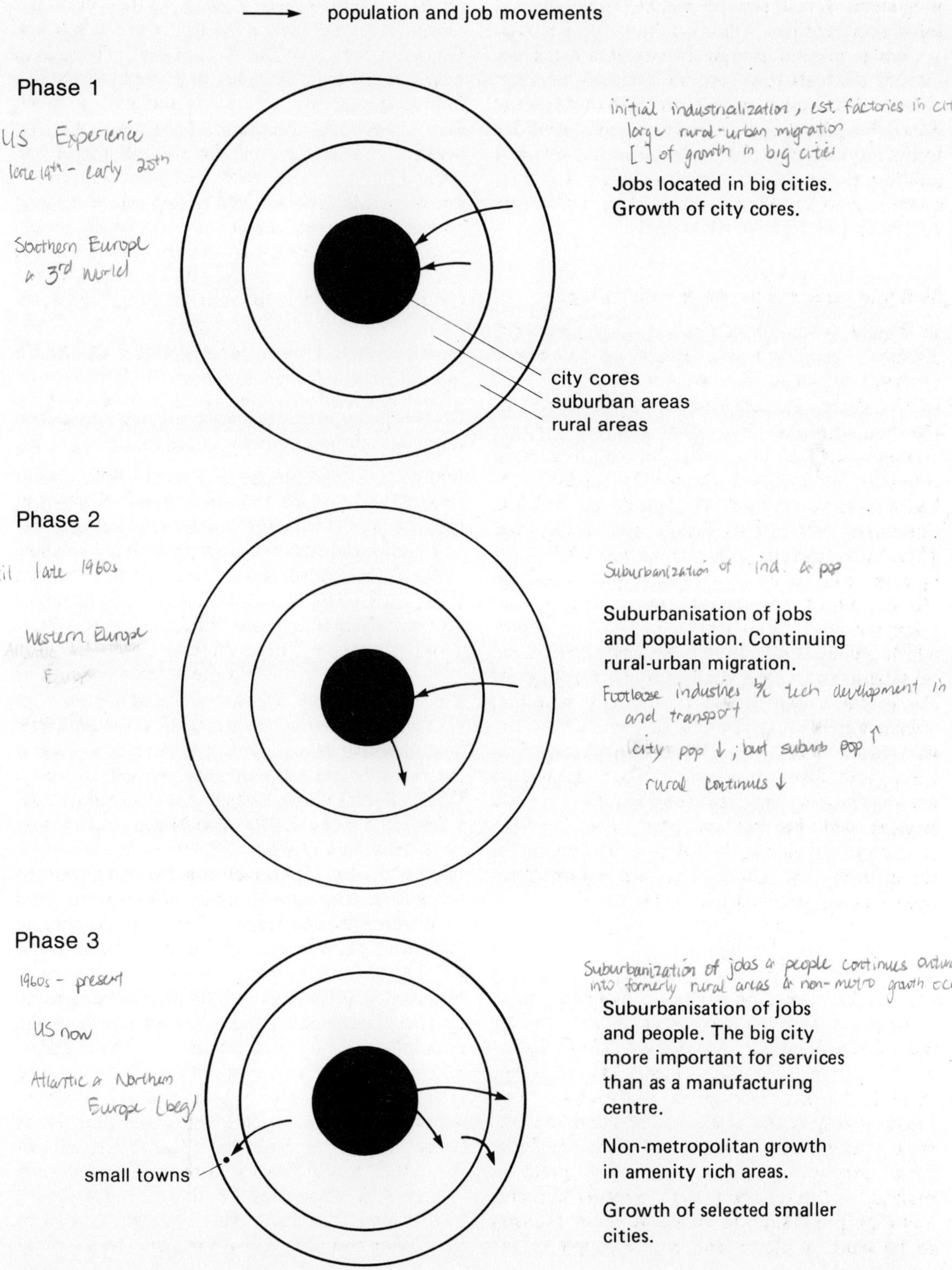

population and job movements
Phase 1
Jobs located in big cities.
Growth of city cores.
city cores
suburban areas
rural areas
Phase 2
Suburbanisation of jobs
and population. Continuing
rural-urban migration.
Phase 3
Suburbanisation of jobs
and people. The big city
more important for services
than as a manufacturing
centre.
Non-metropolitan growth
in amenity rich areas.
Growth of selected smaller
cities.
small towns

Figure 3.21 A general model of urban systems' change

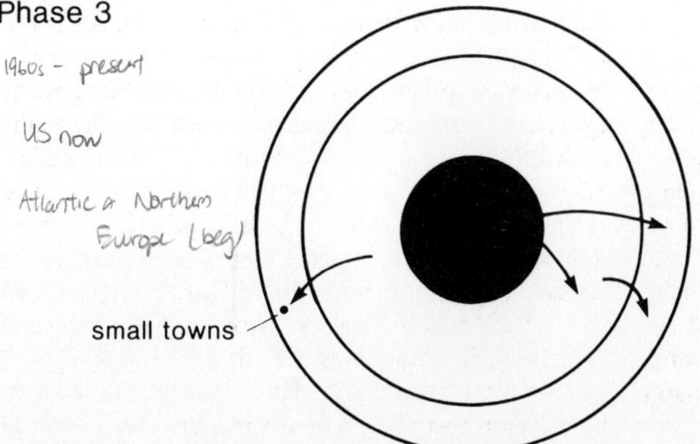

the same scale as has happened in North America or Atlantic Europe.

This simple model should be seen as a description of the unfolding patterns of the US urban system, the likely course for cities in Atlantic Europe and one out of many possible developments for other national urban systems.

GUIDE TO FURTHER READING

On periodic markets see:

Hay. A.M. and Smith, R.H.T. (1980), Consumer welfare in periodic market systems, *Transactions Institute of British Geographers, New Series*, 5, 29-44.

Hill, P. and Smith R.H.T. (1972), The spatial and temporal synchronization of periodic markets: evidence from four Emirates in Northern Nigeria, *Economic Geography*, 48, 345-55.

Smith, R.H.T. (ed.) (1978), *Market Place Trade: periodic markets, hawkers and traders in Africa, Asia and Latin America*, Centre for Transportation Studies, University of British Columbia.

Early work on central place theory includes:

Christaller, W. (1966), *Central Places in Southern Germany* (translated by C. Baskin), Prentice-Hall, Englewood Cliffs, N.J.

Dickinson, R.E. (1932), The distribution and function of the smaller urban settlements of East Anglia, *Geography*, 17, 19-31.

Galpin, C.J. (1915), *Social Anatomy of An Agricultural Community*, Research Bulletin 34, University of Wisconsin Agricultural Experiment Station.

More recent work includes:

Berry, B.J.L. (1967), *Geography of Market Centres and Retail Distribution*, Prentice-Hall, Englewood Cliffs, N.J.

Bromley, R. and Bromley, R.D.F. (1979), Defining central place systems through the analysis of bus services: the case of Ecuador, *Geographical Journal*, 145, 416-36.

Lösch, A. (1954), *The Economics of Location*, (trans. by W.H. Woglom), Yale University Press, New Haven.

Parr, J. (1981), Temporal change in a central place system, *Environment and Planning A*, 13, 97-118.

Preston, R.E. (1971), The structure of central place systems, *Economic Geography*, 47, 136-56.

For a useful introduction to accessibility in 'thinning' central place systems see:

Moseley, M.J. (1979), *Accessibility: The Rural Challenge*, Methuen, London.

Of the many studies linking urban systems and economic growth consider some of the work in:

Bourne, L.S. and Simmons, J.W. (1978), *Systems of Cities*, Oxford University Press, New York.

Pred, A.R. (1966), *The Spatial Dynamics of US Urban-Industrial Growth 1800-1914*, MIT Press, Cambridge, Mass.

Pred, A.R. (1977), *City-System in Advanced Economies*, Hutchinson, London.

Case studies of urban systems include:

Berry, B.J.L. (1973), *Growth Centres in The American Urban System*, 3 vols, Ballinger, Cambridge, Mass.

Bourne, L.S. and Simmons, J.W., *op. cit.*

Chang, S.-D. (1976), Changing systems of Chinese cities, *Annals of The Association of American Geographers*, 66, 398-415.

Gugler, J. and Flanagan, W.G. (1977), On the political economy of urbanization in the Third World: the case of West Africa, *International Journal of Urban and Regional Research*, 1, 272-92.

Hall, P.G. and Hay, D. (1980), *Growth Centres in The European Urban System*, Heinemann, London.

4 The Dynamics of Urban Systems

The urban system is an arrangement of towns held together by flows of people, goods and ideas. These flows constitute the dynamics of the urban system, the system's lifeblood. In the last chapter we looked at the spatial arrangement of the urban centres. In this chapter we will consider the dynamics.

THE MOVEMENT OF PEOPLE

People are continually on the move. Figure 4.1 represents some of the different types of movement. We can distinguish between the very frequent, short-distance moves involved in journeys to work, shop and play, and the infrequent, larger-distance moves which involve a permanent change in residence.

When the permanent relocation is made within the same city, it is termed *intra-urban* migration; this form of migration constitutes two-thirds of all permanent relocations. When the relocation is from one city to another, it is termed *inter-urban* and when the relocation is made from a rural area to a town or city it is termed *rural-urban* migration. In subsequent chapters we will consider intra-urban migration, but for the moment we will examine the characteristics of inter-urban and rural-urban movement.

Rural-urban migration is the predominant form of movement in the third world. It was also important in the developed world of the nineteenth and early twentieth centuries. Throughout the twentieth century in Britain and the USA, for example, the importance of rural-urban migration has declined as inter-urban moves began to predominate. It is a sign of economic development when rural-urban migration is replaced by inter-urban migration as the dominant form of movement.

Table 4.1 Population movement and economic growth

Dominant form of movement	*Stage of economic growth*
rural-urban	early industrialisation
inter-urban	mature industrialisation
urban-rural	late (post) industrialisation

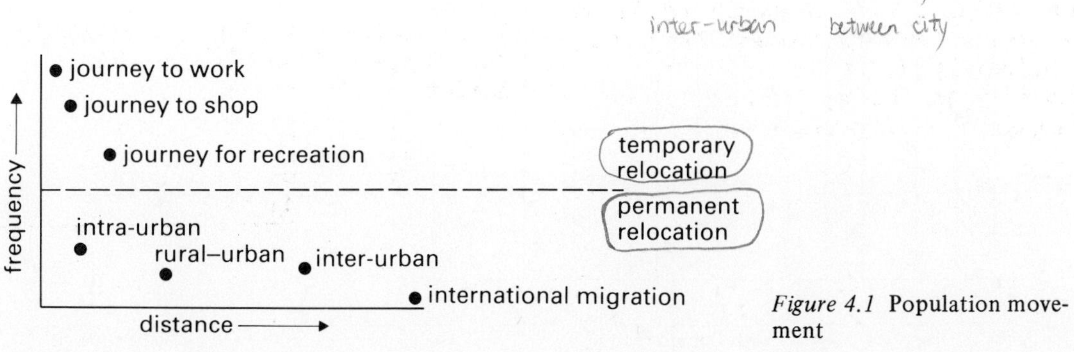

Figure 4.1 Population movement

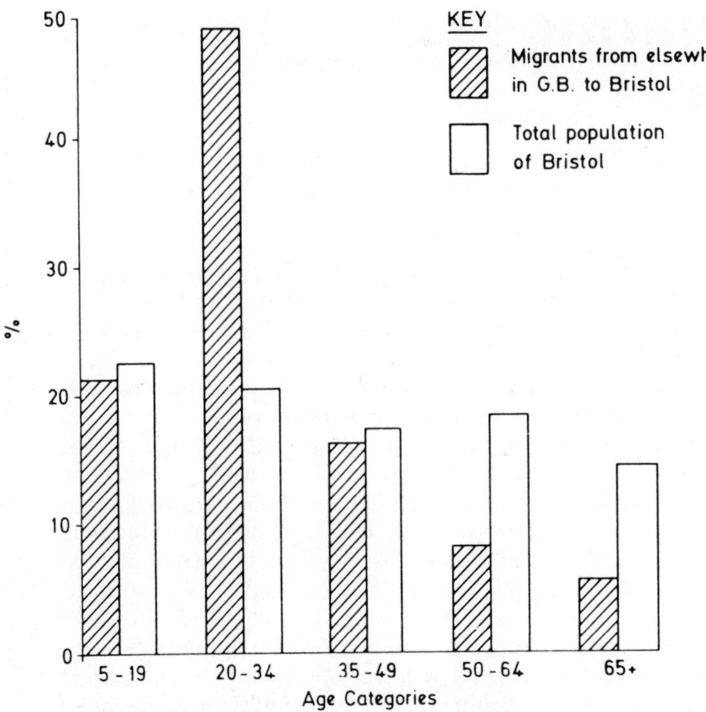

Figure 4.2 Age distribution of immigrants and total population of Bristol

Source: Short, J.R. (1980), *Urban Data Sources*, Butterworth

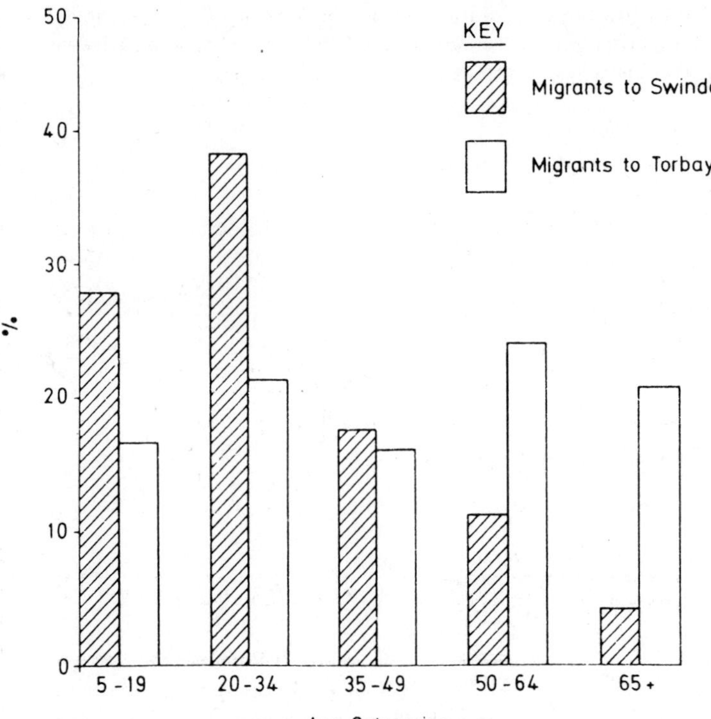

Figure 4.3 Age distribution of immigrants to Swindon and Torbay

Source: Short, J.R. (1980), *Urban Data Sources*, Butterworth

MODELLING POPULATION MOVEMENT 1: DESCRIPTIVE

Ravenstein

In a paper given to the Royal Statistical Society of Britain in 1885 the statistician E.G. Ravenstein sought to expound the laws of population movement. He identified seven:

1 The great body of migrants only proceed a short distance.
2 The inhabitants of the country immediately surrounding a town of rapid growth flock into it; the gaps thus left in the rural population are filled up by migrants from more remote districts, until the attractive force of one of our rapidly growing cities makes it influence, step by step, the most remote corner of the kingdom.
3 The process of dispersion is the inverse of that of absorption and exhibits similar features.
4 Each main current of migration produces a compensating counter-current.
5 Migrants proceeding long distances go by preference to one of the great centres of commerce or industry.
6 The natives of towns are less migratory than those of the rural parts of the country.
7 Females are more migratory than males.

Lee

More recently the sociologist Everett Lee has suggested that the amount of population movement between two cities i and j depends upon the mix of push and pull factors (unemployment and lack of housing in city i would be push factors while the existence of highly paid jobs in j would be a powerful pull factor) and the existence of intervening opportunities. Migrants are hardly likely to move from i to j if just as highly paid jobs can be obtained in a city closer to city i than j. We can translate this description into a single diagram (Figure 4A). The positive and negative signs in the origin i and destination j refer to pull and push factors.

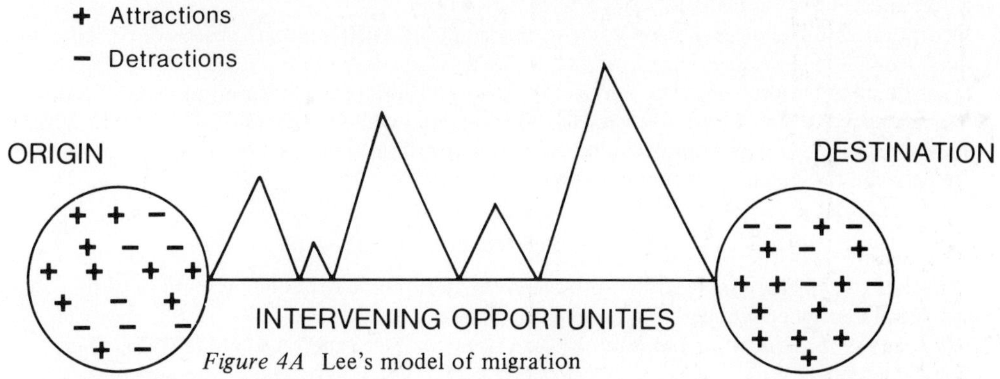

Figure 4A Lee's model of migration

References

Lee, E. (1969), A theory of migration, In Jackson, J.A. (ed.), *Migration*, Cambridge University Press.

Ravenstein, E.G. (1885), The laws of migration, *Journal of The Royal Statistical Society*, 48, 167-227.

MODELLING POPULATION MOVEMENT 2: STATISTICAL

The movement between cities can be examined with reference to the gravity model. The basic gravity model suggests that population movement between city i and city j (we can use the term mij to refer to this movement) is in direct proportion to the populations of city i (P_i) and city j (P_j) and indirectly proportional to the distance D_{ij} between them. We can express the relationship in the following way:

$$mij = k \frac{P_i P_j}{D_{ij}} \quad \text{where k is a constant}$$

This is a useful starting point. However, migrants move in relation to job opportunities. We can add this dimension to our models:

$$mij = k \frac{u_i}{u_j} \cdot \frac{w_j}{w_i} \cdot \frac{P_i P_j}{D_{ij}}$$

where, u_i u_j are the percentage of unemployed in the labour force at i and j respectively and

w_i w_j are the hourly average wages in dollars at i and j

Using a version of this model in a multiple regression framework, I.S. Lowry analysed population flows between 90 SMSAs over the period 1955 to 1960 and obtained an $R^2 = +0.6821$. In other words almost 70 per cent of the variations in population flows was explained by the model.

Ian Masser used a similar model in studying inter-urban population movements in England and Wales over the period 1965 to 1966 and achieved an $R^2 = 0.9395$.

More recent work has been concerned with 2 elements:

1 Incorporating differences in propensity to move amongst different sub-groups in the population.
2 Distinguishing between *net flows* and *gross flows*. If 30,000 people leave j to i and 20,000 move from i to j then the net flow is 10,000 from j to i while the gross flow is 50,000. There are important net flows from declining cities to expanding cities but the largest gross flows are between the booming economies of expanding cities.

References

Gober-Meyes, P. (1978), Employment-motivated migration and economic growth in post-industrial market economies, *Progress in Human Geography*, 2, 207-29.

Lowry, I.S. (1966), *Migration and Metropolitan Growth: Two Analytical Models*, Chandler, San Francisco.

Masser, I. (1970), *A Test of Some Models for Predicting Inter-Metropolitan Movement of Population in England and Wales*, Centre for Environmental Studies, University Working Paper 9, London.

Who moves?

Migration is a selective process. Not all households are represented in the process of movement. In general, it is the younger, more dynamic, more ambitious households who move; it is they who have the necessary get-up-and-go to start afresh. The age selectivity of migration is shown in Figure 4.2 with respect to the age distribution of migrants to the English city of Bristol compared to the city's population. Notice how the modal group for migrants is the 20-34 category.

In rich countries there is also a significant amount of retirement which involves the movement of more affluent households to recreational centres after they have retired from employment. The permanent relocation of retired New Yorkers to Florida and of ageing Londoners to Bournemouth or Majorca are just two examples of such retirement migration. The difference between employment-linked migration and retirement migration is graphically illustrated in Figure 4.3 which compares the age distributions of migrants to the English manufacturing town of Swindon and the resort town of Torbay on the English south coast.

The selectivity of non-retirement migration has a number of consequences for the origin and destination areas. In the origin areas there is a loss of young, dynamic people. In areas of economic growth this is not a major problem, as out-movement is balanced by in-movement. But in areas where there is a net population loss there is a draining away of population resources as the more ambitious, dynamic people leave and an increasing proportion of the remaining population is elderly, more conservative and less willing to innovate. In the rural areas badly affected by rural-urban migration the effects of population loss are even more severe. In the destination areas, by contrast, the local economy gains by the influx of fresh blood. The economy is boosted by the inflow of potential entrepreneurs.

Why people move

In non-retirement migration the predominant reasons for movement are economic. People tend to move where there are jobs and better employment prospects. Secondary reasons include the desire to escape from social and family restrictions, the attraction of the bright city lights which act like a beacon attracting people from the dull boredom of the countryside, and overall a feeling of dissatisfaction with the present allied to the promise of better prospects elsewhere.

Table 4.2 Reasons for movement

Push	*Pull*
unemployment	employment
poor social life	'bright lights'
poor social services	good social services
lack of individual freedom and repression/ discrimination	promise of freedom

Migrants can be divided into two groups: the small groups of early migrants who are the colonisers in so far as they are the first of their ethnic, religious, or social group to move to a particular place; and the majority of migrants who follow in the wake of the early explorers. If the early migrants are successful then news of their success travels home. The initial colonisers provide the source of information which prompts the movement of the majority of migrants. The early arrivals provide sources of information as well as accommodation and defence for the later arrivals. Streams of migration then begin to appear as in the movement of Mexicans to Southern California, Pakistanis to Britain, southern blacks to northern US cities and Irish people to London. The 'colonisers' gain a foothold in the local housing and job markets which provide a platform for later migrants.

Spatial patterns of movement

In the poorer peripheral countries the predominant form of movement in the urban system is *upwards* as people move from rural areas to urban centres and from smaller cities to larger cities. The greatest amount of net in-movement is experienced by the very large cities. In very large countries

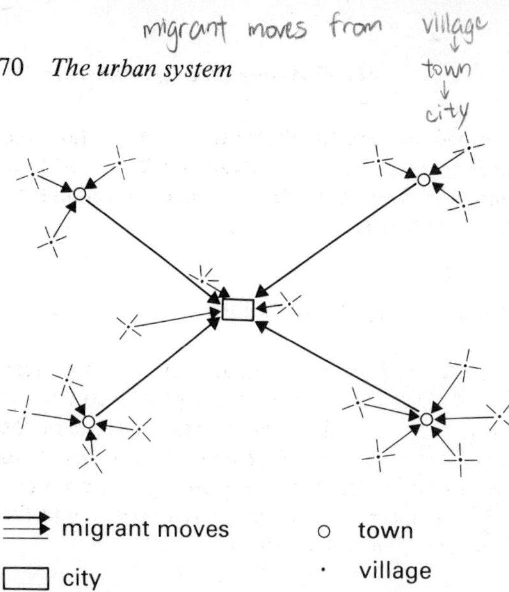

Figure 4.4 Model of step migration

with poor transport links and a number of subsidiary urban centres a definite sequence of step migration can sometimes be discovered. Step migration, identified by Ravenstein in the second of his seven laws, is shown in Figure 4.4. In smaller countries with fewer subsidiary cities migrants may leave rural areas and head for the big city.

In the developed countries net population movement occurs in areas with growing economies, while population loss is recorded in the declining urban regions. The level of net population movement is an indicator of economic success, booming cities attract people, declining cities lose population. But population redistribution is more than just an indicator of economic growth. It can also become a cause of growth. Figure 4.5 highlights the general argument. In urban regions, where population is growing, there is an increased demand for goods and services, more jobs are created, more migrants are attracted who in turn create the need for more goods and services. In growing economies there is a benign circle of cumulative growth. In declining urban economies, in contrast, the loss of population means a loss of purchasing power, less demand for goods and services and overall a further deterioration in the economy. In this case there is a downward spiral of economic contraction.

Figure 4.5a represents the case of population growth leading to sustained economic growth. While this may be true in the short to medium term, in the long term the reverse may happen. The inflow of population may be so great as to put heavy pressure on the housing market and the urban infrastructure. In the core countries spiralling house prices and congested freeways are just two signs of overheated urban economies. If unchecked, the negative externalities associated with such rapid population influx may force some industries to relocate elsewhere. Thus while population inflow may stimulate the economy in the short to medium term it may lead to a slackening of economic growth and perhaps a net

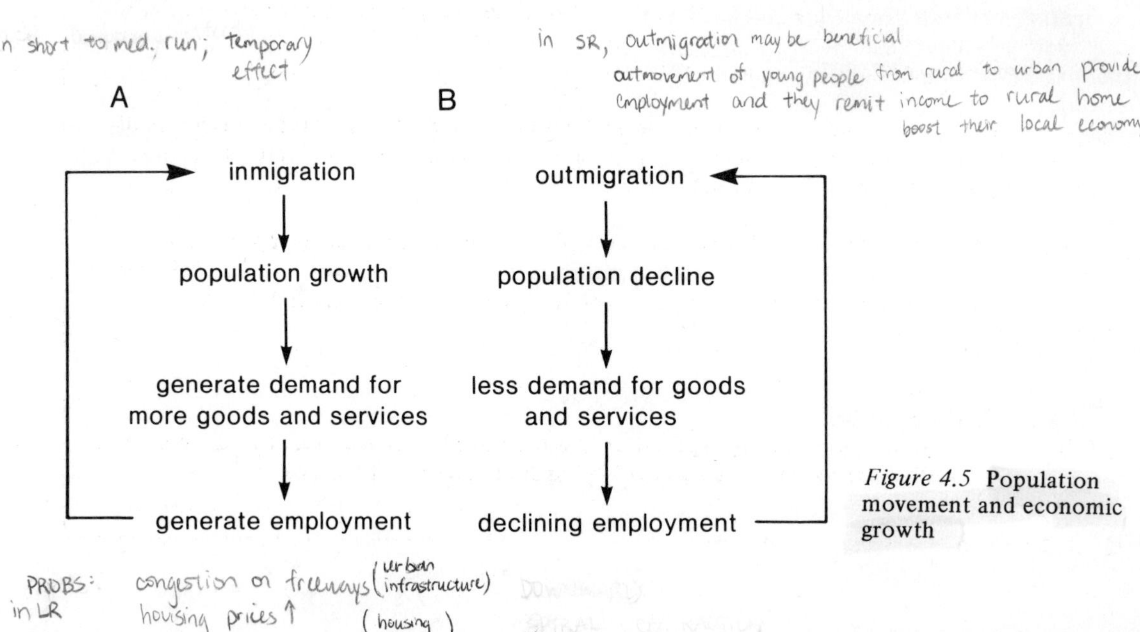

Figure 4.5 Population movement and economic growth

decline. The very large metropolitan economies of North America and Western Europe are now experiencing net loss of jobs as capital, firms and workers move down the urban hierarchy to the smaller centres. In developing countries the flood of immigrants may be greater than the ability of the urban economy to provide jobs and the capacity of the urban infrastructure to cope with such large population influxes. The waves of population in-movement experienced by some third-world cities are swamping the already fragile urban economies.

Similarly, while Figure 4.5b presents a case of rural outmigration having a deleterious effect on origin areas, in the short term outmovement may be beneficial. The outmovement of young people from areas of high rural unemployment to urban centres may provide employment, and the remittances of migrant workers to their home areas may provide much-needed income into the local economy. The economy of Malawi, for example, is kept afloat by the remittances of workers in the South African gold mines. In places as varied as Mexico, Portugal, southern Italy and Turkey the money that migrant workers send back home provides a valuable source of income to rural economies.

THE MOVEMENT OF GOODS

In a very real sense the urban system can be seen as a system of commodity transfer with towns and cities being assembly and transfer points in the circuits of the national economy. Two aspects of the movement of goods are worthy of consideration; the nature of the transport network and the character of the urban nodes.

Transport networks

There is a strong relationship between modes of transport, the nature of the urban system and levels of economic development. When goods are transported by human porterage or rudimentary cart, then the urban system is ill-connected and

THE ULLMAN MODEL

The American geographer Edward L. Ullman suggested that the geography of transport could be considered with reference to three elements:

Complementarity implies that before the transport of commodity x takes place between city i and city j there must be demand for the commodity x in city j and a supply in city i. The greater the complementarity the larger the flow.

Intervening opportunity exchange takes place between city i and city j only if there is a lack of intervening cities which might soak up city i's supply of commodity x. The greater the intervening opportunity between i and j the smaller the flow.

Transferability Even when there is complementarity and a lack of intervening opportunity between city i and city j, if the cost in time and/or money of moving commodity x is very high, transferability is minimal, and there is little interaction. The easier the transferability the greater the flow.

Reference

Ullman, E.L. (1956), The role of transportation and the bases for interaction, In W.L. Thomas (ed.), *Man's Role in Changing The Face of The Earth*, University of Chicago Press.

TRANSPORT NETWORKS

The transport network is an important element in the economic fabric of a country. An efficient network can improve the movement of goods, people and information while an inefficient network can hinder such movement. A city plugged into an efficient network can export and import more easily than a city only poorly connected to other elements in the urban system. A good transport network is a vital requirement for economic growth. But what exactly do we mean when we use the terms 'efficient' and 'good' in relation to networks? These terms are fuzzy. We can be more precise by using indices which measure different aspects of networks.

If a transport network is seen as a graph structure – a set of routes linking a number of nodes (i.e. towns and cities) – then a number of different measures can be calculated.

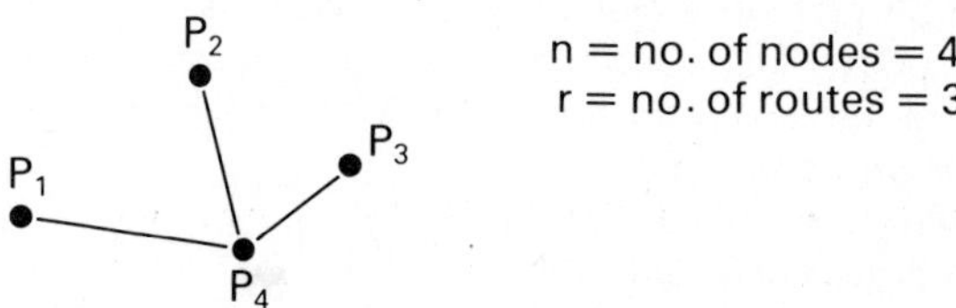

Connectivity

The connectivity of a network is calculated by dividing the observed numbers of routes by the maximum number of routes where,

$$\text{max. nos of routes} = \frac{(n^2 - n)}{2} \quad \frac{12}{2} = 6$$

$$\text{connectivity} = \frac{\text{observed number of routes}}{\text{max. nos of routes}} = \frac{3}{6} = 0.5$$

This value can be interpreted by comparing it with the maximum connectivity of a network which is 1.0, and the minimum connectivity which is $\frac{2}{n}$; in this case $\frac{2}{n} = 0.5$. In this simple case the network displays minimum connectivity.

Centrality

The most central node in any network can be calculated by simple matrix manipulation:

	P1	P2	P3	P4
P1	0	0	0	1
P2	0	0	0	1
P3	0	0	0	1
P4	1	1	1	0
Total	1	1	1	3

where 1 represents a link and 0 represents no link. When added up the node with the largest total number of links is the most central node. In this case P4 is the most central. A node with the lowest number of total links is the least central.

Gamma index (γ)

The amount of connection within a network can be found by calculating the gamma index (γ) where

$$\gamma = \frac{r}{3(n-2)} \times 100$$

In the case of the previous example

$$\gamma = \frac{3}{3(4-2)} \times 100 = \frac{3}{6} \times 100 = 50 \text{ per cent}$$

In this case the network is only half connected.

Eta index (η)

The coverage of a transport network over a particular area of space can be found by calculating the Eta index

$$\eta = \frac{r}{m}$$

where r is the number of routes and m is the total mileage of the network. A high eta value indicates very little coverage and generally speaking the lower the eta index value the greater the transport network covers the particular area of space under investigation.

Reference

Haggett, P. and Chorley, R.J. (1969), *Network Analysis in Geography*, Edward Arnold, London.

economic development is low. Economic growth is predicated upon a growing market which in turn implies good transport groups. With successive improvements in transportation modes, economic growth is stimulated, since the size of the effective market is increased. The major developments in modes of transportation have proved a stimulus to growth and have had specific urban implications.

Rail In the nineteenth century the economic landscape was transformed by the coming of the railways. The railways reduced the cost of transporting bulky commodities. Wheat production and cattle rearing in the United States, for example, were stimulated by the spread of the railways because the interior could then be connected to the world markets. The economic history of the nineteenth-century United States is essentially one of the spreading tentacles of the railway systems, the development of urban centres as assembly points, and the growth of the major ports with the resultant development of the interior. The nineteenth century saw the growth and development of the railway cities such as Chicago.

Automobiles If the story of the nineteenth century was of the railways then the transportation history of the twentieth century is one of the automobile. With the development of motor transport a new flexibility was introduced. Factories which could transport their goods by road no longer had to be

Table 4.3 Transport modes and cities

Type	*Example*
Railway city	Chicago; Crewe
Auto city	Los Angeles; Birmingham (UK)
Airways city	Atlanta; Heathrow, London
Pipeline city	Grangemouth (UK)

THE COMING OF THE MOTOR CAR

The most significant change in transport development in the developed world has been the wide adoption of road transport for freight traffic and individual movement. Car ownership rates have continued to rise and motorways continue to spread through the landscape. The automobile has freed the locational requirements of industry and brought tremendous freedom to car users, enabling them to move pretty much when and where they like. The advantages of automobiles are widely known. What is less well known are the drawbacks to automobile use and road transport in general.

1 It is one of the most dangerous modes of travel. In Britain alone there are approximately 6000 people killed each year and many more seriously injured. Plane crashes or railway accidents tend to be more dramatic but in total kill less people. We now take the slaughter on our roads for granted.
2 The wide-scale use of cars makes it more difficult for non-car users including the poor, the very old and the young.
3 Road building tends to use up a disproportionate amount of public investment in transport leading to the deterioration of other transport models such as the railways.
4 Automobiles use energy. Mass transit schemes and railways use less energy for the same number of travel miles.
5 The large-scale construction of roads leads to environmental damage and loss of amenity.

All transport models involve a mixture of costs and benefits. In any discussion of transport alternatives we have to be aware of the costs of automobile usage and road building. There are powerful interests – the car companies, road builders – who form a strong pressure group urging greater use of automobiles and more highway construction. There are less powerful interests working in favour of a greater use of mass transit schemes. The following table reflects the success of the road/automobile lobby in the USA

	% of federal transport expenditure, 1979
highways	41.6
mass transit	13.6
railroads	13.7
water	10.9
air transportation	20.2

located close to the railway line or the railhead. The coming of the automobile and the spread of the road network meant a spreading out of economic activity and residencies away from the corridors along the railway lines. An increasing proportion of freight traffic now goes by road rather than rail.

Aeroplanes Since 1945 the biggest single improvement in transportation has been in air transport. The real cost of air travel has declined as better jets have been developed and the frequency of flights has introduced a new invisible transport network in the skies which now links the major urban centres. Compared to other modes the use of air transport of freight traffic is prohibitively expensive. However, recent years have seen the growing importance of domestic airways in inter-city passenger traffic. Air terminals now provide a stimulus to growth in surrounding areas as firms locate close to this important transport mode. The recent growth of Atlanta, Georgia, and Heathrow, UK, reflect the economic multiplier effects of air terminus.

Ships Ships are still the most important mode of transporting bulky commodities overseas. And major cities still tend to be ports – three-quarters of all cities with more than 2 million inhabitants are ports. The most important recent development has been the increasing size of ships and the concentration of shipping activities in a few, very large ports. Rotterdam, for example, is now the main oil port of the whole of Western Europe.

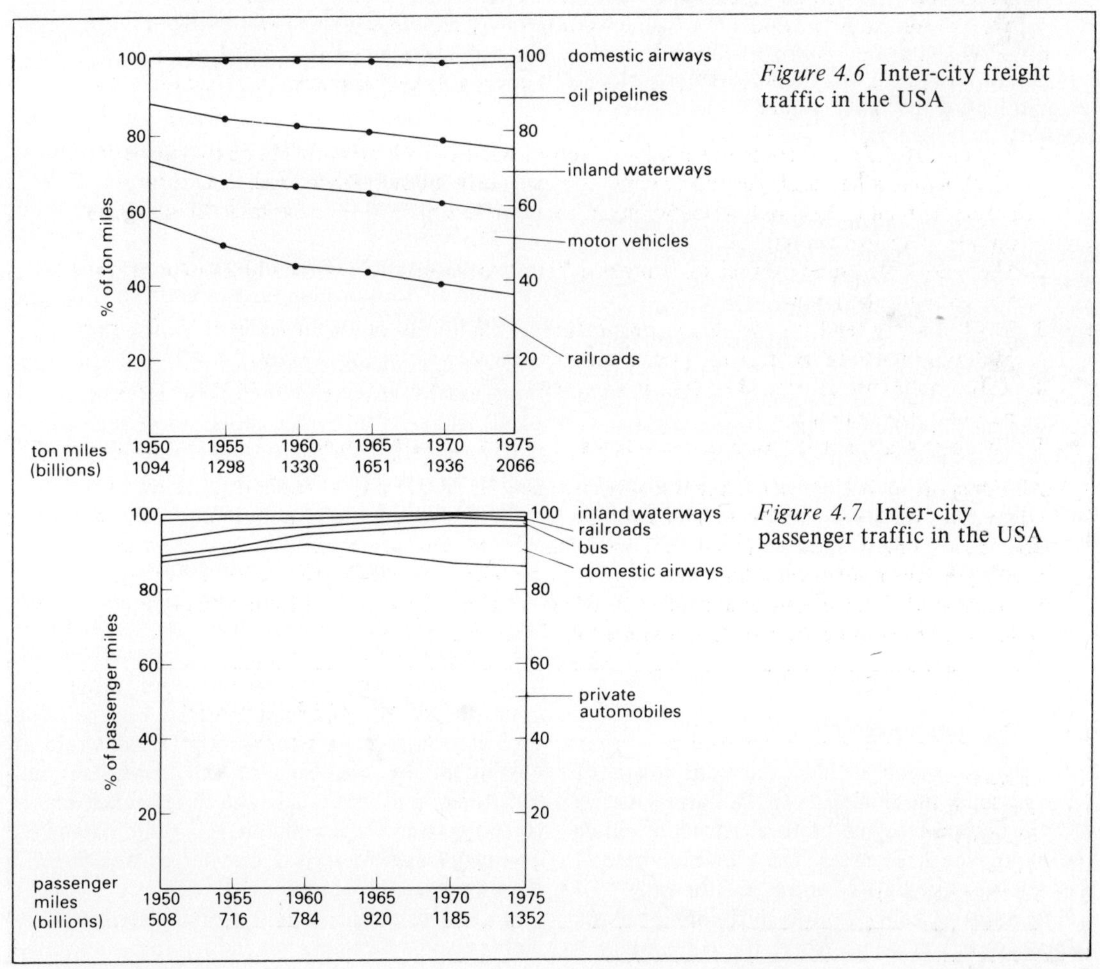

Figure 4.6 Inter-city freight traffic in the USA

Figure 4.7 Inter-city passenger traffic in the USA

Special modes There are a number of special modes of transporting energy. Pipelines, for example, are now used to transport the bulk of oil and gas overland, while electricity lines transmit electric power. These modes of transport do not necessarily stimulate large multiplier effects around the main nodes. A gas-collecting point or oil refinery, once built, can continue to operate without generating large-scale urbanisation effects in the surrounding areas. The gas-storage centres on the Norfolk coast in England, which is the landfall site of North Sea Gas, are situated in rural calm and employ very few people. These special modes of transporting energy have been increasing in importance and Figure 4.6 shows how an increasing proportion of freight traffic in the United States is carried by oil pipeline. This trend is replicated throughout the core.

The different modes of transporting goods are shown with respect to the United States in Figure 4.6 and Figure 4.7. In Figure 4.6 the modes of transport in freight traffic are shown. From this diagram we can see the declining importance of railroads since 1950 and the increasing importance of motor vehicles, inland waterways and particularly oil pipelines. Figure 4.7 shows that in terms of inter-city passenger traffic the private automobile reigns supreme. Since 1950 over 80 per cent of all passenger miles have been in the private automobile although since 1960 this proportion has declined somewhat as domestic airways have increased in importance. The airways are mainly used for long-distance inter-city traffic.

Towns and cities are nodes in the transportation of goods, they are the assembly and transfer points in the circuits of the national economy. We can distinguish urban centres in terms of their role in the transfer of goods. Two main types can be identified – resource-orientated centres and break points.

Resource-orientated centres

Such centres which include the coal towns of Pennyslavania, the mining towns of Latin America and the railhead towns of rural Africa assemble and export local resources. The economic base of the resource-orientated centres is the export of commodities to other centres in the national and international economy. Where the commodity is very bulky and is used as a raw material in a productive process of an industry, then the industry may be attracted to the resource-orientated centre. In the nineteenth century and early twentieth century the distribution of basic raw materials such as coal and iron ore influenced the location of heavy industry. Steel towns, for example, grew up close to sources of coal and iron ore. In the developed world of the twentieth century transport improvements and the cheaper transmission of energy have meant a move away from supply-orientated locations to market-orientated locations. The dynamic sectors of the economy are the footloose industries such as computer technology firms which use very small amounts of raw material and are not 'pulled' to their supply centres.

The development of resource-orientated centres into urban centres with self-sustaining growth can take the form of a number of stages.

(1) The export of commodities to other centres.
(2) The capital which is invested and jobs generated to develop this export base create multiplier effects and causes further growth of local specialised services.
(3) The growth of local-based industries and services.
(4) Expansion of 'local' industries leads to attraction of footloose industries and the widening of the cities' export base.

Resource-orientated centres grow by widening their export bases and replacing the imports of goods and services by the provision of such goods and services by local firms. Resource-orientated centres fail to grow when the export base is not widened and there is no process of import substitution.

There are many resource-orientated centres in the third world but few of them have grown into large cities. Many commentators have argued that this is because the profits and multiplier effects are exported along with the commodities to the core countries of America and Western Europe. The exploitation of resources in the third world is conducted by the large North American and European multi-nationals who have branch plants for processing the raw materials in other countries. In many cases there is a transfer of wealth from the periphery to the core.

From this perspective the central place hierarchy and transport networks which link up the resource-

Plates 11 and 12
Ports as break points:
(11) the container port of Felixstowe, England;
(12) Soya storage warehouse in Amsterdam

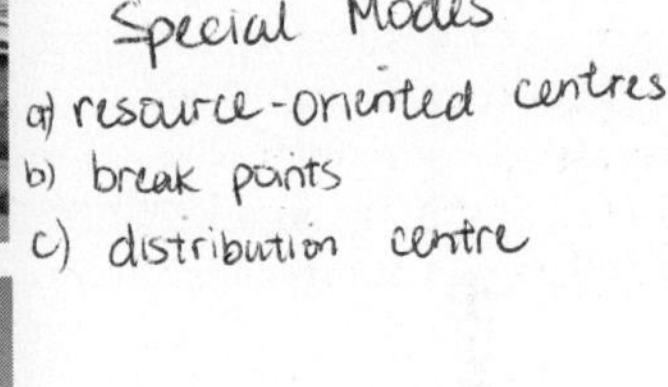

orientated centres with ports and ultimately the international economy form a system of exploitation where wealth flows from the periphery to the richer core. This argument is widely believed in the third world and explains why many peripheral countries seek to control resource development by controlling foreign companies either through nationalisation or by forming cartels. The growth of OPEC stemmed from the response of formerly poor oil-producing countries to the machinations of the big oil companies.

Break points

Break points occur when the transfer of goods involves a change of transport mode. In the case of *ports* goods shipped by sea have to be unloaded and distributed over land or re-exported by other ships. This activity may provide a nucleus for the accretion of further related activity such as storage facilities, manufacturing industries and transport terminals. Examples of associated manufacturing include sugar refining, tobacco processing and oil refining. The majority of world cities are also ports.

Major *airports* now act as break points and thus as stimuli to local growth. The locations of airports present both positive and negative effects. On the plus side they provide a source of jobs and contracts. But on the negative side they are

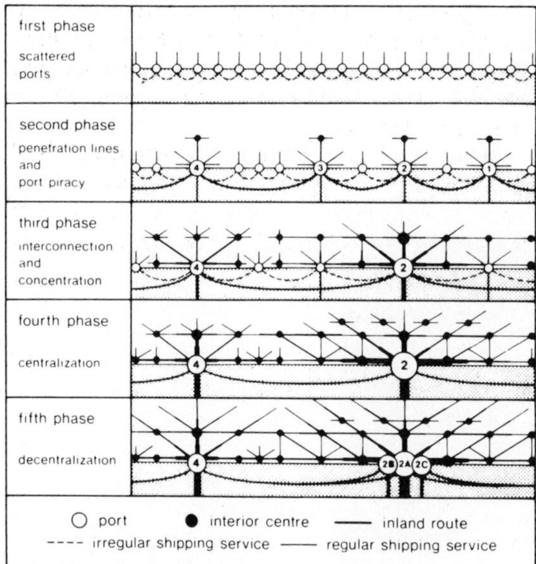

Figure 4.8 A model of port development
Source: Rimmer, 1967

Phase 1 Dispersed pattern of seaports scattered along coast, limited hinterlands, irregular service

Phase 2 Emergence of main landward penetration routes, certain ports expand at the expense of others (1, 2, 3, 4). These four ports develop as foci for separate route networks

Phase 3 Feeders continue to develop until 1, 2 and 3 link; 2, in its central position, captures the trade of the other two, and 1 and 3 revert to former states. 4, unlinked to the other network, survives

Phase 4 The networks of 2 and 4 link up; but 4 gains sufficient momentum (inertia) to survive, despite the centralisation of economic activities at 2, by providing specialised services. Port 2, however, continues to grow at a faster rate

Phase 5 In this final phase, the continuing expansion of the network and of economic activities leads to the provision of specialised functions at ports 2B and 2C, while the initial port (now 2A) concentrates on general cargo services

very noisy places and by attracting labour may create labour shortages in the local labour market. The negative effects are most clearly felt in the immediate environs of the airport while the positive effects are experienced beyond the immediately surrounding areas. The positive effects are most successfully utilised by export-orientated firms.

The categories of resource-orientated centres, break points and the distribution centres which we have already covered in the previous chapter in our discussion of central places are not mutually exclusive categories. The major urban centres such as New York and London are at the same time resource-orientated centres, break points and major distribution nodes in the central place system. The economies of the very large multi-functional cities, unlike those of the resource-orientated centres, also contain the market-orientated industries. These are industries, such as lemonade making, which, because the cost of distributing the finished product is much greater than the cost of assembling the raw material, are attracted towards the market. The big cities are major nodes in the network of the national economy.

THE MOVEMENT OF IDEAS

The urban system is also the pathway for the transmission of new ideas. The transmission of new ideas including such things as the spread of Rotary Clubs, the spread in the use of family planning methods or the increased use of new technology is termed *innovation diffusion*. This process involves the spread of ideas across time and space. Assume there is a new fashion. Take, for example, the wearing of mini-skirts in the 1960s. A few daring souls were the first to bare their knees – these were the innovators; then came the early majority; then the more conservative groups finally succumbed to the pressure of fashion and they made up the late majority. Finally the laggards started wearing mini-skirts by the late 1960s. This distribution, as shown in Figure 4.9, is found in the diffusion of almost all innovators. Once the innovation has reached saturation level new ideas and new fashions may appear which render the old one obsolete. After the mini came the maxi and no self-respecting fashion-conscious young lady in 1975 would have been seen dead in a short skirt.

We will use the term *innovation paracme* coined by the British geographer David Barker with reference to the rejection of former innovations. The relationship between diffusion and paracme is shown in Figure 4.10. In (a) there is a symmetry between the diffusion and the paracme as in the case of mini-skirts. In (b) there is a long steady diffusion and quicker paracme as with the development of the smoking habit which grew slowly throughout the nineteenth and twentieth centuries but is in the process of rapid decline. In (c) there is a quick diffusion and a slow paracme as with the diffusion of the railways throughout Britain and North America.

How does innovation diffusion occur in space? A useful example is the work of Brian Robson, who examined urban growth in nineteenth-century Britain. Robson's work shows that the

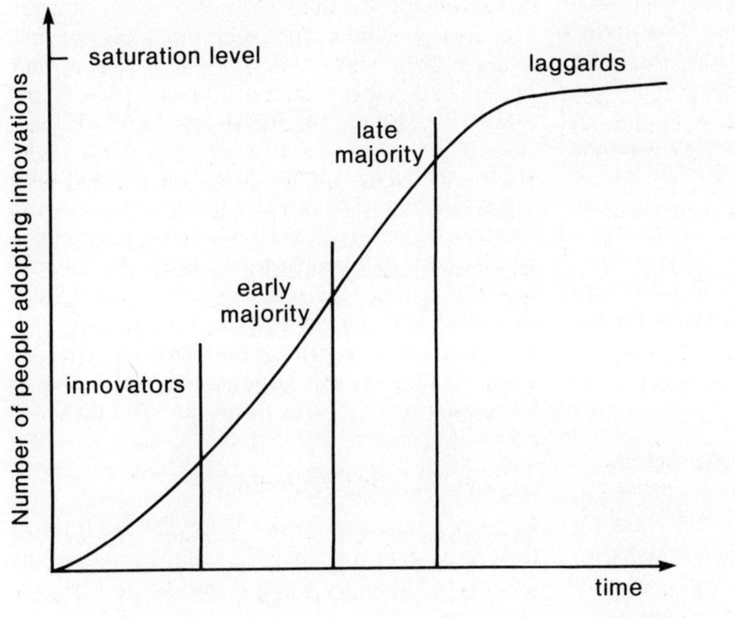

Figure 4.9 The adoption of innovations

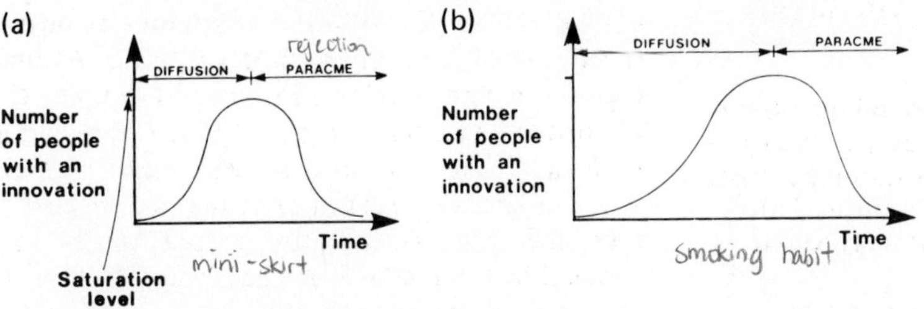

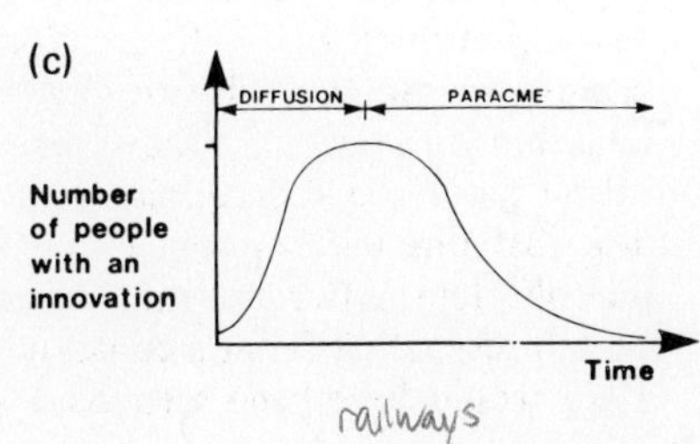

Figure 4.10 Temporal relationships between diffusion and paracme
Source: Barker, 1977

diffusion of gasworks with provided gas lighting had a definite pattern. Gaslights were first seen in 1820 in London. Then the very large urban centres of industry – Bristol, Birmingham, Liverpool Manchester, Leeds – were some of the first places to open gasworks. Later, places surrounding these big cities also opened gasworks. It was not the case that the innovations spread out from centres like the waves produced by dropping a stone in a pond. Rather, it was a case of hierarchical diffusion. Figure 4.11 generalises the process. Most innovations diffuse down the urban hierarchy. Innovations are first seen in the major cities, later in the smaller towns and finally in the rural areas. This pattern applies to most innovations whether it be the use of credit cards, the wearing of mini-skirts or skateboarding. The big cities provide the milieu for the creation of innovations and contain a large proportion of innovators responsive to new ideas and eager to try out new schemes. Lower down the urban hierarchy people tend to be more conservative, more wary of change. The selectivity of migration of people from rural areas to the big cities means that a higher proportion of would-be innovators and the early majority in a typical innovation diffusion are located in the urban centres.

In terms of innovation adoption the major cities are much closer together even though separated by larger distances than they are by smaller cities nearby. The latest ladies' fashions, for example, are almost simultaneously seen in New York, London, Paris and Rome. It takes much longer before they are seen in Albany, Taunton, Nantes or Brindisi.

The urban system can be seen as a set of pathways through which there is flowing a succession of innovation waves. At any one time a whole series of diffusion and paracmes will be at various stages of early adoption by the innovators in the big cities, wider adoption by the early majority in the very large and medium-sized cities and almost saturation point when the diffusion has spread right down the hierarchy.

THE SHRINKING NETWORK

Urban centres are connected by networks in both space and time. The physical linkages of roads and railways tie urban centres in space but the speed in which goods and people travel down the network tie cities in time. Look at Figure 4.12. Here it can be seen that by quickest means it takes three-and-half hours to travel the 2000 kilometres straight-line distance between London and Madrid, but it takes over nine hours to travel the 550 kilometres between London and Stranraer. In space-time terms Madrid is closer to London than Stranraer. New York to London by Concorde now takes less than five hours. New York is now closer to London than Stranraer. The space-time network warps the distances of absolute space.

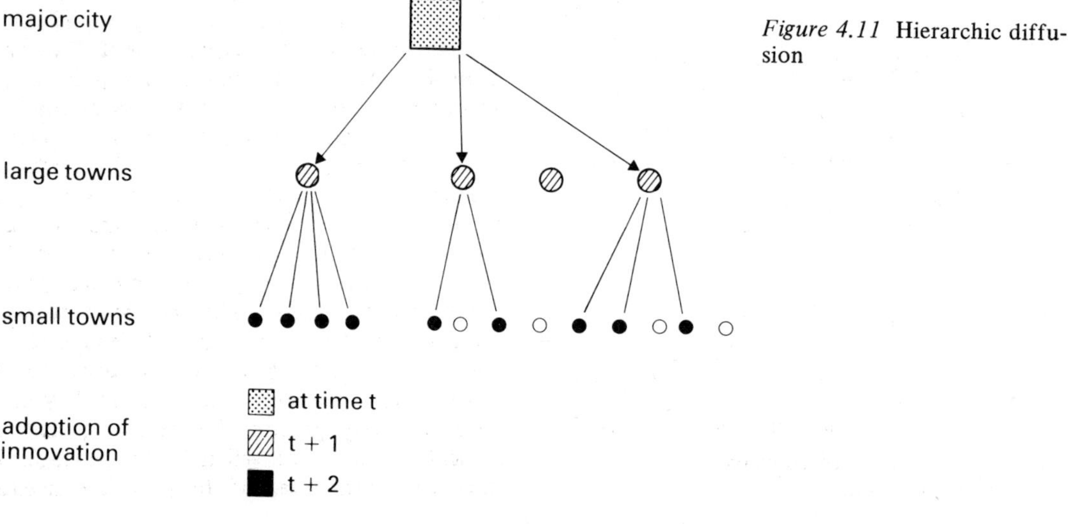

Figure 4.11 Hierarchic diffusion

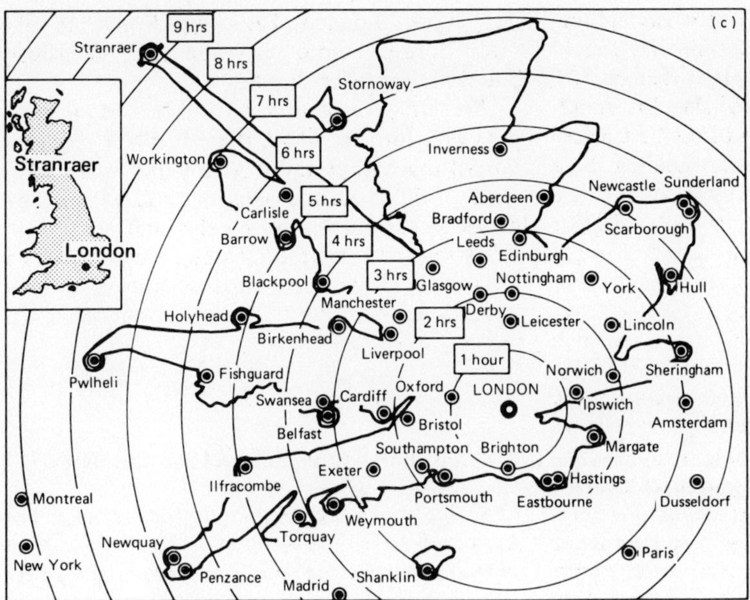

Figure 4.12 London in space-time
Source: Parkes and Thrift, 1980

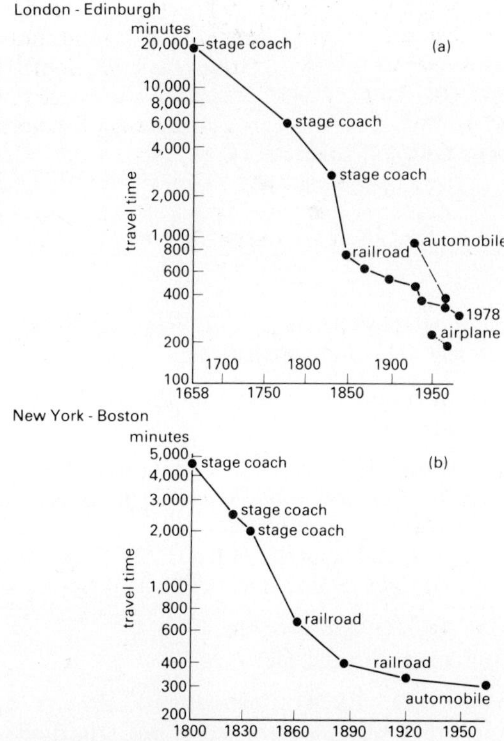

Figure 4.13 Time-space convergence
Source: Janelle, 1968

Because of improvements in transportation cities have been moving closer together in time-space terms. Figure 4.13 shows the speed of this convergence between the two pairs of cities of London and Edinburgh and New York and Boston. Notice how in both cases there has been a dramatic decline in the time taken to travel between these cities. It now takes only hours by plane where before it took days by rail, weeks by coach and months by ship. The world is coming closer together and the centres laced together by airline networks are now only hours apart. This time-space convergence in association with the rapid improvements in communications (telephones, teleprinters, etc.) now means that Marshall McLuhan's concept of a *global village* is now a reality. Within minutes we can find out what is happening on the other side of the world and within hours we can be there. But while we have been coming together in one sense we have also been moving apart. The gap between rich and poor countries is increasing while the chasm between east and west shows little sign of being crossed; if anything the latest spurt to the arms race is making the global village a much more dangerous place. The very process of coming together has brought its dangers as well as its disadvantages. It takes less than a second to press the nuclear

MEASURING TIME-SPACE CONVERGENCE

The rate of time-space convergence between two cities i and j can be measured by the following equation.

$$\frac{(T_{ij})^1 - (T_{ij})^2}{Y_2 - Y_1}$$

where $(T_{ij})^1$ is the travel time between city i and city j in year 1

$(T_{ij})^2$ is the travel time between city i and city j in year 2

Y_1 and Y_2 are the years in question

In 1776 it took 5,760 minutes to travel between Edinburgh and London, but by 1966 this figure had fallen to 180 minutes. Fitting these figures into the equation we get

$$\frac{5,760 - 180}{1966\text{-}1776} = \frac{5580}{190} = 29.4 \text{ minutes per year}$$

Over the period 1776 to 1966 London and Edinburgh were converging at the rate of 29.4 minutes per year. It would seem therefore that the two places are closer together in time. But this is sometimes difficult to believe when you are waiting in a plane stacked above London's Heathrow airport.

Reference

Janelle, D.G. (1968), Central place development in a time-space framework, *Professional Geographer*, 20, 5-10.

button and less than ten minutes for the planet to be annihilated. If travellers in 1800 needed three overnight stagecoach stops to travel between New York and Boston at least they were secure in the knowledge that civilisation could not be destroyed in less time than it takes to cook a hard-boiled egg.

GUIDE TO FURTHER READING

An introduction to the dynamics of urban systems is the collection of papers:

Bourne, L. S. and Simmons, J.W. (1978), *Systems of Cities*, Oxford University Press, New York.

A useful review of the migration literature is:

Shaw, R.P. (1975), *Migration Theory and Fact*, Bibliography Series No. 5, Regional Science Research Institute, Philadelphia.

There are a number of books on the geography of transportation:

Eliot Hurst, M.E. (1973), *Transportation Geography: Comments and Readings*, McGraw-Hill, New York.

Taaffe, E.J. and Gauthier, J.L. (1972), *Geography of Transportation*, Prentice-Hall, Englewood Cliffs, N.J.

Important papers include:

Hoare, A.G. (1974), International airports as growth poles: a case study of Heathrow, *Transactions Institute of British Geographers*, 63, 75-96.

Leinbach, T.R. (1976), Networks and flows, *Progress in Geography*, 8, 197-207.
Rimmer, P. (1967), The search for spatial regularities in the development of Australian seaports, 1861-1901/2, *Geografiske Annaler*, 49B, 42-54.
Taaffe, E.J., Morrill, R.I. and Gould, P.R. (1963), Transport expansion in underdeveloped countries: a comparative analysis, *Geographical Review*, 53, 503-29.

Innovation diffusion in general is examined in:

Brown L.A. (1981), *Innovation Diffusion*, Methuen, London.
Gould, P.R. (1969), *Spatial Diffusion*, Commission on College Geography Resource Paper No. 4, Association of American Geographers.
Hagerstrand, T. (1968), *Diffusion of Innovations*, (translated by Allan Pred), University of Chicago Press.

The paracme is discussed in:

Barker, D. (1977), The paracme of innovations: the neglected aftermath of diffusion or a wave goodbye to an idea, *Area*, 9, 259-64.

Specific examples of diffusion in urban systems include:

Pedersen, P.O. (1970), Innovation diffusion within and between national urban systems, *Geographical Analysis*, 2, 302-54.
Robson, B.T. (1973), *Urban Growth: An Approach*, Cambridge University Press.

The classic paper on time-space convergence is:

Janelle, D.G. (1968), Central place development in a time-space framework, *Professional Geographer*, 20, 5-10.

Reviews of subsequent work include:

Forer, P. (1978), A place for plastic space, *Progress in Human Geography*, 2, 230-67.
Parkes, D.N. and Thrift, N.J. (1980), *Times, Spaces and Places,* John Wiley, London (esp. chapter 7).

5 Managing the Urban System

THE STATE AND NATIONAL URBAN POLICY

The urban system is a system in flux. The overall characteristics and the absolute and relative position of individual cities is constantly changing. Part of this change relates to specific government actions e.g. siting a university or an army base close to an existing settlement will lead to large multiplier effects and hence the expansion of that city's economy and population with a consequent rise in its position in the urban hierarchy. There are also more long-term, large-scale comprehensive government actions which we can subsume under the title of *national urban policy*. The broad nature of urban policy reflects on the nature of the society. We can imagine the variation in societies as a continuum with, at one end, the *private market economies* in which government actions are limited in scope and size, while at the other end are the *centrally planned economies* in which the state is the most important agent and most powerful single institution. Somewhere in the middle of the continuum would be the *mixed economies* of countries like Britain and France, where private market economics are overlain with state intervention. In many *third-world countries* there is the juxtaposition of capitalist economies with strong government intervention. In Brazil, for example, one of the most capitalist of the Latin American nations, over 60 per cent of the largest companies are state enterprises.

Table 5.1 Types of economies

Type of Economy		*Example*
Private market		USA
Mixed economies		France, UK
Centrally planned		USSR
Third world	private market	Brazil
	centrally planned	Tanzania, Vietnam

In private market societies national urban policy is guided by two factors. First, the state reacts to market forces rather than controlling them. Thus, in the United States, for example, a significant element in urban policy has been to resuscitate the economies of frostbelt cities debilitated by the flow of capital towards the sunbelt. Second, the state responds to various pressure groups with state policy reflecting the power of the different interest groups. Thus, urban policy is shaping according to the needs of large-scale corporations rather than to meet the wishes of the poor who have least political clout.

In centrally planned economies the state has a much more important role. The state runs the economy and guides investment. In the Soviet Union a specific urban policy of spreading urban settlements as evenly as possible across the country can be pursued. The Soviets have also tried to limit the size of the very large cities. Because the state is so all-powerful many of these policy objectives can be met.

In the mixed economies the state reacts to the private market forces of uneven development and, by guiding public investment, also attempts to guide the market. The New Town experiment in Britain is both an attempt at balancing the differences in regional growth rates and an attempt by the state to lay the basis for new economic growth.

In the poorer third-world countries there is a variety of political stances adopted in the pursuit

MANAGEMENT OF THE URBAN SYSTEM IN THE USSR

In the Soviet Union there is a high degree of state control over the character of the urban system. Compared to the USA or countries of Western Europe the state has immense power.

The main aims of Soviet national urban policy have been to (1) limit the size of big cities by limiting growth and directing it to the small and medium-sized towns, (2) 'spread' urbanisation throughout the countryside in order to obliterate rural-urban differences and regional variations in rates of urbanisation. This second aim has been pursued because it is a fundamental tenet of Marxism-Leninism that the spread of urbanisation spreads socialism; rural areas are seen as backward and the emergence of towns lifts rural dwellers from a 'life of rural idiocy'. This belief had a basis of fact in the early days of the Soviet Union when Bolshevism was strongest in the towns and cities and weakest in the much more conservative rural districts.

These aims can be pursued through the state's control over:
internal migration – all Soviet citizens need a resident's permit to live in cities;
investment and industrial location – the state controls where money is spent and factories located, and;
wage rates – higher wages have been paid in the more inhospitable eastern areas in order to attempt to attract workers to the small frontier towns in Siberia.

The policies have not been successful. This is because economic criteria have been given a higher priority than questions of national urban policy. Particularly since 1956 there has been growing emphasis on efficiency and maximising rates of return, which has made the external economies of the big cities in favoured regions more attractive. The optimum size of cities suggested by the Soviet urban planners has increased from 150,000 in the early 1950s, to 300,000 in the late 1960s. The concept of optimum city size has now been dropped as issues of economic efficiency have predominated. Ministries in charge of industrial location have favoured the big cities and have thus tended not to locate industries in the smaller towns, especially in the less-developed regions where there is a lack of skilled labour and poor infrastructure. The net result has been for the greatest growth to occur in the largest cities. There are now more than 18 cities in the Soviet Union with a population of over one million and there are still marked regional differences in rates of urbanisation.

References

Harris, C.D. (1970), *Cities of the Soviet Union. Studies in their Size, Density and Growth*, Rand McNally, Chicago.

Pallot, J. and Shaw, D.J.B. (1981), *Planning in the Soviet Union*, Croom Helm, London.

of national urban policies. However, the two most dominant factors which reappear in the different countries despite the political differences are (a) the internal power of the state, the state is the single most important factor in political affairs, and (b) the state's power is limited by the poverty of the country. The state has very little money to make large fixed investments while much of the economy is controlled by foreign enterprises. Crucial decisions affecting the economics of Latin American, African and Asian countries are made in boardrooms in New York and London. In third-world countries the state's actions are important but limited by the lack of finance and by the nature of external control of the economy. National urban policy is therefore limited in scope.

Despite the variations between the urban policies of different countries there are a number of general trends.

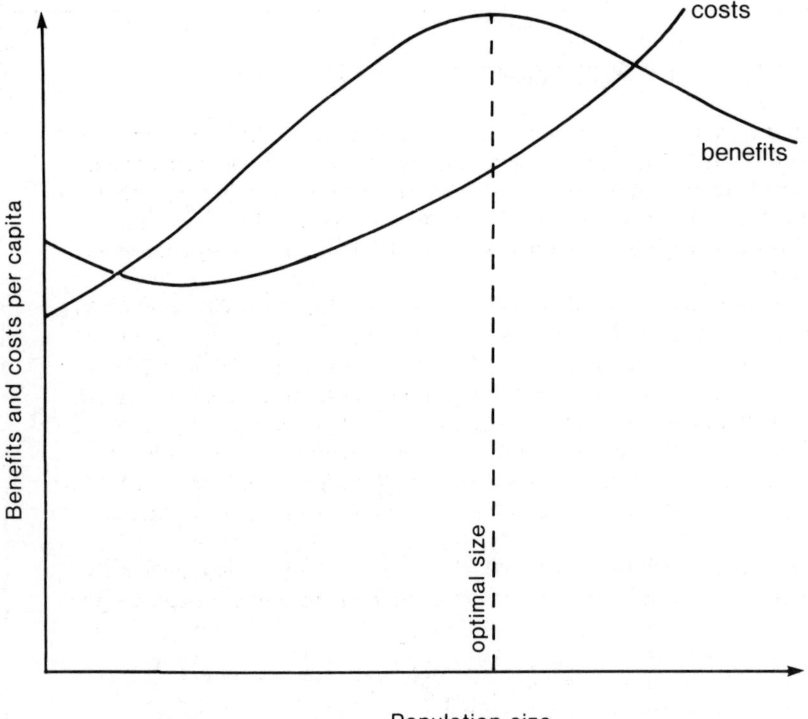

Figure 5.1 Costs, benefits and city size

(1) controlling the apex of the urban hierarchy,
(2) guiding the distribution of the middle-order settlements, and
(3) strategies for dealing with the lower-order settlements.

We will examine each of these in turn.

CONTROLLING THE BIG CITY

One of the biggest planning issues faced by the authorities in many countries is the increasing size of the very large cities. This is a problem faced by countries as far removed as USSR, Mexico, South Korea, India and Brazil. The big city becomes a problem because with increase in size costs may outweigh benefits. Figure 5.1 highlights the general case. The costs which increase with urban size include rents, commuting costs, noise, pollution and crime. The benefits which tend to increase with size include incomes, the provision of consumption goods such as theatres, cinemas, etc. and the provision of public goods such as fire services, police and ambulance services.

The optimum size of the city occurs when benefits are maximised and exceed the costs. The urban economist Harry Richardson has surveyed the literature on the costs and benefits of city size. He suggests that, while there may be no one single optimum city size, there is a series of optima for local government, firms and households.

Local government

In the provision of public goods the costs outweigh the benefits after a population of a quarter of a million has been reached. After this there are administrative scale diseconomies.

Firms

The optima are much larger for firms since they benefit from agglomeration economies. Indeed it is often difficult to think of a specific optimum since many firms continue to thrive and prosper

NEW TOWNS IN BRITAIN

The first new town in Britain was planned by Ebenezer Howard in Letchworth, Hertfordshire, in 1902. Howard wanted to build cities in which a population of about 32,000 would live in garden suburbs, where the land was to be owned by the community. Howard's ideas were the guiding principles of the British Town and Country Planning Association. And it was this association which was instrumental in getting the new town idea implemented by successive British governments since 1945.

Two types of new towns can be identified. The Mark 1 New Towns were designated between 1946 and 1950 with more than half located around London, as part of the attempt to decentralise growth from the metropolis. The Mark 2 New Towns were a feature of the 1960s and early 1970s. They were located around the major conurbations, partly to decentralise growth from the big cities and partly as growth centre strategies to resuscitate the declining economies in the peripheral parts of Britain. We can make a further distinction between the Mark 2 New Towns of the 1960s constructed on greenfield sites and the towns of the late 1960s and 1970s, e.g. Warrington, Peterborough and Northampton, which were new towns grafted on to old established urban centres.

At their best the new towns have provided pleasant urban environments free from congestion and traffic with plenty of green open space. Almost 2 million people in Britain live in the New Towns.

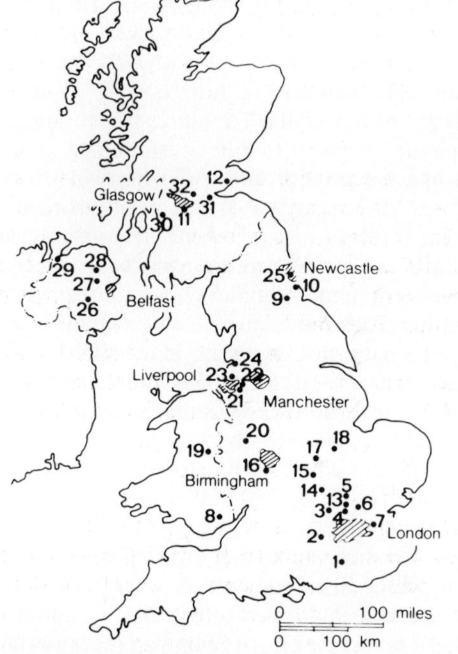

Mark 1 New Towns
1 Crawley '47
2 Bracknell '49
3 Hemel Hempstead '47
4 Hatfield '48
5 Stevenage '46
6 Harlow '47
7 Basildon '49
8 Cwmbran '49
9 Newton Aycliffe '47
10 Peterlee '48
11 East Kilbride '47
12 Glenrothes '48
13 Welwyn Garden City '48

Mark 2 New Towns
14 Milton Keynes '67
15 Northampton '68
16 Redditch '64
17 Corby '50
18 Peterborough '67
19 Newtown '67
20 Telford '63
21 Runcorn '64
22 Warrington '68
23 Skelmersdale '61
24 Central Lancashire '70
25 Washington '64
26 Craigavan '65
27 Antrim '66
28 Ballymena '67
29 Londonderry '69
30 Irvine '66
31 Livingston '62
32 Cumbernauld '55

Figure 5A New Towns in Britain, 1945-1970. The figure after each town is the date of designation. The Mark 1 New Towns were built between 1945 and 1950 around London and in the poorer regions of the country. The Mark 2 New Towns were built during the 1960s around major conurbations

References

Aldridge, M (1979), *The British New Towns: A programme without a policy*, Routledge & Kegan Paul, London.

Schaffer, F. (1972), *The New Town Story*, Paladin, London.

Table 5.2 City size and crime in USA

SMSA size class	Number of reported crimes per 100,000 population (1970)
+ 5 million	4358
3-5 million	4186
2-3 million	3376
1-2 million	3543
0.75-1 million	3369
0.5-0.75 million	2927
0.25-0.5 million	2700
rural areas	927

Table 5.3 City size and income in USA

SMSA size class	Average hourly earnings, $ (1960)
+ 1 million	2.84
0.5-1 million	2.56
0.25-0.5 million	2.43
rural areas	2.00

in the very large cities with more than 5 million population.

Households

The optimum for households is estimated at one million. Below this employment prospects are fewer, incomes lower and provision of entertainment facilities more limited. Above this figure the negative externalities of noise, pollution, high housing costs, high crime rates, and the declining quality of public goods all outweigh benefits. While firms may benefit from cities with more than 1 million population the cost for households and local government outweighs the benefits.

The big city problem has been tackled in a number of ways. The strategies can be divided into the *stick method* and the *carrot technique*. The stick methods are attempts to stop further growth, and range from the Indonesian authorities who prohibit the entry of rural migrants to the capital city of Djakarta, the use of visas by the Soviet government to prohibit rural migrants moving to big Soviet cities, to the British government's previous refusal to grant planning permission for further office construction in London. The carrot techniques are attempts to attract industry, commerce and people away from the big city and they range from the New Town scheme in Britain, where firms were given attractive cheap premises, to the Russian attempts at spreading population distribution by paying higher salaries for workers to go to urban settlements east of the Urals.

While the growth of the big cities has been halted in the core partly through government action and partly through market forces, the big city continues to grow in Latin America, Africa and Asia.

GROWTH CENTRES IN THE URBAN HIERARCHY

One way of decentralising economic activity from the big city is through investment in medium-sized cities located far enough away from the big city to generate independent growth. This is the growth-centre solution. A *growth centre* is an urban centre where industrial and commercial growth is concentrated and which transmits economic growth to the surrounding area. A *spontaneous growth centre* is one which occurs through the operation of private investment and market forces. An *induced growth centre* is based on both public and private investment and is used as an instrument of public policy to direct growth from big cities and as an element in regional policy to deal with poorer cities in declining regions. Under the area development programme in the USA in the 1960s for example, 88 growth centres were selected, where the size of population was only about 38,000. Experience suggests that median city size of 250,000 is needed to generate sustained growth.

By investing capital and locating large industries in selected cities, growth is expected to occur through the multiplier effect and by cumulative causation. A model of cumulative causation is shown in Figure 5.2. According to it the location of a new industry will lead to the expansion of local employment and population which leads to growth of the general wealth of the community and a provision of better infrastructure,

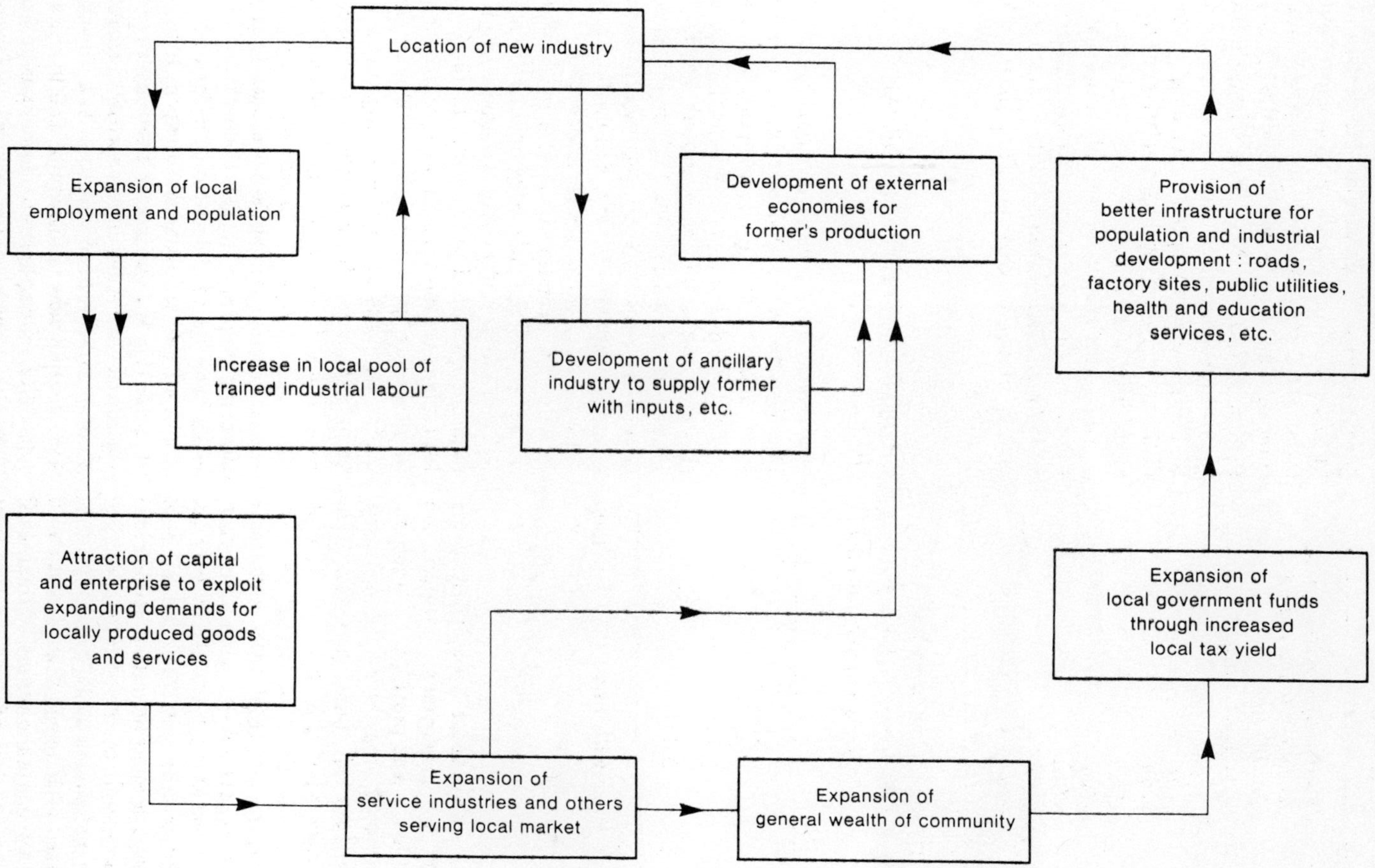

Location of new industry

Expansion of local employment and population

Increase in local pool of trained industrial labour

Development of ancillary industry to supply former with inputs, etc.

Development of external economies for former's production

Provision of better infrastructure for population and industrial development : roads, factory sites, public utilities, health and education services, etc.

Attraction of capital and enterprise to exploit expanding demands for locally produced goods and services

Expansion of service industries and others serving local market

Expansion of general wealth of community

Expansion of local government funds through increased local tax yield

Figure 5.2 Myrdal's model of cumulative causation
Source: Keeble, D.E. (1967), Models of economic development. In Chorley, R.J. and Haggett, P. (eds), *Models in Geography*, Methuen, London

Plates 13 and 14
Induced growth centres: (13) Brasilia, the new capital of Brazil; (14) Nitra, a medium-sized town in Czechoslovakia

all of which provide the basis for the attraction of other firms and industries, and so the cycle begins again.

The induced growth centre is used as one element in regional policy because it is believed that the concentration of investment in one centre and the resultant growth will spread to the surrounding region. The spread effects first mentioned by the Swedish economist Myrdal and independently by Hirschmann include jobs for rural residents, the increased demand for local services and goods and the diffusion from the growth centre of more efficient practices. The converse to spread effects are the backwash effects which refer to the deleterious effects on poor regions of growth elsewhere; these include selective migration and the lack of investment.

Growth centres have been used throughout the world and the British mark two New Towns, the area development programmes of the United States and the settlement schemes of the French Fifth National Plan are all examples. However, it has proved difficult to lure industries and commerce away from the attractive big cities.

EVALUATING THE EFFECTS OF GROWTH CENTRES

Growth centres have been widely used in national urban policies. Their effectiveness has been measured in a number of ways. Researchers have examined the following:

1 *The patterns of commuting* to the growth centre from the surrounding area. If there is an increase after growth-centre designation and policy implementation then this would count as a spread effect.
2 *Industrial linkage* involving the examination of the purchase of materials by firms in the growth centre to see if they have purchased locally and the extent of the use of local sub-contractors.
3 The development of the *service sector* through analysing the pattern of shopping trips by growth-centre workers.

In a study of Georgia it was found that growth emanating from Atlanta was first felt in the other major towns and then eventually spread out to the immediate rural areas. In a comprehensive study of growth centres in the East Anglia region of England Malcolm Moseley found evidence of increased commuting, but industrial linkage occurred mainly with firms outside the region, while the growth of the service sector took place in the shopping centres of the large towns. Growth in this case did not trickle down the hierarchy to the small towns and problem areas of the rural districts. It was only the big towns which gained from the spread effects.

References

Moseley, M.J. (1973), The impact of growth centres in rural regions – II, An analysis of spatial 'flows' in East Anglia, *Regional Studies*, 7, 77-94.

Nichols, V. (1969), Growth poles: an evaluation of their propulsive effect, *Environment and Planning*, A 1, 193-208.

Induced growth centres have to compete against the economic inertia of the existing urban system.

THE LOWER ORDERS

The concentration of investment implied in the concept of practice of growth centres involves the lack of investment elsewhere. To concentrate investment and growth in centre A means denying funds to centres B, C and D. In practice it is the smaller urban centres and villages in particular which are denied funds. Figure 5.3 highlights the case of County Durham, England, where a whole series of villages were earmarked for only minimal investment by the county authorities. The D class villages, as they were called, were starved of funds while investment was channelled to larger settlements and new towns in the region. This type of selective investment policy has two consequences. First, those areas denied funds are likely to experience further decline as the out-movement of capital and population further debilitates the local economy. We can imagine a situation in which the arrow linkages of the cumulative causation model of Figure 5.2 are reversed. In other words the out-movement of industry leads to the decline of infrastructure, declining wealth of the community and declining ability to locate new industry. Second, for those remaining there will be a reduction in opportunity and life changes, as employment prospects dwindle. Opportunities will be dependent upon travelling perhaps long distances, but for those lower-income households without

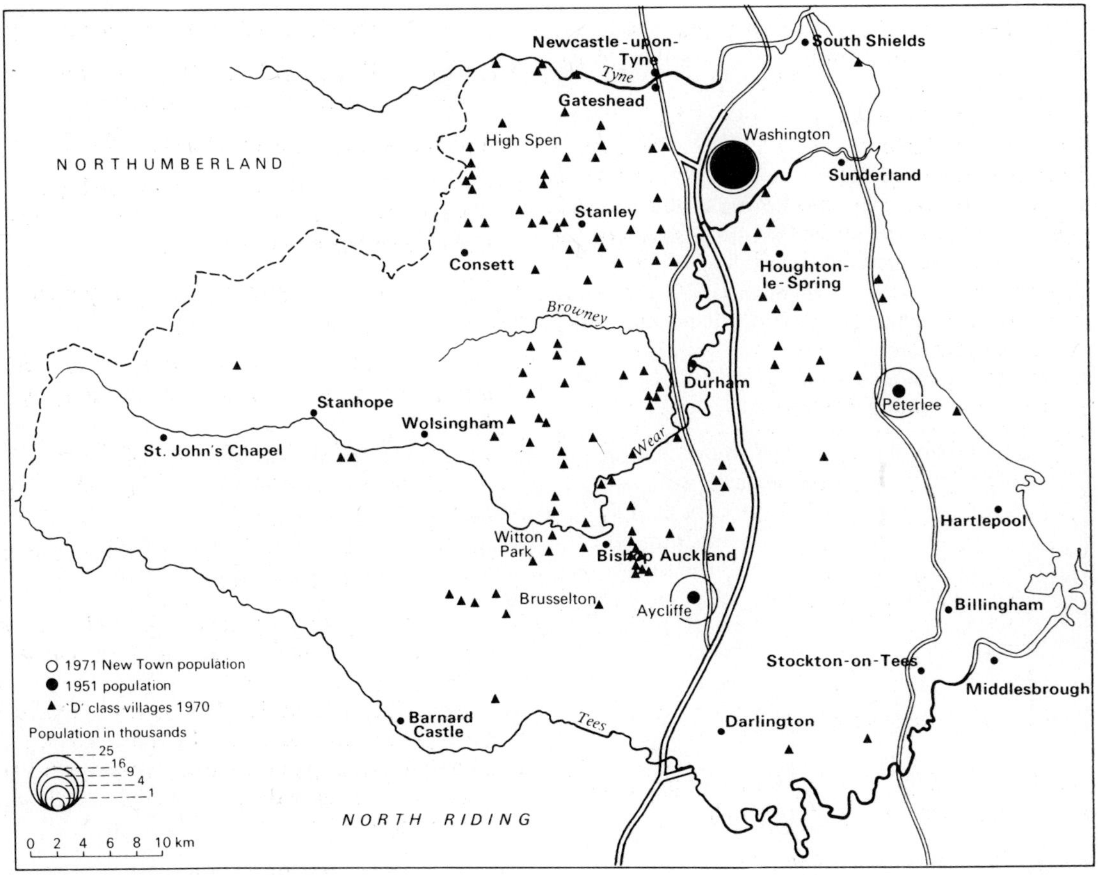

Newcastle-upon-Tyne
Tyne
South Shields
Gateshead
Washington
High Spen
NORTHUMBERLAND
Sunderland
Stanley
Consett
Houghton-le-Spring
Browney
Durham
Stanhope
Peterlee
Wolsingham
St. John's Chapel
Wear
Hartlepool
Witton Park
Bishop Auckland
Brusselton
Aycliffe
Billingham
○ 1971 New Town population
● 1951 population
▲ 'D' class villages 1970
Population in thousands
25
16
9
4
1
Stockton-on-Tees
Middlesbrough
Barnard Castle
Tees
Darlington
NORTH RIDING
0 2 4 6 8 10 km

Figure 5.3 D class villages in County Durham. Designated in 1970, such villages were to receive only minimal public investment
Source: Warren, K. (1973), *North East England,* Oxford University Press

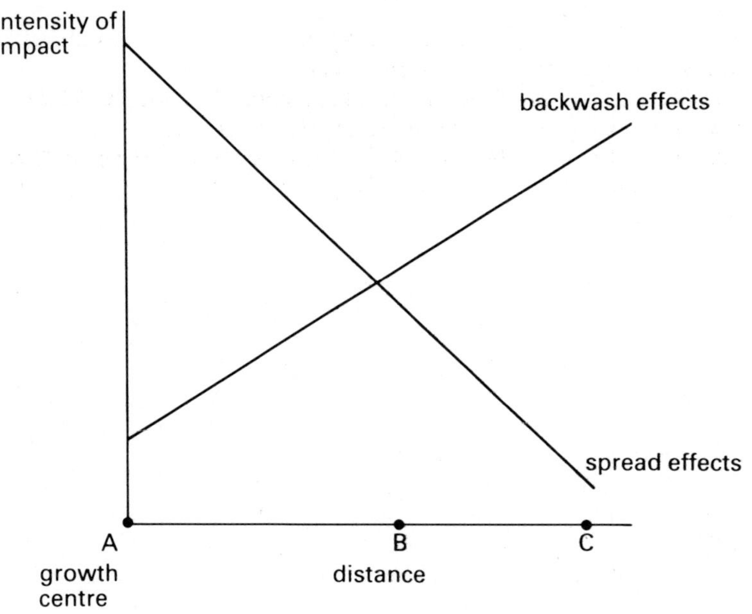

Figure 5.4 The distribution of spread and backwash effects

easy access to private transport this restriction will lead to a reduction in the standard of living.

To some extent the centres within the shadow of a growth centre will gain from spread effects. However, the further a settlement is located away from the growth centre the more backwash effects are likely to outweigh spread effects. In Figure 5.4 the inhabitants in settlement C are likely to experience declining standards of living. This diagram uses absolute distance but the ease of covering distance will vary with income, age, access to private transport and the quality of public transport. Even in settlement B all the people who cannot drive a car will be less able to use the services in the growth centre than the younger, car-owning households. Concentrating growth in selected centres has definite spatial effects and particular social redistributional consequences. The economic efficiency of concentrating growth has to be balanced against the social costs faced by the remaining rural residents.

GUIDE TO FURTHER READING

General introduction to national urban policies regarding settlement patterns include:

Berry, B.J.L. (1976), Comparative urbanization strategies, in Swain, H. and Mackinnon, R. (eds), *Managing Urban Systems*, IIASA, Laxenburg, Austria.

Bourne, L.W. (1975), *Urban Systems: Strategies for Regulation*, Clarendon Press, Oxford.

Richardson, H.W. (1981), *National Urban Development Strategies*, Geography Paper 76, Department of Geography, University of Reading.

The costs of benefits of city size are examined by:

Richardson, H.W. (1973), *The Economics of Urban Size*, Saxon House, Farnborough.

A good introduction to growth pole theory is:

Darwent, D.F. (1969), Growth poles and growth centres in regional planning – a review, *Environment and Planning*, A 1, 5-32.

Models of cumulative growth were first presented by:

Hirschmann, A.O. (1958), *The Strategy of Economic Development*, Yale University Press, New Haven.

Myrdal, G. (1957), *Rich Lands and Poor: The Road To World Prosperity*, Harper & Row, New York.

There have been many evaluations of growth centres. Among the many, see:

Gray, I, (1969), Employment effect of a new industry in a rural area, *Monthly Labour Review*, 92, 29.

Robinson, G. and Salih, K. (1971), The spread of development around Kuala Lumpur; a methodology for an exploratory test of some assumptions of the growth pole model, *Regional Studies*, 5, 303-14.

The decline of lower-order urban settlements is discussed in:

Cloke, P. (1979), *Key Settlements in Rural Areas*, Methuen, London.

Clout, H.D. (1977), *Rural Settlements. Progress in Human Geography*, 1, 475-80.

Moseley, M.J. (1974), *Growth Centres in Spatial Planning*, Pergamon, Oxford.

Part 3

The Internal Structure of the City

Plate 15

6 The City as Workplace

Cities are places where things are made, goods are sold and work is done. In this chapter we will consider the city as workplace.

TYPES OF EMPLOYMENT

The way in which people earn their living is often divided into three categories.

(1) *Primary occupations*: these include the production of raw materials, e.g. agriculture, mining, lumbering.

(2) *Secondary occupations*: which involve the processing of raw materials, the production of goods. This is the manufacturing sector.

(3) *Tertiary occupations*: involve the provision of services rather than the production of goods. The service sector ranges from entertainment, insurance, banking, finance, government, to professional and scientific services.

The growth of capitalist economies can be seen as a progression from the predominance of primary occupations to the rise of tertiary occupations. In the pre-industrial world most people were

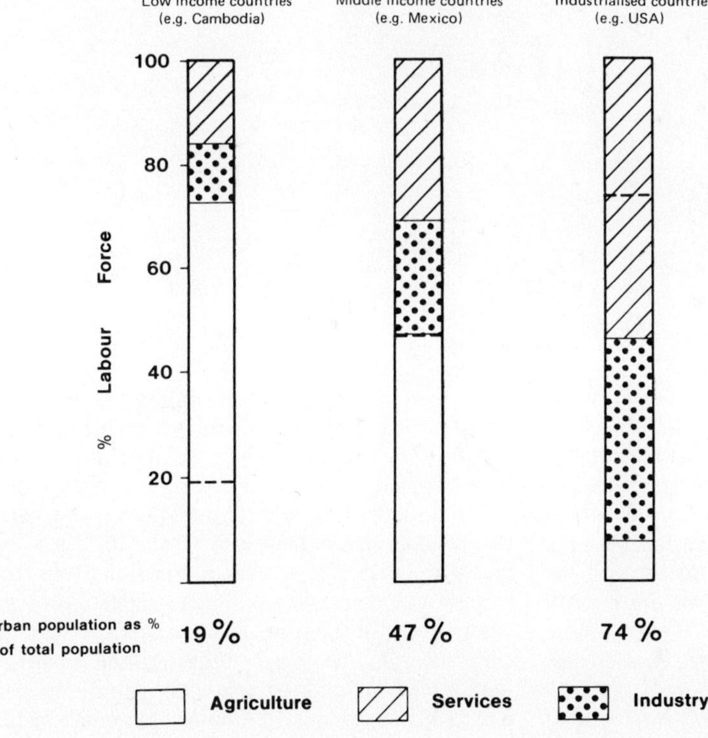

Figure 6.1 Occupational categories and levels of urbanisation

Plates 16 and 17
Employment in third-world cities: (16) an eating stall in Singapore; (17) a fortune teller at work in Khatmandu

involved in the primary occupations of agriculture. Urban centres were few and small. The process of industrialisation involved the growing importance of secondary occupations such as steel-making. Certain industries were attracted to the urban areas and there was a direct relationship between the growth of the manufacturing sector and the rise of cities. As the economy grows the tertiary occupations of the service sector become more important. On top of the industrial base is now laid an urban-oriented service economy.

The trend of primary to tertiary employment has a definite urban manifestation. In the early stages urban centres are small; during industrialisation they expand; while in the more recent stages the cities become more service- than industrial-oriented. The relationship between occupational catagories and levels of urbanisation is shown in Figure 6.1. Notice the progression from low-income countries with the high proportion of the labour force in the primary occupations of agriculture towards the richer industrialised countries with service and industrial workers being important and levels of urbanisation being that much higher.

Table 6.1 City classification, 1871

Class		
Class 1	London	London
2	County or assize town	Reading, Oxford
3	Watering places	
	(a) seaside	Blackpool, Southend
	(b) inland	Bath
4	Seaports	Southampton
5	Manufacturing towns (textile and dress)	
	(a) woollen goods	Halifax
	(b) silk goods	Norwich
	(c) cotton goods	Rochdale
	(d) lace goods	Nottingham
	(e) hosiery	Leicester
	(f) gloves	Witney
	(g) boots and shoes	Northampton
	(h) straw plait	Luton
6	Manufacturing towns (minerals, metals, chemicals)	
	(a) coal mining	Aberdare, Wolverhampton
	(b) iron mining and manufacturing	Derby
	(c) copper and tin mining and manufacturing	Truro
	(d) lead mining	Hexham
	(e) cutlery, tools and metal manufacture	Sheffield
	(f) needle manufacture	Redditch
	(g) nail manufacture	Dudley
	(h) slate quarrying	Bethesda
	(i) salt mining and manufacture	Droitwich
	(j) earthenware and china manufacture	Stoke-on-Trent
	(k) glass manufacture	St Helens
	(l) chemical manufacture	South Shields

Source: Census of England and Wales 1871, General Report

The distribution of these different employment types varies between cities. The service sector tends to be located within the central areas of the larger urban centres. Cities will also differ in relation to the exact mix of employment types; we can make a general distinction between central places – providing a range of services to surrounding regions – and specialised function cities where one activity, be it steel-making, government, etc., predominates. Classification of cities by the type of work they do has long been part of urban studies. In 1871, for example, the Census office in Britain classified 281 towns in England and Wales according to a sixfold division with numerous sub-divisions. Note in Table 6.1 the range of different types of manufacturing detailed in Classes 5 and 6. A hundred years later David Donnison and Paul Soto used the census to classify British towns (Table 6.2).

Table 6.2 City classification, 1971

Group			
Group	1	London	
	2	Regional service centres	Reading, Oxford
	3	Resorts	Blackpool, Southend
	4	Residential suburbs	Solihull, Esher, Crosby
	5	New industrial suburbs	Watford, Worcester
	6	New towns	Harlow, East Kilbride
	7	Welsh mining towns	Aberdare
	8	Engineering	Derby, Sheffield
	9	Textile towns	Rochdale, Halifax
	10	Engineering II	Peterborough, Eton & Slough
	11	Heavy engineering and coal	Wolverhampton
	12	Inner conurbations	Liverpool, Newcastle
	13	Central Scotland	Dundee, Glasgow

Source: Donnison, D. and Soto, P. (1980), *The Good City*, Heinemann, London

THE ECONOMIC CONTEXT

The threefold classification of employment which we have used tells us about the type of employment. It distinguishes between farmers, factory workers and teachers. It does not, however, allow us to say anything about the form of employment, the how or indeed the why of employment. For this we need another classification and one which links the nature of employment to the overall economic context. We can make a twofold distinction between the *capitalist mode of production* and *centrally planned economies*. The capitalist mode of production has two main characteristics. First, goods are produced as commodities to be sold at a profit. The aim of firms and corporations in capitalist economies is to make a profit and from this goal flows the investment strategies and locational shifts of operation. Table 6.3 shows the general set of relationships. The economic pressures operating on a particular firm primarily relate to profitability (either too little or the potential for more) and this provides the stimulus for change in either the production process or the organisation of the labour force which has distinct spatial implications. The geography of recession noted in Table 6.3 is a shorthand notation for the process of plant closures, unemployment and declining economies, while the geography of growth is the notation for new plants opening up, increased employment opportunities and the whole range of positive multiplier effects. The exact location chosen for any particular firm depends upon the spatial variations in profitability. Figure 6.2 shows the location of maximum profit in an idealised example.

Second, workers enter into bargains with their employers and this bargain is constantly changing as employers seek to increase and maintain profits by reducing labour costs, while workers seek to maintain and improve their wages and working conditions. The variation in labour costs and

Table 6.3 Firms and locational outcome

General	Specific: *Lack of profits*	Specific: *Profit potential*
economic pressures operating on firm	e.g. overcapacity uncompetitive overmanning	e.g. undercapacity need for labour
changes required in production process and organisation of labour force	closures, lay-offs rationalisation	new plants, lay-ons expansion
the spatial/locational implications	the geography of recession	the geography of growth

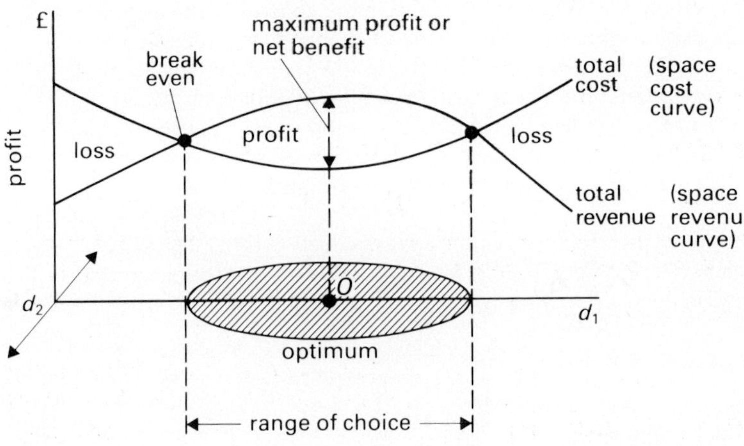

Figure 6.2 Simple model of the location considerations of a single production facility. Source: Smith, D.M. (1977), *Human Geography: a welfare approach*, Edward Arnold, London

management-labour relations has an important role to play in contemporary industrial location. Holding everything else constant, firms tend to go to areas where labour is cheap and docile. The introduction of assembly lines and mass production techniques has involved a deskilling of labour, so manufacturing companies can now produce their goods with unskilled and semi-skilled labour. This allows them to set up plants in areas where there is no industrial tradition and lack of labour militancy. Much of the industrial movement from the north east of the USA to the south, for example, is a move from a highly unionised region to a less unionised one.

The twentieth century has also seen the partial realisation of the prediction of the nineteenth-century social theorists. Karl Marx, in particular, has proved to be the most influential observer and critic of capitalism. He argued for the new order, a society in which people's control over nature would be guided by a communal endeavour. The ultimate aim was a communist society in which there was no unequal division of labour and an equitable distribution of resources which allowed the full flowering of human potential. The goal was to produce a society in which individual members received according to their needs and gave according to their ability. In practice the actually existing socialist societies are planned economies where central planners provide the

LOCATING INDUSTRIES IN CENTRALLY PLANNED ECONOMIES

In centrally planned economies industrial location is a result of planners' decisions not market forces. The principles of industrial location in the Soviet Union can be considered at two scales. At the regional level industrial location reflects both the equity and the efficiency arguments. The adoption of the principles of equity which stress that industrial centres should be dispersed throughout the country has led to a dispersion of industry from the small number of pre-revolutionary urban centres such as Moscow. Soviet industry, compared to industries in advanced capitalist countries, is more dispersed. However, the efficiency argument of maximising national incomes and reducing costs has been an important element. There is a fragmentation of administrative responsibility between regional planners and those in charge of different industries who want to fulfil their quotas and reduce costs. The sector planners, in making location decisions which minimise cost, thus often work against an equitable distribution of industry.

At the urban level the principles of industrial location are to minimise journey-to-work, separate land uses and set up industrial centres. In practice, however, the city planners have been unable to achieve all these aims. In the first place the city planners have little actual control over industrial location. In Moscow, for example, only one-fifth of 1400 industrial enterprises are controlled by the city Soviet. The rest come under the control of the different ministries who are often unresponsive to the arguments of the weak planning authorities. In the second place there has been the legacy of industrial inertia. In the Stalinist period emphasis was on industrialisation, often industrialisation at any cost. Principles of land-use planning did not appear on the agenda. The net result has been for the reality of industrial location in cities to be different from the theory. In Moscow one-third of all industrial enterprises contravene basic zoning regulations. And this is a city with a powerful city government. This situation is worse elsewhere.

In this centrally planned economy therefore we can see a tension between the demands of equity with the claims of efficiency and the conflict between the different institutions in the planning bureaucracy. In achieving their different goals the ministries often pursue contradictory policies.

References

Bater, J.H. (1980), *The Soviet City*, Edward Arnold, London.

Pallot, J. and Shaw, D.J.B. (1981), *Planning in the Soviet Union*, Croom Helm, London.

detailed quotas which enterprises have to meet. In this context a balance has to be struck between efficiency and equity. The planners must ensure that there is a full utilisation of resources, while at the same time ensuring an equitable distribution of opportunities.

In practice many countries and especially many western European countries fall somewhere between a pure capitalist mode of production and a completely centrally planned economy. The mixed economies, as they have become known, are essentially capitalist economies in which firms seek to make profits, but the state has an important role to play in providing goods and services which the private sector does not provide and in maintaining the conditions for further accumulation of capital and the reproduction of labour power. The state in this case has a double facet. On the one hand it maintains capitalist production but on the other it is used as a vehicle to provide welfare facilities. In the following pages of this chapter we will concentrate on the city as workplace in mixed economies. However, it is important to remember that this is only one economic context. There are others.

Table 6.4 Kondratieff cycles

Long wave	*Phases*	*Character of wave*
1 1793-1847	1793-1825 expansive; rising rate of profit	Gradual spread of steam power in production
	1826-1847 slackening, stagnant rate of profit	Growth of towns on coalfields and other power sources
2 1847-1893	1848-1873 expansive	Machine-made steam engine becomes dominant source of power. The first technological revolution.
	1874-1893 slackening	Development of industrial cities
3 1894-1939	1894-1913 expansive	Development of consumer-based industries, the second technological revolution
	1914-1939 slackening	Footloose industries allow industrial development away from coalfields Beginnings of suburbanisation of jobs and residences
4 1940/45-1980?	1940/45-1955 expansive	Acceleration of technological developments, the third technological revolution.
	1966-1980? slackening	Growth of service economy Large-scale suburbanisation of jobs and residences

Source: Mandel, 1975

THE ECONOMY: TEMPORAL CONSIDERATIONS

The capitalist economy is a fluctuating one. The fluctuations take the typical sequence of depression, beginnings of recovery, recovery, boom and prosperity, slump and then the cycle is repeated. A number of different amplitudes have been identified.

(1) Long cycles of about 50 years, termed Kondratieff waves in memory of the Soviet economist who formalised the concept. These are based on major technological innovations.
(2) Business cycles of between 7 and 10 years.

The real reasons behind these cycles are not fully understood. Whatever the exact combination of factors responsible for these cycles they play an important part in economic matters. Table 6.4 shows the timing and character of the main Kondratieff cycles. Notice how each one has a specific set of spatial implications. The form of the different technological innovations made some locations more profitable than others. In the first wave the technological developments allowed the use of steam power. But since transport was rudimentary and energy requirements were high, for those firms seeking profits in the new industries the place to be was beside the coalfields where energy was cheaper and agglomeration economies came into play. The result was the development of industrial cities. Later waves meant new technologies and the changing set of profitable locations. We can imagine each of the long cycles as literally waves which sweep over the economic landscape giving shape to the land in the form of peaks of profitability and valleys of loss. Subsequent waves may be channelled to some extent by this landscape but they all shaped their own particular configuration. In the USA the profitable peaks in the nineteenth century were the steel towns of the north east, while in the 1970s it was the suburbs, small towns and sunbelt cities which gave high profits to the new high technology industries.

In the shorter business cycles firms respond much more quickly. In the up-swing of the cycle firms expand either in situ or by setting up new plants. During recession, economic restructuring takes place in the form of product switching, reducing costs, sacking workers, making workers do more for the same money or through plant closure.

The economic position of individual cities is thus a space-time set of co-ordinates determined by relative location in the complex pattern of economic cycles.

THE ECONOMY: SPATIAL CONSIDERATIONS

The world economy and urban hierarchy

A study of the present time allows us to hold constant the time element in the space-time co-ordinates of urban economic fortunes. In this section let us concentrate on the spatial differences by looking at the relationships between the changing world economy and the urban hierarchy.

Throughout the nineteenth and early twentieth centuries there was a structure to the world economy which had definite urban implications. Basically, the peripheral countries, the South of the Brandt Report's terminology (also sometimes known as third world or underdeveloped) supplied the raw materials to the richer core countries who specialised in manufacturing. The big cities in the peripheral countries were points of extraction, while the main manufacturing centres were in the urban areas of the core. More recently there has been the development of a new international division of labour. It has arisen because of the growth of multi-national corporations who can redistribute their activities according to spatial variations in resource environment, and labour costs and organisation. Capital is mobile while labour tends to be relatively immobile. This new international division of labour has two main elements.

(1) Although the transnational corporations have activities throughout the world, their corporate headquarters tend to be located in the core. Corporate headquarters are located in the major cities of the developed world because of the presence of firms and services with international connections in banking, insurance and capital markets. There has been a development of world cities which are major transaction points in the world economy.

(2) There has been a development of manufacturing in cities of the third world. Multi-national companies are locating their basic production processes in cities of the periphery where labour is cheap and docile, and government grants can be maintained. Moreover the companies have sought

Table 6.5 World centres of corporations and finance

Main centres
New York
Tokyo
London
Secondary centres
Osaka
Rhine-Ruhr
Chicago
Frankfurt
Zurich

Table 6.6 Industrial growth rates: selected countries

	Average annual per cent growth rates in industry	
	1960 – 1970	*1970 – 1977*
Singapore	12.6	8.6
Mexico	0.3	6.2
South Korea	17.2	17.0
USA	5.2	2.3
UK	3.1	0.5

to build factories in these places in order to jump over the tariff walls set up by many third-world countries. The governments of these countries have sought arrangements with international companies in which resources can be exploited in exchange for the setting up of manufacturing activities.

The old pattern of resources being exploited in the periphery and then manufactured in the core is changing. This recent trend has two implications. First, there has been the obvious growth of manufacturing in certain third-world cities. Not all countries have seen the action. It has been concentrated in a few countries. Brazil, South Korea, Egypt, Hong Kong and Singapore have seen tremendous rates of growth, particularly in the period 1960 to 1980. Although there has been some recent slackening in these countries the rates of growth since 1970 have been greater than in the traditional manufacturing countries. This subset of countries has been termed the newly industrialising countries (NICS) and in terms of the spatial expression of their growth we can term them the newly urbanising countries. Consider the cases of Mexico and South Korea (see Table 6.7). Compared to the USA, both countries have experienced larger rates of growth in GNP per capita, larger rates of growth in the manufacturing component of total output and much faster rates of urban growth.

Second, the economic base of some manufacturing cities in the developed world has suffered. The cities and the working population which have grown up around the traditional manufacturing base have suffered from declining demand due to recession and increased competition

Table 6.7 Growth rates in manufacturing and urbanisation

	average annual growth rate of GNP per capita 1960-1977	*% of manufacturing in GDP*		*% urban population*	
		1960	*1972*	*1960*	*1975*
South Korea	7.4	12	25	28	49
Mexico	2.8	23	28	51	63
USA	2.4	29	24	66	70

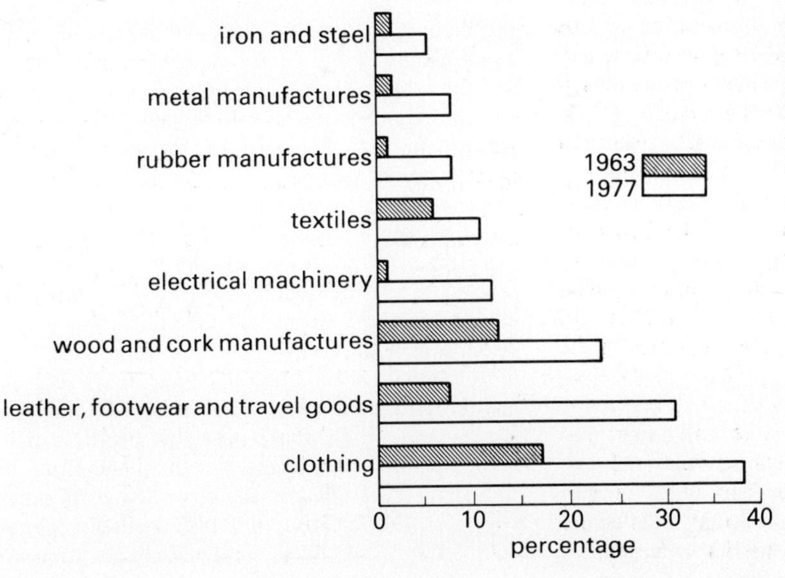

Figure 6.3 The increasing share of OECD imports accounted for by newly industrialising countries
Source: OECD (1979), *The Impact of the Newly Industrializing Countries,* Paris, OECD, chart C

THE BIG FIRM

One of the most important single developments in capitalist economies has been the rise of large companies. Economic activity has been concentrated in a fewer number of very large firms and corporations. This has come about through mergers and take-overs. The general trend in recession has been for the small companies to either go to the wall or be taken over by the big firms.

The modern corporations have several features. First, they are big. There are 15 industrial corporations which had sales greater than the gross national product of 48 nation states. The sales of General Motors, for example, are greater than the gross national products of Austria, Norway, Greece Ireland and Morocco. Second, the big firms have their fingers in many pies. The modern corporation has investments in many sectors, including manufacturing, entertainment, retailing, real estate, etc. Capital is constantly being invested and reinvested in order to achieve the highest rates of return. Third, they are multi-national. Their investments and activities occur throughout the world.

The rise of the big firm has a number of implications:

1 Much of our economic theory is based on the notion of a free market. This is a nineteenth-century view which had some credence when there were a large number of small firms in any one sector. Today, in comparison, the big firms hold a disproportionate market share. In the USA over 90 per cent of the automobile market is in the control of three firms; General Motors, Ford and Chrysler. These firms collude to keep prices high even when cost-cutting techniques have been introduced. Rather than meeting the market, the big firms control it.

2 The macro-economic and regional policies of governments are now affected by the actions of a few companies. In the third world the large companies have sales as big as the host country's GNP. Big firms discuss economic and social matters with host countries' governments on

especially from the newly industrialising countries. Figure 6.3 shows the increase in proportion of imports from the newly industrialising countries into the richer countries of the OECD. The fate of some urban economies in the USA and UK has been made doubly precarious not only through increased competition from the newly industrialising countries but from the strong economies of Japan and West Germany. The economic lifeblood of places like Detroit and the West Midlands is severely threatened.

National economies and the urban hierarchy

At any one time different cities will be differentially placed on the profitability surface which guides capitalist decision-making. As we have noted, the exact position will vary by time both in terms of the different profitability criteria set by the technology of the particular wave and in the exact timing of both the long Kondratieff and the shorter business cycles. At any one time therefore we can identify places where new firms are attracted and existing ones are expanding. We can identify urban winners and urban losers. For the current urban winners the process can be cumulative. Nothing succeeds like success. More technically the urban winners see the operation of the mechanics of cumulative causation outlined in chapter 3. New firms are attracted, population growth generates new demands, more firms are established to meet these demands, more jobs are created and so the beneficial cycle continues upwards. The cities where only low profits can be made are the urban losers. For them new firms are not attracted from elsewhere, while existing ones contract, shed labour and businesses are closed completely. For those workers unable to move

equal terms if not from a superior position. The big firms have enough economic muscle to influence government decisions. Regional policy, for example, is predicated upon the state being able to persuade a firm to move to specific regions. But if the firm can say either let us set up here or we will locate a factory in another country, then the concept of the sovereign state is in jeopardy. Stuart Holland has termed the coming of the big firms as the rise of meso-economic power.

3 The activities of the multi-nationals have distinct locational implications. We can see their operations as a three-level affair. At the apex is the head office, the corporate headquarters. This is located in one of the world cities, for example, New York or London, close to international financial, legal and information-processing centres. Then there are the subcorporate head offices located in main centres where the corporation has business. For example a US multi-national may have its head office in New York and sub-corporate offices in San Francisco, London, Lagos, Delhi, Melbourne, etc. Finally, there are the branch plants where routine manufacturing processes are performed by semi-skilled and unskilled labour. These branch plants are increasingly being located in third-world countries, especially the newly industrialising countries where labour is cheap and docile. What are emerging, therefore, are regions which have a branch-plant economy where the economic base is under external control.

References

Galbraith, J.K. (1973), *The New Industrial State,* Penguin, Harmondsworth.
Holland, S. (1976), *Capital Versus the Regions,* Macmillan, London.
Taylor, M. and Thrift, N. (eds) (1981), *A Geography of Multi-Nationals,* Croom Helm, London,
Watts, H.D. (1981), *The Branch Plant Economy: a Study of External Control,* Longmans, London.

employment prospects become very restricted. In the region as a whole the economy declines, the tax base is eroded and cutbacks in welfare expenditure and local authority spending may occur.

The real losers are of course people. The location and implications of economic process affect different groups of people in different places in differing ways. Those most affected are the unskilled and those trained for jobs which are no longer available. People can in theory move to where jobs are available but if they lack the new skills then there is very little point. Even if they have the skills booming areas tend to have spiralling house prices and tight housing markets. Entry is made difficult especially for the lower income groups.

Table 6.8 Changing manufacturing employment in 245 SMSAs in the United States, 1947-1967

	Employment		*Absolute change*	*Percentage change*
	1947	*1967*		
Central cities	7,356,733	7,063,426	−293,307	− 3.9
Suburban rings	4,141,704	8,044,030	+3,902,326	+94.2
SMSAs	11,498,437	15,107,458	+3,609,021	+31.4

THE CITY CENTRE

The city centre is the biggest single concentration of employment. The central area of cities, commonly referred to as the Central Business District (CBD) is the hub of commercial and retail activity in the city. The CBD can broadly be defined as the area of highest land values. It is not a homogeneous area. The CBD can be considered as consisting of two interrelated parts, the core and the frame. The CBD core is the area of intensive land use with multi-storey dwellings housing offices, retail shops, consumer services, theatres and banks. It has the highest concentration of pedestrian flows and an absence of permanent residential population. The CBD frame is an area of semi-intensive land fringing the core where land use is dominated by warehouses, car sales and services, transport terminals, manufacturing and some institutional uses.

Three sets of jobs are found in the city centre. First, there are the office jobs ranging from management to routine service work such as lift attendant, etc. all associated with the public and private office sector in the commercial areas of the central city. Second, there are those jobs associated with the city centre as a retail and entertainment centre. These jobs are available in shops, cinemas, restaurants, etc. Much of the employment is poorly paid, often done by women. Finally there are manufacturing jobs; these relate to the three main types of industries:

(a) Those industries such as printing and newspapers which require the accessibility to skilled labour and the maximum accessibility for the distribution of their products provided by central city location.
(b) Those industries such as office-machine manufacturing which are attracted to the market provided by the nearby location of offices in the commercial core.
(c) Those industries, generally small-scale concerns, which are located in the inner city simply through inertia. Initially attracted to the central city for a variety of reasons which are now no longer operative, they remain in the central city because of their inability to face the high costs of moving to better locations. It is these types of industries which are experiencing greatest difficulty in the current economic climate.

The biggest change affecting the central area as employment centre has been the suburbanisation of both manufacturing and service industries. In the manufacturing centre there has

Table 6A Births and deaths of firms in Glasgow 1959-1969

Zone	*Distance from city centre*	*A* *Births**	*B* *Deaths†*	*A–B* *Net balance*
1	0–3	46	50	–4
2	3–4	43	25	–18
3	4–6	32	8	+24
4	6–10	65	10	+55

* Includes firms who moved in from other zones
† Includes firms who moved out to other zones

Source: Lever, 1972

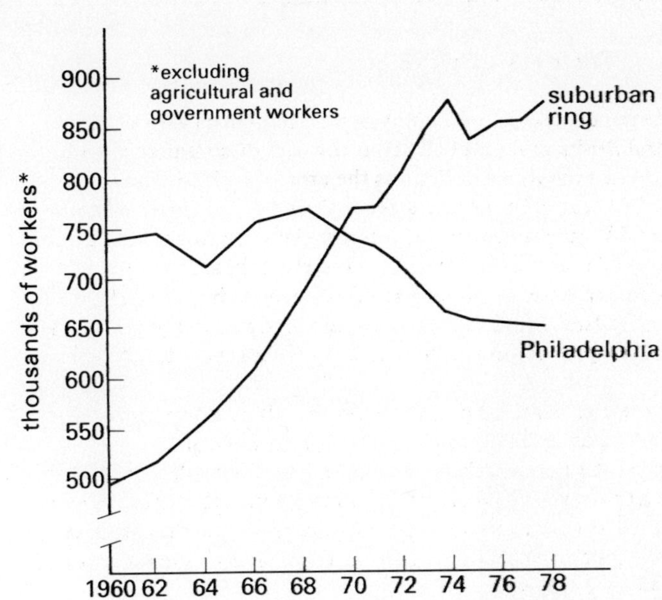

Figure 6A Employment trends in Philadelphia SMSA

been a net decline in the number of firms and the number of jobs in manufacturing. Inner-city firms have been closing more than others due to their uncompetitive position in the market while new firms are setting up in suburban industrial estates or rural locations. Table 6A shows the situation for just one city. This trend has been continuing for some time. More recent, however, has been the decentralisation of retail centres in the form of hypermarkets, and service sectors as offices are relocating to suburban and small town locations. The net effect is to reduce the importance of the central area as an employment centre (see Figure 6A) and to make it more difficult for inner-city residents lacking access to transport to compete in the job market. Inner-city residents can see job opportunies decentralising beyond their reach to the suburbs or to small-town locations.

References

Lever, N.F. (1972), The Intra-Urban Movement of Manufacturing: a Markov Approach, *Transactions of the Institute of British Geographers*, 56, 21-38.

Short, J.R. (1980), *Urban Data Sources*, Butterworths, London.

Sternlieb, D. and Hughes, J.W. (1980), The Changing Demography of The Central City, *Scientific American*, 243, 2, 40-5.

Plate 18
Temples of capitalism in New York's CBD

Plate 19
The mosque dominates the skyline of a Tunisian town

The ebb and flow of investment and the consequently locational implications occur both between cities and within cities. At the intra-urban level the most distinctive features have been the net suburbanisation of manufacturing industry and the relative growth of service-type jobs in the central areas of large cities. Table 6.8 shows the general pattern of central city loss and suburban gain in manufacturing employment.

The decrease in manufacturing has been caused by several factors:

(1) Net plant closures. In inner-city areas there have been fewer new firms being established than existing ones closing. Deaths are greater than births.
(2) Inner-city plants have the oldest machinery and lowest productivity; they are the first to be closed when recession occurs or competition is stiff.
(3) New plants are created in the suburban and small-town areas where land and labour is cheaper, labour is often more malleable and purpose-built accommodation is available and congestion limited.
(4) Firms have been responding to the problems of profitability by cutting down labour costs. Existing plants in the inner city have been shedding labour.

While there has been a decrease in manufacturing employment there has been a relative and sometimes an absolute increase in service employment. Table 6.9 shows a typical pattern for the two English cities of London and Manchester. It seems clear then that the more buoyant retail and service sectors which have been expanding are still locationally tied to the large urban centres. Many of the service-type jobs rely on centrality either because of the need to be accessible to customers (the retail sector) or to maintain close contact with subsidiary services and the need for face-to-face contact with business associates (the business and financial sector in particular). In the booming government sector the white-collar offices have been urban-based, while the growth in manual government employment has been particularly high in the urban municipal sectors. Table 6.10 shows for those US cities with a decline in total employment, how municipal government has been an increasing source of employment. In one sense city governments have soaked up some of the pool of unemployment. As we shall see, the growing high proportion of people employed by city governments especially in declining city regions is part cause and part effect of the urban fiscal crisis. We will return to this theme in a later chapter.

The exact pattern of changing job distribution varies in the urban hierarchy. In the UK, for example, while the decline in manufacturing has been most marked in London and the major cities, manufacturing growth has occurred in the small town and rural areas (see Table 6.11). While all

Table 6.9 Employment change in Greater London and Greater Manchester, by sector of economic activity

Sector	*Greater London*			*Greater Manchester*		
	1971	*Change, 1971-75*		*1967*	*Change, 1967-72*	
	(000)	*(000)*	*%*	*(000)*	*(000)*	*%*
Manufacturing	1049.3	−213.4	−20.3	596.6	−93.8	−15.7
Basic services*	1440.8	− 42.8	− 3.0	363.5	−27.0	− 7.4
Non-basic services**	1246.4	+121.1	+ 9.7	228.5	+38.7	+16.9

* Includes workers in gas, electricity and water; transport and communication; distributive trades; miscellaneous services.
** Includes workers in insurance, banking, finance and business services; professional and scientific services; public administration and defence.

Source: Keeble, 1978

the locational categories shown in this table have increased in service employment, the greatest percentage increase was in the medium-sized cities and small towns.

In summary, then, the pattern in the urban region of the rich capitalist world has been fourfold:

(1) A shift from manufacturing to service employment.
(2) A decline of the manufacturing base in central cities, especially cities in the older industrial regions.
(3) The growth of manufacturing in suburbs, new cities and rural areas.
(4) An increasing proportion of service and government employment in central cities.

In the major cities of the third world the trend has been for an overall increase in manufacturing employment, though there are still very high levels of unemployment and under-employment.

Table 6.10 Percentage change in the number of workers employed in municipal government 1960-70, for 21 declining central cities

City	*employed resident labour force 1960-70*	*resident municipal labour force 1960-70*
1 St Louis	−21%	0%
2 Newark	−16	+45
3 Cleveland	−15	+16
4 Pittsburgh	−13	+ 7
5 Buffalo	−13	+28
6 Chicago	− 8	+18
7 Detroit	− 8	0
8 Boston	− 8	+20
9 Cincinnati	− 8	+40
10 Birmingham	− 8	+43
11 New Orleans	− 7	+11
12 Minneapolis	− 7	+ 1
13 Rochester	− 6	+50
14 New York	− 4	+52
15 San Francisco	− 4	+31
16 Oakland	− 4	+17
17 Philadelphia	− 3	+18
18 Baltimore	− 3	+47
19 Washington, DC	− 2	+101
20 Seattle	− 2	+20
21 Louisville	− 1	+32

THE ROLE OF THE STATE

Even in the most ideologically conservative countries the state plays a huge role in economic matters. In managing the money supply and providing the context for legal transactions the state is an important element in the economic life of a country. In terms of explicit locational outcomes we can identify the three scales of state intervention.

Table 6.11 Employment change by type of sub-region in the United Kingdom, 1959-1975 (%)

	Manufacturing employment	*Service employment*	*Total employment*
London	− 37.8	+ 2.3	− 11.4
Conurbations	− 15.9	+ 5.2	− 4.7
Major free-standing cities	+ 3.4	+16.1	+ 9.9
Smaller free-standing cities	+17.9	+14.3	+17.0
Industrial non-city	+16.3	+28.7	+22.0
Urban non-industrial	+38.8	+13.1	+18.8
Semi-rural	+44.9	+13.8	+19.0
Rural	+77.2	+ 1.2	+14.3

Source: Fothergill, S. and Gudgin, G. (1982), *Unequal Growth*, Heinemann, London

International level

In its trade and commercial negotiations with other states the government sets the context for the international trade relations of enterprises. The state can pursue either of two broad strategies. First, there is the strategy of putting up tariffs in order to protect certain home-based industries. Second, there is the free-market approach which lets the market decide. In practice no country follows a free-market approach. Rather the difference lies in the protection afforded to a differing mix of industries. The exact strategy followed has definite locational impacts. For example, by setting up tariffs to foreign-made cars the state protects domestic car producers and the economies and jobs of car-producing areas, and forces foreign companies to set up manufacturing plants in the domestic market. These tariff-hopping industries can be located with some regard to regional policies.

National and regional

Most capitalist countries have marked regional differences in industrial structure, levels of unemployment and employment opportunities. Two arguments have been made against the existence of such inequality. First, there is the rational argument. This states that such marked regional differences lead to different problems in both declining and booming regions. Table 6.12 shows the macro-regional costs as well as the benefits from an unbalanced resource use in a simplified two-region economy.

Second, there is the more persuasive political argument expressed through the ballot box. The voters in the less-developed regions and their

Table 6.12 Macro-regional cost and benefits from imbalanced resource use (simplified two-region economy)

	More-developed region (MDR)	*Less-developed region (LDR)*
1	Employment of immigrant labour raised and educated in LDR.	Education, and pre-work costs of raising emigrants to MDR.
2	Benefit from inflow of already skilled and adapted immigrants.	Loss of more skilled and better adapted labour to MDR.
3	Labour supply adapted to needs during sustained long-term expansion.	Excess of labour supply over local employment opportunities.
4	Raised full-employment ceiling preventing earlier business cycle downturn.	Loss of capital to MDR preventing sustained initial growth and promoting downturn.
5	Re-emigration of excess labour from region in event of business cycle downturn.	Aggravation of surplus unemployed by re-immigration of MDR labour in event of downturn.
6	Higher proportion of remaining skilled and adapted labour in unemployed during recessions.	Higher proportion of unskilled and unadapted labour in regional reserve of unemployed over long run.
7	Marginal transport cost savings to main national markets for medium and small firms.	Marginal transport cost disadvantages to main national market in MDR.
8	More rapid local communications for small and medium firms to other suppliers.	Less rapid communications to suppliers in MDR for some small and medium firms.
9	Greater social facilities for retention or attraction of middle management in leading firms.	Fewer social facilities for middle management in leading firms, partly offset in some cases by less congested environment.

Source: Holland, S. (1976), *Capital Against The Regions*, Macmillan, London

Figure 6.4 Regional policy areas of Britain
Source: Frost, M. and Spence, N. (1981) 'Policy responses to urban and regional change in Britain', *Geographical Journal,* vol. 147(3), 321-49

political representatives lobby (in association with the various local business interests eager to benefit from increased growth) central government in order to direct government funds and private industry to their areas to create jobs and profits. This is the main cause of regional policy incentives.

In Britain, for example, there has been a series of important regional policy measures since 1945 all based on the carrot and stick principle. Firms wishing to expand their operations in booming regions have been refused planning permission, and attracted by fiscal incentives and tax concessions to locate in the poorer regions. Figure 6.4a shows the distribution of assisted areas prior to 1982. The special development areas (SDAS) have the biggest range of incentives and the intermediate areas have the least. The SDAs are areas of high unemployment and include the older industrial conurbations of Glasgow, Liverpool and Newcastle. Figure 6.4b shows the changed distribution of development areas after the incoming Conservative government in 1979 sought to redirect government expenditure and to give some credence to their free-market ideology.

The operation of regional policy has created jobs. Optimistic estimates suggest that between 1960 and 1976, for example, almost 240,000 manufacturing jobs were created in all development areas although many of the jobs were part-time, poorly paid and provided few training opportunities.

Sub-regional and the urban scale

Government intervention also occurs at the level of individual cities. On the one hand there are the policies pursued by the separate municipal governments. In both Britain and the United States, for example, municipal governments seek to attract firms in order to increase their tax base, generate growth in the local economy and provide employment. This has been termed *boosterism*. On the other hand, there are also the national government policies designed for the specific urban regions. These have become particularly important in recent years. In Britain, for example, the 1970s saw the creation of various government schemes. In the *partnership schemes* local authorities worked with central government, the *urban development corporations* were newly created bodies to deal with the severe inner city problem areas while the *enterprise zones* were established to attract jobs (see Figure 6.5). Enterprise zones are also used in the USA (for a general discussion see the special issue of the *International Journal of Urban Regional Research* 1982, vol. 6, no. 3).

Figure 6.5 Urban policy measures
Source: Short, J.R. (1982) Urban policy and British cities, *Journal of the American Planning Association*, vol. 48, no. 1, 39-52

EMPLOYMENT AND INCOME

There are two important aspects of employment. First there is the overall distribution of different types of jobs. We have already seen how in advanced economies there is a move towards more service employment than manufacturing. The exact mix of different types of jobs depends upon the overall state of the economy and the position in the various cycles. Second, there is the important aspect of who fills the particular slots in the job market. Not all forms of employment are the same. Different jobs are paid different incomes. A top executive receives on average sixteen times more than a garbage collector. Different groups tend to be in different types of jobs and thus receive different levels of income. Let us consider the main groupings.

Sex Women are over-represented in poorly paid jobs and under-represented in the higher paid, decision-making types of employment.

Race In both the UK and USA blacks are in poorer-paid jobs than whites. In the USA, for example, median family income for blacks is only two-thirds that of white households. In certain countries, e.g. South Africa, this differential is institutionalised.

Occupation Non-manual workers are paid more than manual workers and unskilled manual workers are paid least of all. The spatial variation of differentially paid occupation groups leads to variations in income over space. This variation occurs at the national, regional and urban level.

We can picture the job market as a continuum. At one end are the good, well-paid jobs with good working conditions, job security, higher levels of

WORK AND TOIL

For many people work is the most boring, tedious part of the day. As one worker in an English chemical factory said:

> 'You move from one boring, dirty, monotonous job to another boring, dirty, monotonous job. And then to another boring, dirty monotonous job. And somehow you're supposed to come out of it all "enriched". But I never feel "enriched" – I just feel knackered.' (Nichols and Benyon, 1977, p. 16)

The distinction made by William Morris in the last century between useful work and useless toil still seems appropriate. Although there are people doing useful things, much paid employment involves monotonous jobs. The factory system is well known for producing routinised activities into which individuals have to fit. Here machines dominate human actions. But even in laboratories and offices where the rhythm of the assembly is less insistent, people's loss of control over their work leads to alienation. Ask any person involved in routine typing. I think that when Thoreau noted that, 'the mass of men lead lives of quiet desperation' he was primarily referring to their work.

Some denied expression in their workplace resign themselves to the fact, but some fight the system in all sorts of ways. Strikes and works-to-rule are the more obvious examples. But there are also more common, less news-catching activities. In factories throughout the world workers do 'homers', making things for their own use. As Haraszti (1977, pp. 140-3) discovered:

> . . . homers are seldom useful things . . . . Here the passion is for nothing other than work, work as an end in itself . . . . It is the antithesis of our meaningless 'real' work . . . . By making homers we win back power over the machine and our freedom from the machine.

References

Haraszti, M. (1977), *A Worker In a Worker's State: Piece Rates in Hungary*, Penguin, Harmondsworth.

Nichols, T. and Benyon, H. (1977), *Living with Capitalism: Class Relations and the Modern Factory*, Routledge & Kegan Paul, London.

See also:

Braverman, H. (1974), *Labour and Monopoly Capital*, Monthly Review Press, New York.

Terkel, S. (1975), *Working*, Wildwood, London.

training, good prospects, all with fringe benefits. At the other end there are the bad jobs which pay low wages, offer little security or training, provide poor working conditions and few career prospects. Different groups in society are differentially placed in this continuum of job opportunity. In the labour markets of the big cities there have been two trends of recent years. First some good jobs in the business, government and education sectors have remained in the central area. There is a twofold residence pattern for the good job workers: either in the suburbs involving long-distance commuting, or inner city areas, increasingly in the gentrified neighbourhoods.

Second, the loss of good jobs in manufacturing (caused by suburbanisation of industry) has not been replaced by good jobs in the service sector. For many inner-city residents the only jobs available within reasonable travelling distance are the poor jobs in the basic service sector as postmen, bellhops, cleaners, porters, etc. within the public and private sectors.

In the smaller cities and suburban areas the new manufacturing jobs have been created as corporations are setting up factories in places with either weak union or non-union labour force. Because of technological improvements, many of these jobs are on assembly lines involving routinised work practices requiring little or no skill. The 'new' manufacturing jobs are deskilled in comparison to the old manufacturing jobs.

Unemployment One of the most important trends in recent years has been the growing level of unemployment. Figure 6.6 shows the overall trend in four countries, which, although differing in levels of unemployment, all share the same rising trend. Part of the reason lies in the downturn in the world economy. As the recession deepens there is less demand for goods and less need for labour. Firms reduce their workforce and do not take on any new workers. Another part of the reason and one that is more disturbing is the fact that modern capitalist economies are absorbing less of the population as workers. Industry is now run with less workers as firms introduce labour-saving machines. The age of the microchip is one of computer-programmed machines. The rising levels of unemployment in the post-war period may therefore be a constant factor in capitalist economies. Mechanisation and continued technological developments may ensure a long-term, large pool of unemployed.

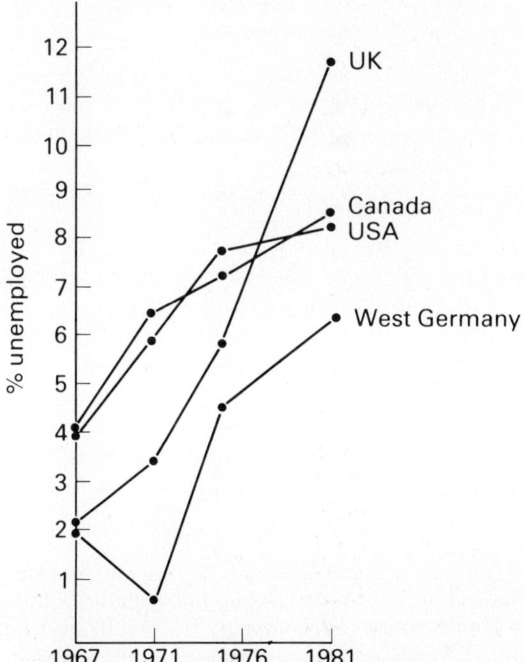

Figure 6.6 Unemployment in capitalist countries

The incidence of unemployment is inequitably distributed. Unemployment rates are highest amongst blacks, young people, women and unskilled workers. In inner-city areas where these groups are concentrated, the highest unemployment rates are recorded. There is thus emerging an increasingly large proportion of the population, concentrated in certain areas, who are reliant upon welfare payments. Attempts to reduce welfare expenditure raise major social and political questions. The questions will be sharply posed in the inner cities.

THE OTHER ECONOMIES

The unemployment statistics refer to the formal economy, the economy in which transactions are recorded and taxes are paid. But there are others. We can make the following distinctions:

The formal economy

This is the one which is recorded and measured in official returns. It involves the sale of labour power in the market. This economy has been contracting and unemployment has been rising.

The informal economy

This involves transactions which are not recorded. This is the economy beyond the reach of the inland revenue service. A number of sub-types can be identified.

Illegal informal economy. Activities in this sector include prostitution, drug pushing and other criminal activities. This sector, like the formal economy, has its big corporations. The mafia is the General Motors of the illegal economy. In certain inner-city districts this illegal economy is the main source of employment. While the formal economy recedes, the importance of the illegal informal economy often increases.

Semi-legal informal economy. This involves operations such as car washing, building work, etc. which in themselves are not illegal, but for which no taxes are paid. This activity is not recorded in official statistics. In third-world cities with high levels of unemployment and under-employment, it is the main source of living for a majority of urban residents.

The communal economy. This involves the cashless exchange of services, generally it occurs within neighbourhoods and between family groups.

Domestic economy. In which people do things themselves.

We can illustrate the types of economies with respect to two examples. If a couple wanted to redecorate a room they could:

(1) Employ a decorator, the transaction being recorded and the appropriate taxes being paid. This is the formal economy.
(2) Employ a decorator but payment is not recorded in official statistics and no taxes are paid. This is the semi-legal informal economy.
(3) A friend does it as part of a general system of reciprocal favours. This is the communal economy.
(4) They do it themselves. This is the domestic economy.

Take another example. If a man and woman with two children want to go out for the evening and need a baby-sitter they could:

(1) Employ an official baby-sitter with the transaction being recorded and taxes being paid.
(2) Pay someone to do it, with the transaction not being recorded.
(3) Get a friend or use people in their baby-sitting circle.

Most people will use (2) or (3). All the evidence we have, and as you can imagine hard evidence is difficult to collect about these things, suggests that the informal economy is growing. As formal employment decreases more and more people use the informal sector.

GUIDE TO FURTHER READING

A good general introduction to geographical perspectives in the labour market is:

Dicken, P. and Lloyd, P.E. (1981), *Modern Western Society*, Harper & Row, London (especially chapters 2 and 3).

A brief but stimulating account of the spatial implications of Kondratieff waves is:

Hall, P. (1981), The geography of the fifth Kondratieff cycle, *New Society*, March, 535-7.

See also Mandel, E. (1975), *Late Capitalism*, New Left Books, London.

For the implications of the emerging world economy see:

Cohen, R.B. (1981), The new international division of labour, multinational corporations and the urban hierarchy, In M. Dear and A.J. Scott (eds), *Urbanization and Urban Planning in Capitalist Society*, Methuen, London.

There is a wealth of literature on the geography of investment flows, industrial restructuring and locational outcomes. See:

Keeble, D. (1978), Industrial decline in the inner city and conurbation, *Transactions of the Institute of British Geographers, New Series,* 3, 101-14.

Massey, D. and Meegan R. (1982), *The Anatomy of Job Loss*, Methuen, London.

Mandel, E. (1975), *op. cit.*

Sternlieb, G. and Hughes, J.W. (eds) (1975), *Post-Industrial America: Metropolitan Decline and Inter-Regional Job Shift,* Centre for Urban Policy Research, Rutgers University, New Jersey.

Walker, R. and Storper, M. (1981), Capital and industrial location, *Progress in Human Geography*, 5, 473-509.

The rise of the service economy and the locational implications are discussed in:

Clark, T.A. (1980), Regional and structural shifts in the American economy, In S.D. Brunn and J.O. Wheeler (eds), *The American Metropolitan System: Present and Future*, Edward Arnold, London.

Daniels, P.W. (1975), *Office Location: An Urban and Regional Study*, Bell, London.

A discussion of the other economies is contained in:

Burns, S. (1977), *The Household Economy*, Beacon Press, London.

Gershuny, J.I. (1979), The informal economy – its role in post industrial society, *Futures*, February 3-15.

Pahl, R.E. (1980), Employment, work and the domestic division of labour, *International Journal of Urban and Regional Research*, 4, 1-20.

7 The City as Residence

People live in cities. The next section seeks to discover who lives where, and why and how they live there. To answer these questions we have to consider the housing market, since this is the arena in which different groups are allocated to different types of housing in different areas of the city.

THE HOUSING MARKET

The production of housing

We can identify four modes of housing production.

Self-produced housing. This mode of housing production involves people producing their own accommodation. It arises as a form of meeting individual needs when either there is no alternative or through choice. In third-world cities it constitutes an important element as many people build their own housing because there is no alternative supply. The level of technological sophistication is low. Owner-occupation is the main type of tenure associated with this mode of housing production although there may be some sub-leasing of individual rooms or spaces.

Individual contract production involves the immediate consumers hiring building firms to construct individually designed dwellings. It is a minor form of housing production as only the very rich can afford to employ builders on individual contracts.

Institutional contract production. Here institutional landlords (including the state, local authorities, very large landlords) hire building firms to construct a large number of dwellings. A form of this mode of housing production is also found in socialist countries. Building firms tend to be very large and the level of technological sophistication is high. Housing for rent is the predominant tenure form.

Speculative production. This mode is found in capitalist societies when builder-developers build housing for the mass market. The builder-developers sell their dwellings directly to the consumer. Since housing must be produced before it is sold, builder-developers need external sources of finance to maintain their operations. And because housing is so expensive consumers need to obtain funds to purchase dwellings. The speculative mode of housing production is thus directly affected by credit facilities. When money is tight builders find it difficult to obtain credit and buyers are unable to raise house purchase loans. This form of housing production is cyclical in response to booms and slumps in the economy. The form of tenure most likely to be associated with this is owner-occupation.

The supply of housing

A general distinction can be made in the housing market between housing supplied by private markets and housing provided by the state, the public sector. In the *private sector* housing is allocated on the ability to pay. The rich get the best, most desirable housing in the most-favoured locations while the poor get the worst housing in the least-favoured places. The overall quality of housing depends on the state of the economy (in the richer countries of the world housing quality tends to be much better than in the poor countries) and on the distribution of wealth, which determines the difference between the very best and the very worst housing.

Plates 20, 21 and 22
Income and housing in Mexico City; low-income dwellings (20); middle-income residences (21); a high-income area (22)

HOUSING IN THE THIRD-WORLD CITY

In comparison to the cities of the rich developed countries, housing in the third-world city is of much poorer quality. The world band of poorest-quality housing stretches either side of the equator, covering the countries of Latin and Central America, Africa and Asia.

The most single distinctive feature of third-world cities is the existence of self-built shelter. In the core countries of the world economy most housing is produced either by the state or by specialist building firms. In the third world, by contrast, the demand for housing is great and the supply so low that many people have very little option but to build their own accommodation. These dwellings, known variously as slums, shanty towns or squatter settlements, are an

Table 7A Extent of peripheral settlements (1978)

	City	*City population*	*Peripheral settlements as % of city population*
Africa	Dakar	500,000	18
	Lusaka	194,000	27
Asia	Calcutta	6,700,000	33
	Djakarta	2,906,000	25
	Karachi	752,000	33
South America	Santiago	2,184,000	25
	Lima	2,800,000	36
	Caracas	1,590,000	35

Source: United Nations

important feature in third-world cities. Table 7A shows their relative and widespread importance. All the evidence we have suggests that they are increasing in size. In Mexico City they housed 15 per cent of the population in 1952 but 40 per cent by 1970. Their population growth rate was between 10 and 15 per cent per annum between 1950 and 1980 while the city's overall growth rate was only 6 per cent per annum. These self-built settlements vary in location and character. We can distinguish between different types in terms of degrees of security of tenure and type of physical construction, from the nomadic illegal squatter in a temporary, hastily-constructed building to a legal resident in a relatively high-standard property. John Turner has made a further distinction between:

1 *Low-income bridgeheads* housing the low-income recent arrivals in poor-quality central-city locations.
2 *Low-income consolidators* of greater stability, larger residence and better-quality housing.
3 *Middle-class status-seekers* comprising those with more money and greater security. Location close to high-status groups is an important consideration.

At a fundamental level we can distinguish between slums of hope and slums of despair. The former are the self-built housing areas where migrants are consolidating their position in the urban informal economy, standards of housing provision are being improved and overall things look, if not great, at least improving. The slums of despair occur when there are few oppor-

Plates 23 and 24
Squatting: (23) squatters close by the Kuala Lumpur Hilton; (24) resettlement

tunities for low-income households to improve and upgrade their dwellings. This occurs when incomes are low, rents are high and/or when the settlement and its inhabitants feel insecure about their occupancy either because of leasing arrangements or environmental factors. In Mexico City, for example, a distinction is made between the *Colonias Paracandistas* located on the periphery, housing almost a third of the city's population, and the more dismal inner-city neighbourhoods of the *Ciudades Perdidas*. The Colonias Paracandistas are the slums of hope, and the Ciudades Perdidas are the slums of despair.

References

Turner, J.C.F. (1970), Squatter settlements in developing countries, In D.P. Moynihan (ed.), *Towards a National Urban Policy*, Basic Books, New York.

Turner, J.C.F. and Fichter, R. (1972), *Freedom to Build*, Macmillan, London.

Ward, P.M. (1982), *Self-Help Housing: A Critique*, Mansell, London.

HOUSING IN THE SOCIALIST CITY

The system of housing allocation is different in socialist countries from that in North American and West European countries. The difference lies in the degree of state control. In the USA, for example, the vast majority of housing is produced by the private sector and housing is allocated by income. In socialist countries the state sector is much more important and housing is allocated by position in the queue.

There are a number of studies which allow us a housing snapshot of before and after successful socialist revolutions. In his study of Havana, the French writer Jean Pierre Garnier highlights the impact of the 1959 revolution on urban structure. Before the Castroite revolution the housing market was dominated by filtering and shanty towns. The few rich people lived in large houses, which eventually filtered down the income scale, but rural migration was so high and housing provision so inadequate that shanty towns circled Havana. After the revolution housing was allocated by need rather than income and the old socio-economic pattern of segregation was radically altered. Housing problems did not, however, disappear. Mateju, Vecernik and Jerabek (1979) show a similar pattern for Prague. After the socialist take-over in Czechoslovakia the allocation of housing was taken over by the state and socio-economic segregation lessened. The social ecology of the city was transformed.

The USSR provides a useful case study of housing in a socialist country. When the Bolsheviks took state control in 1917 housing conditions were bad. Indeed one reason the Bolsheviks gained urban support was because of the poor living conditions of the industrial workers. After 1918 all urban land was municipalised, rents were frozen in 1919 and housing was allocated by the local soviets. Within six years over half a million people were rehoused in existing buildings by reallocation of dwelling space. In 1922 a standard of 9 square metres of living space per person was laid down.

Between 1918 and 1950 over 350 million square metres of housing were built in the USSR. Even this scale of building did not meet all needs and in 1950 the average amount of living space per person was 4 square metres, less than half the statutory minimum. In this period housing, like all consumer goods, was given low priority. The emphasis of the Soviet planners lay on building up a strong industrial base. The priorities began to change in the mid 1950s as the effects of war damage were slowly being righted and to meet the undercurrent of criticism. From 1957 onwards a huge housing drive was put into operation. By 1977 the total urban housing fund had reached 2,000 million square feet, whereas in 1950 it was only 513 million. Between 1960 and 1975 1.55 billion square metres of housing had been produced and two-thirds of the Soviet Union's population had been rehoused. This had been achieved through a concentration on prefabricated building techniques and a centralisation of the building industry. By 1976 average living space per person had reached 8.1 square metres, still some way below the standard of 9 square metres but a vast improvement on the 4 square metres per person of 1950. This average figure masked variation within the Soviet Union ranging from 11.6 square metres in Minsk in Belorussiya to 6.2 square metres in the Azerbaydzhan city of Evlakh.

In the contemporary Soviet city there are three types of tenure arrangements. First, there is the state sector which controls over 70 per cent of all housing in the Soviet Union. State housing is mass produced, mostly in the form of apartment blocks. The term 'state' does not imply unified control. Within the state sector there is a variety of different institutions, the city soviet and the range of different ministries and government departments. Although in the very large cities the city soviet is gaining almost total control, in other cities unified control

Table 7B Housing stock in selected Soviet cities

City	*Housing space* *Square metres per person*	
	1971	1977
Moscow	9.5	10.3
Leningrad	8.3	9.1
Kiev	8.8	9.1
Tashkent	5.6	6.3
Minsk	7.4	8.0
Tbilisi	7.5	8.1
Omsk	7.3	7.5
Riga	9.4	9.7

is absent. Each large government ministry has its own stock of housing which is used to attract and reward workers. There is thus occupational segregation. This proliferation of control (and overall there is a 50-50 split between city soviet and departmental housing), had led to problems in co-ordinating the provision of necessary infrastructure.

Second, there is co-operative housing which, after being frowned upon in the Stalinist era, was legalised again in 1962 as part of the strategy to solve the housing crisis. By the mid 1970s there were 25,000 co-operatives housing 2.2 million people. In housing co-operatives the state provides between 40 and 60 per cent of the cost of construction and in each scheme participants are limited to 60. Since the participants have to put in some money, it has been a tenure form limited to the wealthiest urban residents. Co-operative housing apartments contain a high proportion of members of the upper echelons of the Party, scientists and engineers.

Finally, there is the private sector. Private housing is particularly important in rural areas, where it forms the majority of the housing stock. Even in urban areas it forms about 25 per cent of private housing. Private housing is typically of wooden construction, detached, low density and often of very poor quality since it is not plugged into the municipal services. Although a suspect category to the Soviet ideologists, it has been encouraged by the planners. In 1972 loans were given by the government to encourage private house-building.

References

Barry, D.D. (1969), Housing in the USSR, cities and towns, *Problems of Communism*, 18, 1-11.

Bater, J.H. (1977), Soviet town planning: theory and practice in the 1970s, *Progress in Human Geography*, 1, 177-207.

DiMaio, A.J. (1974), *Soviet Urban Housing: Problems and Policies*, Praeger, New York.

Garnier, J.P. (1973), *Une Ville, Une Révolution: La Havane*, Maspero, Paris.

Mateju, P., Vecernik, J. and Jerabek, H. (1979), Social structure, spatial structure and problems of urban research: the example of Prague, *International Journal of Urban and Regional Research*, 3, 181-202.

Plates 25 and 26
Residential differentiation in Bratislava, Czechoslovakia

Thus, in poor countries with a very inequitable distribution of income the overall quality of housing is poor with a world of difference between housing for the rich and the shelter available for the poor.

A secondary distinction can be made between the different tenure categories of the private sector. In the case of *private renting* a tenant purchases accommodation from a landlord in the form of regular rent payments. The quality of accommodation varies by rent levels; the more you pay the better the accommodation. Conversely, the poorer you are the less rent you can afford and the poorer the quality of your accommodation. The segregation and housing space reflect differences in rent-paying ability.

There is a possible social conflict between tenants and landlords. Landlords want to charge as much rent as possible while tenants want to pay as little as possible. The urban story is studded with tenant/landlord conflicts. The most famous perhaps is the Glasgow rent strike of 1914/15 when a rent strike arose in the Scottish city after a 23 per cent increase in rents. The rent strike was called, industrial workers went on strike for a day and 15,000 workers in all threatened further strike action. The government of the day closely followed the events and in order to maintain armaments production and vitiate social unrest, a bill was rushed through Parliament. The 1915 Rent and Mortgage Act limited the amount of rent increase and it laid the basis for a succession of rent controls in Britain.

In most developed countries the private rented sector is declining as public housing and owner-occupation is increasing. In 1914 nine out of every ten British households lived in private rented accommodation, but by 1980 less than two out of ten were private renters. Although there has been a shrinking in the private rented sector, in large cities and especially in inner-city areas the private rented sector is still very important. At the two ends of the private rented inner-city housing market are the penthouse suites for the rich and the slums for the poor.

In the *owner-occupied* sector households purchase ownership rights as well as accommodation. The immediate purchase of the average house, however, is beyond the reach of all but the very rich. For owner-occupation to become anything more than the preserve of the wealthy it is necessary to have some form of house-purchase finance. These sources allow the household to buy the property and then pay back the loan over a period of years. In the USA the savings and loans associations, the commercial banks, mutual savings banks and various government agencies are important. In Britain the building societies, the clearing banks and the local authorities are the main institutions.

The implementation of the policies of the different institutions shape the housing market. By giving mortgages to some and not others the financial institutions respectively confer benefits and impose constraints on different sets of households and by giving mortgages in some areas rather than others they structure the housing geography of the city. Although they vary in detail we can look at the broad similarities in the operation of these institutions. In order to get a loan to buy a dwelling it is often necessary to earn above a certain income level. Thus, the poor are denied access to house-purchase finance and they therefore have to move into the private rented sector or public housing. Entry is also based on race. In both the USA and UK, for example, there is strong evidence that blacks are discriminated against in mortgage applications. This is partly due to the income requirements, but the evidence also suggests at least for the USA, that even when blacks have similar income and comparable applications they are 20 per cent more likely to be denied mortgage funds.

We can consider the allocation of mortgages with respect to households, dwellings and residential areas. *Households* obtain house-purchase loans in relation to their income. As a rule of thumb the British building societies give mortgages up to two and a half times annual gross income. Thus, if a family earns £10,000 before tax they should be able to get a mortgage for £25,000 and a family earning £8,000 could get a mortgage up to £20,000. There is definite relationship between income, loan and house purchasing power. The richer households obtain bigger mortgages and can afford to buy the more expensive housing. As in the private rented sector there is segregation by income.

LAND-USE MODELS OF THE PRIVATE HOUSING MARKET

Perhaps the two most famous models in urban geography are the Burgess and Hoyt models of urban land use. Their spatial expression is shown in Figures 7A and 7C. In the literature they are often discussed as general models of urban land use. This is incorrect. What they describe are the spatial outcomes of particular housing market processes.

The Burgess model is a concentric ring structure with a progression from the central business district which is continually expanding into the mixed land-use area of the zone in transition. Thereafter successive zones have increasing housing quality and rising status the further towards the suburbs. The process which underlies this pattern is one of *invasion and succession* as migrants to the city centre move out to the next zone, which has a knock-on effect (see Figure 7B). The Burgess model is a model of cities experiencing large-scale migration and in which

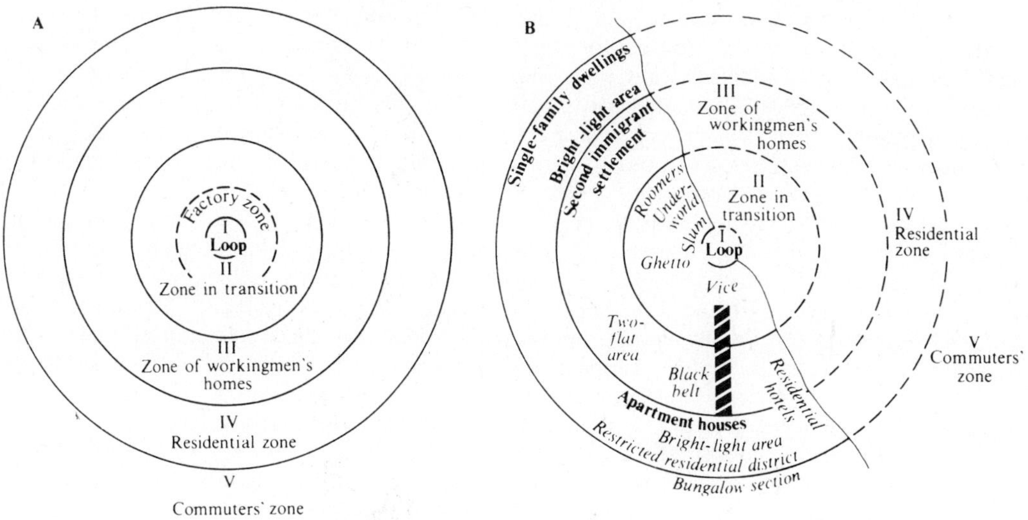

Figure 7A The Burgess Model and contemporary Chicago
Source: Burgess, 1925

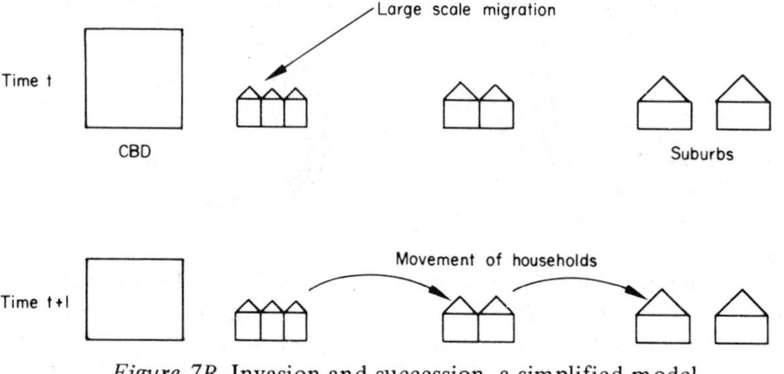

Figure 7B Invasion and succession, a simplified model

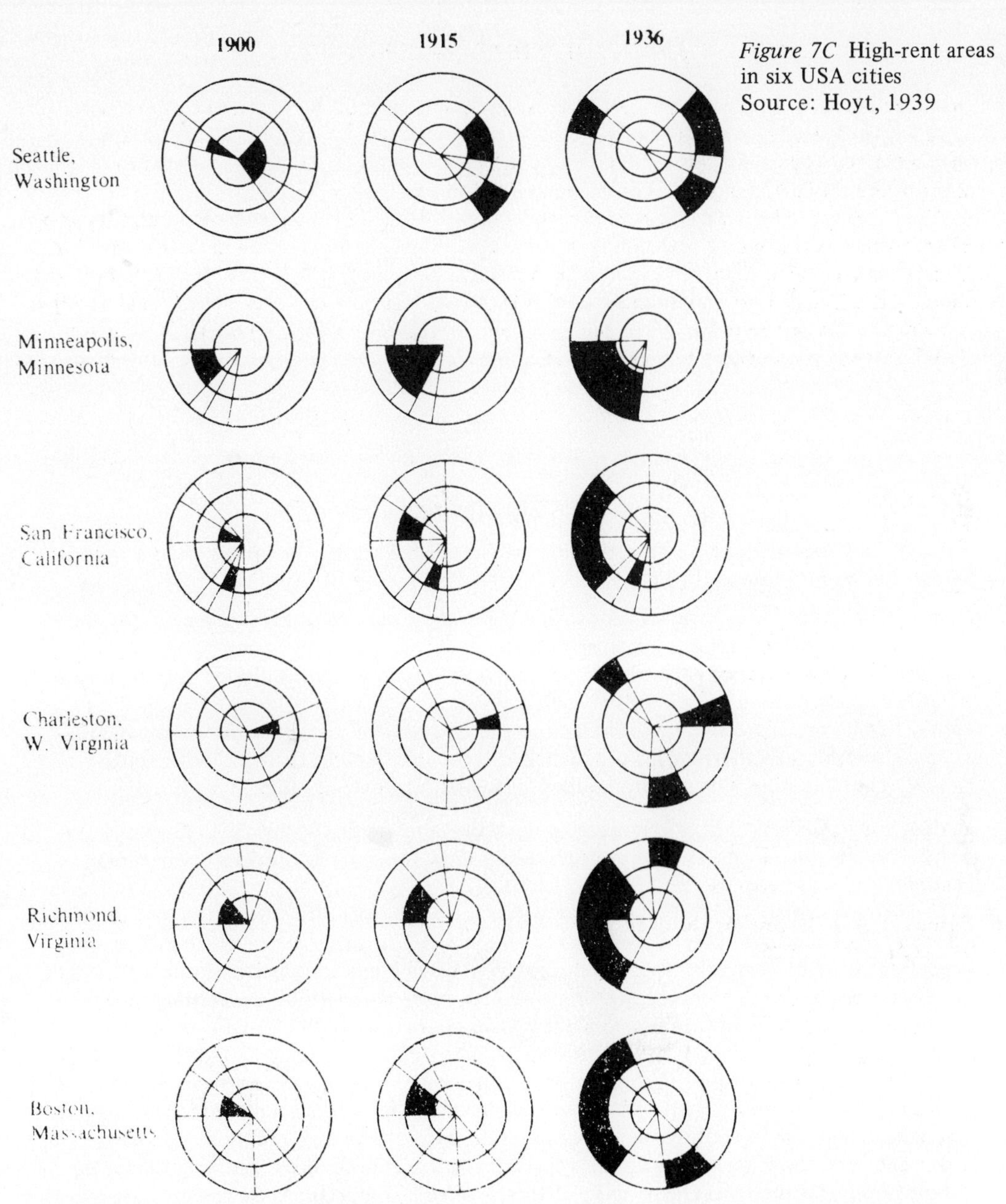

Figure 7C High-rent areas in six USA cities
Source: Hoyt, 1939

the housing market is dominated by the private sector. It was used to describe the experience of Chicago in the first third of the twentieth century. It has less relevance where migration levels are low and public sector housing is important. Tests of the model by Schnore have shown that the pattern of increasing status towards the suburban edge is not found in all US

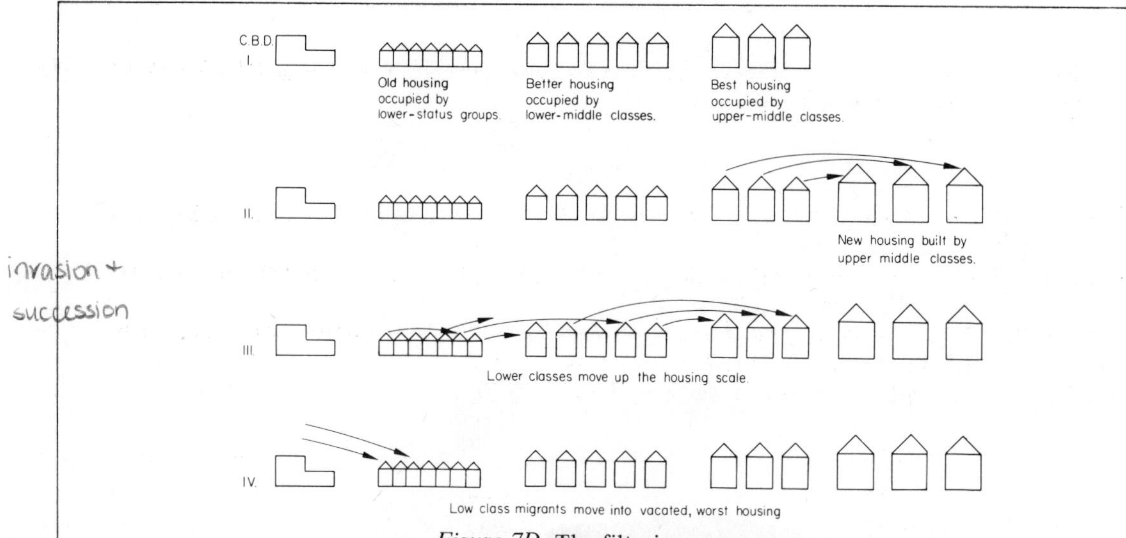

Figure 7D The filtering process

cities. On the basis of empirical investigation into the distribution of income groups Schnore classified cities into four groups:

Type A The 'Milwaukee' type, which showed the Burgess pattern of high-income groups in the suburbs and low-income groups in central areas.
Type B The 'New Orleans' type which had both high- and low-income groups in the centre and middle-income groups in the suburbs.
Type C The 'Fort Smith' type where high-income groups were located in the centre and low-income groups in the suburbs. This type is also commonly found in Latin American cities.
Type D The 'Des Moines' type with no identifiable pattern.

The Burgess model was only of relevance to the older, larger cities of the USA. The newer, smaller, rapidly growing cities did not necessarily follow the patterns Burgess discovered in Chicago.

The Hoyt model is of a sectoral land-use pattern. On the basis of investigation into residential areas, Hoyt suggested that high-status residential districts form sectors which radiate outwards from the CBD along transport routes towards the home of community leaders. Maintaining this pattern was the process of *filtering*. The high-income households, according to Hoyt, moved continually to new housing. This left vacancies which were filled by lower-income groups. In effect the housing filtered down the income and status hierarchy (see Figure 7D). The Hoyt model assumes continual movement. But a number of researchers have pointed to the stability of high-income residents and the permanence of high-status neighbourhoods. Boston's Beacon Hill, and London's Hampstead, for example, continue to maintain their exclusivity. More important, the Hoyt model assumes that lower-income households can only obtain the cast-off housing of the rich. The context of Hoyt's work is important in this respect. He was a vigorous free marketeer who saw public housing as creeping socialism. His work is, in effect, arguing for the efficacy of leaving things to the market. In other words the state according to Hoyt should not provide public housing. The filtering mechanism is an irrelevancy in housing markets where public housing is important. An important distinction has to be drawn between the processes and patterns of the models. While the patterns may be still found today, this does not imply that the models are correct. The processes may well have changed. Different types of process can produce similar patterns.

References

Bassett, K.A. and Short, J.R. (1980), *Housing and Residential Structure,* Routledge & Kegan Paul, London.

Burgess, E.W. (1925), The growth of the city, In Park, R.E., Burgess, E.W. and McKenzie, R.D. (eds), *The City*, University of Chicago Press.

Hoyt, H. (1939), *The Structure and Growth of Residential Neighbourhoods in American Cities*, Federal Housing Administration, Washington, D.C.

Schnore, L.F. (1965), *The Urban Scene*, Free Press, New York.

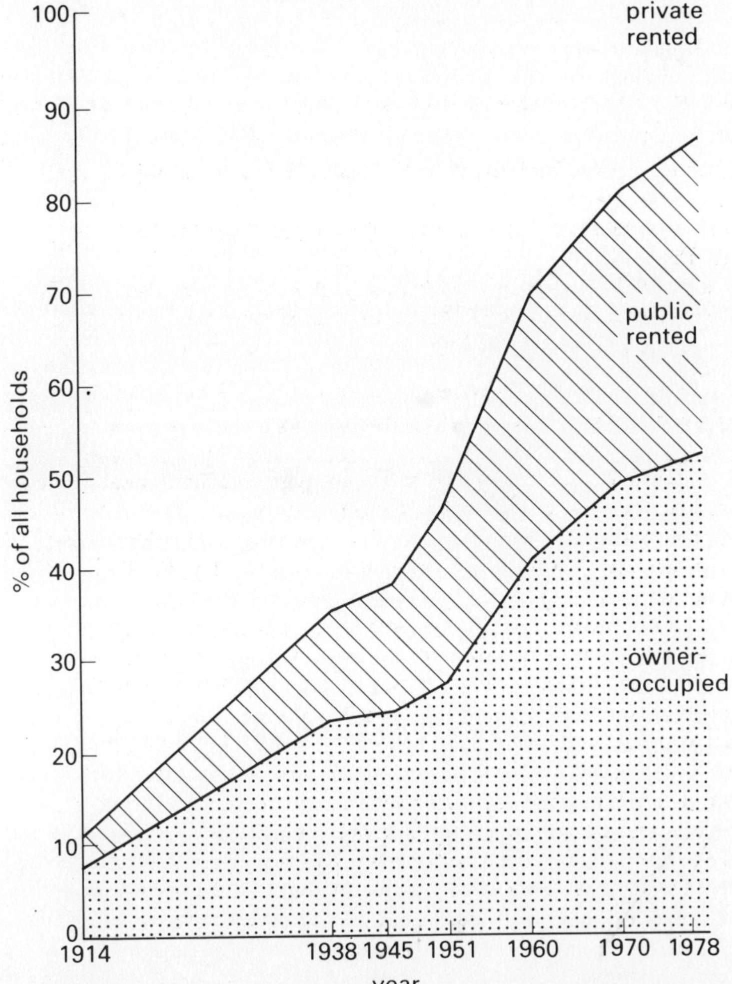

Figure 7.1 Housing tenure in Britain

Table 7.1 Source of house-purchase finance in UK and USA in 1975 (%)

Source							*Total*
UK	Building societies	Insurance companies	Banks	Local authorities	Other public institutions		
	75	2	2	16	5		100
USA	Savings and loan assocs	Insurance companies	Commercial banks	Mutual savings banks	Government agencies	Other	
	46	4	16	10	13	11	100

In terms of *dwellings* the financial institutions prefer to lend on standard properties of single or two-storey, detached or semi-detached family-type housing than the converted accommodation in blocks of flats. It is much easier to get a mortgage for the former than the latter.

The lending policy of institutions with respect to households and dwellings is clearly seen when we consider the distribution of mortgages by *residential areas.* There are two extremes. At one end there are the well-favoured areas where mortgages are easily available, typically the middle- to higher-income suburban areas where both the applicants and dwellings reflect the lending preferences of the institutions, and at the other extreme there are those inner-city areas housing low-income groups where the housing is of poorer quality. Here the institutions are loath to lend. The areas, the typical applicants and the quality of housing are all considered bad risks. The explicit policy of refusing to lend in certain areas is termed red-lining. Red-lining can vary in impact from the outright denial of mortgages to the more subtle policy of demanding higher down-payments or higher interest rates for the small number of mortgages allocated in red-line areas. The red-lining policy can become a self-fulfilling prophecy. By refusing to grant mortgages the institutions take away the lifeblood of the housing market. Owners and landlords find it difficult to sell, there is no incentive to improve property and the net result is for housing deterioration to continue, providing further argument for the institution's red-lining policy. Some inner-city areas are caught in a downward spiral of red-lining/continued deterioration/less mortgage financing/continued deteriorations/red-lining. Red-lining further disadvantages those, typically the poor, who live in red-lined areas. They find it difficult to obtain finance for house purchase and the quality of their accommodation is often poor and of deteriorating quality.

Mortgage finance tends to flow to suburban areas while it is denied to certain inner-city areas. The flows of house-purchase finance structure the housing market. By denying funds to inner-city areas the institutions create the preconditions for further deterioration and by readily granting mortgages for suburban property they lubricate the process of suburbanisation. The spatial distribution of the very sources of mortgage finance in one US city is shown in Figure 7.2. Notice how in the inner-city area of Baltimore cash transactions are the most important single category. This is evidence of red-lining.

The role of the state in the private sector

The private housing sector is subject to a whole variety of government actions. The two most important are the control of the private rented sector and the encouragement of owner-occupation. The degree of rent control varies by country and within the USA even by state. In some states there are no limits on rent levels and market forces dominate. In other states of the union as in Britain

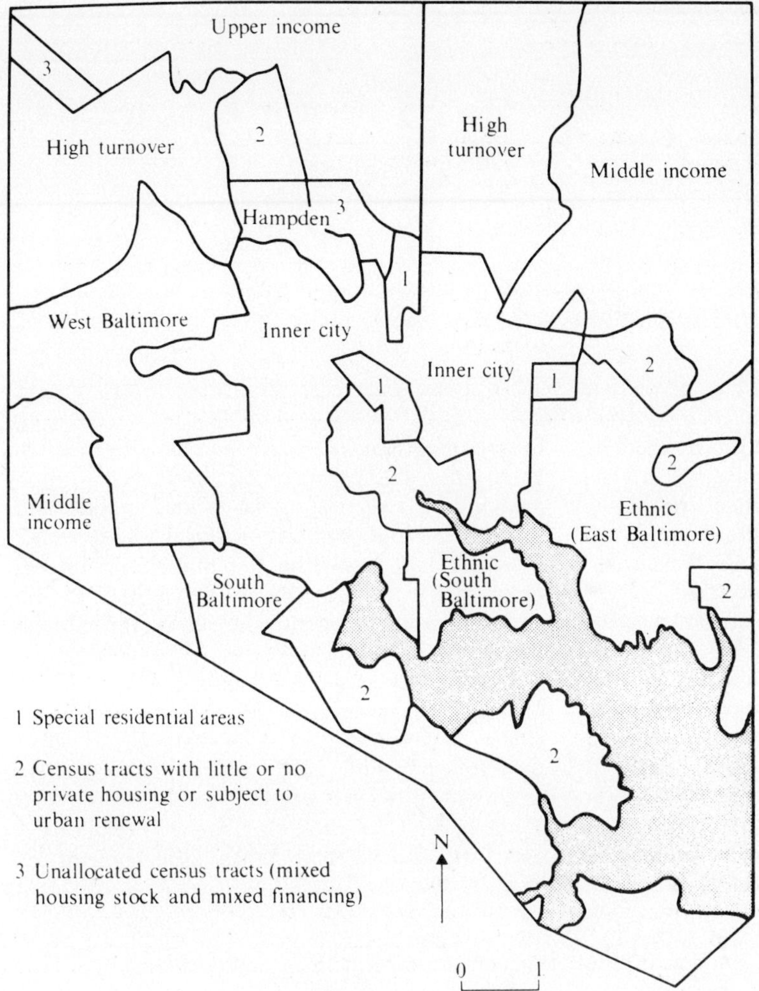

Figure 7.2 Housing finance
Source: Harvey, D. (1975), The political economy of urbanization in advanced capitalist countries, in Gappert, G. and Rose, H.M. (eds) *The Social Economy of Cities*, Urban Affairs Annual Review 9, Sage, Beverly Hills, Ca.

	Inner city	*Ethnic*	*Hampden*	*West Baltimore*	*South Baltimore*	*High turnover*	*Middle income*	*Upper income*
*% Transactions by source of funds**								
Cash	65.7	39.9	40.4	30.6	28.3	19.1	20.8	19.4
Private	15.0	—	—	12.5	—	—	—	—
Federal S and L	—	—	18.2	12.1	22.7	13.6	29.8	23.5
State S and L	12.0	43.2	26.3	11.7	13.4	14.9	17.0	10.5
Mortage bank	—	—	—	22.3	13.4	32.8	—	—
Community bank	—	—	—	—	—	—	—	—
Savings bank	—	—	—	—	—	—	—	21.1
% FHA insured	2.9	2.6	14.1	25.8	22.7	38.2	17.1	11.9
Average sale price ($)	3,498	6,372	7,059	8,664	8,751	9,902	12,760	27,413

*Figures of less than 10% are not recorded.

Table 7.2 The rise of owner-occupation

Country	*% owner-occupation* 1950	1973
Sweden	45	40
West Germany	42	35
The Netherlands	30	33
UK	26	52
France	35	45
USA	50	62
Canada	60	60
Australia	45	66

there are very strong controls. In Britain there has been a series of rent controls since 1915 which have given security of tenure to tenants and limited the amount of rent that the landlord can charge. In association with the rise of other investment opportunities these controls have made private renting relatively unprofitable and have been an integral part of the spectacular decline in the amount of private rented accommodation.

There has been less variation between advanced capitalist countries in their attitude to owner occupation. Most governments have sought to encourage owner-occupation. This has been achieved by giving tax relief to owner-occupiers' mortgage repayments and by state involvement in the provision of house purchase finance. In Britain the state has afforded a privileged position to building societies in the money market and through the local authority mortgage schemes has extended the possibilities for low-income owner-occupation. In the United States the federal government encourages owner-occupation through the activities of three agencies – the Government National Mortgage Association, the Federal National Mortgage Association and the Federal Home Loan Mortgage Corporation – which generate and guide credit to the house-purchase sector and through specific measures. Section 235 of the Home Ownership Programme of the Department of Housing and Urban Development for

Table 7.3 Percentage distribution and beneficiaries of federal government financing by income group within the metropolitan system

Income group ($)	*Mortgage interest deduction*	*Property tax deduction*	*Capital gains*
0–9,999	2	2	1
10,000–19,999	16	15	16
20,000–49,999	63	55	64
50,000–99,999	15	19	12
100,000–199,999	4	6	2
200,000 and over	1	3	5
TOTAL	100	100	100

Source: U.S. House of Representatives. Tax Exempt Bonds for Single Family Housing. Subcommittee on the City of the Committee on Banking, Finance, and Urban Affairs 96th Congress, 1st Session (Washington, D.C.: GPO, 1979), pp. 76-7

example assists low- to medium-income households to purchase new or rehabilitated dwellings.

It is difficult to speak of a housing market since the term's connotations of economic transactions being predominant and state involvement being minimal simply do not apply. The state is intimately involved in the housing market. In seeking to encourage owner-occupation the government is eager to produce a tenure form which, with its property connections, chimes with the dominant ideology in capitalist society. It has also been argued that owner-occupation provides people with a stake in society; they are more likely to work hard, to be less radical, and overall owner-occupation is seen by many as an important source of stability. However, encouraging owner-occupation has its disadvantages. In creating a significant proportion of the population with a stake in the housing market the government at the national level becomes locked into further fiscal ventures which involve keeping interest rates down and channelling funds to the residential sector. At the local level owner-occupiers become important elements in planning decisions, often seeking to fight against land-use planning changes and proposals from City Hall which may affect their property values. To encourage owner-occupation is to create the conditions for further state involvement.

The form of state involvement in the owner-occupied sector has been regressive. By giving fiscal advantages to owner-occupiers, the government have been aiding the wealthier sectors of society. And even within the owner-occupied sector it is the richer owner-occupiers who have gained most. As Table 7.3 shows, at least for the United States, the poorest households have not gained from federal government financing. Rather it has been the middle- and upper-income groups who have gained most.

Public housing

The state is directly involved in the housing market through the provision of housing. Such housing is termed state housing or public housing. As a proportion of the housing stock it varies between 2 per cent in the USA, 31 per cent in the UK and 36 per cent in Sweden. Public housing is allocated on need rather than the ability to pay. Access is determined in the way in which housing need is measured and the circumstances of the household. In Britain the local authorities allocate public housing to those on their housing waiting lists. Position on this list is determined by number of points, which are gained for such things as size of household in relation to existing accommodation, quality of existing housing, medical considerations and length of time on waiting lists, etc.

The size of the public housing sector reflects a number of factors. At a national level it reflects the varying strength of socialist political parties. Where these are strong, as in Britain, France and Sweden, the public housing sector is large. Good-quality public housing has long been a working-class demand and a consistent item on socialist parties' agendas. In North America, by contrast, where socialist parties are small and weak, private sector housing remains predominant. The tenants of public housing in the USA are overwhelmingly poor and predominantly black. The public sector is used to house those who find it difficult to find other accommodation. It is a residual tenure category housing the very poorest – even in contrast with the public housing sectors in other countries.

In Britain, by contrast, public housing accommodates a much wider income spread and is not so stigmatised as in the United States. There are three basic types of purpose-built public housing in Britain. First, there is the more suburban, low-density, two-storey housing found around the edges of the cities. The larger estates were built since 1945 and before 1965. Second, there are the inter-war estates built between 1919 and 1939 and they contain some of the best and also some of the worst public housing. The best was built immediately after the First World War when there was a political need to provide 'homes for heroes'. Later periods of the inter-war era saw cutbacks in housing expenditure and reductions in housing standards. Finally, there is the post-1965 housing found predominantly in inner-city sites. Two elements can be distinguished. On the one hand there are the high-rise tower blocks of the 1960s and 1970s which have proved very unpopular and they are now no longer built. On the other hand there is a high-density low-rise building. Public housing in Britain is very varied in style, quality and hence desirability.

The variations in housing stock are used by the housing managers in allocating dwellings to housing. The tenants classified as 'more responsible'

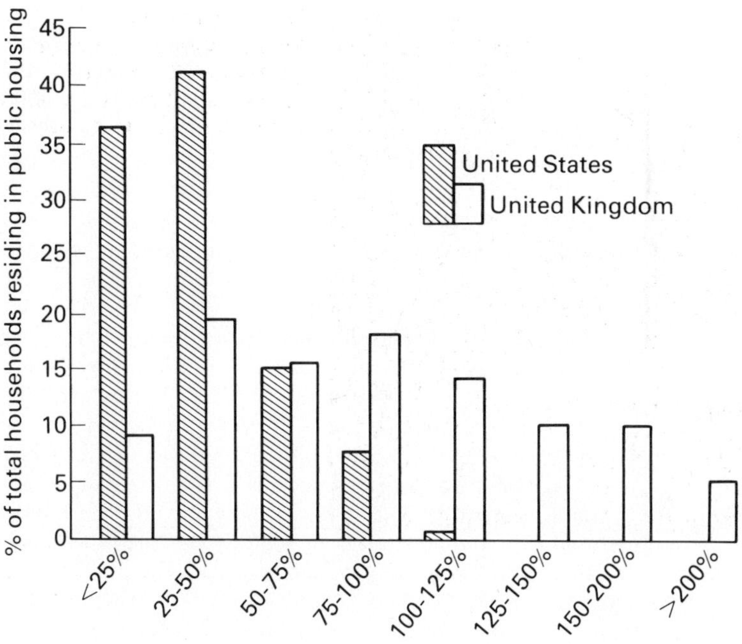

Figure 7.3 A comparison of the distribution of public housing tenants by income, US and UK, 1972
Source: Wolman, 1975, cited in Bourne, 1981

and 'better' are given the best-quality housing on the favoured estates. The poorly graded tenants are given the worst housing. In the public housing sector the housing managers are important in allocating housing to households and thus in structuring the social geography of the city.

The demand for housing

We can make a useful distinction between need and effective demand in understanding the housing market. Almost everyone needs some form of accommodation because shelter is a basic human requirement. But the private sector market responds to purchasing power not need, i.e. it responds to effective demand. The demand for housing varies across the population. Different sub-groups have a differing mix of constraints and choices in the housing market. The main dimensions of variation are income, ethnic status and stage in the life cycle.

Income In the private sector the greater the income of a household the greater the effective choice, and the poorer the household the less choice available and the greater the constraints. Richer households thus pre-empt the more favourable parts of the housing market, while the poor take what is left. We can see the housing market in the city very much like seats in a theatre or arena. The rich enter first and pick the best seats. People then follow in order of income levels. The poor come in last and have to take what is left.

Ethnic status The demand for housing also varies by ethnic status. The greater the difference between an ethnic minority and the general population then the greater the segregation. There are both choice and constraint factors involved. Many ethnic minorities are discriminated against in the housing market and they thus find it difficult to obtain mortgages outside of their own area. Estate agents (realtors) often guide different ethnic groups to different parts of the city. Ethnic groups live segregated one from another because they find it difficult to do otherwise in the housing market. But there are also other reasons. The continued concentration of immigrant groups in certain parts of the city reflects the need for collective groupings. A location amongst people of the same religion or ethnic status provides a familiar milieu in a strange society, a buffer

Plates 27 and 28
Public housing projects in (27) Gothenburg and (28) Amsterdam. Is one of better design than the other?

against a society which may not be understood and a defence mechanism against perceived or actual threat. The classic case is of the Jewish ghetto which not only reflected discrimination but also the need for defence and the desire to maintain old customs. For subsequent arrivals the immigrant neighbourhood provides a point of entry to the new society, a source of shelter and information and a staging post for further advancement. The greater the difference between the immigrants in the new society the greater the need for a collective grouping and thus the creation of distinct neighbourhoods and a high degree of residential segregation.

The history of many cities has been one of a succession of immigrant waves. The immigrants, often poor, first entered the housing market at its easiest point of entry – the private renting areas of the inner city. They formed distinct clusters. If the immigrants achieve material success then the second-generation immigrants advanced within the new society. There was less need for the sons and daughters to live in the old ethnic neighbourhoods. The process of absorption of

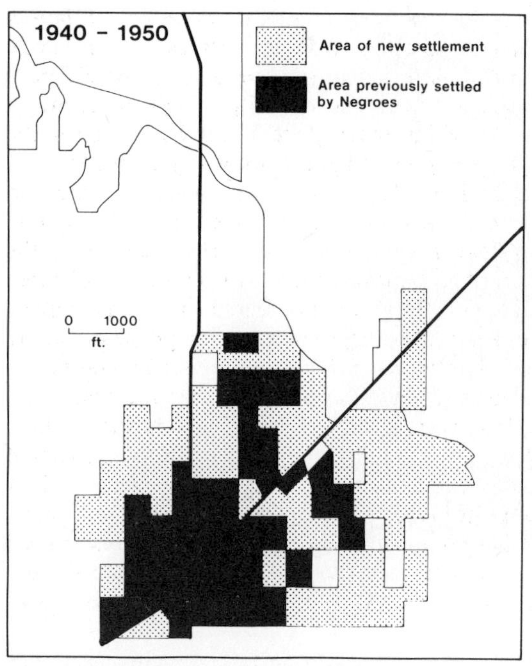

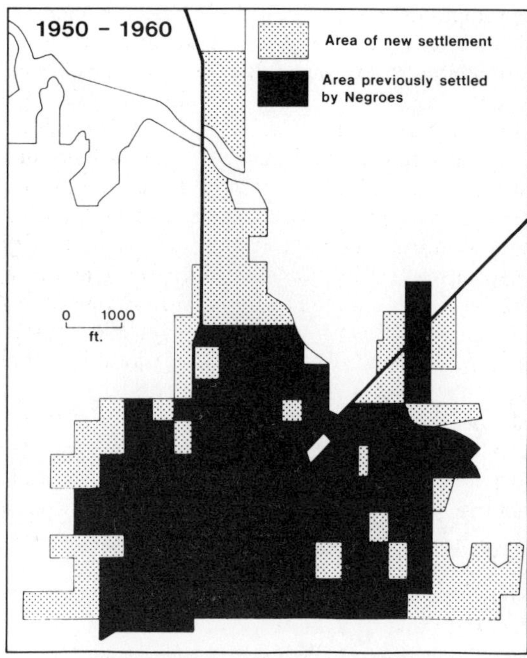

Figure 7.4 Ghettoes on the move: the case of Negroes in Seattle
Source: After Morril, R. (1965), The negro ghetto: problems and alternatives, *Geographical Review*, 55, 339-61.

Plate 29
Ethnic areas in the city: Chinatown in Kuala Lumpur, Malaysia

the migrants into the new society was reflected in the scattering of the second- and third-generation immigrants outwards from the old neighbourhoods. Inner-city neighbourhoods of major US cities have seen a succession of west European, east European, south European, black and hispanic migrants. In the past migrant absorption was possible because many of the immigrants took part in the booming economy. Rising real incomes aided absorption. During recession, however, the rising escalator of economic growth and standards of living stops. Those at the bottom see little chance of improvement and cannot move upwards in the socio-economic hierarchy and outwards from the old neighbourhoods. This proves the tinder for social unrest. The riots in Britain in 1981, for example, were a response against the multiple deprivation felt especially by the young blacks in the rundown inner-city areas.

Stage in the lifecycle The demand for housing varies through time. For the private housing sector we can imagine the lifecycle of the typical household as shown in Table 7.4. The first stage involves a person leaving their parents' home. Their space demands and income are limited and the only form of housing they can afford is a cheap central city apartment. The next stage of the household lifecycle will be setting up a family. This involves greater space requirements, entailing the need to move to a larger apartment or small house. Subsequent stages involve children and greater space requirements until the later stages of the household's lifecycle. Different stages of the cycle involve different space requirements and different housing types. The majority of residential moves made within the city are caused by changes in the lifecycle prompting new space requirements. Residential mobility in the private housing market can be seen as a response to changes in the family lifecycle. The formation of a new household, the arrival, growth and eventual departure of children all cause changes in household space requirements and relocation can be seen as the process whereby households move in order to obtain housing in conformity within their space requirements. Not all households can move so freely, however. Many have invested a large amount of emotional capital in their existing accommodation while others find the cost and trouble of moving too much. These households will experience changes in their lifecycle in terms of lengthening queues for the bathroom in the morning rather through residential moves.

In the public housing sector the degree of residential mobility depends upon the size and variation in the housing stock. In cities where the stock is large and varied enough to allow tenants to move, the changes in their lifecycle would be met by transfers within the public housing sector. But when the housing stock is limited in size there is less flexibility and households may not be able to move so easily in response to changing space requirements.

Table 7.4 Housing needs associated with different stages of the lifecycle

Stage in lifecycle	*Housing needs/aspirations*
1 pre-child stage	relatively cheap, central city apartment
2 child-bearing	renting of single-family dwelling close to apartment zone
3 child-rearing	ownership of relatively new suburban home
4 child-launching	same areas as (3) or perhaps move to higher-status area
5 post-child	marked by residential stability
6 later life	institution/apartment/live with children

MEASURING SEGREGATION

We can measure the degree of segregation in the city by a number of indices.

1 *Index of dissimilarity* This index provides a measure of the similarity in the spatial distribution of two sub-groups of the population. It is obtained by the following equation:

$$ID_{XY} = \frac{\Sigma(X_i - Y_i)}{2}$$

where X_i represents the percentage of the X population in the ith area, Y_i represents the percentage of the Y population in the ith area and ID_{XY} is the index of dissimilarity. To calculate the index we must add up the difference between the percentage of each group in all the areas and divide by 2. Table 7C provides an example of the calculation of this index. The ID value ranges from 0 to 100. When the ID value is close to 0 this implies that the two populations have similar spatial distributions, the closer the calculated value is to 100 the more dissimilar are the two spatial distributions and hence the greater the degree of residential segregation. The ID value can also be interpreted as a measure of the percentage of one population who would have to move in order to reproduce the distribution of the other population.

Table 7C Calculation of the index of dissimilarity

Area	*X* *Percentage persons in socio-economic groups A*	*Y* *Percentage persons in socio-economic groups B*	*(X – Y)* *Difference*
1	35	10	25
2	30	15	15
3	20	35	15
4	15	40	25
Total	100	100	$\Sigma(X - Y) = 80$

$$ID_{XY} = \frac{\Sigma(X_i - Y_i)}{2} = \frac{80}{2}$$

$$ID_{XY} = 40$$

Table 7D Indices of dissimilarity for occupational groups by census tracts, Chicago, 1950
Source: Duncan and Duncan, 1955

	a	b	c	d	e	f	g	h
a Professional workers	–	13	15	28	35	44	41	54
b Managers, officials		–	13	28	33	41	40	52
c Sales workers			–	27	35	42	38	54
d Clerical workers				–	16	21	24	38
e Craftsmen and foremen					–	17	35	35
f Skilled manual						–	26	25
g Service workers							–	28
h Semi- and unskilled manual								–

Table 7D presents the results of an analysis of residential segregation in Chicago which used the index of dissimilarity. The figures show the correspondence between social and spatial distance for different occupational categories. The two ends of the social spectrum of occupational categories, the professional workers on the one hand and the semi- and unskilled manual workers on the other, record the highest index of dissimilarity: 54 per cent of professional workers would have to move to another area in order to match the spatial distribution of semi- and unskilled manual workers. As a general conclusion we can note that the closer the occupational categories are in social terms, the greater the similarity in their spatial distributions.

2 *Index of segregation* This index measures the extent to which a specific sub-group has a similar distribution to the spatial distribution of the total population. It is obtained in the following formula:

$$IS_{XY} = \frac{ID_{XY}}{1 - \Sigma Y_i \mid \Sigma X_i}$$

where, ID_{XY} is the index of dissimilarity between the total population X and the subgroup Y, ΣY_i represents the total number of the sub-group Y in the city, ΣX_i represents the total population of the city. An example of the calculation of the index of segregation is shown in Table 7E. This IS value ranges from 0 to 100 with values closer to 100 indicating a greater degree of residential segregation.

Table 7E Calculation of the index of segregation

Area	*Y* *Percentage of Y sub-group (absolute nos)*	*X* *Percentage of total population (absolute nos)*	*Difference*
1	40(80)	15(150)	25
2	35(70)	25(250)	10
3	15(30)	35(350)	20
4	10(20)	35(350)	25
Total	100(200)	100(1000)	80

$$ID_{XY} = \frac{\Sigma(X_i - Y_i)}{2} = \frac{80}{2} = 40$$

$$IS_{XY} = \frac{ID_{XY}}{1 - \Sigma Y_i | \Sigma X_i} = \frac{40}{1 - 200/1000}$$

$$IS_{XY} = 50.0$$

Table 7F shows the results from the aforementioned study of Chicago. When occupational categories are listed in order of income and prestige, the indices of segregation form a u-shaped pattern as shown in Figure 7E.

The indices of dissimilarity and segregation can also be used with reference to birth place and ethnic groups. They can also be used in temporal study with successive indices over time indicating the extent of increasing or decreasing segregation.

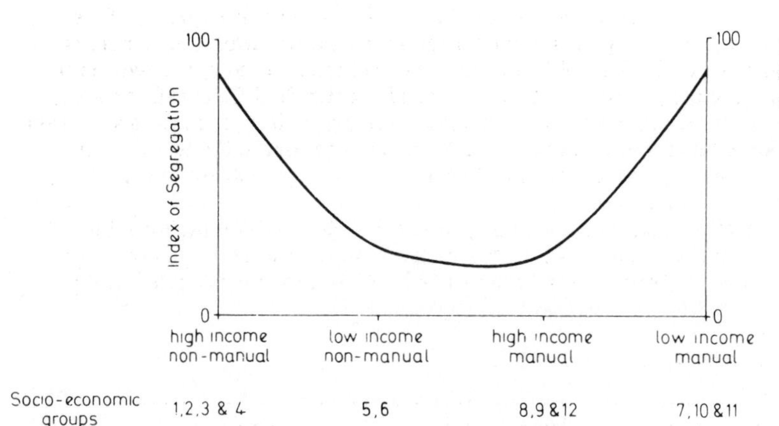

Figure 7E Segregation index and socio-economic status

Table 7F Indices of segregation for occupational groups by census tracts, Chicago, 1950

Major occupation category	*Index of segregation*
Professional workers	30
Managers, officials	29
Sales workers	29
Clerical workers	13
Craftsmen and foremen	19
Skilled manual	22
Service workers	24
Semi- and unskilled	35

3 *Location quotient* The degree of concentration of particular groups is measured by the location quotient. It is calculated by dividing the percentage of the sub-group of the population in an area by the percentage of the total population in the same area. An example of the

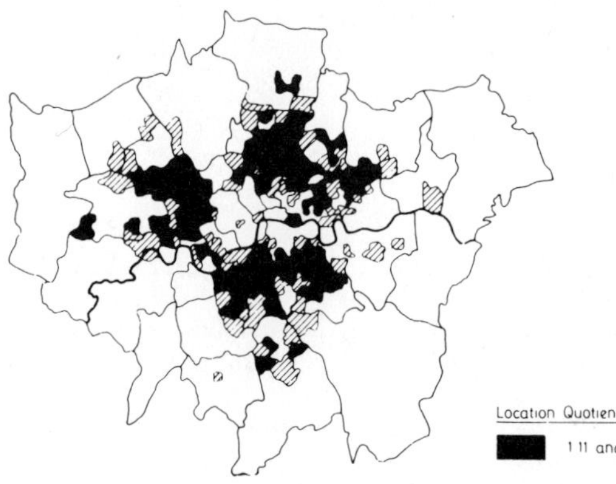

Figure 7F Distribution of West Indian-born population in London by location quotient

calculation of the location quotient is shown in Table 7G. If an area has an LQ value of less than 1 this indicates that the sub-group of the population under investigation is under-represented in that particular area. If an area has an LQ value greater than 1 then the sub-group of the population is over-represented in that particular area. The larger the LQ value of an area, the greater the concentration of the sub-group under investigation in that particular area. In the hypothetical case considered in Table 7G areas 1 and 2 are over-represented in terms of the proportion of the population born in Timbuktu, while areas 3 and 4 are under-represented; the greatest concentration is found in area 2.

An example of the use of the location quotient is shown in Figure 7F which shows the distribution of LQ values for the West-Indian-born population in the wards of London (Lee, 1973). This map reveals that the West-Indian-born population was very concentrated in the inner areas of London.

Table 7G Calculation of the location quotient

Area	*Percentage born in Timbuktu*	*Percentage total population*	*Location quotient*
1	35	25	(35/25) 1.40
2	40	25	(40/25) 1.60
3	20	25	(20/25) 0.80
4	5	25	(5/25) 0.20
Total	100	100	

The measurement problem

The results from the application of the three indices are dependent on the size of the observation unit. Figure 7G shows, from data taken from a study of Asian segregation in Huddersfield (Jones and McEroy, 1978), how the index value varies according to the scale of analysis. Large observation units may mask patterns of segregation which occur at street and block level.

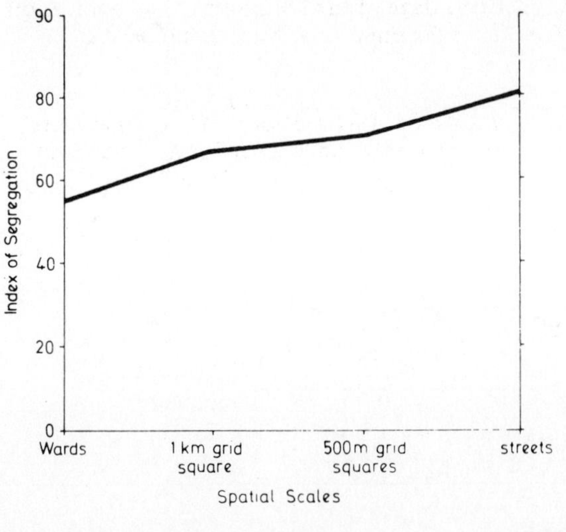

Figure 7G Effects of scale on indices of segregation

References

Duncan, O.D. and Duncan, B. (1955), Residential distribution and occupational stratification, *American Journal of Sociology*, 60, 493-506.

Jones, R.P. and McEroy, D. (1978), Race and space in cloud-cuckoo land, *Area*, 10, 162-6.

Lee, T.R. (1973), Ethnic and social class factors in residential segregation, *Environment and Planning A*, 5, 477-90.

For individual households the process of moving dwelling takes the form shown in Figure 7.5. Once the decision to move is made households define an aspiration region which is the set of housing types and prices which they want and can afford; they then search the various information sources such as newspapers and estate agents to obtain information on dwelling vacancies. They then examine vacancies, match these to their aspiration region and then choose a specific vacancy or redefine their aspirations or decide not to move. The aggregate pattern of residential moves takes the form of distinct channels of movement. These channels can be considered as streams of households of particular socio-economic status or ethnic status into particular areas of the city. These channels can be seen as the process by which socio-economic and ethnic segregation in the city is maintained.

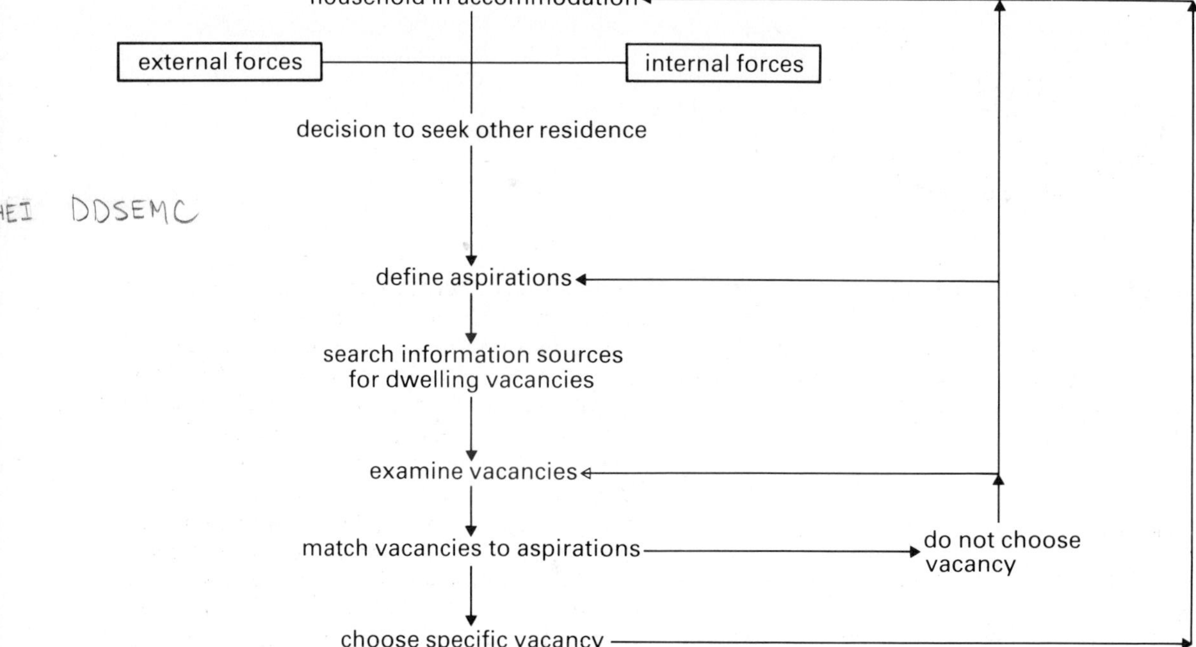

Figure 7.5 The decision-making process of residential mobility

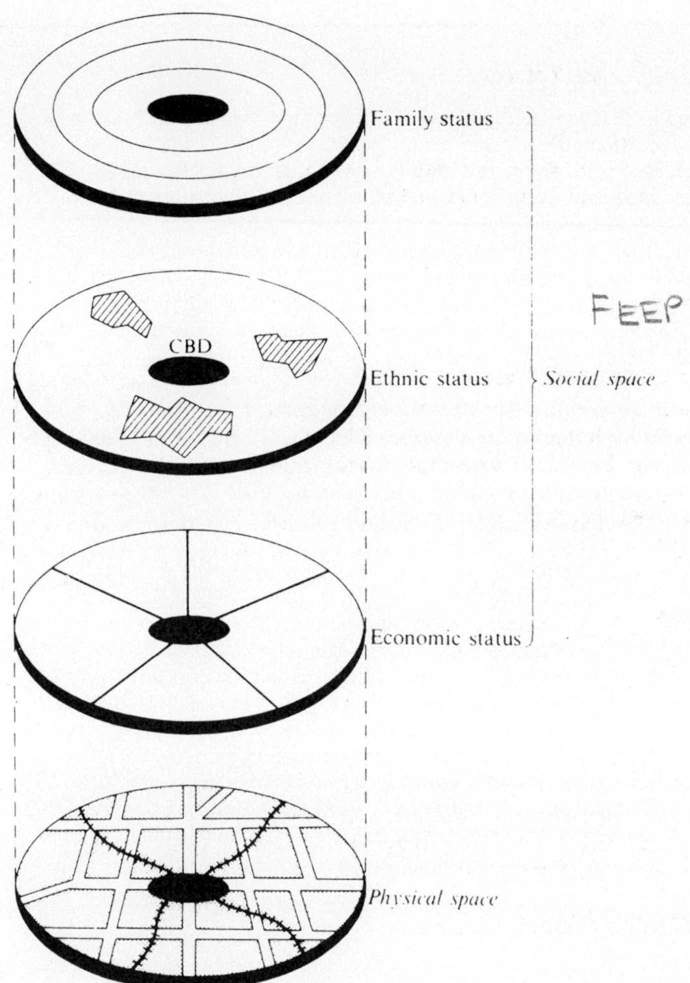

Figure 7.6 The spatial dimensions of the residential mosaic
Source: after Murdie, R.A. (1969), Factorial ecology of metropolitan Toronto, *Research Paper 116*, Department of Geography, University of Chicago

THE RESIDENTIAL MOSAIC

The meshing of housing supply and housing demand produces a patchwork quilt of different types of residential areas, which we can term the residential mosaic.

A general model

Generalising from a whole series of studies, we can suggest a general model for the residential mosaic in the private housing sector of cities in advanced capitalist countries. Figure 7.6 catches the essentials of the model. Superimposed on the physical space of streets, buildings and roads are the three dimensions of social space. **Family status** distinguishes between households at different stages of their lifecycle. Younger, single-person households are found in the private renting areas while the nuclear family of mum, dad and the two kids is located in the suburbs. A transect from the city centre to the city's edge would be a move from stage 1 to stages 4 and 5 in the lifecycle model shown in Table 7.4. **Economic status** differences occur through variations in income. In most major cities there is a distinct sectoral pattern with definite high-income and low-income sectors. **Ethnic** groups are found clustered together in selected neighbourhoods throughout the city.

FACTORIAL ECOLOGY

In the early 1960s the growing use of quantification in urban geography, aided by developments in computer technology, merged with the rising interests in examining urban residential patterns. The use of factor analysis in the analysis of residential differentiation is termed factorial ecology.

The data input for a factorial ecology is a set of variables related to the different sub-divisions of the city. Table 7H shows the list of variables, used in a study of the city of Bristol, taken from the 1971 Census. The observation units were the 821 enumeration districts shown in Figure 7H. These districts had an average population size of 500. They were the units used to collect census information, and the US equivalent is the census tract. The initial data in this case thus consists of eleven variables for 821 observations – a huge data set. The aim of factor analysis is to collapse this data set to something more manageable without losing valuable information. The technique does this by reducing the amount of information for retaining the essence. We can see how it does this by looking at the output from the application of a factor analysis, in this case a variant known as principal components analysis, to the data set. We will treat the technique itself as a black box; for those interested in the internal workings of the analysis see amongst others Johnston (1978).

Principal components analysis reduces the initial data to a set of new components which summarise the initial information in a much-reduced, more-manageable form. The *eigenvalue* for each component tells us to what extent the new component captures the information of the initial data set. The *component loading* which is a measure of the relationship between the new component and the initial variable allows us to identify what the new component is actually measuring. The *component scores* are the values of the component in each of the spacial units of observation. Table 7I summarises the output. In this case the eigenvalue is expressed as a cumulative percentage of total variance. The first component measures 25.1 per cent of the total variance. In other words this new component on its own measures just over a quarter of the total variance. The pattern of component loadings shows that the component is measuring socio-economic status and high positive scores indicate high socio-economic

Table 7H Variables used in the principal components analysis

Variable number	*Description*
1	Percentage of population aged 0-14
2	Percentage of private householders living at densities greater than 1.5 persons per room
3	Percentage of private householders in owner-occupation
4	Percentage of private householders renting from local authority
5	Percentage of private householders renting unfurnished accommodation
6	Percentage of persons born in New Commonwealth
7	Percentage of population retired
8	Percentage of persons economically active and retired in socio-economic groups 1, 2, 3 and 4
9	Percentage of persons economically active and retired in socio-economic groups 5 and 6
10	Percentage of persons economically active and retired in socio-economic groups 7, 10, 11 and 15

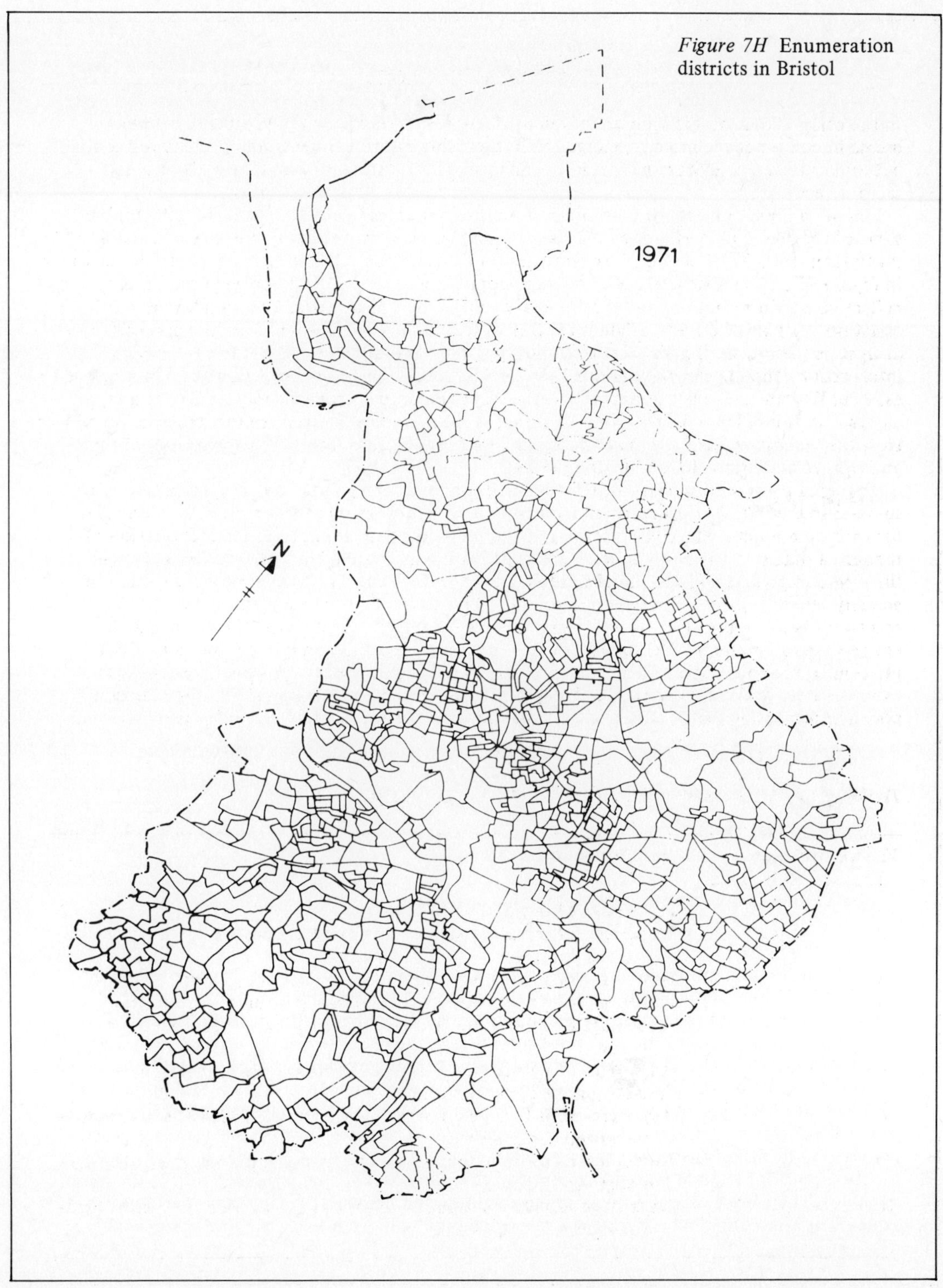

Figure 7H Enumeration districts in Bristol

Table 7I Summary of results from principal components analysis

Component number	*Description*	*Variable*	*Component loading*	*Cumulative percentage of total variance*
1	Socio-economic status	8	0.76	25.11
		9	0.75	
		10	– 0.85	
		6	– 0.48	
2	Tenure	5	0.83	48.37
		2	0.63	
		3	– 0.93	
		1	– 0.44	
3	Stage in lifecycle	1	0.76	64.70
		6	0.50	
		7	– 0.81	

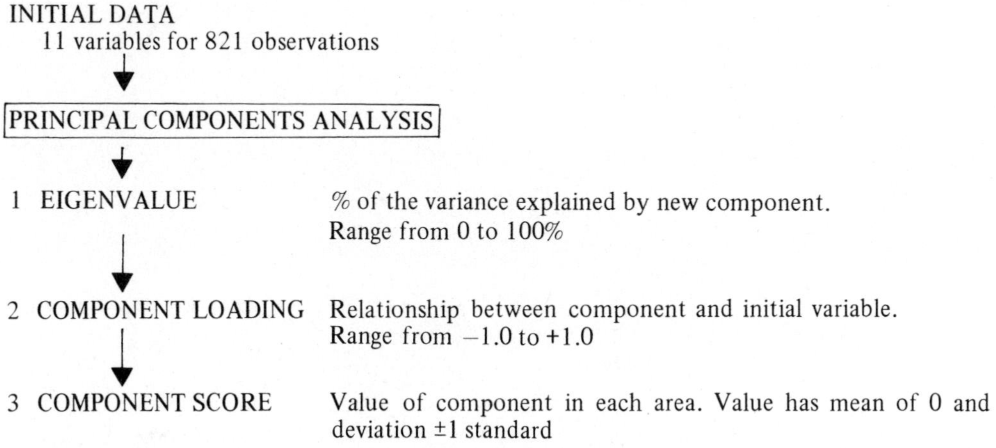

INITIAL DATA
11 variables for 821 observations

↓

PRINCIPAL COMPONENTS ANALYSIS

↓

1 EIGENVALUE — % of the variance explained by new component. Range from 0 to 100%

↓

2 COMPONENT LOADING — Relationship between component and initial variable. Range from –1.0 to +1.0

↓

3 COMPONENT SCORE — Value of component in each area. Value has mean of 0 and deviation ±1 standard

Figure 7I Stages in the principal components analysis

status. The component scores in Figure 7J show a distinct sectoral pattern for the location of high-status areas. Low-status areas are grouped around the city centre. Component 2 is measuring tenure and the pattern revealed in Figure 7K highlights, through picking out areas of high positive scores, the areas of private renting in the city. Notice the distinct inner-city location. Further out are found the areas of public housing and owner-occupation. Component 3 measures stages in the lifecycle with high positive scores, indicating areas where there are large families. The pattern revealed in Figure 7L is reminiscent of the concentric pattern suggested in the family-status dimension depicted in Figure 7.6. The three components together captured almost two-thirds of the initial information.

The observant student would have noticed that the components produced reflect the initial variables. There are two well-known principles in factor analysis, the Gigo and the Lilo principles. The Gigo principle is if you put garbage in you will get garbage out. And under the

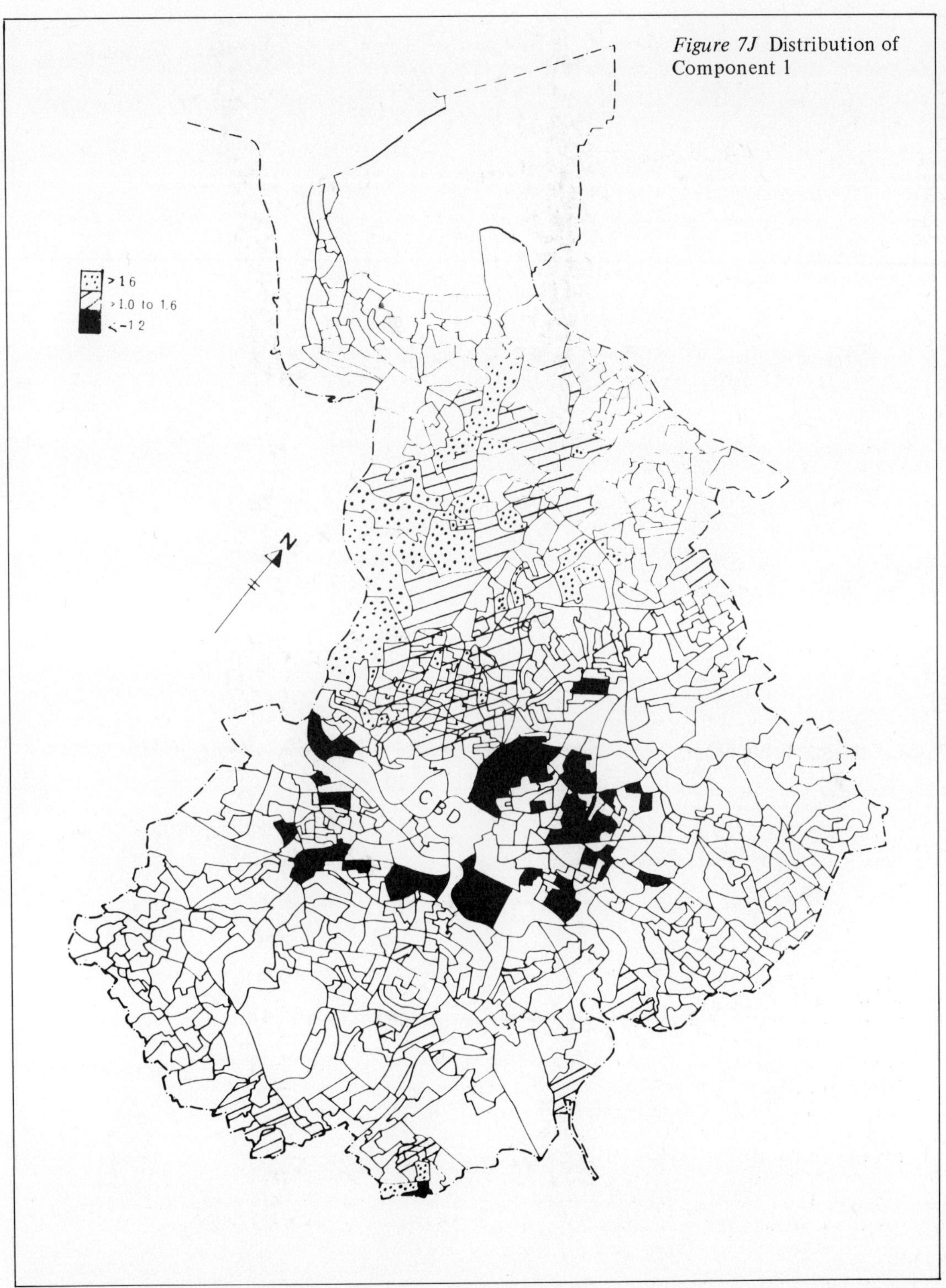

Figure 7J Distribution of Component 1

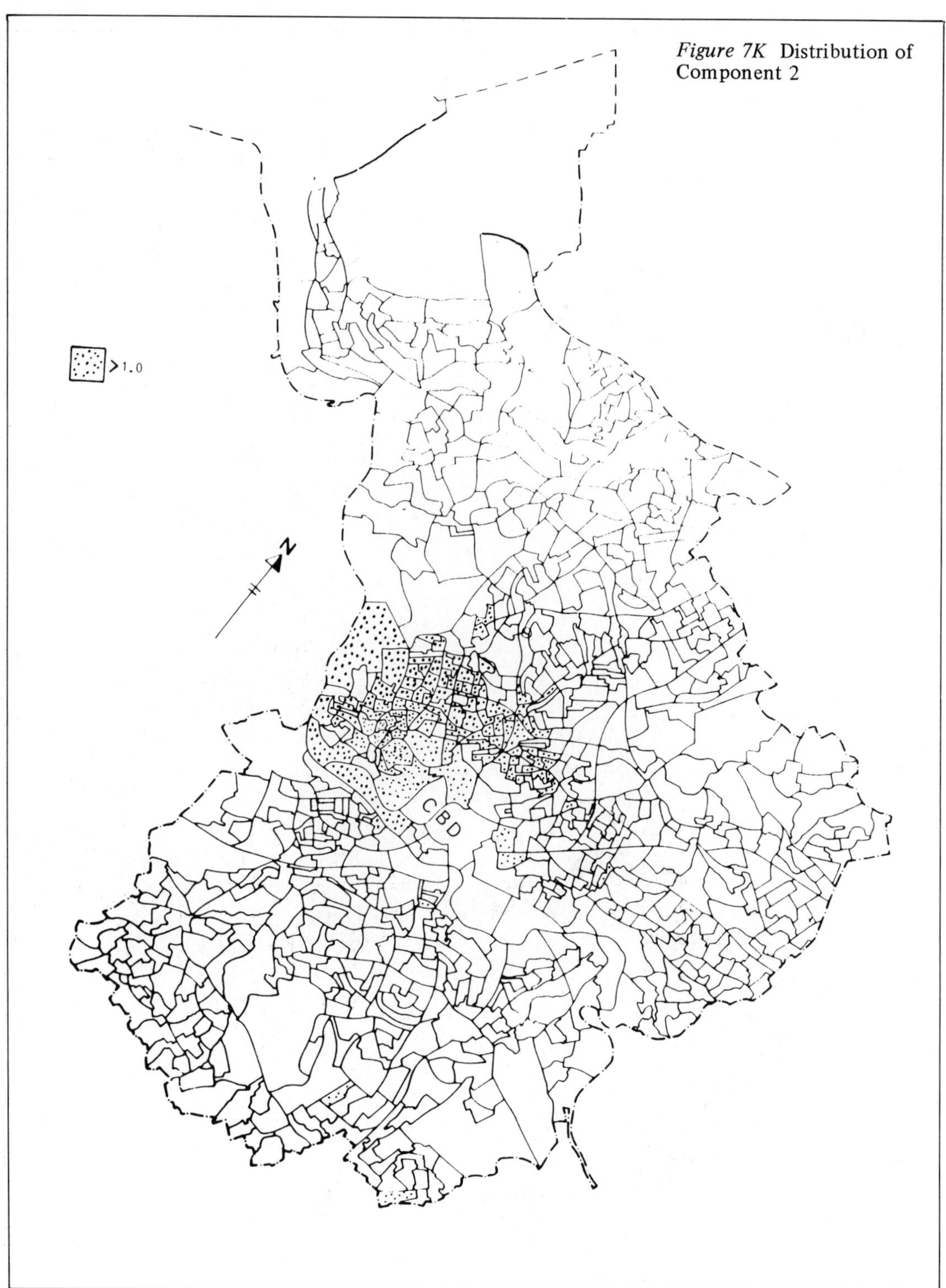

Figure 7K Distribution of Component 2

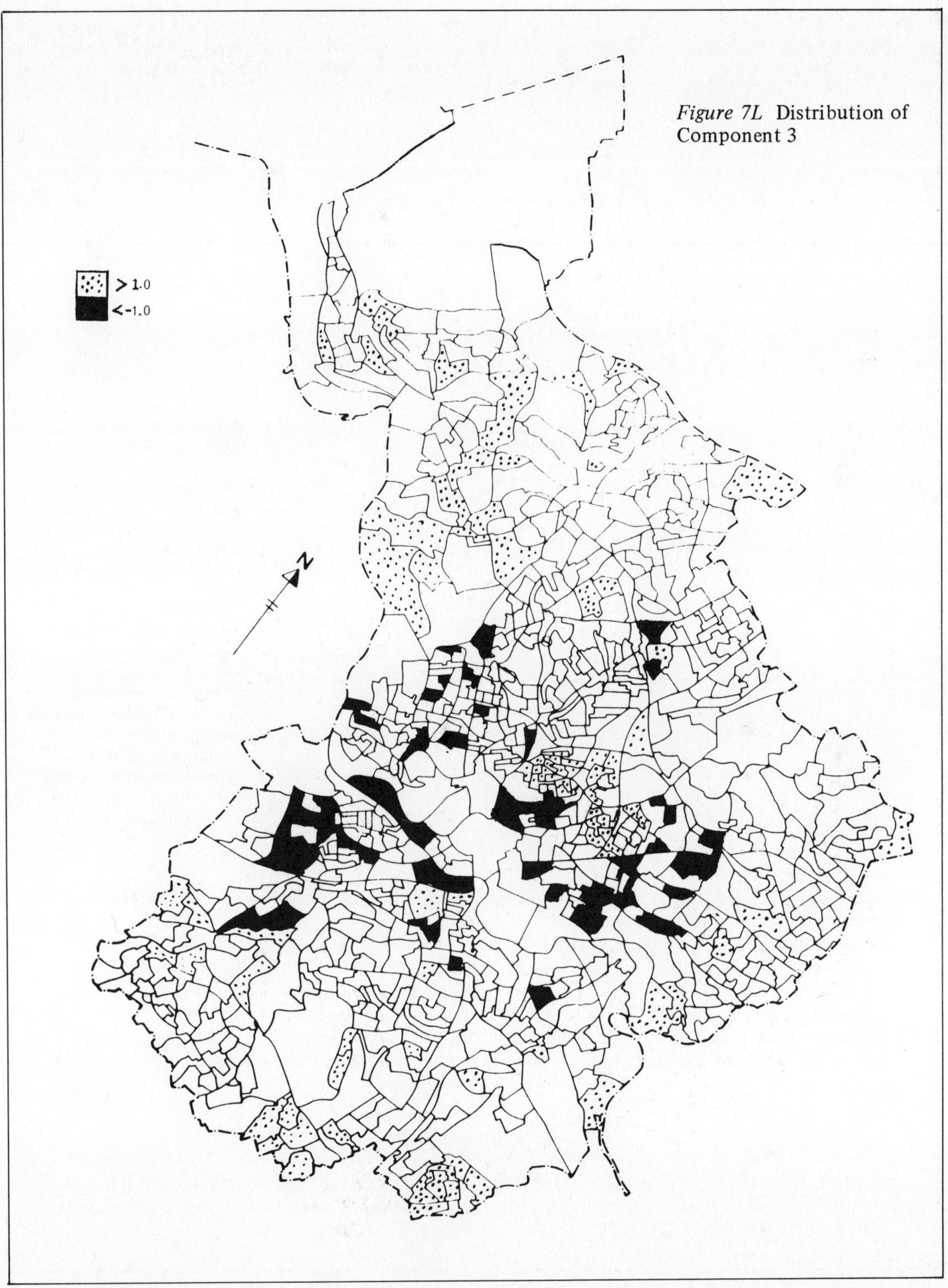

Figure 7L Distribution of Component 3

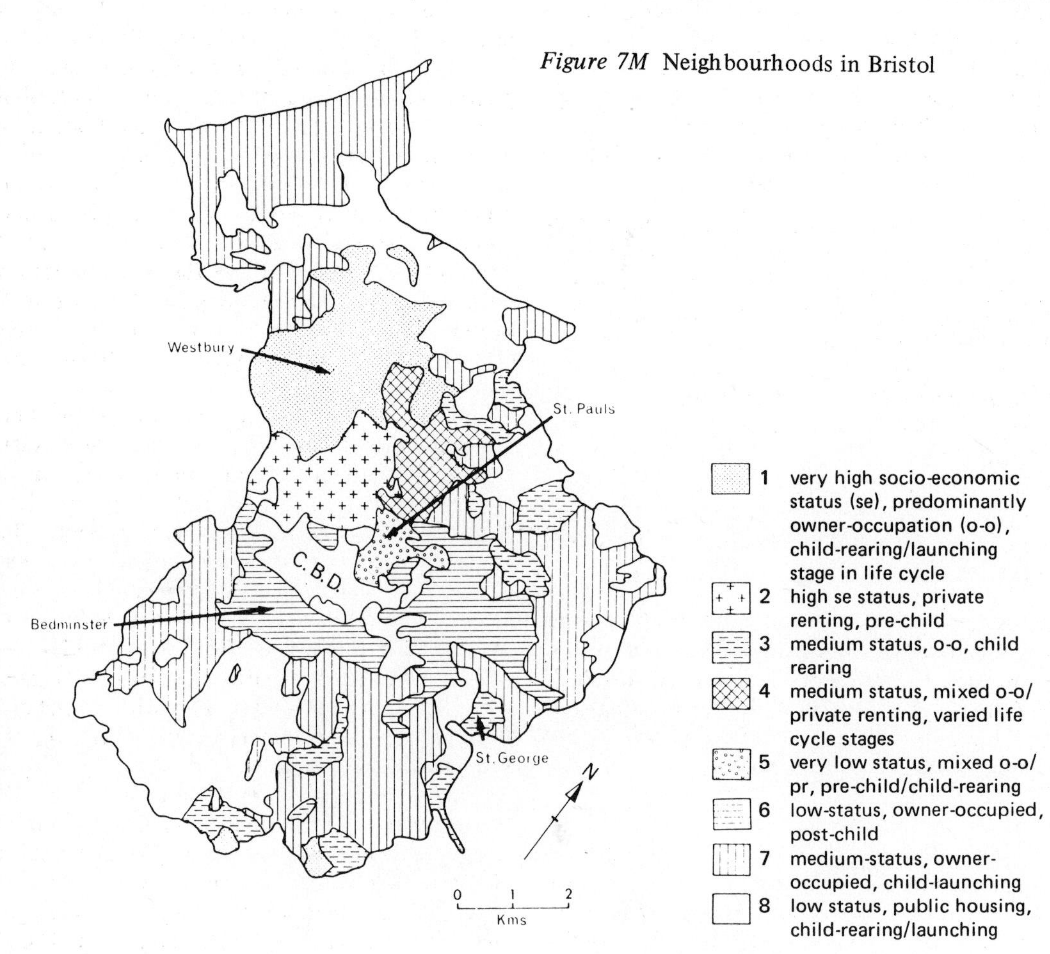

Figure 7M Neighbourhoods in Bristol

Lilo principle if you put lots of data in you get lots of data out. Factor analysis is only as good or as bad as the initial data.

Factor analysis has been widely used in urban geography and it has provided the basis for further work. The component scores have been used as the basis for defining residential areas. Figure 7M, for example, shows the result of a grouping of the three component scores. These residential areas were then used as a sampling frame for research into residential mobility; inmigrants to the four named areas were identified and interviewed. The neighbourhood typology produced from factor analysis can be used as a starting point for a whole range of investigations.

References

Johnston, R.J. (1978), *Multivariate Statistical Methods in Geography*, Longman, London.

Short, J.R. (1978), Residential mobility in the private housing market of Bristol, *Transactions of the Institute of British Geographers, New Series*, 3, 533-47.

The superimposition of these dimensions on the physical fabric of the city produces the residential mosaic. We can locate most types of neighbourhoods with respect to each of these dimensions. Combining family and economic status, for example, we can identify four distinct types:

(1) *High economic status, early stage in the life-cycle* – found in the penthouse flat districts of the inner-city, housing the cosmopolitans.
(2) *Low economic status, early stage in the life-cycle* – the rooming house district housing transient households.
(3) *Low economic status, later stages in the life-cycle* – the low- to middle-income suburban areas.
(4) *High economic status, later stages in the life-cycle* – the exclusive suburbs housing the middle-income and wealthy child-rearing households.

These residential types only refer to the private housing market. In Britain and Sweden, for example, we have to introduce the other dimension of public housing. In Britain low-income groups are found both in the central city areas and in the peripheral public housing estates.

Social areas

The different residential areas provide the milieux in which people grow up and are socialised. The residential area is the social basis of our everyday life. The neighbourhood influences behaviour through providing a context for shared assumptions and attitude.

The influence of the neighbourhood varies with different groups in the population. For the people who work in a different part of the city the neighbourhood may constitute only a small part of their urban life. For the transient worker the neighbourhood is simply an area of the city in which they live at the present time. But for those tied to the home – e.g. unemployed, old people, very young and housewives – the neighbourhood is the main locale for social behaviour and for the long-established home-based resident the neighbourhood is of great social and emotional significance. Amongst male adolescents, for example, local areas can provide the basis for gang territoriality. Figure 7.7 shows turfs in Glasgow.

We can see the influence of the neighbourhood in a number of ways. First, in the USA at the local level, the politics of place dominate over the politics of class, and neighbourhood politics are very important, partly because neighbourhood groups have been set up by the federal government and partly as a response to urban renewal and other programmes against which residents have mobilised. The revolt against urban renewal in US cities in the 1960s and 1970s was primarily a neighbourhood affair involving community mobilisation. The urban sociologist John Mollenkopf (1981) provides case studies from Boston and San Francisco.

Second, the local area can provide the basis for shaping attitudes. Brian Robson (1969) undertook a study of the city of Sunderland. Different residential areas were identified by principal components analysis and these provided the sampling areas for a questionnaire study into attitudes to educational attainment. The results showed that the people of similar status but living in different areas had different attitudes and people with differing status but living in the same area held similar attitudes. The urban social area seemed to have an independent effect on the individual's social outlook.

Finally, political attitudes are shaped by the life experience of the voters, including the characteristics of their neighbourhood. The independent effect of the neighbourhood on voting patterns is termed the *neighbourhood effect*. It has been identified in a series of studies. It is often difficult to separate the neighbourhood effect from other variables affecting political disposition. However, Table 7.5 shows the neighbourhood effect in action. The results are taken from a study of nine towns classified into three broad groups according to general political disposition. Individual people were also classified after an interview. Note how the percentage of respondents classified as of low-economic status and voting Republican is greater in neighbourhoods classified as high status. Similarly, a greater proportion of high-status people in low-status neighbourhoods vote democrat. A similar type of effect is noted in Table 7.6, which shows for Britain the different voting behaviour of middle- and working-class households in resort towns and mining areas. The latter have a greater socialist/militant tradition; the neighbourhood effect in this case is a radicalising one.

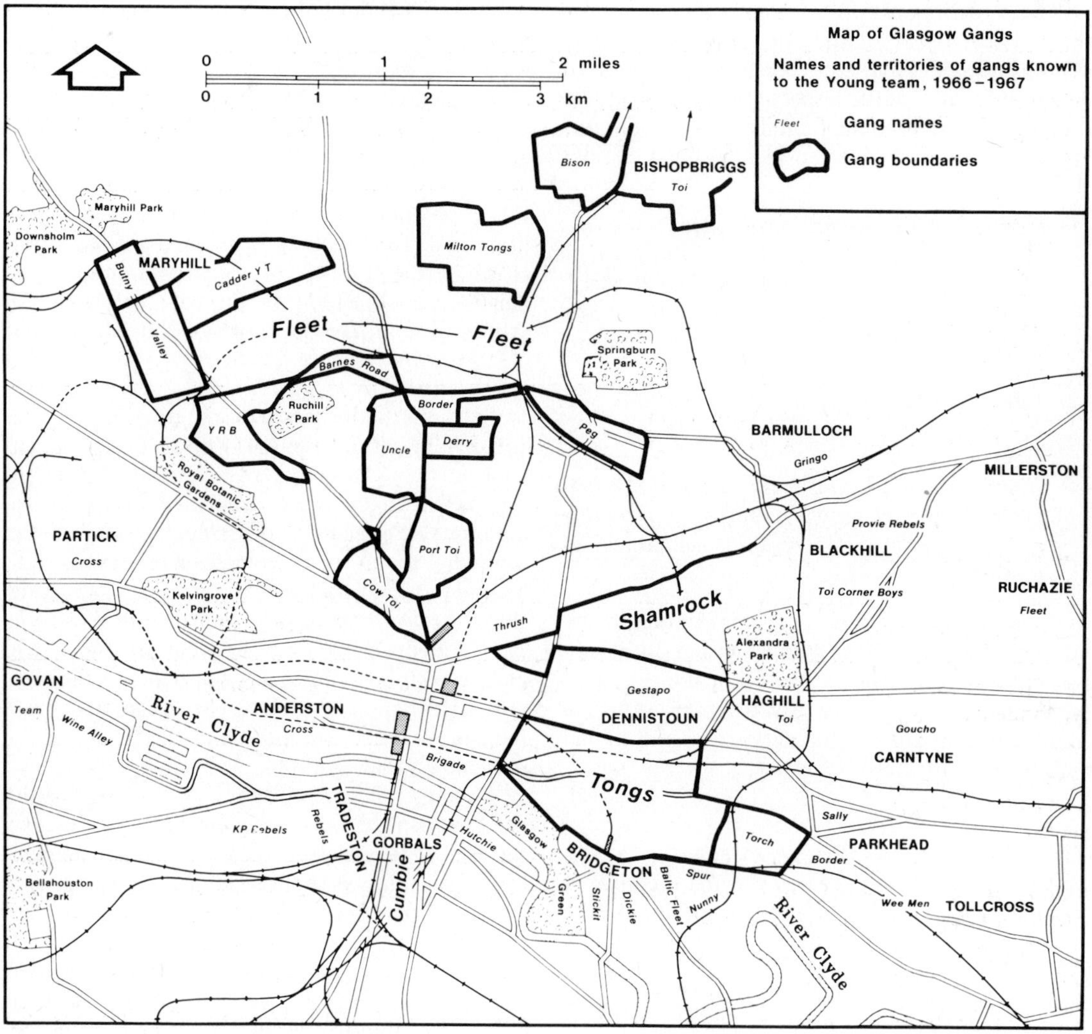

Figure 7.7 Turfs in Glasgow
Source: after Patrick, J. (1973), *A Glasgow Gang Observed*, Eyre Methuen, London

MAJOR TRENDS

The two most important changes in the city as residence have been the growth of the suburbs and the more recent trend of urban renewal and gentrification. We will consider each in turn.

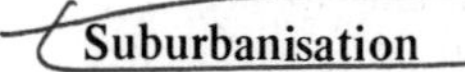

Suburbanisation

The single most important change in urban form in advanced capitalist countries in the twentieth century has been the growth of the suburbs. The 'great camp', as J.K. Galbraith has termed it, has arisen around the edges of major towns and cities. Galbraith's term captures the essence of the suburb; it is an area of residence, a neighbourhood of houses rather than the mixed land-use type of neighbourhood found in the city proper.

There are a number of preconditions for

Table 7.5 Class, neighbourhood and urban context: Republican voting patterns

Political characteristic of town	*Strong Democrat*		*Mixed*		*Strong Republican*	
Neighbourhood socio-economic status	*Low*	*High*	*Low*	*High*	*Low*	*High*
Respondents' socio-economic status						
Low	16	29	20	43	49	67
High	22	36	37	65	65	89
(entries are percentage voting Republican)						

Source: Segal, D.R. and Mayer, M.W. 1969. The social context of political partisanship in Dugan, M. and Rokkhan, S. (eds), *Quantitative Ecological Analysis in the Social Sciences,* MIT Press, Cambridge, Mass.

Table 7.6 Constituency type and voting in Britain

Type of constituency	*Mining*		*Resort*	
perceived class of respondents	middle	working	middle	working
% voting				
Conservative	64	9	93	52
Labour	36	91	7	48

Source: Butler, D.E. and Stokes, D.E. (1969), *Political Change in Britain: Forces Shaping Electoral Choice*, Macmillan, London

suburbanisation. Since suburbanisation implies a separation between home and workplace, perhaps the most important is relatively cheap transport. Waves of suburbanisation have occurred with developments in transport; streetcars, railways and now the automobile and rapid transit systems have produced their own suburban areas. Each improved transport system has extended the distance of the suburbs from the central city. Other preconditions include land for building and effective demand for suburban housing. But these are all preconditions not causes. To understand why we have to consider the actors involved. The *producers* of the suburbs include the banks, road builders, auto-companies, house builders, transport companies and land speculators. They make their profit out of building suburbs. Then there is the *state*. It is lobbied by the producers to aid their operations. The state has also looked at the suburbs in a favourable light. Many politicians have argued that by encouraging owner-occupation in suburban residencies a stable society is produced. If urban has the connotation of radicalism and rural of conservatism then the suburbs have one of political apathy. Finally there are the *consumers*. For those with effective choice the action of the producers in association with the state has made it economically rational to choose a suburban location. It is easier to get a mortgage, tax relief is greater and the quality of suburban life is much better. Consumer choice has been shaped by the producers and the state. The consumers also seek

Plates 30, 31, 32 and 33
Contrasting views of urban Britain: (30) inner-city neighbourhood in Reading; (31) suburban Horsham in Sussex

Contrasting views of urban America: (32) Harlem; (33) typical middle-income suburbia

Table 7.7 The relative growth of the suburbs in USA

	% share of US population	
	Central cities	*Suburbs*
1950	34.6	24.4
1960	37.0	33.2
1970	31.4	37.6
1975	29.6	39.1

to influence the state to limit further residential growth and to maintain the exclusivity of the suburbs.

We can see this triadic relationship operating in post-war America. Since 1945 the rate of suburban growth in the USA has been tremendous. Suburban house-building was aided by the growing concentration of building activity in even larger house-building companies. These larger builders could mass-produce houses. They therefore required the large tracts of land generally found at the city's edge. The production of the suburbs was also promoted by the road builders and the banks and mortgage-lending agencies keen for business. The suburbs were a better investment for these institutions than the central city. The state also aided the process of suburbanisation, partly as a response to lobbying by road builders and house builders but partly to meet the macro-economic policies of the post-war era. In the immediate post-war period another slump like the inter-war one was feared and the federal government sought to lubricate the building of roads and buildings in order to maintain aggregate demand in the economy. Through Federal Housing Administration mortgages and other schemes, the federal government stimulated suburban house production.

For the consumer with effective choice this new built form provided better housing in more attractive areas. People flocked to the suburbs and more pressure was put on the state to ease their path. Having moved to the suburbs, the consumers sought to maintain their position. They did this by seeking to halt further residential developments – arguments of self-interest mingled with general pleas about environmental quality to stop the in-movement of lower-income groups who it was feared would reduce property values and lower the quality of the neighbourhood. The better-organised consumers operated through the zoning boards, municipalities and special districts to maintain the status of their areas by exclusionary zoning. Zoning ordinances, which placed minimum price limits, excluded cheaper housing and thus lower-income groups. The result has been for the process of suburbanisation to be a differential one. Not all the population has been equally affected. Suburbanisation in the USA has been an overwhelmingly white, predominantly middle- to upper-income phenomenon. The lower-income ethnic minorities have to all intents and purposes been excluded.

In other countries the pattern of suburbanisation has differed. In Britain, for example, there are stronger land-use controls which have been used to stop suburban sprawl. However, although differing in detail, the broad picture remains the same. Figure 7.8 shows the spread of the population around Bristol. As in the USA the process of suburbanisation has been a differential one. We can measure this by compiling an index of home/workplace separation. A high value on this index reflects a large separation between home and workplace and the socio-economic group with the highest value has the greatest separation between home and workplace, i.e. it is the most suburbanised socio-economic status category. Figure 7.9 shows the index of separation for the different socio-economic groups in the Bristol region. Notice how the managers and professional workers are much more suburbanised than lower-income non-manual and manual workers.

Table 7.8 Suburban-central city differences 1975

	median family income ($)	*% black population*
Central city	11,343	60
Suburbs	14,007	17

Urban renewal

Whilst suburbanisation has been occurring at the edge of the city, important processes have been in operation at the city centre. The most important has been *urban renewal*. This has involved

Journey to work, 1961

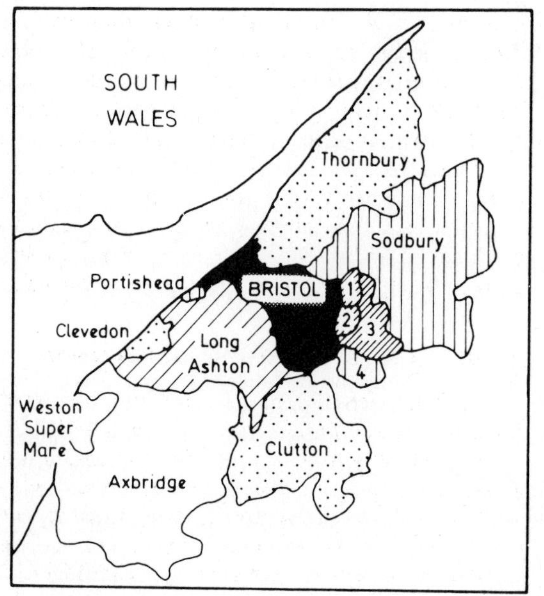

Journey to work, 1971

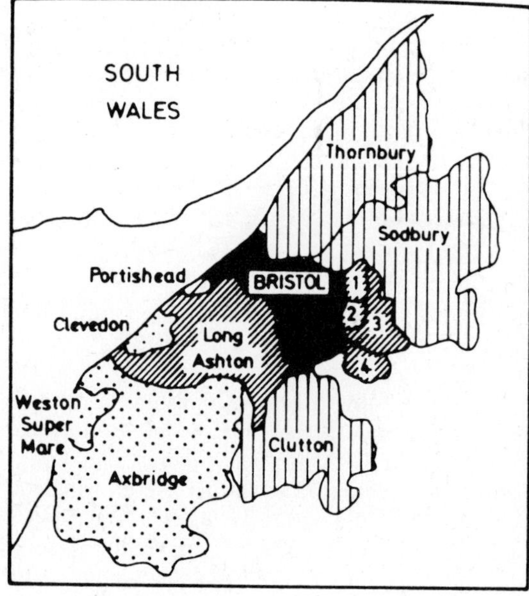

1 Mangotsfield 2 Kingswood 3 Warmley 4 Keynsham

KEY TO % OF ECONOMICALLY ACTIVE POPULATION WORKING IN BRISTOL

+40 % +30 - 40 % +20 - 30 % +10 - 20 %

Figure 7.8 Suburbanisation in the Bristol region 1961-1971

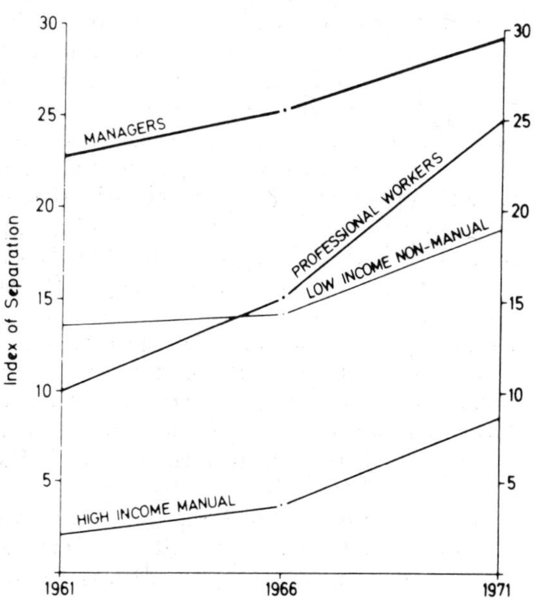

Figure 7.9 Home–workplace separation by socio-economic status

public and private interests which seek to reshape the structure of the central city. The centrality of the city centre is an important resource. In a capitalist society it is a commodity to be bought and sold, a very valuable commodity because it is limited in supply. Owners of city-centre land therefore have a monopoly over a scarce commodity.

Urban-renewal projects in the major cities of capitalist countries have shown two major characteristics. First, it has involved the clearance of low-income housing. In the USA from 1945 to 1968 over one million dwellings were demolished and 600,000 households were displaced as part of government programmes. In Britain under the comprehensive redevelopment schemes over 600,000 dwellings were demolished between 1960 and 1974. The scale of housing destruction has been large. The housing which has been demolished has been the old, inner-city properties, housing low-income households. Second, urban renewal schemes have prompted a community response. Many communities have established residents' associations, pressure groups and defence organisations against the destruction of their neighbourhoods. Local politics in inner-city areas during 1960s were dominated by the fight against urban renewal. It was often an unequal struggle. The poor neighbourhoods had few resources to fight against the combined pressure of business interests and the government. Some limited successes were achieved but mainly in the much better-organised, richer neighbourhoods with more articulate residents.

The exact form of urban renewal has varied across the different countries. In the USA urban renewal involved the demolition of low-income dwellings and in its place the construction of middle- to upper-income accommodation, commercial property and shopping precincts. The poor and especially the poor blacks shouldered the burden of urban renewal, having their homes demolished and their neighbourhoods torn down while the benefits went to the construction companies and property development agencies. When low-income housing was demolished and the area cleared, land was given cheap to the property and construction companies who developed it in the construction of more-expensive housing and commercial retail establishments, all for very large profits. In effect urban renewal was black renewal and a subsidy by the state to private interests.

In Britain, by contrast, while this kind of thing happened in certain cities in others the onus for urban renewal came from the local authorities eager to construct public housing. In the conurbations the Labour party has often been in control and the central plank in their manifesto has been a willingness to provide public housing. Although there have been some commercial developments, much of the land has been given over to public housing. Municipal socialism in Britain has tempered the business dynamic of urban renewal.

Improvement, gentrification and displacement

The urban-renewal projects were the dominant force affecting central cities in the late 1950s, 1960s and early 1970s. Although still important in certain cities, the government-sponsored projects are of less importance. The most recent impact refers to the revitalisation process involving *housing improvement* and *gentrification*. The former refers to an increase in housing quality without any change in neighbourhood composition. In many countries the emphasis in state housing policy has switched from urban renewal to housing improvement. In Britain, for example, since 1969 households have been able to obtain grants from the government to improve their property. Housing policy has switched from demolition to rehabilitation partly as a cost-cutting exercise. Gentrification, in contrast, refers to housing improvement associated with the change in neighbourhood composition, a displacement of low-income by higher-income households. Gentrification is now taking on significant proportions. In the USA most of the major cities are now experiencing varying levels of gentrification in their central-area neighbourhoods. In Britain the process has been occurring in a few selected cities such as Bristol and London. The reasons for the process are many. In essence it is a process involving young, middle-income, well-educated households who work and play in the central city. Unlike their predecessors they are not making the trek to the suburbs, their jobs and whole way of life is urban rather than suburban-orientated. The process has been lubricated by the property companies, realtors, developers and downtown business interests eager to benefit from trade. It has also been encouraged by certain city governments eager to increase their tax base. Gentrification is the mirror image of suburbanisation. And like suburbanisation it creates its own sets of conflicts. The most important is between the middle- and upper-income households and the displaced residents, as the low-income households are effectively forced out as rents and house prices escalate beyond their buying power.

A GUIDE TO FURTHER READING

There is a mass of literature on the housing market. But see:

Bassett, K. and Short, J.R. (1980), *Housing and Residential Structure*, Routledge & Kegan Paul, London.

Bourne, L.S. (1981), *The Geography of Housing*, Edward Arnold, London.

The literature on residential mobility is reviewed in:

Short, J.R. (1978), Residential mobility, *Progress in Human Geography*, 2, 419-47.

Descriptions of the residential mosaic include:

Johnston, R.J. (1971), *Urban Residential Patterns*, Bell, London.

Timms, D.W.G. (1971), *The Urban Mosaic*, Cambridge University Press.

While social segregation in urban space is examined by the papers in:

Peach, C. (ed.) (1975), *Urban Social Segregation*, Longmans, London.

Studies which analyse various social and political aspects of residential areas include:

Mollenkopf, J. (1981), Community and accummulation, In Dear, M. and Scott A.J. (eds), *Urbanization and Urban Planning in Capitalist Societies*, Methuen, London.

Robson, B. (1969), *Urban Analysis*, Cambridge University Press.

Taylor, P.J. and Johnston, R.J. (1979), *Geography of Elections*, Penguin, Harmondsworth.

There is an ocean of material on the major trends of suburbanisation, urban renewal and gentrification. See Bassett and Short (1980) and Bourne (1981).

Dip your toes in the following:

Anderson, M. (1965), *The Federal Bulldozer*, MIT Press, Cambridge, Mass.

Cybriwsky, R.A. (1980), Revitalization trends in downtown-area neighbourhoods, In Brunn, S.D. and Wheeler, J.O. (eds), *The American Metropolitan System*, Edward Arnold, London.

Muller, P.O. (1980), *The Outer City*, Prentice-Hall, Englewood Cliffs, N.J.

Short, J.R. (1982), *Housing in Britain: The Post-War Experience*, Methuen, London.

Walker, R.A. (1981), A theory of suburbanization: capitalism and the construction of urban space in the US, in Dear, M. and Scott, A.J. (eds), *Urbanization and Urban Planning in Capitalist Society*, Methuen, London.

8 Movement and Transport

CITY STRUCTURE AND URBAN TRANSPORT

There is a close relationship between urban structure and forms of transport. Transport opportunities and travel constraints give shape to the city, while the structure of the city affects the form and character of transport. There is a reciprocal relationship. This is not to say that transport causes changes in urban form. It is too facile to say that transport improvements, for example, cause urban expansion. They are a necessary precondition but not necessarily a cause. We can untangle some of the complex interrelationships by considering the sequence of urban growth in terms of dominant transport modes.

The pedestrian city

The first cities were pedestrian cities. Up until 1800 the dominant mode of urban transport was walking. Journeys to work were small, if non-existent, and the size of the cities was circumscribed. The limits of the spatial accretion to the city were severe and urban growth took the form of increasing densities rather than spatial extensions. Between 1780 and 1820 the city of Glasgow in Scotland quadrupled its population, but the extent of the city remained unchanged. Urban growth was felt in rising densities, further subdivisions of dwellings and increases in congestion.

The age of mass transit

The mid to late nineteenth century saw the beginnings of mass-transit systems. In Britain horse-drawn trams and buses first made their appearance on city streets in 1870. The capital city of London opened the first steam-powered underground railway in 1863 and the first electric-powered underground railway – the tube – in 1890. By the beginning of the First World War most major cities in North America and Western Europe had relatively cheap mass-transit systems in the form of electric trams, motor buses, railways and underground systems. In the USA the streetcar became an important part of the turn-of-the-century urban scene.

The age of mass transit was an age in which more and more people could travel further. The new transport systems were part cause and part effect of rapid urban growth and expansion. The effects of the new, cheaper transport modes were fivefold.

(1) Urban growth could now occur through spread as much as by density increases. And as city populations grew, cities expanded. Figures 8.1 and 8.2 show respectively the spread of Toronto and London.

(2) Transport movements allowed a growing separation between home and workplace. Mass

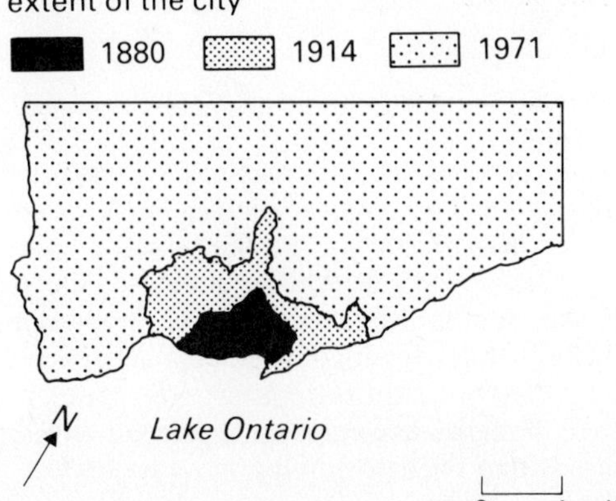

Figure 8.1 Growth of metropolitan Toronto

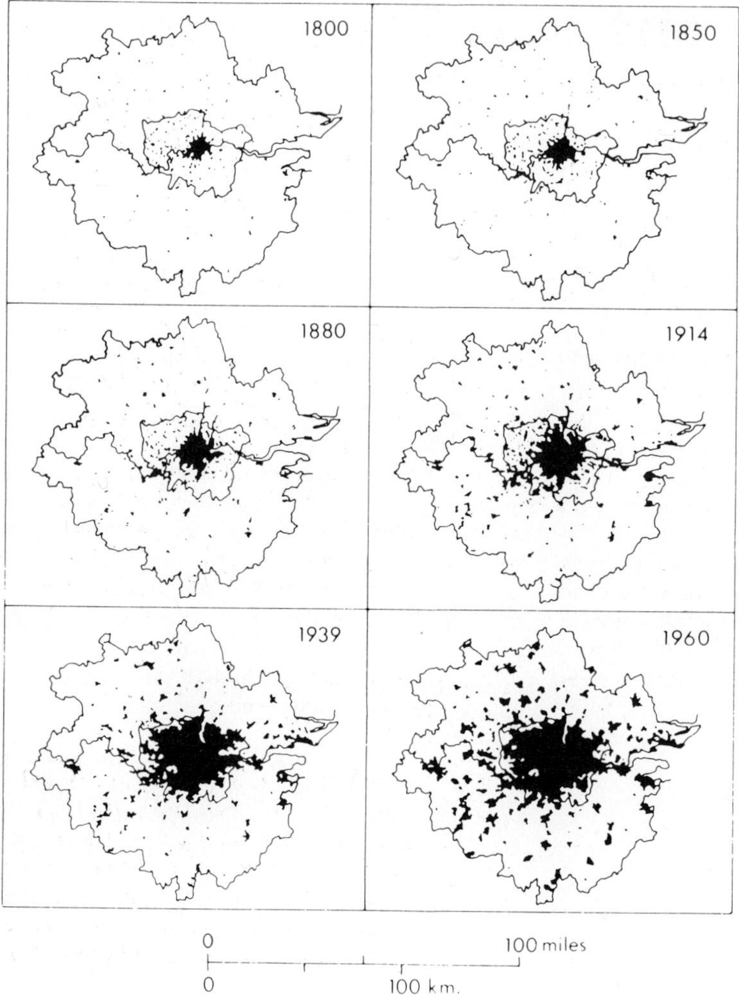

Figure 8.2 Growth of London. Notice how growth is limited after 1939. This is because of the use of greenbelt to reduce urban sprawl
Source: Hall, P. (1975), *Urban and Regional Planning*, Penguin, Harmondsworth

transit was a precondition of large-scale suburbanisation.

(3) This process of suburbanisation was not equally recorded amongst all sectors of the population, but was essentially an upper- and middle-income phenomenon. Within the streetcar suburbs there were subtle differences between neighbourhoods. Builder-developer-constructed, finely graded neighbourhoods and segregation of residents occurred both between the inner and outer city and also within the new suburbs.

(4) Because house construction could now occur at the periphery of the city, there was intense land speculation. The owners of the land which was converted from rural to residential use made substantial gains. The land market thus became the scene of intense activity. The process of residential development and land-use conversion became a highly profitable enterprise.

(5) Finally, the new transport systems became an important feature of the urban scene. They had a physical presence which was an important feature of the landscape and their construction had a huge impact on the immediate areas. The construction of railways in nineteenth-century London, for example, was perhaps the biggest single cause of dwelling demolition, community disruption and forced population relocation.

Table 8.1 City structure and dominant modes of transport

The pedestrian city >1800	limited spatial extent growth occurs through density increase movement is slow medium-distance travel is expensive
The mass transit city 1880 – 1920	increased spatial extent growth occurs through spatial extension movement is faster medium-distance travel becomes less expensive
The auto city 1920 – ?	wide spatial extent, growth of urban regions growth occurs through accretions at the periphery movement is normally fast, but slow at peak periods medium- to long-distance travel becomes relatively inexpensive

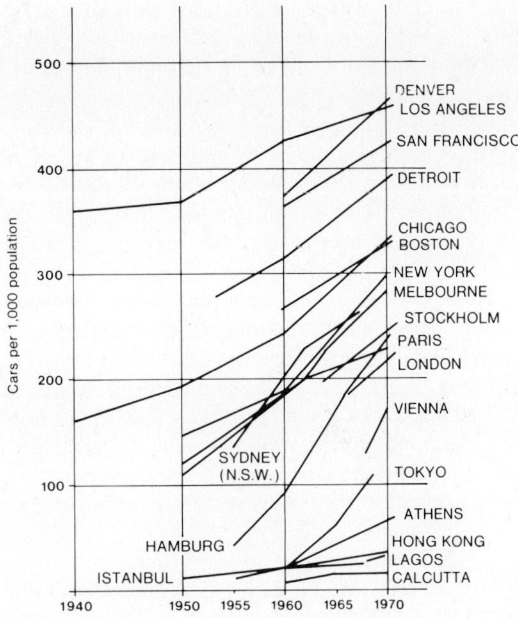

Figure 8.3 Rates of car ownership
Source: Thomson, J.M. (1977), p. 79

The coming of the automobile

In 1863 in the small town of Greenfield, Michigan, Henry Ford was born. His birth was not recorded at the time as a major event but in 1903, when Ford started his motor company, he set the scene for a dramatic change in twentieth-century living. His model T Ford was the first mass-produced motor car. The impact of the automobile has been enormous.

The twentieth-century North American city, and, to only a slightly lesser extent, the Western European city, is the city of the motor car. Since 1900 rates of car ownership have increased, and the shape of the city has been dramatically transformed. The automobile has extended the range of commuting and led to a further extension of urban areas. The city has now become an urban region in which the automobile allows the penumbra of the city to fall far beyond the administratively defined city limits. The automobile has been a precondition of large-scale suburbanisation which has been prompted by builder-developers, land speculators, auto and construction interests and the federal government. The impact of the automobile has been felt throughout the urban system. Its widespread use has been part cause and part effect of the highway-construction programme which has radically altered the appearance of cities and the lives of communities affected by the march of the motorways. The use of the motor car by a large number of individuals has increased individual

Table 8.2 Auto ownership in the US

Year	*Auto ownership ratio (population/auto registrations)*
1900	9511.3
1910	196.6
1920	13.1
1930	5.3
1940	4.8
1950	3.8
1960	2.9
1970	2.3
1980	1.4

Source: US Bureau of Census

mobility but also increased problems of congestion, energy conservation, pollution, traffic accidents and led to the decline of public transport systems in many cities. There have been marked redistributional consequences. Autos are expensive to buy and maintain. The poorest members of society cannot afford them, but because the life of the city moves at the beat of the motor car, people denied access to autos are denied accessibility to jobs and recreation.

At a certain stage the problem of the automobile cities may outweigh the advantages. If energy costs rise, congestion worsens and transport becomes more expensive, and slower forms of mass transport may then provide a partial solution. The automobile city will then become a thing of the cheap energy, non-ecologically conscious past, a brief period in the evolution of city structure.

POPULATION MOVEMENT IN THE CONTEMPORARY CITY

There are many types of movement. Goods, people and ideas move within and between cities. In this section we will concentrate on the movement of people.

Types of movement

People are always on the move. The prime reason for population movement in cities is the separation of activity centres. Within the home, for example, people move from bedroom to bathroom to kitchen in order to do different tasks, fulfil different functions and do different things. It is the same with movement outside the home. The greater the separation of activities within an urban area the greater the movement. The wider the spread of activities the longer the journeys.

Table 8.3 Types of movement

Home-based movements	*as % of all weekly trips*
Journey to and from work	32.5
Journey to and from social recreation centres	19.7
Journey to and from shop	8.4
Journey to and from school	3.3

The greatest amount of movement either begins or ends in the home. Although there are other types of movement, we will concentrate on this home-based type. We can identify four different forms. Their relative importance as discovered in a traffic study of Chicago is shown in Table 8.3 while their relative cost is illustrated in Table 8.4.

1 The journey to work The journey to work is based on the separation between home and workplace. This separation has increased as a function of suburbanisation, aided by land-use zoning which separates residential areas from industrial and commercial centres. The journey to work is a diurnal movement. People tend to leave for work

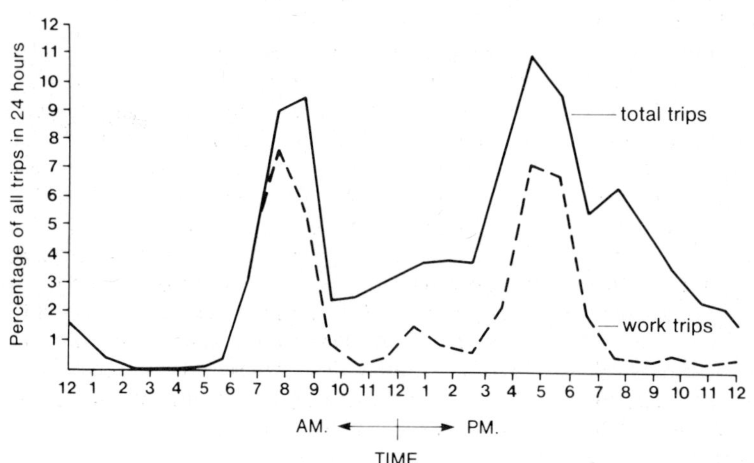

Figure 8.4 Work trips
Source: After Metropolitan Toronto and Region Transportation Study (1966), Toronto, Government of Ontario, Fig. 41

Plates 34 and 35 Routeways in the city: (34) a suburban railway in London; (35) a path in the old Scots town of Culross. The large stones in the middle were reserved for the local gentry; everyone else had to walk on the smaller stones

in the morning and return in the evening. Because workplaces and worktimes are concentrated, this produces a problem of congestion as people try to reach their workplaces at approximately the same time. A number of solutions have been proposed to solve the problem. We can consider just two. First, work times could be staggered. The use of flexi-time would enable people to travel at different times, thus spreading their load and lessening the congestion. Second, workplaces should be less concentrated. Much of the congestion arises because workplaces are concentrated in small areas. Many people are thus converging on restricted areas at the same time. If the workplaces could be separated, then congestion would be less. The difficulty with this solution is that it is difficult to move existing workplaces. There are powerful business interests at work and locational inertia is difficult to overcome.

2 **The journey to play** Much social activity takes place outside the home. People meet in bars, go to cinemas or the theatre or to football matches. These trips form almost 20 per cent of all urban trips. For adults and school children they are concentrated in the two periods of 11.30 to 2.30 and in the evening from 6.00 to 12.00 peaking at 8.00 p.m. Again congestion may occur as people converge at selected recreational points at similar times. For pre-school children the journey to play is a constant activity outside the home as they explore and recreate urban environments.

3 **The journey to shop** Shopping trips tend to be shorter than either journeys to work or to play and they are more evenly spread throughout the working day, although shoppers tend to travel further for higher-order goods and very expensive items. The journey to shop has been radically transformed from the early part of this century as the widespread distribution of small retail centres has been replaced by the concentrated location of large centres. The ultimate expression of this tendency is the large out-of-town hypermarket. This distribution disadvantages those households located far from the big stores and without access to good transport facilities.

URBAN TRANSPORT MODELS

Mathematical models of the urban system have been developed on a large scale since 1945. These models describe aspects of cities through mathematical equations in order to simulate urban spatial structure and urban spatial processes. They have been developed in order to predict likely outcomes and to evaluate the effect of new developments, e.g. the traffic generated by a new hypermarket, a rise in petrol prices, etc.

Let us consider two types of urban transport model which have been developed. The first is the *doubly constrained transport model* which allocates activities to zones and determines the journey-to-work trips (termed 'interaction' in the literature) between zones. The general form is:

$$Tij = A_i \, B_j \, O_i \, D_j \, f\,(cij) \qquad (1)$$

where

$$Ai = (\Sigma \, B_j \, D_j \, f\,(Cij))^{-1} \qquad (2)$$

$$Bj = (\Sigma Ai \, O_i \, f\,(cij))^{-1} \qquad (3)$$

with

Tij = trips from origin zone i to destination j
O_i = trips generated from origin zone i
D_j = trips attracted to destination zone j
cij = a measure of the cost of travelling between zones i and j
f (cij) = some function of travel cost, generally $\exp(-\lambda cij)$ where λ is a parameter

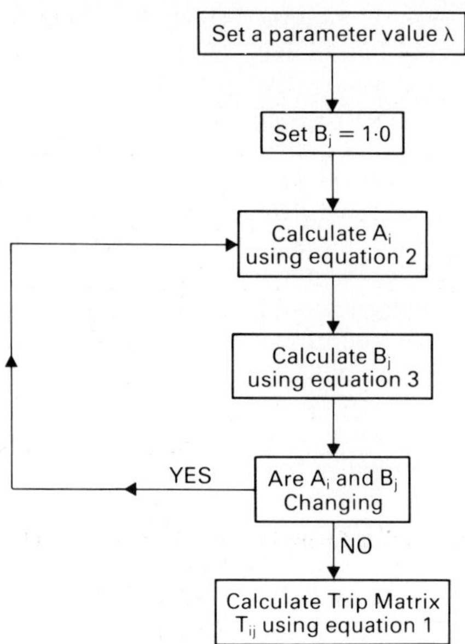

Figure 8A The iterative procedure for solving the doubly constrained model

The model is used in the manner shown in Figure 8A, and the actual and estimated trip patterns are compared. The model is then used to predict travel patterns at future dates. The trip patterns can then be assigned to the road networks to show where congestion may occur and how new transport networks can best be developed.

The second type of model is formulated as a *linear programming model.* This type of model seeks to find the optimal distribution of trip movements (Tij) in order to minimise the overall travel costs or journey times. This is done in the following manner. Assume three residential areas with a journey-to-work pattern and travel times as shown in Tables 8A and 8B. (The example is taken from Foot, 1981.)

Table 8A The journey-to-work trip matrix

	Residential zone			
Work zone	*A*	*B*	*C*	*Totals*
A	3530	1110	180	4820
B	440	1690	50	2180
C	150	60	190	400
Totals	4120	2860	420	7400

Table 8B The travel times (minutes) between 3 zones

	Residential zone		
Work zone	*A*	*B*	*C*
A	1.4	5.2	5.6
B	5.2	1.8	10.7
C	5.6	10.7	1.3

The notation for the zones used in this formulation is shown in Table 8C

Table 8C The formulation of the transport problem

	Residential zone			
Work zone	*A*	*B*	*C*	*Totals*
A	T11	T12	T13	4820
B	T21	T22	T23	2180
C	T31	T32	T33	400
Totals	4120	2860	420	7400

The aim is to minimise

$$Z = 1.4T_{11} + 5.2T_{12} + 5.6T_{13} + 5.2T_{21} + 1.8T_{22} + 10.7T_{23} + 5.6T_{31} + 10.7T_{32} + 1.3T_{33} \qquad (4)$$

Subject to

$$\begin{aligned} T_{11} + T_{12} + T_{13} &= 4820 \\ T_{21} + T_{22} + T_{23} &= 2180 \\ T_{31} + T_{32} + T_{33} &= 400 \\ T_{11} + T_{21} + T_{31} &= 4120 \\ T_{12} + T_{22} + T_{32} &= 2860 \end{aligned}$$

and $T_{11}, T_{12}, T_{13}, T_{21}, T_{22}, T_{31}, T_{32}, T_{33}, \geqslant 0$.

Using the simplex method of minimising Z we get the following results –

Table 8D The optimal journey-to-work pattern to minimise overall travel time

	Residential zone			
Work zone	*A*	*B*	*C*	*Totals*
A	4120	680	20	4820
B	0	2180	0	2180
C	0	0	400	400
Totals	4120	2860	420	7400

The comparison of actual and optimal travel times is shown in Table 8E.

Table 8E Actual and optimal travel times

	Actual (Table 8A)	*Optimal (Table 8C)*
Total travel time	19,316 minutes	13,860 minutes
average travel time	2.6 minutes	1.87 minutes

This type of exercise can be used to plan the location of employment centres and new housing areas in order to achieve optimal journey to work patterns. In an energy-scarce world the ability to minimise travelling is an important one.

References

The best general introduction to urban models and modelling is:
Foot, D. (1981), *Operational Urban Models*, Methuen, London.

More advanced texts include:
Batty, M. (1976), *Urban Modelling: Algorithms, Calibrations, Predictions*, Cambridge University Press.
Wilson, A.G. (1974), *Urban and Regional Models in Geography and Planning*, Wiley, London.

For a critique of this methodology see:
Sayer, A. (1979), A Critique of Urban Modelling, *Progress in Planning*, 6, 187-254.

4 The journey to school All of you reading this book will have experienced this type of trip. It is an age-specific journey occurring at specific times.

Modes of travel

There is a variety of modes of travel. *Walking or running* is the most convenient for very short trips. It is perhaps the healthiest form of travel and definitely the least polluting. It becomes less feasible the larger the distance to be covered. *The bicycle* is a useful form of transport for short to medium distances. This is another healthy form of transport in principle but in practice, with roads dominated by cars, it can be a dangerous way of getting about. There are cities in Western Europe and Asia where it is the predominant form of personal movement. The *automobile* is used most for short to long trips. It is a convenient form of personal transport but it requires land for roads, it uses up non-renewable resources, it pollutes the atmosphere and promotes urban sprawl. There is variety of *mass-transit schemes* including buses, trams, subways and tubes. They are less energy wasteful than automobiles and cheaper though not so convenient.

The breakdown of movement by the different modes of transport is termed *modal split*. The modal split will depend upon the length and purpose of the journey to be made and the type of transport available. The journey-to-work modal split, for example, in the USA in 1975 and the UK in 1971, is shown in Table 8.5. Notice the much larger percentage of journeys by private transport in the USA compared to the UK. This reflects the general affluence of the USA, the direction of

Table 8.4 Illustrative costs of urban travel by different modes

	Speed miles per hour	*Persons per foot width per hour*	*Total costs* per person US cents per mile*
Footway, 4 feet wide	2.1	1,100	negligible
Bicycle track, 4 feet wide	8	450	0.3
Urban street, 44 feet wide, mixed traffic			
Car with driver only	15	39	16.5
Taxi with 4 passengers	12	160	4.3
Minibus with 10 passengers	10	190	2.7
Bus with 30 passengers	8.6	410	2.0
Urban expressway (capacity per foot-width is independent of width)			
Car with driver only	40	180	16.4
Taxi with 4 passengers	40	720	4.1
Minibus with 10 passengers	40	1,200	2.6
Bus with 40 passengers	40	2,000	1.5
Metro (22,500 passengers per hour)	21	1,700	3.9
Urban railway (22,500 passengers per hour)	30	1,700	2.2

*Includes total capital costs, track maintenance costs and vehicle operating costs.

Note: The figures used in this table, like all assumptions, need to be treated with caution. Their calculations can be found in World Bank (1975) *Urban Transport: Sector Policy Paper,* Washington, D.C.

transport planning and the successful lobbying in the US of the highway construction-auto industries. These figures are of course aggregates. Within the UK there are even substantial variations in modal split figures between the major cities. Table 8.6 shows the variation between three of them. Notice two things:

(1) The different proportions going to work by public and private transport. Central Clydeside has the highest public transport component.
(2) The differences between the two broad categories of public and private transport. The highest proportion of people travelling by public transport in London do so by train; in the west Midlands and Clydeside, in contrast, buses are of greater importance.

While the different modes may be complementary (e.g. people may drive their car or take a bus to the local railway station, take a train and then a subway before walking to their appointment) there is often modal conflict within cities. This conflict takes a number of forms. First, there is the conflict generated between on the one hand builders and users and on the other, neighbourhoods affected by attempts to secure the routes for certain types of transport modes. The mirror image of the creation of auto suburbs is the destruction of inner-city areas in order to make room for freeways and urban highways. Much of local

Table 8.5 Modal split of journey to work (%)

	UK (1971)	*USA (1975)*
Public transport	31.9	6.2
train*	6.2	1.9
bus**	24.8	3.8
other	0.9	0 1
Private transport	37.3	84.6
car	35.8	73.2
other	1.5	11.4
Other modes	30.6	9.2
walk/none	20.3	7.9
bike	4.2	1.3
other	6.3	
total	99.8	100

* Includes subways, electric rail and railroads.
** Includes streetcars.

Totals do not necessarily add up to 100 because of rounding.

urban politics in the 1960s and 1970s in the major cities of the Western world revolved around community attempts to fight the motorway solutions to urban transport problems. Doug Hart (1976), for example, shows the rise and fall of the motorway transport plan in London in the early 1970s in relation to community struggles and local elections.

Second, there is also the conflict between the different users and adherents of different modes. This tension occurs because the different modes are often seen as conflicting. The encouragement of individual motor transport in the USA has meant the steady decline, at least until recently, of mass-transit systems. This has occurred because, as more people travel by private automobile, the costs to the remaining users increases. Unless there is a subsidy the increase in cost makes it an even less attractive mode of transport. In many cities in the advanced capitalist countries, particularly in North America, mass-transit systems have seen a downward spiral of decline in demand→increase in costs→less service→less customers→increase in costs→decline in demand.

The choices which individuals make are structured by business interests and the state. The automobile has become an attractive mode of transport because the full costs – including construction and maintenance of highways, provision of traffic police, costs of accidents, environmental costs – are not met by the individual user. In North America the costs of private transport are socialised while the benefits accrue to the individual user. With public transport, the costs are borne by the individual user. In many Western European cities,

Table 8.6 Modal split of journey to work

	Greater London	*Central Clydeside*	*West Midlands*
Public transport	49.8	53.9	35.9
train	27.8	7.7	1.5
bus	20.5	45.1	33.3
other	1.5	1.1	1.1
Private transport	28.5	25.6	38.4
car	27.4	25.4	37.4
other	1.1	0.2	1.0
Other modes	21.7	20.4	25.7
walk/none	15.2	17.2	18.6
bike	2.0	0.5	2.5
other	4.5	2.7	4.6
Total	100	99.9	100

Totals do not necessarily add up to 100 because of rounding.

Table 8F Major forms of urban transportation

Type	*Advantages*	*Disadvantages*
1 Walking or running	Freedom of movement Convenient for short trips Free Provides exercise Conserves energy and matter resources Requires very little land Non-polluting	Slow and difficult for long trips No protection from weather, noise, and air pollution
2 Bicycle	Freedom of movement Convenient Just as fast as car in urban trips less than 8 km (5 miles) Very inexpensive to buy and operate Provides exercise Conserves energy and resources Requires little land Non-polluting	Rider not sheltered from weather, noise, and air pollution Carries only 1 or 2 persons Less protection from injury Slow for trips greater than 8 km (5 miles)
3 Motorcycle and moped	Freedom of movement Convenient Less expensive to buy and operate than car Uses and wastes less matter and energy resources than car Requires relatively little land Less pollution than car	Rider not sheltered from weather, noise, and air pollution Carries only 1 or 2 persons Less protection from injury
4 Automobile and taxi	Freedom of movement (door-to-door service) Convenient Can carry one or several people	Requires much land (highways, parking areas, etc.) Wastes energy and matter resources Pollutes air Promotes urban sprawl Increasingly expensive to buy and operate or to hire
Mass transit		
Railroad and subway (heavy rail systems)	Handles large number of passengers Rapid once boarded and if on time Safer than car Fairly inexpensive for rider Uses fewer matter and energy resources than car Requires much less land than car Less pollution than car	Economically feasible only along heavily populated routes Lacks door-to-door service Fixed routes

Type	*Advantages*	*Disadvantages*
Trolley and streetcar (light rail systems)	Handles large number of passengers Fairly rapid once boarded and if on time Safer than car Fairly inexpensive for rider Uses fewer energy and matter resources than car Requires less land than car Relatively little pollution if electric Cheaper to build and operate than railroad and subway	Economically feasible only along heavily populated routes Lacks door-to-door service Fixed routes
Bus	Handles large number of passengers More flexible routes than railroad and trolley Safer than car Fairly inexpensive for rider Uses fewer energy and matter resources than car Requires less land than car Normally cheaper to build and operate than railroads	Lacks door-to-door service Fairly restricted freedom of movement Can be crowded and noisy Pollutes air
Para transit		
Carpools and vanpools	Carries small group of people Saves money Wastes fewer energy and matter resources than car Provides social interaction	Fairly inconvenient Promotes urban sprawl Restricts freedom of movement Requires much land Pollutes air
Dial-a-ride (mini-buses, vans, and shared taxicab systems)	Handles small to moderate number of passengers Safer than car Moderately inexpensive for rider Usually provides door-to-door service Uses fewer energy and matter resources than car Requires less land than car Cheaper to build and operate than railroad Very useful for the poor, young, elderly, and handicapped	Can require long waits Can be crowded and noisy Pollutes air

by contrast, the costs of public transport are socialised in the form of subsidies. And in these cities, the integrated Paris metro and bus system, for example, public transport is used much more and is an attractive mode of transport.

Table 8.4 attempts to show the different costs of the different modes of urban transport. While walking is the cheapest form of transport, it is the slowest. But notice how individual car driving is by far the most expensive form of transport. In terms of total costs personal car driving is far and away the costliest mode of urban transport. Mass-transit systems are cheaper and in terms of moving persons per hour much more efficient. Now these figures have to be treated with caution, as they are based on a series of assumptions. What they suggest, rather than prove, is that the benefits of mass-transit systems perhaps outweigh the costs of the private automobile.

ACCESSIBILITY

In large urban areas there is a separation of activities. Jobs tend to be located away from homes, shops and cultural facilities. The ease with which a household can overcome the distances between the different centres of activity can be termed a measure of its accessibility. Accessibility is an important factor in any consideration of quality of life. Accessibility is a resource and an element in the real income of households. As a rough generalisation, we can note that the greater the accessibility the greater the power over resources. People who can move easily around the urban area can buy at the cheapest shops, look for the best value for housing and can search widely for jobs. As the distribution of activities has become further separated and public transport has declined, then accessibility has become increasingly a function of car ownership. There is a fundamental difference between car-owning and non-car-owning households. The distribution of cars, like the distribution of other consumer goods, reflects the distribution of income. Richer households have more cars and thus greater accessibility. Even within car-owning households, however, the very young, the very old and the unlucky do not have access to an automobile. Household car-ownership is not the same thing as personal car availability. In Britain, work for the Political and Economic Planning group has shown how levels of car access are much lower than simple car-ownership rates would suggest. Hillman et al. (1973, 1976) found that in a typical inner London district, while the percentage of car-owning households was 43, only 26 per cent of adults had access to a car. The position for young people and particularly adolescents is especially bad.

As public transport has worsened and activities centres continue to separate out then problems of accessibility loom large. As jobs, shops, services and better educational facilities have moved outwards, then those trapped in the inner city have seen a deterioration in their life chances. In the suburbs those with poor access find it difficult to move widely through the urban area and even in better-off households individual members of a family may be denied good accessibility. As the life of the city speeds up and disperses outwards, accessibility becomes both a function and a reflection of real income.

TRANSPORT PROBLEMS

In an important book the transport expert Michael Thomson (1977) has identified seven major sets of transport problems in the large cities of capitalist countries. They are:

Traffic congestion caused by the large number of vehicles in relation to the capacity of the road network. This programme is particularly acute at peak periods. Peak-hour traffic speeds in city centres are now approximately 16 kilometres per hour.

Accidents on urban roads are a serious problem. Table 8.7 gives a comparative estimate of road accidents. These figures conceal the large amount of non-fatal injuries, the need for costly medical facilities and the depth of the anguish caused. In 1978 alone, 52,653 people died in the USA from motor vehicle accidents.

Public transport The problems for public transport systems are: (a) inadequate financing which makes even more difficult the problem of (b) the widely fluctuating demand of peak-hour crowding which involves heavy investment in rolling stock with a subsequent lack of use in non-peak periods generating little income.

Table 8.7 Road accidents in metropolitan areas

City	*Deaths per 100,000 population*
Los Angeles	17.5
Detroit	14.7
Chicago	10.5
Paris	12.5
London	10.2
Tokyo	7.2
Manila	8.4
Karachi	8.6

Pedestrians The city is being shaped and planned for motor cars and it lacks pedestrian accessibility and pedestrian facilities. Walking and to some extent bicycling are and could be important forms of transport, especially for short distances. Yet transport schemes are built for roads and cars not for people as walkers. As Thomson notes:

> Most of the people professionally responsible for urban transport are car owners and drive to their offices everyday. The most powerful transport authorities are usually highway engineering departments occupying premises provided free parking space to which most of the senior staff commute by car. The senior managers of public transport companies are more likely to arrive by car than by one of their own buses. And one of the first tasks of a team of consultants engaged to undertake an urban transport study is to acquire a fleet of private cars. It is beyond dispute that most important decisions affecting urban transport are made by people whose personal viewpoint of the problem is largely behind the wheel of a car. (Thomson, 1977, p. 15)

Environmental impact The growth of motor vehicles in urban areas has caused the twin problems of air pollution and noise pollution.

Parking Automobiles are not always on the move. Their stationary position takes up space and the more cars there are the greater the space taken up. Parking difficulties are greatest in the central city where there is the disparity between the number of parking spaces and the number of cars. Limitations on car parking have been used to indirectly limit the number of cars coming into the central city areas. In contrast *park and ride* schemes involve a collar being placed around the central city area beyond which private automobiles are discouraged. There are transit places at various points around the collar in which car drivers can park and then ride into the centre on a bus.

Although the mix of these problems may vary, most large cities in capitalist countries suffer from severe traffic congestion especially at peak periods, the inadequacy of parking spaces, failing public transport systems, poor conditions for pedestrians, environmental pollution and unacceptable accident rates. These problems have been

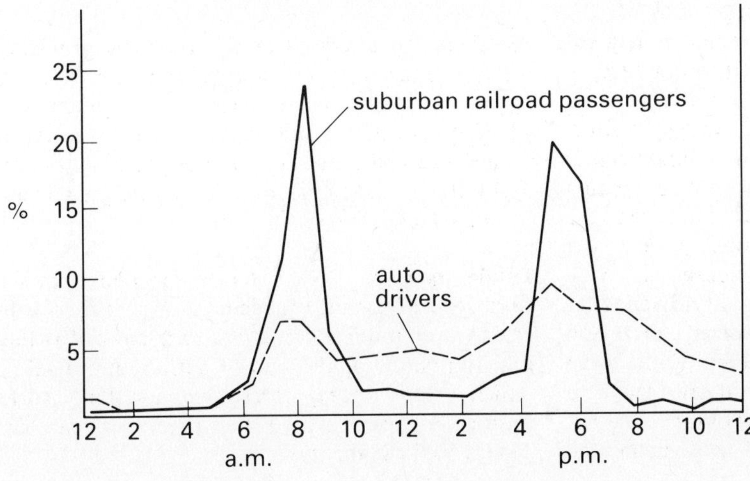

Figure 8.5 The peaking of public transport modes compared to private autos

ACCESSIBILITY

The urban area can be seen as a surface of opportunity. The location of jobs determines the spatial pattern of employment opportunities while the location of schools and health facilities determines the spatial pattern of educational and medical opportunities. People in different places are differentially located with respect to these centres and thus have different degrees of accessibility. A great deal of work has been done on measuring access to public locations such as health clinics, etc. We can measure this accessibility by determining *access opportunity scores* using the formula,

$$A_{oi} = \Sigma \frac{S_j}{t^{b_{ij}}} \qquad -(1)$$

where

A_{oi} is the access opportunity at i
S_j is the size of facility j (in employee hours or some other measure)
t is the distance and/or time taken to travel from residential location i to j
b = an exponent

The larger the scores the greater the accessibility.

Drs Andrew Kirby and Kelvin Jones, working at the University of Reading, have used this equation (with b=1) to measure the access opportunity of people in Reading to the primary health facilities of doctors and dentists. Figures 8B and 8D show the distribution of doctors and dentists (the S_j in equation (1)) and Figures 8C and 8E show the distribution of respective access opportunity scores computed for each enumeration district. Notice how those living in the central areas have better access than those living on the periphery of the city. Figure 8F picks out those places where people are living more than 1 km from both doctors and dentists. These areas comprise 28,000 people.

The differences in accessibility relate to spatial patterns but they have definite *social outcomes*. The maldistribution of resources affects both individual and group welfare.

References

Jones, K. and Kirby, A.M. (1982), Provision and wellbeing: an agenda for public resources research, *Environment and Planning A*.

More general treatments are:

Hodgart, R.L. (1978), Optimising access to public services, *Progress in Human Geography*, 2, 17-48.

Massam, B. (1975), *Location and space in social administration*, Edward Arnold, London.

Smith, D.M. (1977), *Human Geography: A Welfare Approach*, Edward Arnold, London.

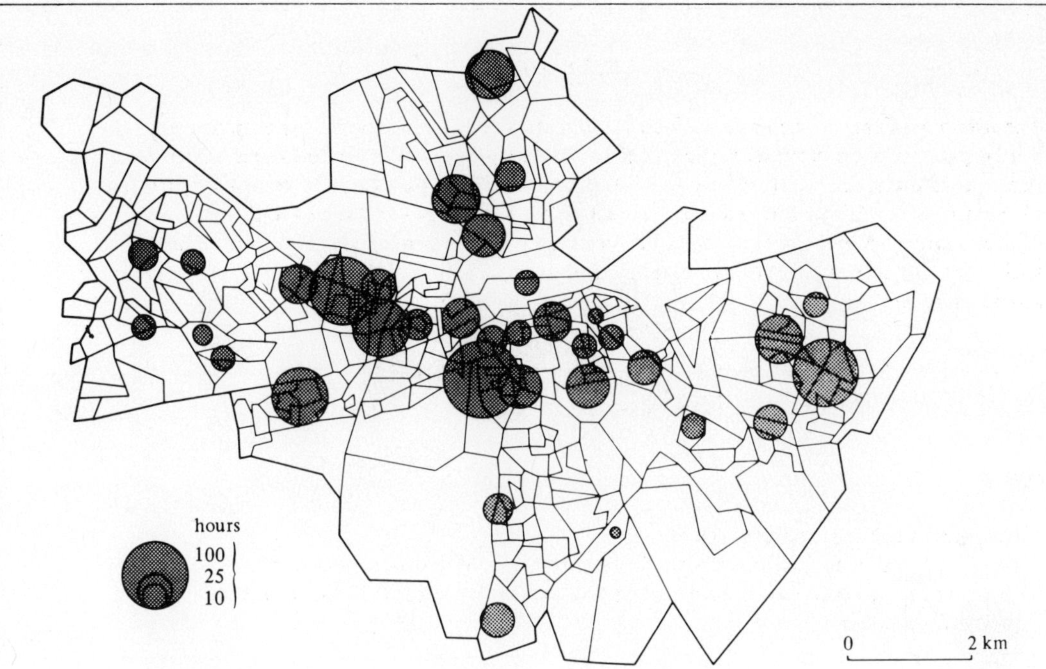

Figure 8B Distribution of general medical practitioners by number of hours worked per week
Source (8B-8F): Jones and Kirby (1982)

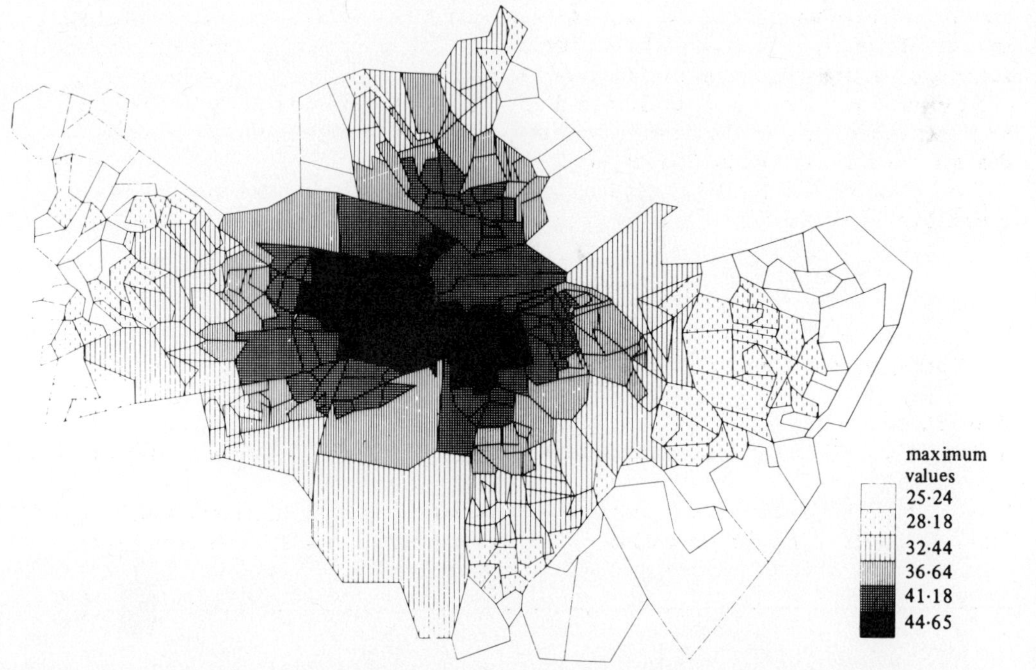

Figure 8C Distribution of access opportunity scores for general medical practitioners

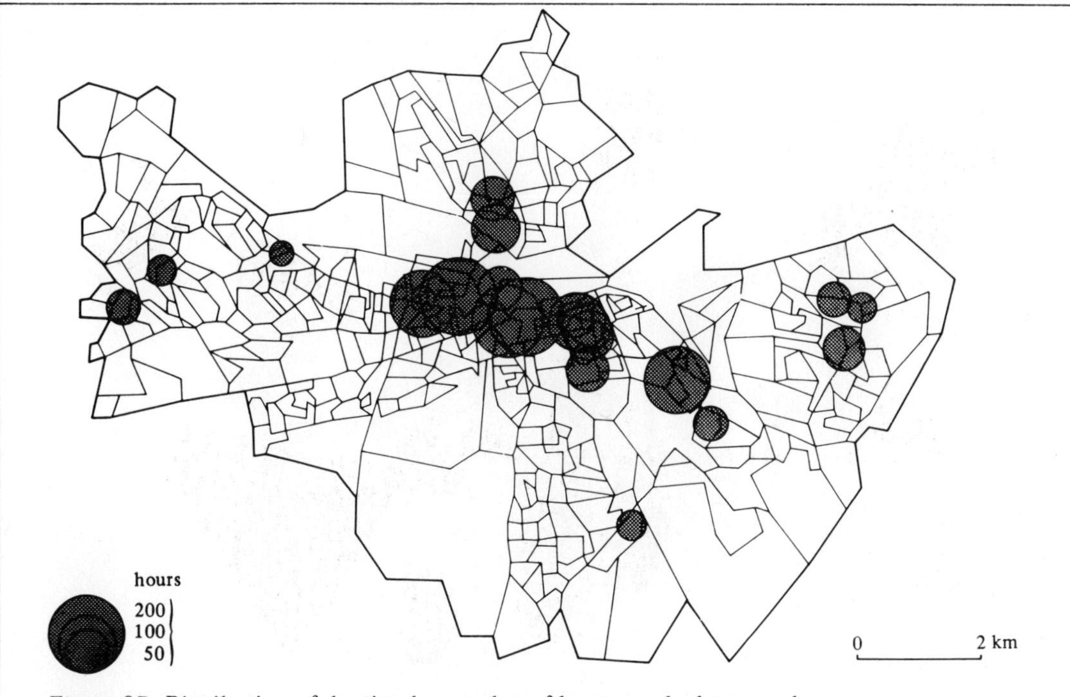

Figure 8D Distribution of dentists by number of hours worked per week

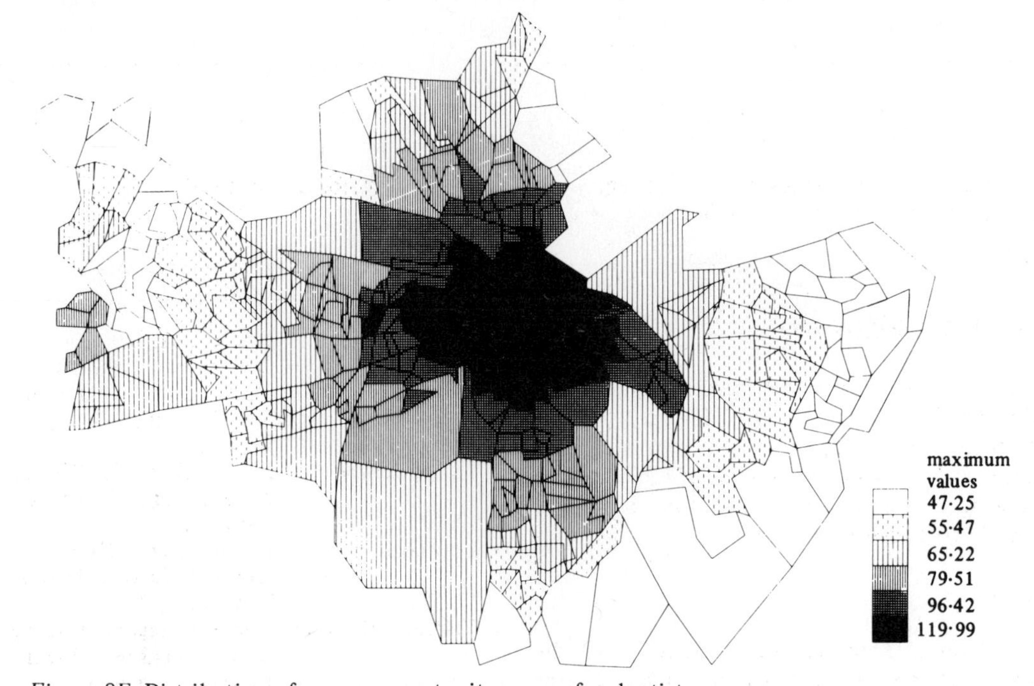

Figure 8E Distribution of access opportunity scores for dentists

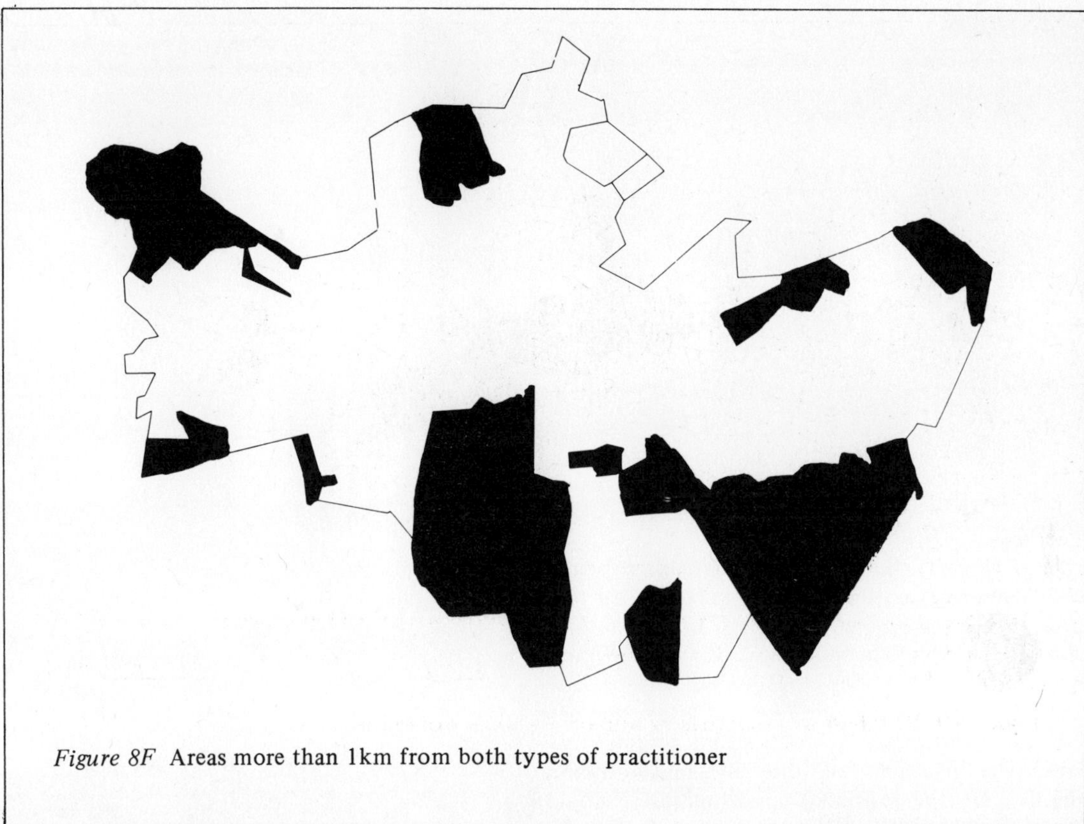

Figure 8F Areas more than 1km from both types of practitioner

made worse as car ownership and use increases and the decline of public transport continues apace.

TRANSPORT SOLUTIONS

There are as many transport solutions as there are urban problems. The difference between policies reflects differences in pressure-group activity, past history and present socio-economic conditions. Following Thomson we can identify five major types of urban transport solutions.

1 Full motorisation

A full motorisation solution implies that the private automobile becomes the main source of transport, there is a large enough motorway

Table 8.8 Urban transport policies

Policy	*Exemplar cities*
1 Full motorisation	Los Angeles, Detroit, Denver, Salt Lake City
2 Weak centre	Melbourne, Copenhagen, San Francisco, Chicago, Boston
3 Strong centre	Paris, Tokyo, New York, Athens, Toronto, Sydney, Hamburg
4 Low cost	Bogota, Lagos, Calcutta, Istanbul, Karachi, Manila, Teheran
5 Traffic limitations	London, Singapore, Hong Kong, Stockholm, Vienna, Bremen, Göteberg

Plates 36 and 37
Banishing the car: pedestrianisation schemes in (36) Sweden, and (37) Perth, West Australia

system to carry the peak loads and there is no one dominant centre. The archetypal case is Los Angeles, where a system of urban motorways (the first urban motorway was built in Los Angeles in 1941) ties together the dispersed activity centres. A precondition and a function of full motorisation is a lack of a strong central city area. The problems of the full motorisation solution are the restricted opportunities to non-drivers, and over half of Los Angeles's population have either no car or limited access to a car. Moreover, the heavy auto usage is a polluting and wasteful form of transport, in terms of non-renewable resources.

2 Weak centre

There are powerful centrifugal tendencies in capitalist cities; the outward spread of jobs and retail establishments has lessened the pull of the central area. Where the central area is still of some restricted importance, the transport patterns follow the weak-centre strategy which is a balance between railroads and freeways leading into the centre and of freeways linking the large number of suburban centres. The weak-centre pattern can be seen as a transition catagory capturing the experience of cities as they move from the strong centre to the full motorisation pattern. The problems found in this type of urban-transport solution include the expense of the commuter railroad system because of peaking.

3 Strong centre

As the name implies, in strong-centre cities the central area dominates the employment, commercial and retail structure of the urban area.

Plates 38 and 39
Transport experiments: (38) a bus lane in Marin County, California; (39) a railway-road conversion in Edinburgh

The transport system is designed to carry people in and out of the central area by both rail and road and there is very little provision for radial routes. Because of the heavy demand public transport systems are important. The main problem with these strong-centre structures is the very high loading and consequent congestion at peak periods.

4 Low cost

In third-world countries the mass of population are poor and cannot afford a car. Expensive transport schemes or the full motorisation solution are thus out of the question. Thomson suggests that the archetypal low-cost strategy should be one in which the city is kept within narrowly circumscribed boundaries and existing roads are used to carry people cheaply on buses and trams. At present there is no perfect example of a low-cost strategy. The transport policies like other policies in the periphery are devised and implemented by a small urban elite who express a life-style and a set of preferences which have little resemblance to the experience of the rest of the population.

MASS-TRANSIT SYSTEMS

Most mass-transit systems of transport – railways, subways, buses, trams and tubes – make a loss. While there is a need for such systems in capitalist societies no corporation will invest because no profits can be made. Most mass transit systems are thus owned by the state, the local authority or some representative board.

Two things make such systems expensive to operate. First, because of the heavy load at peak periods there is a need for large amounts of rolling stock and handling capacity which outside of peak periods is not used. Second, there has been a steady shift from public mass-transit systems to private forms of transport, particularly the automobile. Many public transport systems are caught in a downward spiral of losing customers, which makes it even more expensive for the remaining passengers, which makes private transport an even more attractive proposition. But since private transport cannot meet all the transport requirements there is still a role for the publicly owned mass-transit systems.

Recent years have seen something of a revival of mass-transit systems as would-be transport solutions. In London the Jubilee underground line was opened in May 1979 and the city of Newcastle in England saw the construction of a new metro system of underground railway, opened in 1980. One of the largest systems of recent years was the Bay Area Rapid Transit (BART) scheme built in San Francisco. A case for a rapid transit system in the Bay Area was first made in a consultant's report in 1956. After the three counties of San Francisco, Alameda and Contra Costa gave their endorsement (San Mateo and Marin counties rejected the proposals), the scheme began construction in 1962. It was to be a new space-age-technology type of mass transit in which air-conditioned, lavishly carpeted trains would glide elegantly along tracks driven by computers, passing through plush, architect-designed stations. There were technical snags and the costs escalated. In January 1971 the total costs of BART had risen to $1.6 billion. The system began to take paying passengers in 1972. In practice the scheme did not live up to expectations and in 1976 only 51 per cent of the forecast population was being carried by the elegant carpeted train. People did not give up their cars so easily. In the year 1977-8 the taxpayer was paying $2 for every $1 raised in fares.

We can draw a number of conclusions from the BART experience. First, new mass-transit schemes are expensive. They therefore have to be costed more effectively. Second, big schemes have high capital and running costs, and they are risky propositions. So much money is put into one scheme that if this scheme is unsuccessful then the initial capital investment is lost and running costs constitute an open-ended commitment to lose more money.

A choice can often be made between the large schemes which **may** provide the answer but could cost a fortune and a series of small schemes, such as bicycle routes, making it easier for people to form carpools, etc., which cost less, and are thus less risky. The small scheme never attracts the broad popular appeal. Big schemes, in contrast, fire the political imagination. But perhaps in transport policy as much as in other areas of life, small is beautiful.

5 Traffic limitations

Traffic-limitation schemes seek to minimise the volume of traffic by reducing the need to travel. This is done first by creating and maintaining a hierarchy of centres – at the base are the neighbourhood centres serving the local community, then there are suburban centres where much routine shopping is done, and the sector centres where major shopping centres coexist with office employment. Major corporations are located and very specialist shopping centres are found in the city centre.

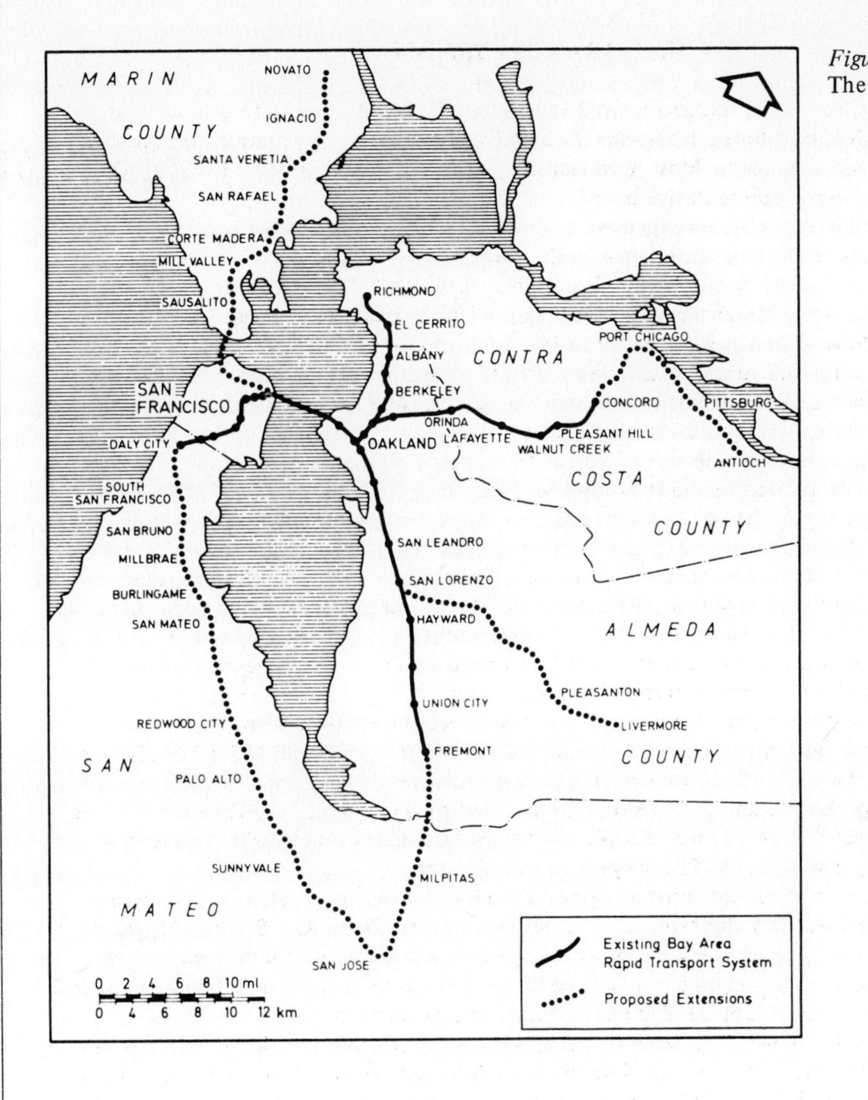

Figure 8G
The BART System

References

Hall, P. (1980), *Great Planning Disasters*, Weidenfeld & Nicolson, London.

Second, it can be achieved by introducing a series of traffic-control measures such as high parking charges, prohibition of cars from a large number of certain streets, priority lanes for buses, cyclists and pedestrians.

The traffic-limitation solution implies good public transport systems. Because of peaking there is a need for some form of subsidy to the public transport system. The political debate over the size of the subsidy to public transport is the main urban transport debate in cities where the traffic-limitation strategy has been used.

The five schemes are ideal types. In practice no one city fulfils all the archetypal requirements. Transport policies in individual cities are likely to consist of a variety of schemes of varying success. It is important to realise, however, that transport solutions are not technical solutions. Despite the hard technical base of empirical analysis and civil engineering expertise transport policies are political choices. They are not the inexorable conclusion drawn from technical considerations. Transport policies are devised by people and reflect material interests. The different transport solutions have a differing mix of costs and benefits to different sections of the community. The full motorisation scheme, for example, benefits highway construction/auto industries and car owners in an energy-rich society. It works against poor households without access to a motor car. The strong-centre solution, in contrast, aids businesses and institutions with interests and especially land-use interests in the existing central area. Transport policies have distinct redistributional consequences.

GUIDE TO FURTHER READING

The best general introduction to urban transport is given by:

Thomson, J.M. (1977), *Great Cities and their Traffic*, Victor Gollancz, London.

Other general introductions include:

Daniels, P.W. and Warnes, A.M. (1980), *Movement in Cities*, Methuen, London.

Rothenberg, J.G. and Heggie, I.G. (1974), *Transport and the Urban Environment*, Macmillan, London.

There is a huge literature on the role of motorways and automobiles, the following is only a very small sample:

Brown, L.R., Flavin, C. and Norman, C. (1979), *The Future of the Automobile in an Oil-Short World*, World Watch Paper 32.

Roth, G. (1972), *Paying for Roads*, Penguin, Harmondsworth.

Townroe, P.M. (ed.) (1974), *Social and Political Consequences of the Motor Car*, David & Charles, Newton Abbott.

Tyme, J. (1978), *Motorways Versus Democracy*, Macmillan, London.

Interesting studies of transport planning include:

Adams, J.G.U. (1981), *Transport Planning: Vision and Practice*, Routledge & Kegan Paul, London.

Grant, J. (1977), *The Politics of Urban Transport Planning*, Earth Resources Research Publicasions, London.

Hart, D.A. (1976), *Strategic Planning in London: The Rise and Fall of the Primary Road Network*, Pergamon, Oxford.

Owen, W. (1976), *Transportation for Cities*, Brookings Institute, Washington, D.C.

Starkie, D. (1982), *The Motorway Age*, Pergamon, Oxford.

Some of the relationships between transport and accessibility are covered by:

Owen, W. (1972), *The Accessible City*, Brookings Institute, Washington, D.C.

Schaeffer, K.M. and Scalar, E. (1975), *Access For All: Transportation and Urban Growth*, Penguin, Harmondsworth.

Hillman, M., Henderson, I. and Whalley, D. (1973), *Personal Mobility and Transport Policy*, Broadsheet 542, Political and Economic Planning, London.

Hillman, M., Henderson, I. and Whalley, D. (1976), *Transport Realities and Planning Policy*, Broadsheet 567, Political and Economic Planning, London.

Urban transport matters are covered by papers published in *Traffic Quarterly* and *Transportation Research.*

9 The City as Investment

In capitalist societies many things become commodities to be bought and sold at a profit. What in pre-capitalist times were prized for their use value become measured by their exchange value in capitalist society. This happens to urban land and buildings and signals the development of places as if money mattered. In this chapter we will be concerned with the character and effects of the use of urban land and property as investment. We will note two important aspects: the impact of past patterns of investment and the character of contemporary ones.

BUILDING CYCLES

We can imagine the urban property market as only one sector for investors. Others include government bonds, securities, company shares, etc. Investment flows into the built environment when relatively high and secure returns can be made and is withdrawn when higher returns can be made elsewhere. The character of contemporary cities owes a great deal to this switching on and off of investment. The urban fabric of the city is the result of past building cycles, which can be seen as the outcome of investment into the built environment.

The building cycle

Researchers have discovered the existence of *building cycles*. These are similar to the Kondratieff and business cycles discussed in Chapter 6 in that there is a definite cadence to activities. In the case of the building cycle, which tends to occur every twenty years, there is a pattern of fluctuation in construction activity in association with the inflow of investment. The different elements of the cycle can be examined in turn.

The trough. In the trough of the building cycle there is only limited construction. Higher returns and profits are being made elsewhere so little capital is invested, and thus very few houses, business premises or offices are built.

The up-swing. The up-turn occurs for a number of reasons. The small number of dwellings built in the trough means that if population and incomes are increasing then there is a rise in effective demand. The price of existing dwellings increases, there is a large market for houses and offices and more profits can be made for builders. Capital is thus drawn into the construction sector and the building cycle begins its upward movement.

The peak. At the peak of the building cycle a large number of dwellings are constructed and a large proportion of total investment goes into the built environment. Land prices increase and speculative activity is feverish.

The down-swing. The down-turn occurs when most of the effective demand is met, profits decrease and capital is invested into more profitable enterprises. The scale and pace of construction eases off.

The composition of the building cycle changes through time. During the down-turn and the trough, when urban land prices are cheaper, relatively more public buildings (schools, hospitals, etc.) are built. When land values increase, the public sector is outbid by the private sector.

Each building cycle is also associated with distinct changes in transportation. The building boom of 1900 to 1920, for example, was associated with the motor car. Since each building cycle is associated with a distinct type of trans-

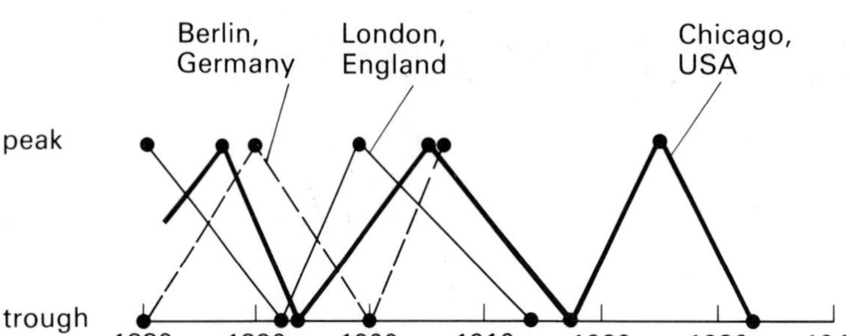

Figure 9.1 Building cycles in three cities
Source: after Gottlieb, 1976

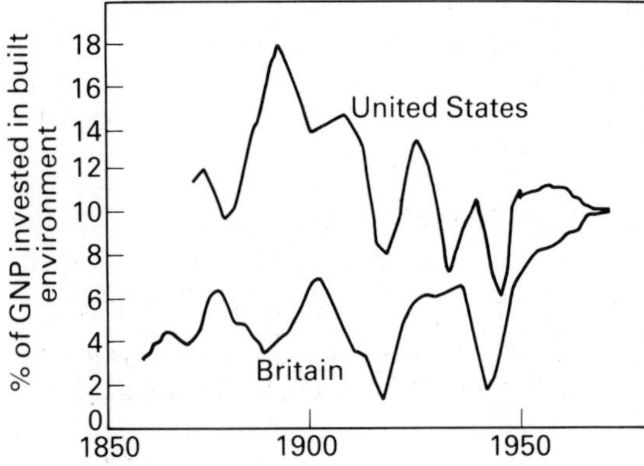

Figure 9.2 Investment in built environment, USA and Britain
Source: Harvey, 1978

portation which gives shape and substance to the layout and disposition of buildings, rather than a building cycle we can think of a transport-building cycle.

There is not one building cycle affecting all cities at the same time. Figure 9.1 shows the variation between cities in different countries. There is some evidence to suggest a relationship between building cycles in North America and Britain. Figure 9.2 shows the rhythm of investment in both these countries over a period of years. Notice how they are phased; a high peak in the USA is matched by a trough in Britain. It seems that investment was switched across the Atlantic. When profits and building were high in the USA, capital flowed in and some of it from Britain. Conversely, when profits were high in Britain, capital from North America was invested in the British building cycle.

The driving force of the building cycle is the different opportunities afforded to capital investors. When profits are high capital is invested and construction activity increases. When high profits are available elsewhere, capital is withdrawn and construction activity declines.

The impact of building cycles

Cities in North America and Western Europe have been affected by a number of building cycles. Each one has left its mark and individual cities bear the imprint of successive cycles. The spatial imprint of these cycles on a typical mid-west city has been modelled by John Adams. Figure 9.3 shows the main outlines: each successive building cycle is linked with a particular urban transport era which gives shape and direction to the building activity. On the ground these cycles can be seen as successive rings of buildings, with the most recent furthest away from the city centre. Into this model we can fit a number of extra variables. The spatial pattern shown in Figure 9.3, for example, would have to be altered if planning restrictions limited the areas where residential development could take place. Suburban municipalities may also limit the amount and type of new building by exclusionary zoning practices.

Each building cycle occurs at a different point in time when architectural tastes and design standards have altered. Each building cycle is thus associated with their particular style of building. Streetcar suburbs of the 1890s differ from the auto suburbs of the 1950s, and the public buildings of the 1860s differ in size and style as well as function from the government offices of 1983. The building cycles leave in their wake mute testimony to previous styles and fancies. The journey from the city centre to the suburbs is like flicking through the pages of a textbook on architectural

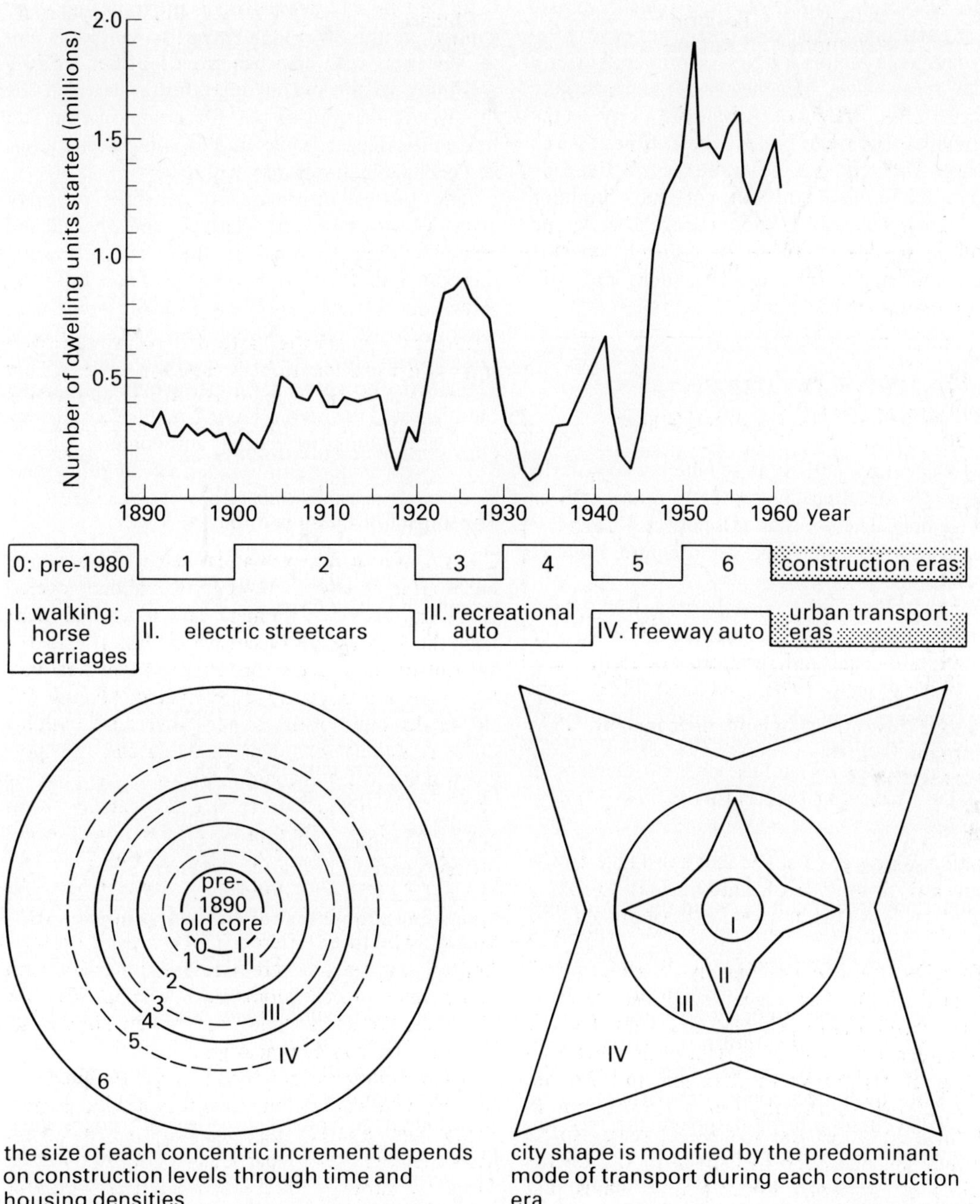

Figure 9.3 Building cycles, urban transport eras, and city shapes in the United States, pre-1890 to 1960
Source: Adams, 1970

design. Since some cities saw their rates of expansion at particular times, different cities have different dominant building styles. Florence is a city of the renaissance, Manchester is an essentially Victorian city, while Los Angeles is a city of the automobile. Cities can be located in times as well as space. The temporal co-ordinates are fixed by the range and dominance of particular building types. Each successive building cycle locks up capital in specific types of building in specific places. Capital is frozen into the bricks and mortar of the built environment.

THE CONTEMPORARY URBAN PROPERTY MARKET

Cities concentrate activity in selected areas and the process of urbanisation confers importance on selected sites. These pieces of scarce land increase in value and the fewer there are the more valuable they become.

We can make a distinction between the owners of urban property (the term property will be used to cover both land and the associated buildings), the property sector which includes those firms directly concerned with the manipulation and structuring of urban land, and the users of urban land. The process of land-use changes involves all three. Let us examine each in turn.

Property owners

A distinction can be made between those who own property as an investment and those who own property in order to use it.

Owners as investors. Property investors seek to maintain or increase their return from their investment. Their ability to do so depends upon the overall state of the economy, the particular type of land they hold and the nature of the relationship with land users. As an example let us consider the case of housing landlords. They can be defined as investors in rental residential property. Their return comes in the form of rent payments and the level of return is the rent payments minus maintenance and loan charges. Since they are unable to influence loan charges, in order to increase their return they can either increase rents and/or reduce maintenance expenditure. Their ability to do this is limited by the degree of tenant resistance. The conflict in this case is between the landlords and the tenants, with the balance of power shifting according to the overall relationship between the supply and demand of rental accommodation and the political-legal framework in which rent levels and occupancy levels may be set.

The greatest returns accrue to those property investors who buy land relatively cheaply and sell at a much higher price. In the property market this comes about through a change of use. Table 9.1 shows the different revenues from different land users in British cities. Notice how more revenue is gained from shops and offices than from houses. The astute property developer would thus make the highest return from buying rental housing property and selling it for retail and commercial use. This is the logic behind much of contemporary land-use changes. Two specific areas of activity can be identified.

Table 9.1 The relationship between land use and revenue in British cities, 1976

Land use	*Gross annual revenue over 1000 sq. ft of site* (£)*
housing (private renting)	400
factories/warehouses	1000
shops	3000
offices (provincial cities)	16,000
offices (central London)	60,000

*Including allowances for differences in plot ratio.
Source: Ambrose, 1977

(1) *City centre and urban renewal* Around the central area of most large cities there is intense property speculation in land-use changes as vacant or housing land is bought up, and planning permission sought to construct office and commercial property which is then let out at high rent levels. The return to investors is very high. This activity has been lubricated by the increase in most cities of the service sector with its need for prime sites. In Britain the process has also been aided by the growth of the large pension funds who are able to finance the hugely expensive operations and are quite willing to take a long-term perspective. The pension funds can afford to wait for long-term

steady returns rather than the high profits of the quick kill.

The story of urban renewal has really been one of housing destruction and retail/commercial/ luxury housing construction; the whole process emanating from the drive of profit investment.

(2) *Urban fringe and residential development* At the urban fringe there is the possibility for agricultural land or other non-urban land use to be turned into residential and other forms of urban land use with a promise of large gains. There is a great deal of speculative activity as land is bought in anticipation of rural-urban land-use conversion. This activity has caused the reassessment of the typical urban fringe land-use model. This model shown in Figure 9.4a is a variant of the von Thünen model in which a transect from the city's edge outwards shows a progression from capital and labour-intensive agriculture such as market gardening to much more extensive agricultural practices such as cattle rearing and wheat farming. The whole basis of the model is the locational advantage of being close to the market. But after examining land-use patterns at the edge of mid-west cities of the USA, Sinclair (1967) has suggested that the typical city follows the pattern outlined in Figure 9.4b. Because of speculation and the fear of urban encroachment there is very little investment in the rural-urban fringe. Immediately surrounding the city's edge there is a lack of investment. Sinclair's model assumes no planning controls or zoning ordinances. If land use in the rural-urban fringe was zoned permanently for agricultural land, then we would expect capital-intensive agriculture. In areas zoned for residential and development the heavy shadow of land-use conversion is pronounced imminent and agricultural investment all but ceases.

Planning is very important, since it determines which land is to be used for particular uses. By indicating where residential development can take place, for example, the land-use planning process favours some sites and hence some landowners more than others. In a review of British land-use planning since 1947, Peter Hall and associates have shown the positive and negative effects of planning. On the positive side land-use planning policies were largely successful in slowing down the rate of rural to urban land-use conversion. On the negative

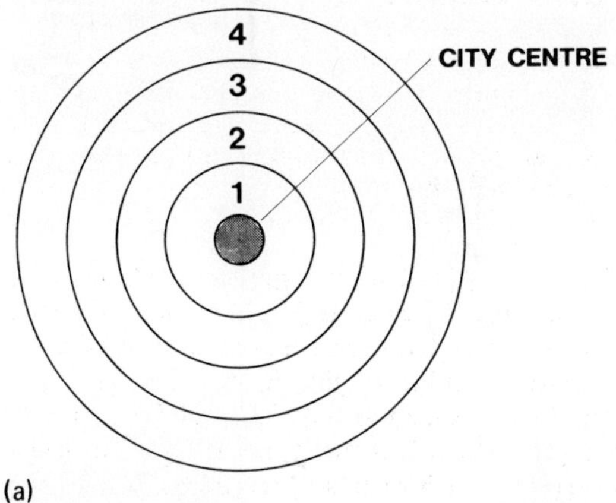

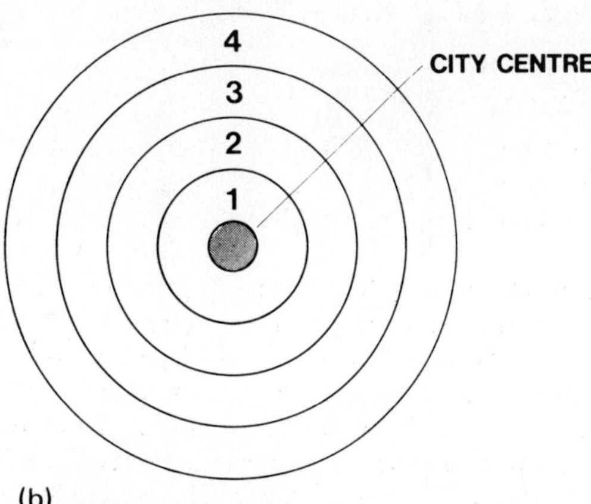

Figure 9.4 Two models of land use on the urban fringe

side, however, planning constraints pushed up land and property prices. Owners of land given planning permission were given a monopoly power which, when translated into land-use sales, led to increased prices. The planning process had distinct redistributional consequences. Owners of land given planning permission saw a dramatic increase in the market price of their land, upper-income owner-occupiers in the protected green belts had their quality of life protected and their property values assured, while the middle- to low-income households purchasing new property were forced to buy more expensive, higher-density housing (Hall et al., 1973).

Owners as users Not all property owners use land as investment. There are some, like manufacturing companies, who own land in order to do something else. We can make a distinction between private institutions including firms and corporations, and private individuals, who own or are buying their residential property. Since they have invested a significant proportion of their earnings into the property, they are concerned at the least with maintaining property values if not improving them. Owner-occupiers are concerned with both the use value and the exchange value of their housing. As a group, owner-occupiers seek to influence urban policies and urban planning in order to increase their property values, through maximising positive externalities and minimising negative ones. Hence, they seek to fight against motorway schemes and the introduction of lower-income residents into their area which may, at least in the minds of the residents, bring down their house prices. Much of local urban politics is

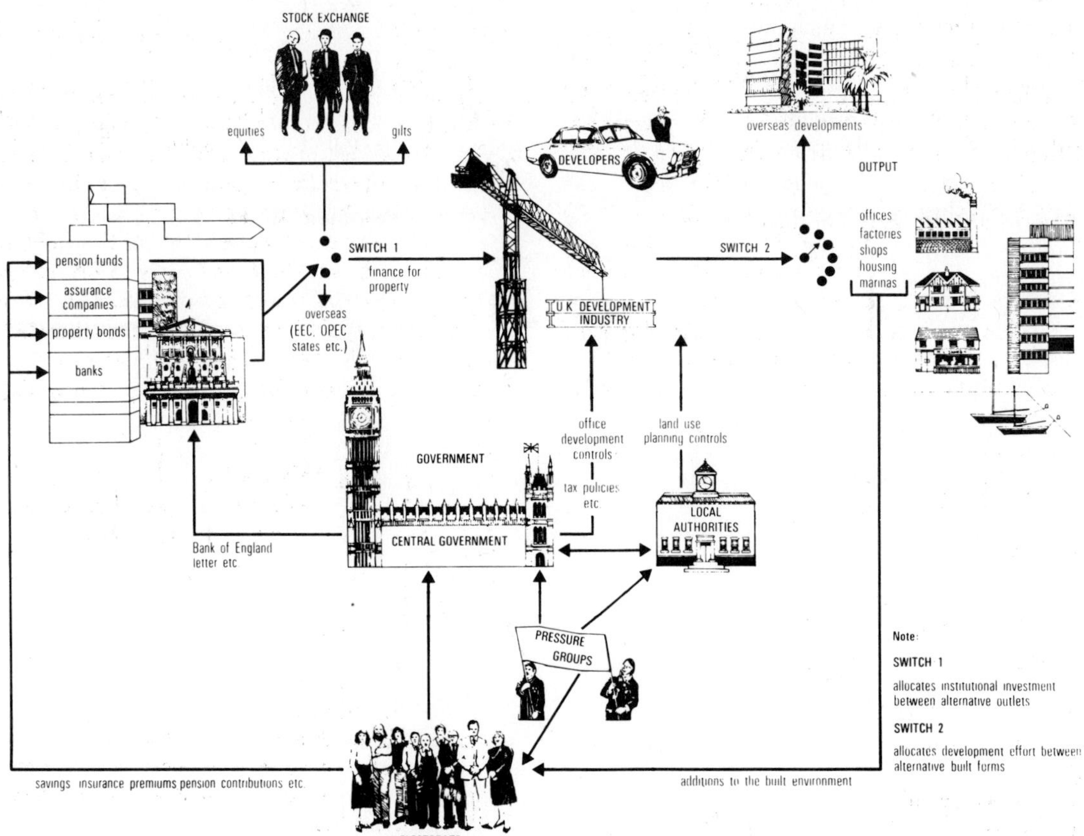

Figure 9.5 The land development system
Source: Ambrose, P. (1976), 'Who Plans Brighton's Housing Crisis?' *Shelter Land Report* No. 1

concerned with the attempt by residents to influence events in order to increase or maintain the exchange value of their housing.

Of course there are owner-occupiers and owner-occupiers. The most successful are the richer households with sufficient resources and connections to influence urban policies to suit their objectives. The fat cats of the very high-income suburbs do very well. Less successful are the poorer inner-city residents who lack the money, the influence and the appropriate language to manipulate the planning process.

The property sector

There are a number of different types of corporations and firms, we will call them agents, involved in the development of urban land.

The range of agents in the property sector is shown with respect to Britain in Figure 9.5. Although varying in detail throughout the countries of the capitalist world, the general picture will remain approximately the same.

Financial institutions are concerned with getting high and safe returns on their investment. Often there is a trade-off between yield and risk, very high returns are made in risky deals which may fail, while lower returns are often made in safe investments. In general, finance flows to those investments yielding good returns. Thus it is much easier for a developer to obtain finance for lucrative office development than to provide low-income housing. Different institutions may adopt slightly different strategies. Insurance companies and pension funds can afford to take a long-term view, and seek safe investments yielding medium returns over long periods. Speculators go for the quick, risky kill. The overall level of capital investment depends upon the returns from alternative investments. Property booms are periods when returns are high, lots of capital is invested and there is a great deal of change in the urban landscape. Figure 9.6 shows one of the indicators of the 1969 to 1973 boom in Britain. The effects of this boom on the urban landscape and internal politics in two cities are discussed in Ambrose and Colenutt (1975).

The development industry can sometimes be divided into two distinct sectors: the construction companies who build the offices, shops and dwellings, and the property developers who assemble their land, obtain finance and planning permission and then either sell or lease the site. In many cases the distinction becomes inappropriate because many very large property companies are also construction firms. In this case we can use the term builder-developer.

The additions and changes to the built environment affect local communities. If they are well organised and rich in resources, they may be able to influence the character and timing of the development through the political process. If weak they may have little success. One of the saddest urban stories of the 1960s and early 1970s was of the destruction of inner-city communities by urban renewal schemes. The voices of local residents were rarely heard in the decision-making chambers.

Most development takes place within a planning

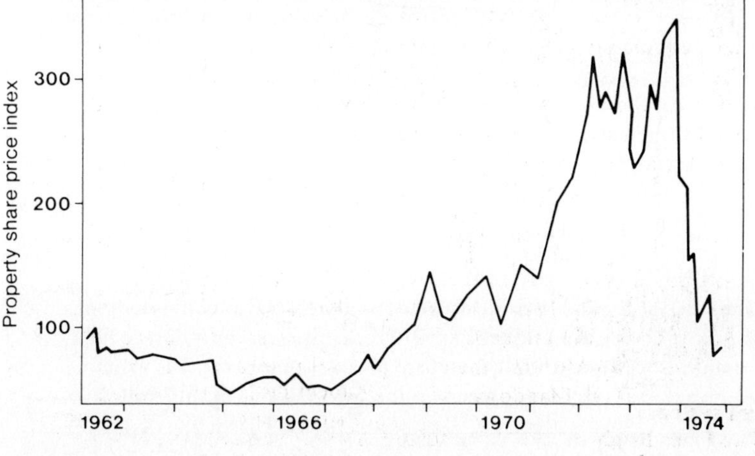

Figure 9.6
The property boom in Britain
Source: Harvey, 1978

LAND RENT

Land or property rent is the payment made by users to property owners. It has been treated differently in the various economic approaches. In neo-classical economics, rent is treated as a rationing device which allocates land to the highest bidder, with rent levels being a function of accessibility. Rent is highest in the areas of highest accessibility and since the city centre is taken to be the point of maximum accessibility there is a definite rent gradient falling from the city centre outwards.

Recent years have also seen the resuscitation of marxist rent theory. Contemporary marxists have argued that neo-classical rent theory masks the social reality of rent; it ignores the form and character of the social relationships involved in the creation and maintenance of rent.

For Marx, who in volume 3 of *Capital* was entirely concerned with agricultural land, land represents a condition of production. By itself it does not produce wealth, but it is necessary for the creation of wealth to take place. In the marxist schema outlined in Figure 9A, capital

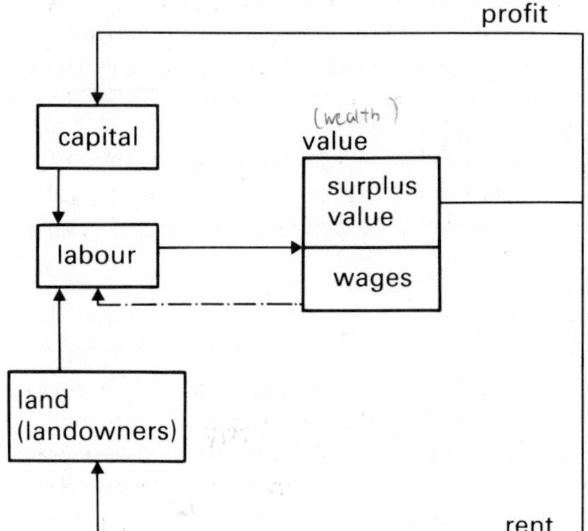

Figure 9A A marxist schema

employs labour in order to produce wealth which is termed value. Part of this value is paid to labour in the form of wages. However, labour does not receive all the value that it produces, the amount not paid to labour is termed surplus value. The existence of monopoly control over land conferred by the institution of private property means that surplus value can be extracted by landowners in the form of rent. In the marxist schema rent is the fraction of surplus value paid to landowners. Marx defined three categories of rent. The categories are defined with reference to the form of the social relationship.

Differential rent

Within this category Marx distinguished two types. In the case of differential type 1, as originally mapped out by Marx, the values and prices of production are determined by labour required for the production of crops in the worst-quality soil. Production on more fertile land, or land closer to the market, requires less labour and therefore produces more surplus value. Some of the surplus value can be extracted by landowners in the form of rent. Landowners automatically receive this rent, since farmers will compete for more fertile land or land closer to the market. This model is similar to the von Thünen model. In the urban case we can see this form of rent occurring when factories or shops closer to the market make higher profits, some of which may be siphoned off by the landowner in the form of rent.

In the case of differential type 2, varying amounts of capital are invested by the user to produce more surplus value which the landowner will attempt to extract. In this case landowners do not necessarily receive the extra rent, since there will be no competitive bidding as improvements will be built into the selling price. Conflict thus occurs in differential type 2 land in the renegotiation of leases, with no certainty that the landowners will get the extra rent.

Monopoly rent

Monopoly rent is received by landowners who let out land for the production of goods sold under monopoly conditions. Marx provides the example of a vineyard producing unique, high-quality wine which, due to the lack of competition, can be sold at very high prices. Since the land is an essential element, the landowner can claim some of the surplus profit in the form of monopoly rent. Planning and zoning confers monopoly power on landowners with land zoned for residential development or office use. They can thus charge high prices which the developers have to incorporate into the eventual selling price of the project.

For both differential and monopoly rents the landowner intercepts the surplus profit which would have otherwise gone to the users. For both types of rent the rent level will be set by the difference between the production and market price of the commodities produced on the land. The rents have no effect on prices.

Absolute rent

This is the more contentious of Marx's categories. Absolute rent, according to Marx, arises from the power of landowners to maintain scarcity and can be defined as rent which derives from the monopoly power of landed property and their ability to create and increase rent payments. Unlike the other two categories, absolute rent does have an effect on prices. In effect absolute rent increases prices and landed property itself has created rent.

The translation of marxist categories to the urban areas has just begun. There are a number of difficulties. Land in the urban context, for example, is only rarely used for the production of wealth. And there are many agents involved in the process of buying, selling and using land. Unlike the simple agricultural case where there are only farmers and landowners, in the urban context there are developers, builders, landowners, planners and a whole host of intermediaries. Overall, then, the urban land market is a much more complex case than the one used by Marx. Although a simple translation of Marx's theory into the urban case is not possible, the theory does provide some illuminations into the dense undergrowth of the urban land transactions. The work of David Harvey, for example, has begun to show how marxist categories can be used with respect to the relationships between landowners and tenants in inner-city housing markets.

The most important point to bear in mind, however, is that marxist categorisation brings into sharp relief the social relationships involved in rent payments. Rent in the marxist category is not an asocial phenomenon. It is a social relationship derived from particular property arrangements in which tensions and conflicts arise. The urban land market and subsequent rent levels are not something natural, god-given, sacrosanct. They are the result of social processes and social conflict.

References

Bassett, K.A. and Short, J.R. (1980), *Housing and Residential Structure* Routledge & Kegan Paul, London.

Edel, M. (1976), Marxist theory of rent; urban applications. In Political Economy of Housing Workshop, *Housing and Class in Britain*, London.

Harvey, D. and Chatterjee, L. (1974), Absolute rent and the structuring of space by government and financial institutions, *Antipode*, 6, 21-36.

Harvey, D. (1982), *The Limits To Capital*, Basil Blackwell, Oxford.

system. Although this may vary (theoretically Britain has a much stronger land-use planning control system than the United States) there is a basic similarity in the planning system of capitalist countries. Even in the strong planning system of Britain, urban planning has been hampered by an inability to take strong positive leads. Planning has been a negative activity, able to refuse developments but unable to stimulate desired investments and spatial outcomes. Successive failures of land-use planning in Britain to capture stronger power over land has made it of nuisance value, able to refuse the most outrageous planning applications, tidy the mediocre ones but unable to challenge the immanent logic of the land-development system. But planning does have an important role, however, in providing the context for property investment decisions. By allowing development to take place in some areas rather than others, the planning system confers monopoly power and lucrative rewards on some landowners and property investors rather than others. The planning system provides the decision-making environment in which property investment takes place.

Users of urban land

Since land is leased out or sold to the highest bidder, we can identify different land users by their ability to pay. Four broad categories of urban land uses can be identified.

(1) *The retail sector* Firms in this sector require accessible sites in order to attract customers. For most shops the more accessible the site, the more customers and hence the greater the profit. Firms in the retail sector are thus willing to pay greater sums for accessible locations. Within the retail sector a distinction can be made between those firms specialising in high, quick-turnover markets, such as clothing shops, etc. and those involved in the more irregular, lower-turnover speciality goods such as high-quality jewellery. The former seek and can pay for more accessible sites than the latter.

(2) *The commercial sector* In this sector accessibility to other offices, financial and other service facilities is important for face-to-face contact in business dealings and to maintain prestige. A distinction can be drawn between prime office centres in the heart of the commercial core of the city and non-prime sites on the outskirts. Rents for prime sites are much higher and here are found the offices of major corporations.

(3) *Residential sector* This sector consists of households seeking accommodation. While some households may desire a central-city location in order to reduce their journey-to-work costs (if their work is in the central area), they cannot afford to outbid retail or commercial firms.

The rent-paying ability of the previous three land-use types can be expressed as a bid-rent function, defined as the amount of rent a firm or household can afford to pay at different locations. These are depicted in Figure 9.7a. This is the simplest case. Figure 9.7b shows the complication of a secondary point of accessibility A formed by an intersection of a radial route and a major highway into the city centre.

(4) *The manufacturing sector* Apart from those industries, for example port-related industries, tied to specific sites, the exact location of manufacturing firms is only of minimal importance in

Plates 40 and 41
The urban land market:
(40) pressure for space leads to mixing of land uses. In this case Mammon has clearly outbid the competitor for the more accessible groundfloor site; (41) speculative office development, fuelled by capital investment. This office block in Reading had lain empty for almost 2 years

this sector. Indeed, accessibility considerations for manufacturing industry have been declining as improvements in transport have been undermining the friction of distance at least over the short-to-medium distance. Manufacturing firms do not need to pay for expensive sites and can be located on the suburban edges of the city.

There is a constantly changing relationship between land users and rent-paying ability. If property rents rise, the weaker firms in the retail and commercial sector may be forced to close and to relocate while lower-income households will be unable to afford the higher house prices. If the rents go so high, there may be large-scale relocation. If office rents become so high then new offices may be set up elsewhere. The very high price of office space in London, for example, has caused many firms to set up their premises in the western suburbs or in the small towns of Maidenhead, Reading and Newbury strung out along the M4 motorway. Similarly, many manufacturing firms have either been forced to close or relocate to the suburbs because of the high cost of sites.

Figure 9.7 Bid-rent functions
Source: Short, J.R. (1980), *Urban Data Sources,* Butterworth

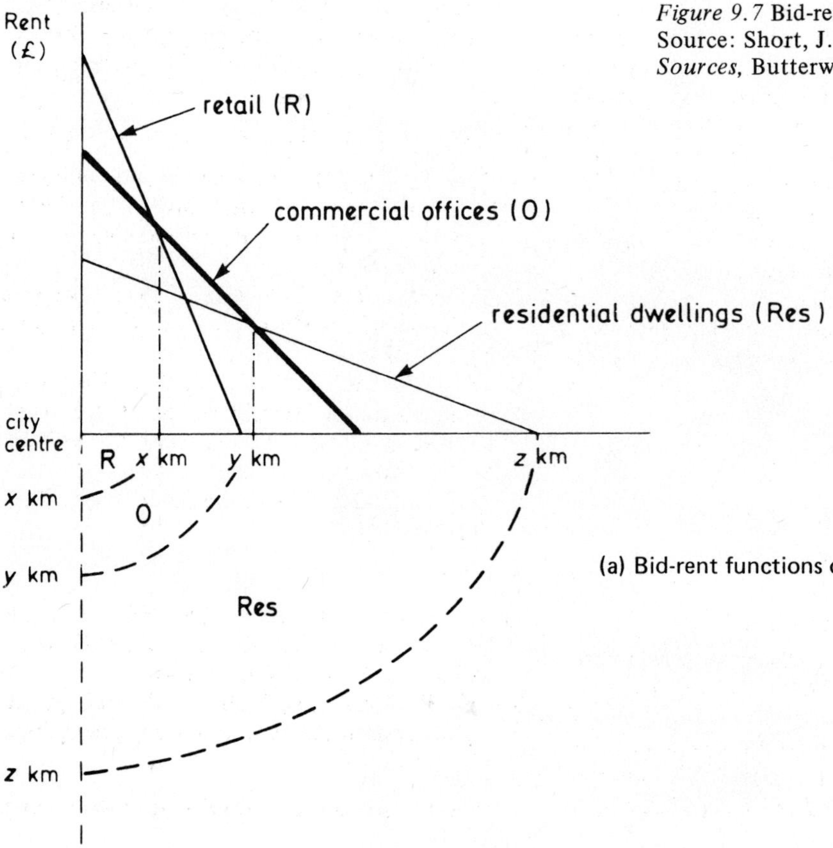

Rent
(£)
retail (R)
commercial offices (O)
residential dwellings (Res)
city
centre
R
x km
y km
z km
x km
O
y km
Res
z km

(a) Bid-rent functions of three land uses

Rent
(£)
retail (R)
commercial offices (O)
A
residential dwellings (Res)
city
centre
distance

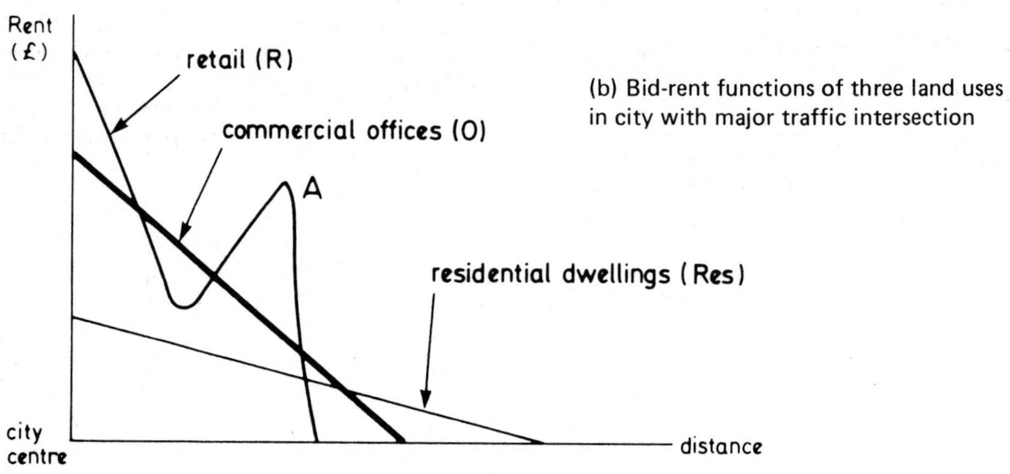

(b) Bid-rent functions of three land uses in city with major traffic intersection

The urban property market is constantly changing and land users are sifted and sorted accordingly. The urban land market is a dynamic one. Looking back over the past twenty years, the dominant trend has been the upgrading of central-area land sites from residential and low-rent commercial uses to high-rent commercial uses. The process of urban renewal has involved the destruction of communities and the construction of offices and high-income residencies. The low-income residents have gained least and the property dealers have gained most. The process of urban renewal has been a regressive one.

GUIDE TO FURTHER READING

Work on building cycles includes:

Gottlieb, M. (1976), *Long Swings in Urban Development*, National Bureau for Economic Research, New York.

Harvey, D. (1978), The urban process under capitalism: a framework for analysis, *International Journal of Urban and Regional Research*, 2, 101-31.

Lewis, J.P. (1965), *Building Cycles and Britain's Growth*, Macmillan, London.

Parkes, D.N. and Thrift, N.J. (1980), *Times, Spaces and Places*, John Wiley, Chichester.

Thomas, B. (1972), *Migration and Urban Development, a Reappraisal of British and American Long Cycles*, Methuen, London.

Case studies include:

Adams, J.S. (1970), Residential structure of midwestern cities, *Annals of the Association of American Geographers*, 60, 36-62.

Whitehand, J.W.R. (1972), Building cycles and the spatial pattern of economic growth, *Transactions Institute of British Geographers*, 56, 39-55.

The urban land market is given general treatment in:

Ambrose, P. (1977), The determinants of urban land use change, Unit 26 Course D204, *Fundamentals of Human Geography*, Open University, Milton Keynes.

Form, W.H. (1954), The place of social structure in the determination of land use, *Social Forces*, 32, 317-23.

Roweis, S.T. and Scott, A.J. (1981), The urban land question, In Dear, M. and Scott, A.J. (eds), *Urbanization and Urban Planning in Capitalist Society*, Methuen, London.

Scott, A.J. (1981), *The Urban Land Nexus*, Pion, London.

See also:

Hall, P., Gracey, H., Drewett, R. and Thomas, R. (1973), *The Containment of Urban England*, PEP and Allen & Unwin, London.

Sinclair, R. (1967), Von Thünen and urban spread, *Annals of Association of American Geographers*, 57, 72-87.

Amongst the many case studies of urban renewal see:

Ambrose, P. and Colenutt, B. (1975), *The Property Machine*, Penguin, Harmondsworth.

Boddy, M. (1981), The property sector in late capitalism: the case of Britain, In Dear, M. and Scott, A.J., op.cit.

Haas, G. and Heskin, A.D. (1981), Community struggles in Los Angeles, *International Journal of Urban and Regional Research*, 5, 546-63.

Hayes, E. (1972), *Power Structure and Urban Policy: who Rules in Oakland*, McGraw-Hill, New York.

10 The City as Political Arena

One of the most significant features of the twentieth century has been the rise of government. Governments have been growing in size and importance. In centrally planned economies the government is now the principal actor in social and economic affairs. In capitalist countries the introduction of New Deals, the rise of the military-industrial complex and the growth of social welfare have extended the boundaries of government involvement. In modern capitalist society the government is a major actor.

With growing involvement of government has come the politicisation of issues. What previously was seen as the domain of the private market is now placed firmly on the political agenda. Take the case of urban planning. With the growth of the nineteenth- and early twentieth-century capitalist cities came problems of poor living conditions and urban congestion. Far-sighted reformers argued the need for collective responsibility, while the victims wanted an improvement in their lot. The result was the growth of urban planning and zoning ordinances. Thus, the quality of the urban environment became a public issue rather than a private concern. To see the politicisation of issues in the interaction between institutions and groups in the pursuit of their aims is to see the city as a political arena.

A useful distinction can be drawn between the realm of formal politics – the rules of the game in the political arena – and the informal politics of the interaction between the major parties; this is the action of the political arena.

FORMAL POLITICS: THE RULES OF THE GAME

There are several dimensions to the city as a formal political unit. We will consider just three.

1 The degree of relative autonomy

The degree of independence of urban governments from the central or federal authorities varies

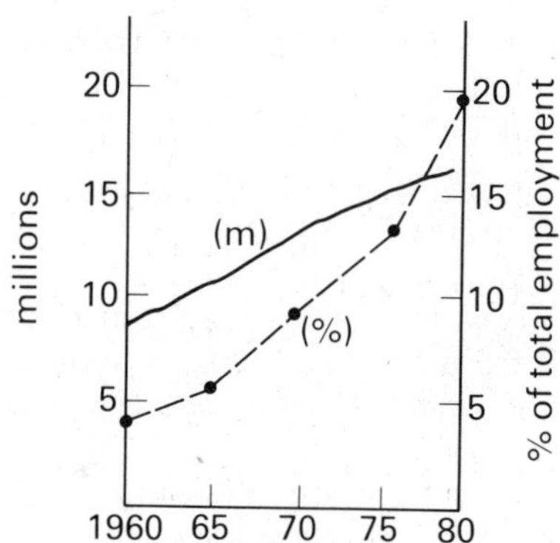

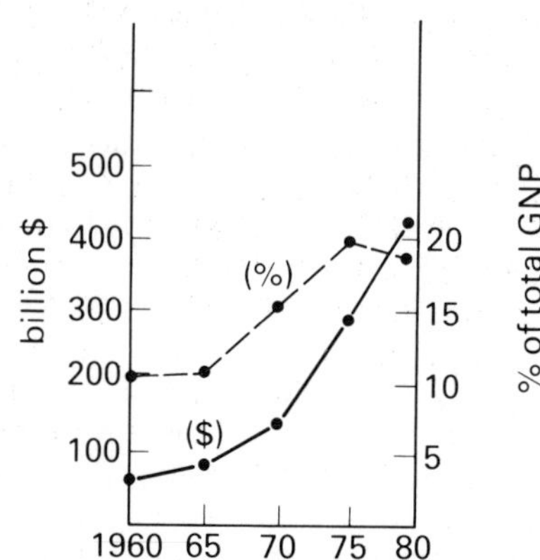

Figure 10.1 The rise of government employment and expenditure
Source: US Census

throughout the world. In most cases, however, ultimate power resides with central government. The rise of government in the twentieth century has been the rise of big centralised government. The independence of all local authorities, including municipal ones, is thus a relative one. This is what we mean by the term relative autonomy.

Table 10.1 The relative autonomy of urban governments

		degree of local autonomy in defining policy goals	
		high	*low*
degree of local autonomy in financing and spending decisions	high	1	2
	low	4	3

The typology shown in Table 10.1 indicates the two main dimensions which structure the level of relative autonomy. The exercise of political power involves both the setting of policy goals and objectives, and the ability to achieve them. Of the variety of means to achieve any given end, we tend to think of fiscal means as the most important. Urban governments vary along each of these dimensions. In the case of 1, the urban government can set objectives and has the fiscal independence to achieve them. In the case of 4, by contrast, the authority has power to identify goals but lacks the fiscal wherewithal. Table 10.1 provides a useful framework to categorise different types of urban governments. It can also be used with reference to a range of policy areas. In the case of Britain, for example, the urban authorities are normally in control of the police, but in practice the level of central control places them in position 3, while their relationship to central government with regard to housing provision places them in 4.

The position also varies over time. In Britain there has been a steady loss of local authority control over financing. In order to sweeten the pill the central authorities have given local authorities a measure of greater control over deciding how much should be spent but keeping strict control over the total amount. There is thus a tension between central and local authorities over the tricky problem of financing.

We can to some extent measure the degree of relative autonomy by examining patterns of spending. If urban governments were simply neutral transmission belts for central government policies then we would expect to see little or no variation between urban authorities in the implementation of these policies. For the USA and UK, at least, all the evidence suggests a substantial variation. Table 10.2, for example, shows the variation between some urban authorities in England and Wales in the level of expenditure on child clinics and family planning; the data has been standardised in order to aid comparison. Notice the substantial variation.

Table 10.2 Welfare expenditure in 25 UK cities (1976)

City	*A*	*B*
London	5.1	10.1
Birmingham	2.3	0.0
Liverpool	1.1	26.9
Manchester	3.0	16.0
Sheffield	3.6	35.8
Leeds	2.9	5.8
Bristol	10.6	28.4
Teeside	2.7	0.0
Coventry	3.0	4.4
Nottingham	2.1	0.0
Bradford	6.7	0.0
Hull	2.2	47.5
Leicester	1.1	0.0
Cardiff	2.5	37.7
Wolverhampton	2.4	0.0
Stoke	3.7	6.5
Plymouth	1.2	0.0
Newcastle	3.4	0.0
Derby	1.1	0.0
Sunderland	2.4	3.2
Southampton	3.1	13.6
Portsmouth	3.8	0.0
Dudley	3.4	0.0
Walsall	2.2	0.0
Swansea	3.4	0.0

A Local authority expenditure (£'s) on child clinics and centres per child under 5 years of age.

B Local authority expenditure (£'s) on family planning per 1000 people.

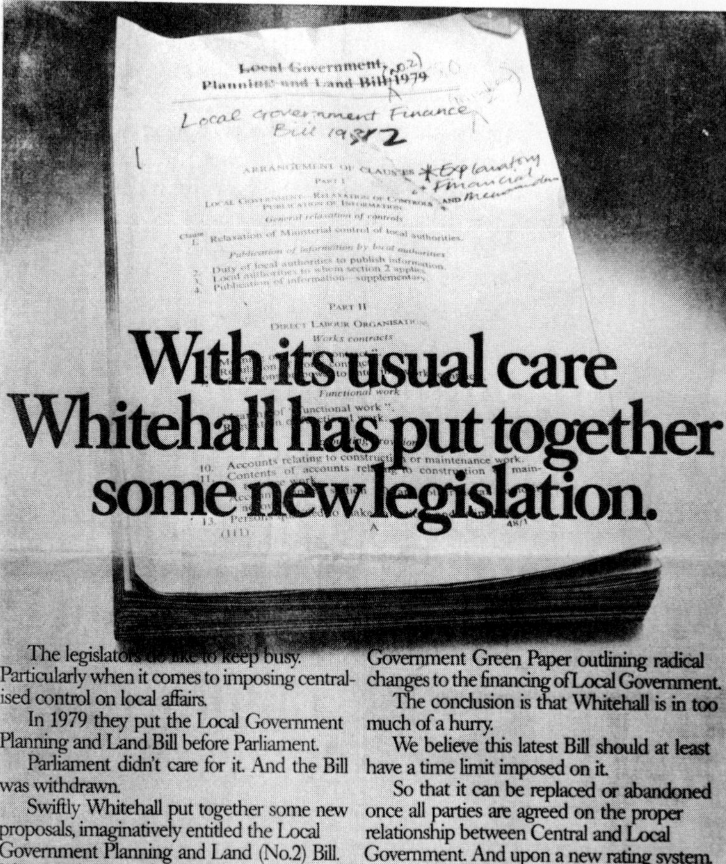

Plate 42
Central-local state difficulties: part of the Association of Metropolitan Authorities' publicity campaign against central government

The main source of variation in urban spending relate to needs, resources and dispositions.

Needs There is a variation in the demands placed on municipal governments in different places. For example, some cities contain a higher proportion of poor people and thus there is a greater need for welfare expenditure.

Resources How much money a municipal authority has determines how much is spent. The greater the resources, the greater the ability to meet demands and hence satisfying needs. Here we come upon an interesting paradox. The richer municipalities have the greatest ability to pay because of their wider and deeper tax base, but less need for welfare services, while the municipali-

URBAN POLITICS IN THE SOVIET UNION

The formal arena of urban politics in the Soviet Union is the city soviet. This is an elected assembly in all settlements with a population of more than 10,000 inhabitants or 2,000 electors. There is approximately 1 soviet member for each 1,500 voters. No non-communist parties are allowed to offer themselves for election. The soviets are large; the Moscow Soviet, for example, has 1,100 delegates. The soviet ratifies decisions made by the executive committee, which is the decision-making body in charge of administration. Members of the 3- to 15-person committee include senior communist party members, heads of municipal departments and some elected members from the soviet.

Although the soviet, through the executive committee, is in charge of the municipal departments, e.g. land-use planning, there is no control over non-municipal enterprises such as a metal factory which is controlled by republic committees or national government departments. The degree of power wielded and control exercised by the executive committee of the city soviet is limited by the fact that many local enterprises owe their allegiance and financial base to other political and administrative bodies. The bulk of municipal budgets, for example, come from higher regional authorities. Some municipal authorities are facing their own form of fiscal crisis as funds do not keep pace with rising costs.

References

Friedgut, T.H. (1978), Citizens and soviets: can Ivan Ivanovich fight city hall, *Comparative Politics*, July.

Taubman, W. (1973), *Governing Soviet Cities*, Praeger, New York.

Oliver, J.H. (1968), Citizen demands and the Soviet political system, *American Political Science Review*, 63, 465-75.

ties which have the greatest need generally have the least ability to meet these needs. In government structures where the central government operates to minimise variation in local public finance this may not be a problem. In the UK most money spent by urban authorities is provided by the central exchequer and there is a definite policy of sharing the funds according to needs. In the USA, by contrast, where most of the local spending is locally raised, variations in resources have a marked effect on the ability to meet needs. Table 10.3, for example, shows the relationship between income levels, tax base and spending on education for the city of Oakland and four neighbouring communities. Notice the variation in the tax base, where the poorer city of Oakland has less resources than the richer suburb of Emeryville. The result is for the richer suburb of Emeryville to be able to spend three times more per child.

Table 10.3 Tax base and education spending in Oakland, California and surrounding communities

	Tax base per child ($)	*Spending per child ($)*
Oakland	$ 12,008	$ 587.54
Fremont	5,245	545.46
Hayward	11,718	517.45
Piedmont	11,718	825.44
Emeryville	95,122	1694.51

Source: After Levy et al., 1974

Dispositions Local authorities vary in political disposition and these variations have marked fiscal differences. In Britain, for example, Labour-controlled central and local authorities tend, holding everything else constant, to spend more on welfare type services such as education and public housing than Conservative-controlled authorities: Table 10.4 shows the typical relationship between central and local political disposition and resultant patterns of spending. Although not so clear cut, the evidence from the USA suggests that Democratic parties are bigger welfare spenders than Republicans.

Two models have been proposed to handle the relationship between disposition and spending. In the *adversary model* it is assumed that the local political party carries out its policies whatever the extent of the electoral victory. The *vote-buying model* suggests that local politics are sensitive to their local electoral position and will spend more when they are in marginal positions in order to buy votes. As a hypothesis it has been suggested that the adversary model is more relevant in the case of urban government in Britain with its clearly defined political and class divisions but the vote-buying model is much more important in the USA. No firm conclusions have yet been reached because it is difficult to separate the close ties between needs, resources and disposition. The voters in greatest need, for example, will tend to vote for parties which promise to spend most. It thus becomes difficult to sort out the precise effect of needs and disposition. It is difficult to separate out the independent effect of each of the three factors.

Table 10.4 Central: local political disposition and probable local patterns of spending

Local government	*Central government*	
	Labour	*Conservative*
Labour	high local expenditure	medium local expenditure
Conservative	medium local expenditure	low local expenditure

2 Areas of jurisdiction

In previous chapters we have noted how the concept of the city needs to be replaced by the notion of the urban region. The functioning urban region often extends beyond the boundaries of urban government. In the case of many metropolitan areas political boundaries fail to match urban reali-

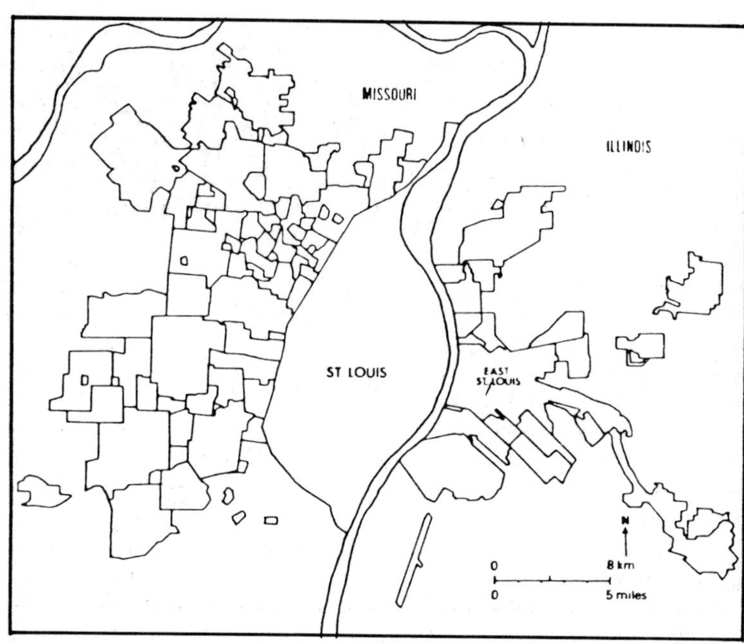

Figure 10.2 Jurisdictional fragmentation in the St Louis Metropolitan Area

ties. There are two reasons for this. First, there is the slow political response rate compared to rapid urban growth. To change political boundaries is a long, often complicated procedure, while urban growth in the extension of the urban region continues apace. Second, there are the political and material interests at stake. Many firms and households have sought to escape from central city taxes by moving to the suburbs. And they have sought to maintain their position by building political fences behind their escape routes in the form of creating and maintaining separate areas of political jurisdiction.

In the USA the metropolitan scene is one of political fragmentation. Most large cities, especially those in the frostbelt, are composed of a central city municipality hemmed in by suburban municipalities. This political division is overlain by differences in income and welfare needs. In general, the central-city areas have a higher proportion of lower-income households and greater demands are placed on welfare services. In the suburban areas, in contrast, there is a much stronger tax base and less need for welfare services. There is thus a disparity in the political units between the welfare demands and the ability to meet these demands. This has been termed the central-city/suburban fiscal-disparity problem. It refers to the imbalance in the need for public services and the ability to finance these services. The spatial distribution of the disparity in the United States is shown in Figure 10.3. The problem is most severe in the frostbelt areas of the city where the urban economies are weak and there is a higher proportion of poorer households, and strong barriers to central-city annexation and incorporation of suburban municipalities. In the sunbelt cities the economies and tax base are stronger and there are fewer barriers to annexation.

Although separated by political boundaries, the central and suburban municipalities are joined by

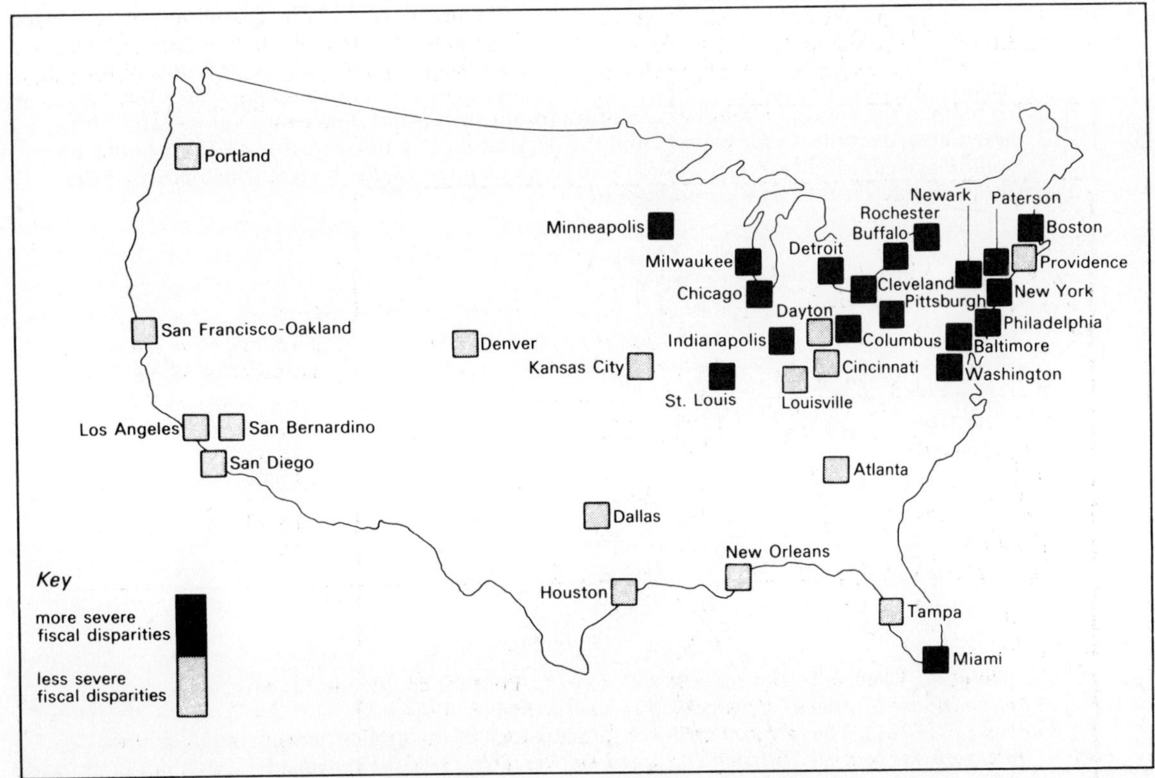

Figure 10.3 Fiscal disparity in the USA

THE URBAN FISCAL CRISIS

Many US cities have been faced with a crisis in meeting expenditure from revenues: the growing gap constitutes the urban fiscal crisis. This crisis has been aided by the overall nature of urban government in the USA. Two features are important.

1 There is an imbalance between demand-making for services and welfare expenditure, which tends to occur at the urban level, and tax-raising ability which is greatest at the federal level. The municipalities experience the greatest expenditure demands but lack strong revenue-generating powers.
2 The pattern of metropolitan fragmentation creates a central city-suburban fiscal disparity.

Within this context municipal spending has been increasing in the USA as business has called for infrastructure investment, municipal unions have bargained for higher wages, while residents have called on government to maintain and improve municipal services. The imbalance between expenditure and revenues began to be sharply felt in many frost-belt cities as the recession led to firms closing and taxations revenue being reduced while demands for municipal services steadily increased. The problems were exacerbated in cities where the suburbanisation of economic activity was draining away the economic lifeblood of the urban economy.

As the squeeze tightened in the early to mid 1970s the three main groups responded accordingly – business resisted tax increases, municipal unions fought to keep their jobs and wages levels, while city residents pressed for existing services to be maintained. The fiscal strains were declared fiscal crises by the municipal authorities in order to wield the budgetary axe. In New York the authorities' response was twofold:

1 To take the budget out of the electoral control, through the creation of an emergency finance board in 1975. By this method it was hoped to disenfranchise the political demands of the various residents' groups.
2 To redirect the reduced level of expenditure to suit the powerful interest groups. Table 10A shows how, over the 4-year period from the declaration of a fiscal crisis in 1975, spending on welfare and education services was reduced more than the capital budget which provides the infrastructure for the city's corporations.

Table 10A Budget cuts in New York City

	Spending fiscal year 1979-80 (million of dollars)	*% change from fiscal year 1975-76*
Social services	1233	–41.37
City university	244	–34.31
Hospitals	199	–52.84
Capital budget	1032	–18.03
Total	6346	–23.75

References

Friedland, R., Piven, F.F. and Alford, R.R. (1977), Political conflict and the fiscal crisis, *International Journal of Urban and Regional Research*, 1, 447-73.

Marcuse, P. (1981), The targeted crisis: on the ideology of the urban fiscal crisis and its uses, *International Journal of Urban and Regional Research*, 3, 330-55.

a whole series of transactions and flows. If the suburbanites use central-city facilities, for example, parks, cultural centres, etc. without paying the central-city taxes, then they are termed *free-riders.* They are getting a free-ride at the expense of the central city. If, on the other hand, suburbanites spend money in the central areas, the net effect on the central municipality is positive. Much work has gone into assessing the net effects of central-city/suburban relations. Table 10.5 shows the result of just one example, in this case a study of Detroit and surrounding suburban municipalities. In this case the term free-rider would seem to be appropriate.

Table 10.5 Suburban/central-city exploitation: Detroit ($)

Municipality	*1 Median family income*	*2 Per capita benefits from Detroit*	*3 Per capita payments to Detroit*	*4 Per capita benefits-payments (2-3)*
Allen Park	9420	9.86	3.34	6.52
Birmingham	12850	18.22	5.64	12.58
Dearborn	8500	9.25	2.53	6.72
Gross Point Park	13250	16.53	9.75	6.78
Highland Park	5620	3.96	2.23	1.73
Roseville	7870	13.09	3.32	9.77

Source: after Neenan, 1973

In the UK there is less metropolitan fragmentation. However, there are still disparities between functioning urban regions and local political boundaries. Since local government reform in 1974, England and Wales has had three types of local government which administer planning, transport, police, fire, education and welfare. These are counties, metropolitan counties and the Greater London Council (see Figure 10.4). In this particular context the important point to note is the relationship between the thirty-nine counties and the districts. Many of these districts are substantial cities in their own right. Bristol, for example, is a city with a population of approximately 400,000, yet it comes under the control of the county of Avon. A logical solution was proposed by one member of the Royal Commission which was set up to enquire into local government reform. Derek Senior urged the government to set up urban regions as the basic unit of government. His proposals were not acted upon. The Conservative rural counties were fearful of being swamped by central urban areas with large numbers of Labour voters, while the central Labour authorities were wary of being submerged in a sea of rural conservatism. The 1974 system, as outlined in Figure 10.4, constitutes a compromise. Because of the central origin of much local-authority spending there is less of a central-city/suburban fiscal disparity problem such as there is in the United States. But because of the central control the ruling political party in central government can manipulate the formula under which the grants are calculated in order to aid its political home lands. This happens. Thus Conservative governments tend to channel more money to the rural counties while successive Labour governments have sought to aid the metropolitan districts.

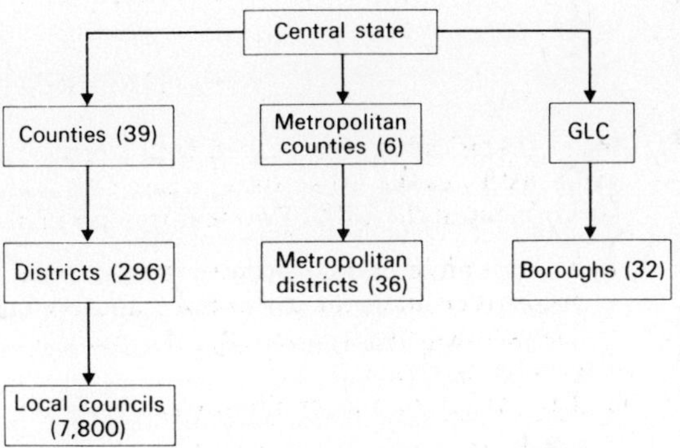

Figure 10.4 **Local government structure in England**

3 Forms of urban government

The form of urban government varies by country. The sources of variation are many but in this section we will seek to highlight these differences by comparing and contrasting the experience of the USA and UK.

The USA There are approximately 19,000 urban

WHO RULES IN THE URBAN ARENA?

The question of who wields effective power in the city has long been an important topic in urban research. Three positions can be identified. The *elitist* position states that a self-conscious business elite effectively runs the city. The *pluralist* position states that power is diffused among a number of competing centres. No one interest or pressure group, according to the pluralists, dominates all aspects of policy. Dahl's work in New Haven, for example, seeks to show that pressure-group influence varies according to the policy issue. Dahl's analysis of the three issues of urban redevelopment, public education and party nominations partly undermines his own case. Different individuals and pressure groups were involved in each of the three areas of public debate, but the analysis pointed to the overwhelming importance of middle-income and business interests albeit expressed by different individuals in separate organisations. The *neo-elitist* position was formulated in response to the arguments of the pluralists. It asserts that power does not lie at the level of pressure-group activity but resides in the ability of certain groups to exclude a wide range of issues from public debate. Hayes's (1972) study of urban renewal in Oakland, California, for example, showed that urban renewal was promoted by business interests and the issue of the destruction of low-income housing and the displacement of the inner-city black population was not raised on the political agenda.

The positions differ because of the different modes of analysis used. The pluralist approach takes a one-dimensional view of power, with its emphasis on the behaviour of pressure groups and the conflict generated by particular issues. The neo-elitist position adopts a two-dimensional view of power since it focuses not only on decision-making and issues but also nondecision-making and potential issues. A three-dimensional view of power in contrast would incorporate an understanding of observable and latent conflict, subjective and real interests, and issues and potential issues, since it is only such a wider view that can lay bare the relations of power within society.

Table 10B Perspectives on power

one-dimensional	*two-dimensional*	*three-dimensional*
behaviour	behaviour	behaviour
decision-making	decision-making, nondecision-making	decision-making, nondecision-making and control of political agenda
issues	issues and potential issues	issues and potential issues
observable conflict	observable conflict	observable and latent conflict
subjective interests	subjective interests	subjective and real interests

References

Dahl, R. (1961), *Who Governs?*, Yale University Press, New Haven.
Hayes, E. (1972), *Power Structure and Urban Policy: Who Rules in Oakland?*, McGraw-Hill.
Lukes, S. (1974), *Power: A Radical View*, Macmillan, London.
Short, J.R. (1982), *An Introduction to Political Geography*, Routledge & Kegan Paul, London.

municipalities in the USA. There are three main types of urban government.

In the *mayor-council* form the municipality is divided into wards for electoral purposes. The electorates vote by wards for the mayor and members of the council. In the strong-mayor system the mayor appoints heads of the municipal departments. In the weak-mayor system the council runs the departments by committee and many of the municipal officers are voted into and out of public office. The mayor-council system is the main form of urban government in the large frostbelt cities. It was the main form of urban government in the era of Boss politics which saw its heyday from the last third of the nineteenth century up until the present day in some cities especially in the frostbelt. The Boss system, sometimes known as machine politics, was based on the control of votes as votes gave power. Through their political machine the bosses controlled votes and they kept these votes by dispensing favours and services and by manipulating ward boundaries (termed gerrymandering) in order to favour their support.

In the *commission form of government* the electorate vote in city-wide, non-partisan elections for members of a commission who in turn run the municipal departments. This form of government was proposed by the reformers of the late nineteenth and early twentieth centuries who sought to dispense with boss politics and emasculate the political power of the urban working class.

In the *council manager form of government* there are city-wide, non-partisan elections for members of a council who elect a manager who in turn is the chief executive of the municipality.

Both the commission and the council manager forms of government are important forms of government in the newer, smaller cities of the sunbelt where there is no history of Boss politics and

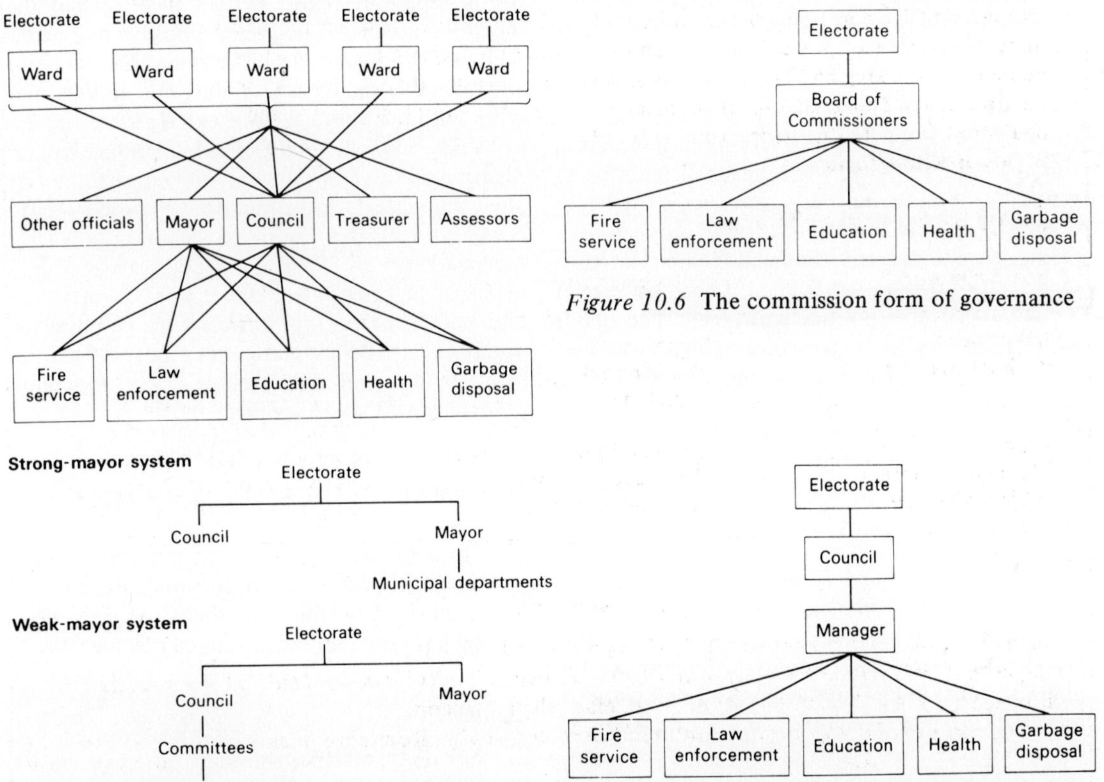

Figure 10.5 Mayor-council of governance

Figure 10.6 The commission form of governance

Figure 10.7 The council-manager form of government

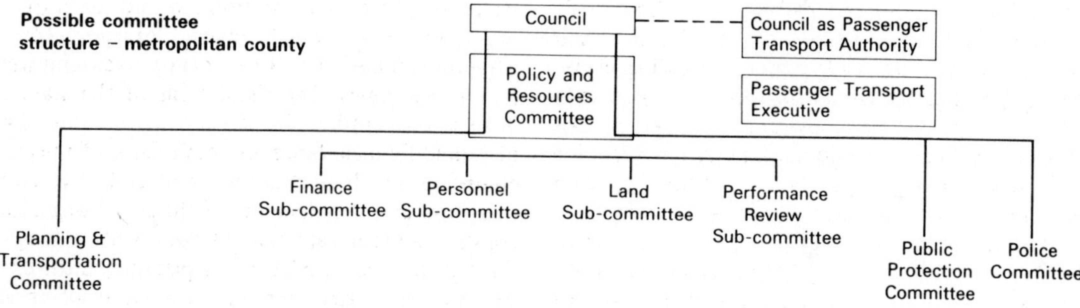

Figure 10.8 Committee structure of local government

a weaker working class. It is the most important form of government in the richer municipalities.

The city-wide election system, sometimes termed 'at-large' elections, works against lower-income and ethnic groups concentrated in particular parts of the city while the non-partisan nature of politics tends to place more emphasis on the language of efficiency and cost reduction than the vocabulary of politics and redistributional consequences.

The UK In most British cities elections occur on a ward basis. These are units varying in population from 8,000 to 30,000 with the small units being found in the older inner-city areas while the larger ones are found in the more recently growing peripheral parts of the city. Councillors are elected to represent a ward on the council. Urban politics in Britain is national politics writ small. The major political parties – Conservative, Labour, Liberal and Social Democratic – all fight in local elections. The electoral language of urban politics is the language of national political ideologies. If urban politics in the USA is the politics of place then the politics of class dominate the urban scene in Britain.

A full council meeting is the set-piece affair of local politics. The real decisions are made by the committees. The committee structure of a metropolitan authority is shown in Figure 10.8. The chairmanship of the committee is a powerful political position and one which is in the hands of the political party which has gained a majority of council seats. These committees are serviced by the municipal bureaucracy. The planning and transportation committee, for example, obtains its information and monitoring reports from the planning and transport departments staffed and headed by full-time permanent, non-elected officials. The appointed officials are thus in a position of considerable power. They are permanent experts, as opposed to part-time political representatives, and they are the main interpreters of central-government directors and major sources of information. Some writers have argued that much of urban public-policy impacts (e.g. urban renewal) owes a great deal to departmental power and bureaucratic initiatives. But bureaucrats must work with the political representatives. Rather than a crude councillor/bureaucrat division we can identify a powerful political elite consisting of the chief bureaucrats and committee chairpeople. This is not to deny that considerable power is wielded independently by both senior politicals and senior officials. In cases where direct political interest is minimal then the senior officials will be important initiators of policy proposals, but if political interests are clearly indicated then the senior politicians will take a leading role.

INFORMAL POLITICS: THE MAIN AGENTS

The form of urban government provides the context in which different groups and interests seek to maintain and improve their position. At a general level three broad groups can be identified.

Capital

In capitalist countries business interests have a considerable role to play in the urban political arena. The interest of capital are twofold:

(1) To reduce costs. Profit-seeking firms seek to

minimise expenditures which do not directly aid profits. Thus, most firms seek to minimise their rent levels and levels of taxation. Holding everything else constant firms will tend to (re)locate in areas where costs are lowest. Much of the net suburbanisation of economic activity has been due to firms and corporations seeking cheaper accommodation, cheaper labour and lower taxation levels.

(2) To benefit from publicly financed services. An individual firm would find it impossible to pay for its workforce's housing, education and transport. But firms need schools, hospitals and roads in order to educate, heal and transport workers.

The Spanish sociologist Manuel Castells suggests that we can analyse the city as a unit of collective consumption. Those essential services such as roads, hospitals and schools are the collective means of consumption. They are collective, argues Castells, in that they are provided by the state, although they are used by capitalist firms. Different firms seek at the same time to use these services but avoid paying (too much) for them. Much of the growth of public services therefore has come from the private sector seeking to obtain these essential means of consumption without having to provide them themselves.

Labour

The institutions of organised labour, like those of capital, are concerned with production and reproduction. Thus their interests are twofold:

(1) Labour wants to maintain a supply of jobs and increased wages. A desire to maintain jobs often means an alliance with capital while the demand for higher wages often means a conflict.

(2) At the point of reproduction organised labour, especially in those countries with a socialist tradition, seeks to maintain and improve the education, health and general social welfare of workers. These goods and services, termed the social wage by some writers, are sometimes the same as those sought by capital.

Capital and labour each have interests outside the factory gates and office walls. Sometimes there is a congruence of interests. Better education facilities are often demanded by both capital and labour, although disputes may arise over the funding and the direction of the programme. In other cases there is explicit conflict. Capital often seeks to direct expenditure to aid its profits (e.g. motorways which reduce transport costs) while organised labour often wants to extend welfare programmes. The fiscal crisis of the state is in reality a conflict over the amount and direction of public finance. Since the built form of the city comprises much of the means of collective consumption and the elements of the social wage, the conflict between capital and labour is often fought through the medium of urban planning as the city becomes the arena for the resolution of these conflicts.

Households

In particular cases households, as consumers of urban public services, have a role to play in informal urban politics. Much of urban politics is concerned with the tension between municipal officials and unions on the one hand and on the other households as consumer trade unionists. Households also play a role as residents. We can imagine the city as a constantly changing externality surface. A new road which links up a suburban housing area with a downtown is a new positive externality to the suburbanites, but the construction of the freeway through the city, with the consequent noise, pollution and destruction of the local community, is a negative externality to the inner-city resident. Alterations in the distribution of both public and private goods and services create a constantly changing externality surface. Much of residents' involvement in urban politics is concerned with manipulating this surface in order to maintain or improve their positive externalities and minimise or deflect the negative ones.

Residents respond in two main ways, the so-called exit/voice choice. On the one hand, they can move in order to escape the real or perceived negative externality such as high crime rates, the presence of low-income households, poor schooling, falling property values. This is the rationale behind the white middle-income flight to the suburbs. Those who have beaten the path to the suburbs have sought to impede the influx of later, lower-income, would-be suburbanites by exclusionary zoning. On the other hand, the residents who stay put either through choice or constraints, can voice their approval and try to mobilise political support and influence political decisions. The relative success of residents'

Plates 43 and 44
Political dialogue in the streets: (43) London: (44) Barcelona

groups will depend upon organisational skill, contacts with influential people and key decision-makers, the stakes involved and the strategies they adopted.

In any particular issues which arise in the urban political arena there will be a variety of interests involved. There will be the politicians, the municipal unions and a range of groups affected. In general business interests will seek to reduce their tax load and direct public spending to meet their needs and residents will want to maximise positive externalities and minimise negative ones. Often there is conflict between members of the same broad categories. Downtown business interests will want to see urban-renewal projects which secure their financial viability, while business interests elsewhere will not want to see too much public expenditure going to subsidise their competitors.

How are disputes resolved in the urban political arena? Generally, on political strength. The strongest, the large corporations and powerful unions, have the economic muscle to get most of their interests satisfied. And the richer residents have better resources and organisation than lower-income residents' groups to achieve their goals. The players in the urban arena are not equal.

OUTPUTS AND OUTCOMES

The net result of the demands of capital and the needs of labour and the political mobilisation of households as both consumers and residents has been a tremendous growth in the role of the local state. Public goods and services now constitute a significant element in contemporary cities. Michael Teitz captures the public nature of the modern city. Although his comments also apply to modern urban woman.

> Modern urban man is born in a publicly-financed hospital, who sees his education in a publicly-supported school and university, spends a good part of his life travelling on publicly-built transportation facilities, communicates through the post office or the quasi public telephone system, drinks his public water, disposes of his garbage through the public removal system, reads his public library books, picnics in his public parks, is protected by his public police, fire and health systems; eventually he dies, again in the hospital, and may even be buried in a public cemetery. (Tietz, 1968)

The British political scientist Patrick Dunleavy has constructed a typology of the variety of urban goods and services. Let us take it a step at a time. Dunleavy first of all makes a distinction between consumption goods and services and non-consumption activities (Figure 10.9). He makes a further distinction between state-managed consumption goods and services, where the state

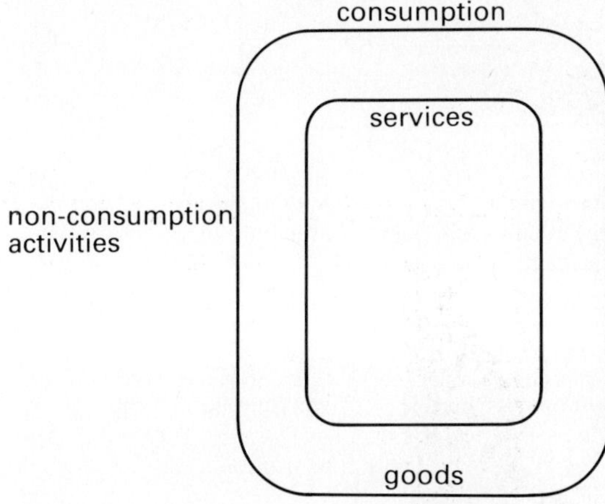

Figure 10.9 Consumption/non-consumption goods and services

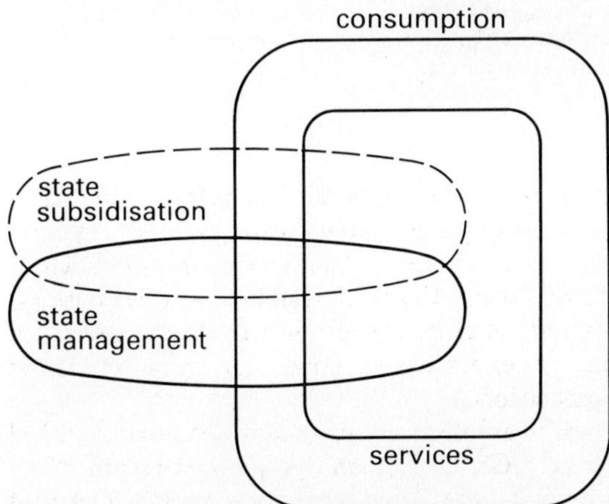

Figure 10.10 State subsidisation and management

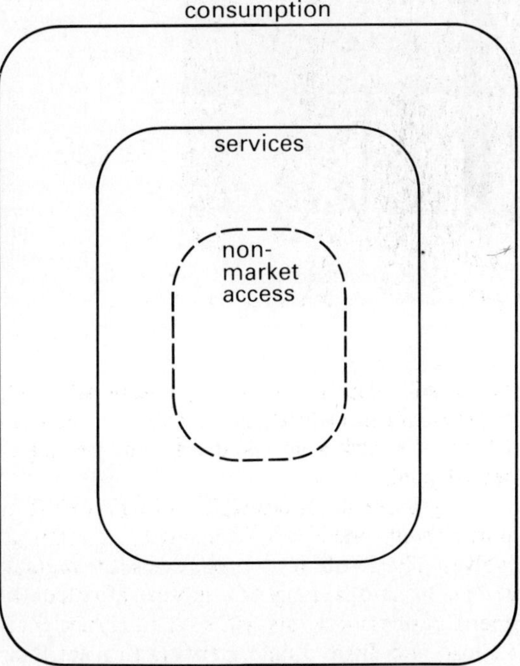

Figure 10.11 Market and non-market access

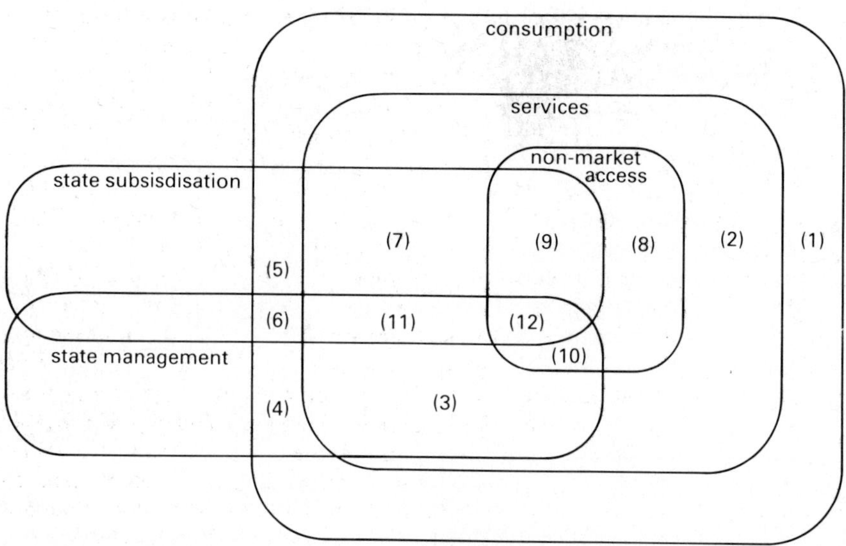

No.	Description		Examples	Category
1	private goods consumption		consumer durables	individualised consumption
2	private service consumption		commercially supplied services	
3	public commercial services		public utilities (UK)	
4	state-organised goods consumption		?	
5	state-subsidised goods		owner-occupier housing (UK, USA), company cars (UK), food stamps (USA)	quasi-individualised consumption
6	state-organised and subsidised goods consumption		?	
7	state-subsidised commercial services		low income private renting (UK), cultural services (UK), much mass transit (USA), Medicaid programmes (USA)	
8	private non-market services		National Trust, RNLI (UK) philanthropic groups (USA), private open spaces	quasi-collective consumption
9	state-subsidised, private non-market services		youth, welfare, community groups (UK, USA), housing associations	
10	state-organised non-market services		future public housing? (UK)	collective consumption
11	state-subsidised public services		urban mass transit (UK)	
12	non-market, state-subsidised public services			
		charged services	public housing (UK, USA)	
		'need' services	health services (UK) personal social services (UK, USA)	
		'merit' services	higher education (UK)	
		free services	highways, school education, public protection, urban planning and environmental services (UK, USA)	

Figure 10.12 An extended typology of forms of consumption

organises consumption, and state-subsidised goods and services where the state also subsidises this consumption (Figure 10.10). The final distinction is drawn between market access to consumption goods and services, where what you get is determined by what you can pay for, and non-market access which is not conditioned by people's willingness to pay (Figure 10.11). The net result is to produce an extended typology of consumption forms. This typology shown in Figure 10.12 can be used to place most outputs of the urban political arena. It can also be used to locate the changing position of different consumption goods and services and to compare the level and range in different countries and different cities in the same country. We would expect, for example, at first glance to find more of items 10 in centrally planned economies than capitalist ones and more in capitalist countries with a strong socialist tradition, for example Britain, than countries such as the United States which lack this tradition. The typology provides a useful framework in which to measure and compare the level of outputs.

We can differentiate between the outputs of the urban political arena, that is the number of streets built, the amount of money spent, etc., and the outcomes which are the distributional consequences of public-policy outputs. There are four main types of outcomes.

(1) *To them who hath* (Figure 10.13a) Regressive outcomes are those which aid the better off. The urban renewal schemes of the last twenty-five years, for example, have aided powerful business interests. This outcome in general arises from the political and economic muscle wielded by powerful interests. Indeed very powerful groups may not even need to exercise power, as their interests may be seen as the national or indeed the general interest. In many cities business interests are seen as synonymous with the public interests and in this

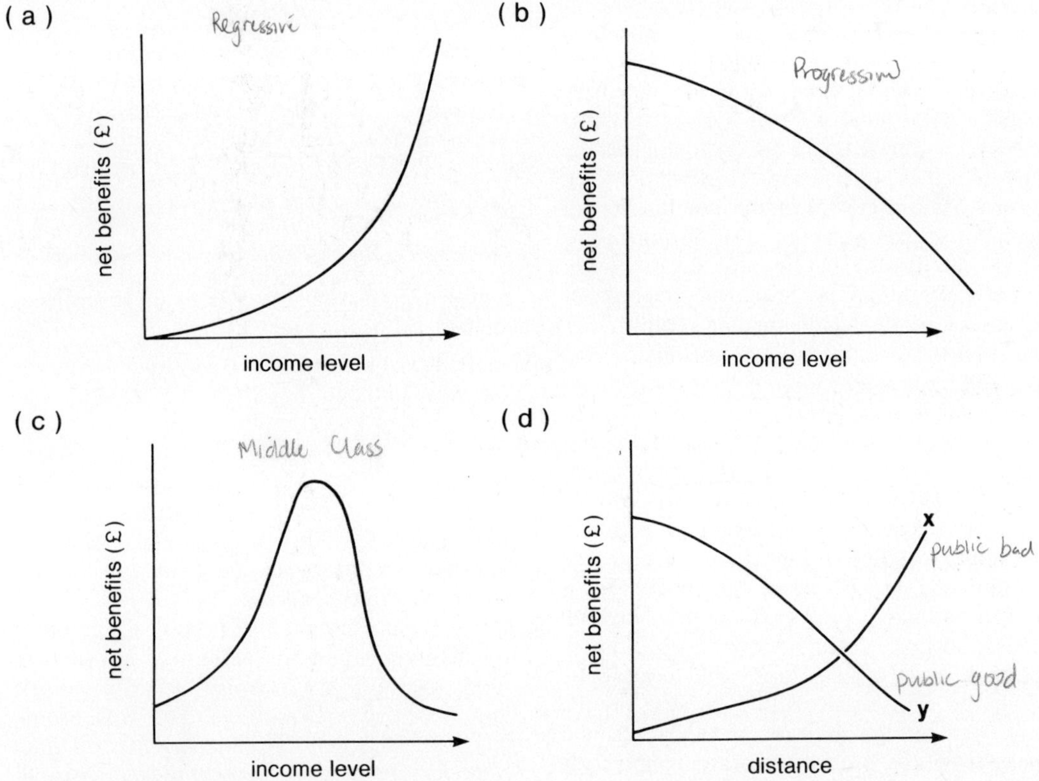

Figure 10.13 Distribution of outcomes

case business does not need to be involved in the political process directly since its interests are already being seen to.

(2) *Compensatory* These outcomes are redistributional because they provide most benefits to the lower-income groups (see Figure 10.13b). Many of the welfare programmes have a compensatory outcome. Poorer groups can obtain compensatory outcomes through their weight of numbers in the political process and through direct action. Inner-city riots have done more than anything in both Britain and the United States to produce some welfare programmes with redistributional consequences. In order to maintain some measure of social harmony most governments in capitalist society have to produce some compensatory outputs in order to reduce the inequalities produced by the private market.

(3) *The sharp elbows of the middle class* A number of studies of public policy outcomes have pointed to the sharp elbows of the middle-income groups. In some social-policy programmes you obtain what you ask for, for example grants for housing improvement, the use of subsidised facilities such as sports centres and libraries. The rich have their own facilities, while the poor have to compete with the articulate, organised middle-income groups who have the ability to operate the system to their advantage (Figure 10.13c). Professor Le Grand (1982) of the London School of Economics examined the distributional outcomes of the British public policies in health, education and housing. He found the greatest net beneficiaries were the middle-income groups.

(4) *Locational* Some outputs have distinct spatial outcomes. We can identify *public goods* which are facilities which provide positive externalities to the surrounding areas' population; for example hospitals, schools, libraries, etc. and *public bads* which are facilities which impose negative externalities on the surrounding areas, for example, factories producing noxious fumes. Line x in Figure 10.13d sketches out the distribution of net benefits for a public bad and line y for a public good. Much of locational politics in the urban arena is of different groups seeking to benefit from the location of public goods. Tension is caused because groups can only gain at the expense of others. If one group, for example, seeks to relocate a public bad it can only do so at the expense of another area.

The rise of government involvement has meant that our lives are dominated by the impact in outcome of public-policy programmes. The attempt to generate programmes which benefit material interest is the very stuff of urban politics and constitutes the contemporary city as a political arena.

GUIDE TO FURTHER READING

These are a number of books on urban politics. General treatments include:

Cox, K.R. (1973), *Conflict, Power and Politics in the City: A Geographic View*, McGraw-Hill, New York.

Cox, K.R. (1979), *Location and Public Problems*, Maaroufa Press, Chicago.

Dunleavy, P. (1980), *Urban Political Analysis*, Macmillan, London.

Friedland, R. (1982), *Power and Crisis in the City*, Macmillan, London.

Johnston, R.J. (1979), *Political, Electoral and Spatial Systems*, Oxford University Press.

Lineberry, R.L. and Sharkansky, I. (1977, 3rd edition), *Urban Politics and Public Policy*, Harper & Row, New York.

Saunders, P. (1979), *Urban Politics*, Hutchinson, London.

Short, J.R. (1982), *An Introduction to Political Geography*, Routledge & Kegan Paul, London.

A useful introduction to patterns of government spending is:

Bennett, R.J. (1980), *The Geography of Public Finance*, Methuen, London.

On metropolitan fragmentation see:

Neenan, W.B. (1973), Suburban-central city exploitation thesis: one city's tale. In Boulding, K.C., Pfaff, M. and Pfaff, A. (eds), *Transfers in an Urbanized Economy*, Wordsworth, Belmont, California.

Zeigler, D.J. and Brunn, S.D. (1980), Geopolitical fragmentation and the pattern of growth and need: defining the cleavage between sunbelt and frostbelt metropolises. In S.D. Brunn, J.O. Wheeler (eds), *The American Metropolitan System: Present and Future*, Edward Arnold, London.

An interesting introduction to local government reform in Britain is:

Dearlove, J. (1979), *The Reorganization of British Local Government*, Cambridge University Press.

General studies of the city as political arena include:

Castells, M. (1977), *The Urban Question*, Edward Arnold, London.

Castells, M. (1978), *City, Class and Power*, Macmillan, London.

Castells, M. (1983), *The City and The Grassroots*, Edward Arnold, London.

Cox, K.R. (1981), Capitalism and conflict around the communal living space, In M. Dear and A.J. Scott (eds), *Urbanization and Urban Planning in Capitalist Society*, Methuen, London.

Harloe, M. and Lebas, E. (1981), *City Class and Capital*, Edward Arnold, London.

Particular studies include:

Simmie, J. (1981), *Power, Property and Corporation*, Macmillan, London.

Dahl, R.A. (1961), *Who Governs*, Yale University Press, New Haven.

Gottdiener, M. (1978), *Planned Sprawl: Private and Public Interests in Suburbia*, Sage, London.

Studies of public goods and urban outcomes include:

Kirby, A.M. (1979), *Education, Health and Housing*, Saxon House, Farnborough, Hants.

Kirby, A.M. (1982), *The Politics of Location*, Methuen, London.

Levy, F.S., Meltsner, A.J. and Wildavsky, A. (1974), *Urban Outcomes: Schools, Streets and Libraries*, University of California Press.

Le Grand, J. (1982), *The Strategy of Inequality*, Allen & Unwin, London.

Teitz, M. (1968), Towards a theory of urban public facility location, *Papers of the Regional Science Association*, 21, 35-51.

Part 4

People and the Urban Environment

Plates 45 and 46

11 Perception and Activity in the City

PERCEPTION AND EVALUATION

People's behaviour in the urban environment depends upon their perception. Their actions are conducted in the environment as perceived. How do people perceive the urban environment?

Key elements

According to the American urban researcher Kevin Lynch the building blocks of environmental knowledge are paths, edges, nodes, districts and landmarks. *Paths,* sidewalks, roads and canals, are the thoroughfares along which people travel. We gain knowledge in our travels. *Edges* are the boundaries between different districts; they include railway lines, shore-lines, breaks in the sizes of buildings and the boundary at the city's edge between rural and urban land uses. *Nodes* are junctions of concentrated activity such as railway stations and main squares. *Districts* are named areas of the city with definite edges and distinct characteristics. Non-residential districts include the downtown area while the residential areas of the city are a mosaic of residential districts with different names and characteristics. *Landmarks* are recognisable features generally smaller than nodes. Striking buildings and famous statues are examples of landmarks. Edinburgh's castle and Paris's Eiffel Tower are just two of the more famous landmarks.

These five elements allow us to put some order into our perception of the city. Superimposed one upon another, the elements provide us with a mental map of the city. The mental map we have of a city is continually being modified. The longer we live in a particular city and the more we travel in the city the more our knowledge increases and the size of our mental map expands. The size of the mental map thus varies by length of residence, travel patterns, income and stage in the lifecycle. Distinct differences have been uncovered in the mental maps of different groups. Figure 11.2, for example, shows variation in the mental map of Los Angeles held by three different income and ethnic groups. In a very real sense they inhabit three different urban worlds.

Our knowledge of the city affects our evaluation. We tend to like the bits we know and this affects our behaviour. Once we have established a travel route from home to workplace, home to school or home to shops, for example, we tend to stick with it. People do not search through all possible routes every time they are travelling, evaluating each very carefully. Rather, once people have established an acceptable route as quickly as possible their behaviour and activity becomes routinised. A similar pattern is found in residential mobility. When people are looking for a new house or apartment they do not search all possible vacancies within their budget constraint. Rather they search very few places in areas with which they are familiar. We operate in the tightly circumscribed world of our mental map. Most households have a dome of knowledge concerning areas in the city centring on their present residence. This knowledge is gained in the process of living in the area and may be reinforced by the nearby location of friends, local shops and schools. Most activity takes place within this awareness space. The bias in our perception is apparent on the national as well as the urban scale. Figure 11.3, for example, shows the USA as seen from the point of view of a New Yorker and a Bostonian. Notice how for the New Yorker Brooklyn figures very largely, while Texas is placed in the peripheral role on the edge of their awareness space. For the Bostonian Cape Cod figures very largely, while the interior of the USA is *terra incognita.*

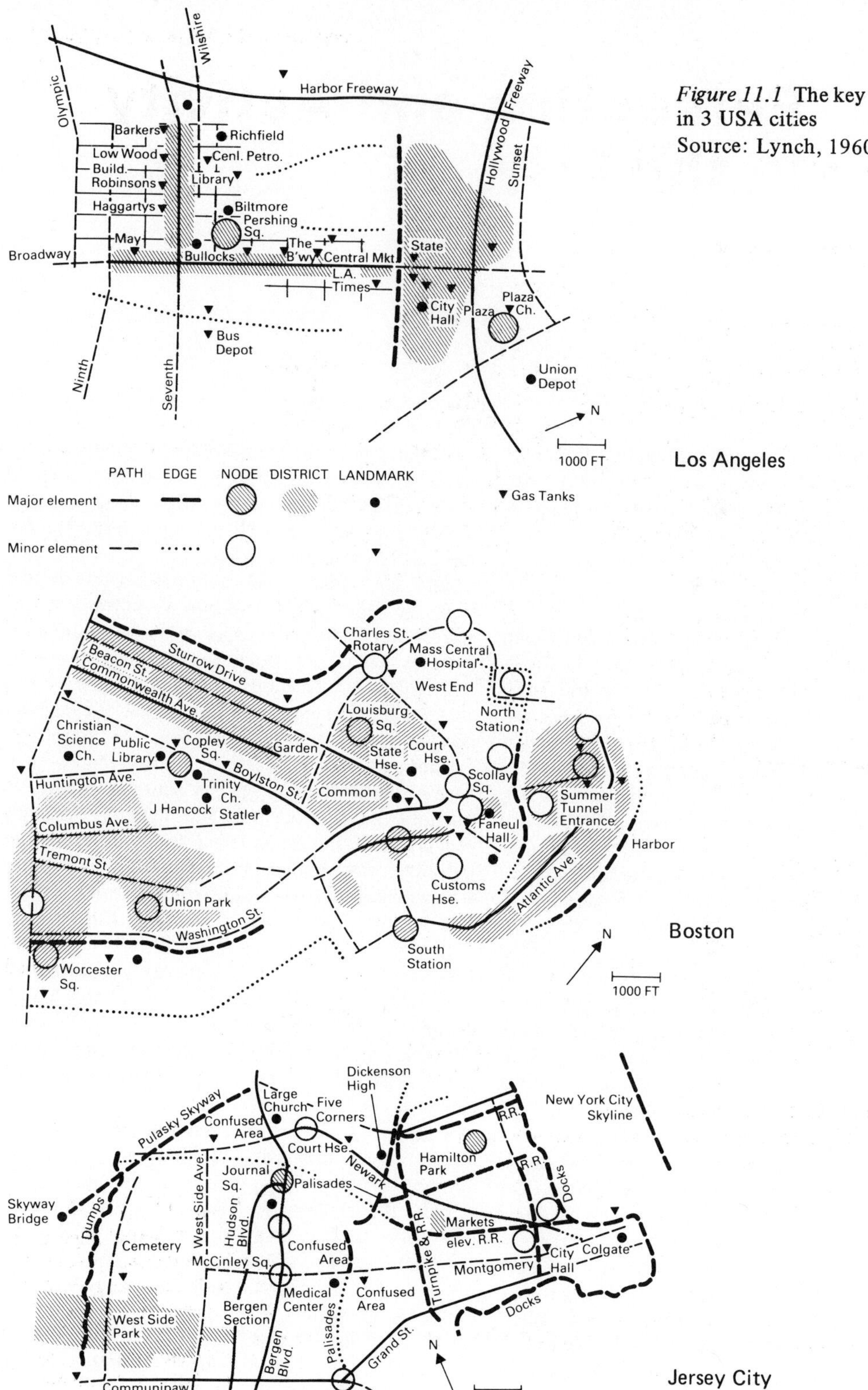

Figure 11.1 The key elements in 3 USA cities
Source: Lynch, 1960

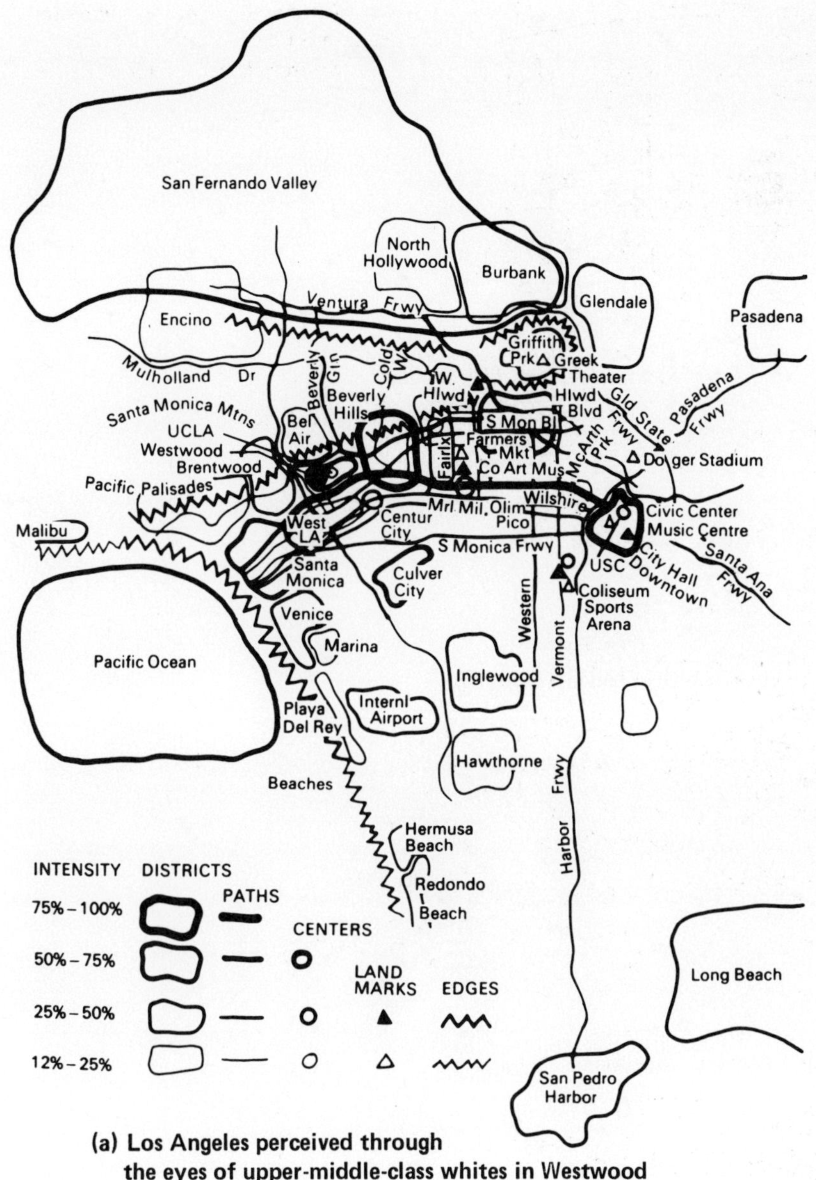

(a) Los Angeles perceived through the eyes of upper-middle-class whites in Westwood

Figure 11.2 Los Angeles
Source: after Orleans, P. (1967), Differential cognition of urban residents: effects of social scale on mapping, *Science, Engineering and the City,* Publication No. 1498, National Academy of Engineering, National Academy Press, Washington, DC

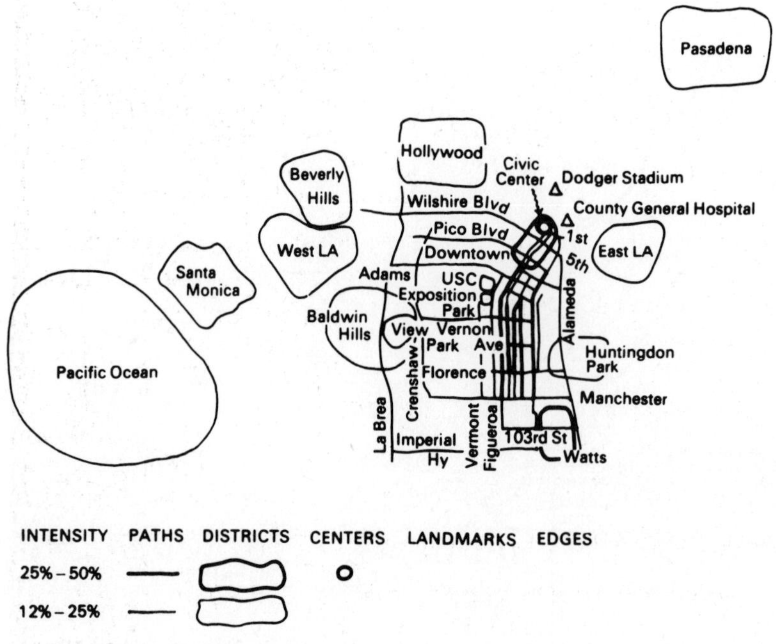

(b) Los Angeles through the eyes of black residents in Avalon

INTENSITY	PATHS	DISTRICTS	CENTERS	LANDMARKS	EDGES
50% – 75%	▬▬			▲	
25% – 50%	──				
12% – 25%	—	▭	○	△	

(c) Los Angeles through the eyes of Spanish-speaking residents in Boyle Heights

Figure 11.2 cont.

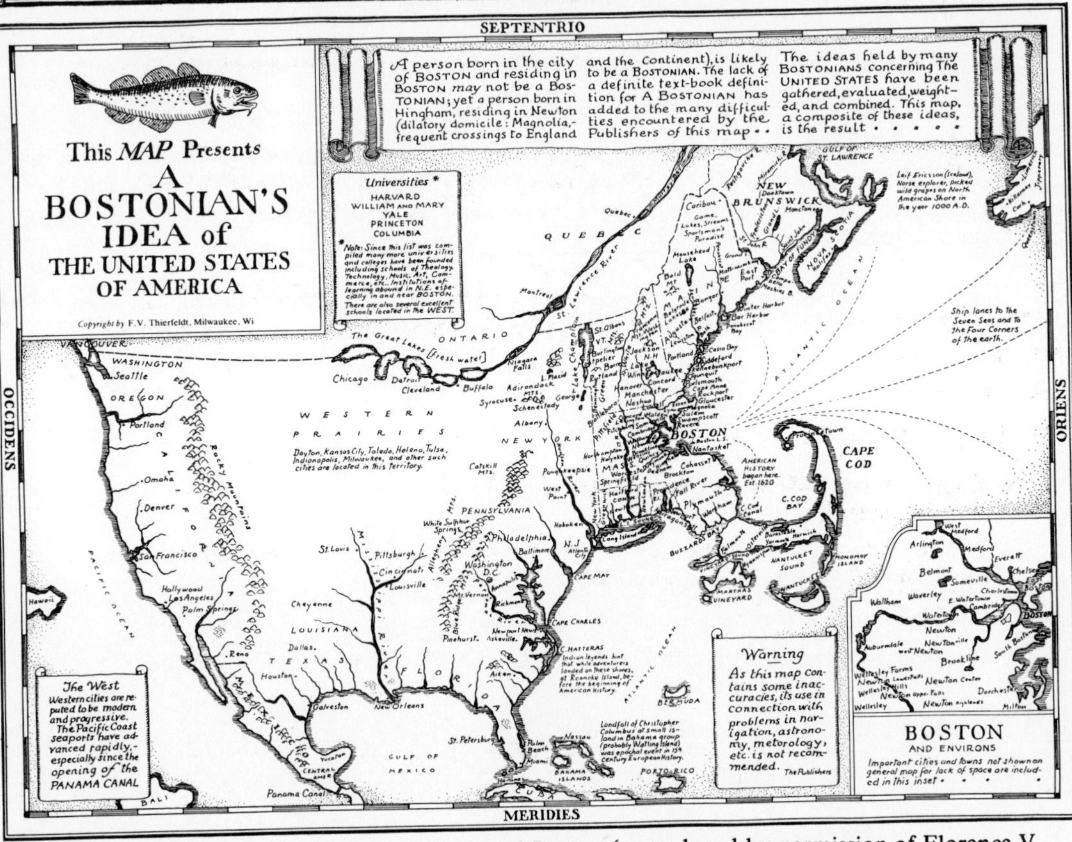

Figure 11.3 The USA as seen from New York and Boston (reproduced by permission of Florence V. Thierfeldt)

THE LYNCH METHOD

In order to elicit environmental knowledge Kevin Lynch conducted a three-part study with a sample of people. First, there was an office interview lasting almost 1½ hours. The following questions were asked, and the answers were taped. In this case the city being studied was Boston.

1 What first comes to your mind, what symbolises the word 'Boston' for you? How would you broadly describe Boston in a physical sense?

2 We would like you to make a quick map of central Boston, inward or downtown from Massachusetts Avenue. Make it just as if you were making a rapid description of the city to a stranger, covering all the main features. We don't expect an accurate drawing – just a rough sketch. (Interviewer is to take notes on the sequence in which the map is drawn.)

3 (a) Please give me complete and explicit directions for the trip that you normally take going home to where you work. Picture yourself actually making the trip, and describe the sequence of things you would see, hear, smell along the way, including the pathmarkers that have become important to you, and the clues that a stranger would need to make the same decisions that you have to make. We are interested in the physical pictures of things. It is not important if you can't remember the names of streets and places. (During recital of trip, interviewer is to probe, where needed, for more detailed descriptions.)

(b) Do you have any particular emotional feelings about various parts of your trip? How long would it take you? Are there parts of the trip where you feel uncertain of your location? (Question 3 is then to be repeated for one or more trips which are standardised for all interviewees, i.e. 'Go on foot from Massachusetts General Hospital to South Station,' or 'Go by car from Faneuil Hall to Symphony Hall.')

4 Now, we would like to know what elements of central Boston you think are most distinctive. They may be large or small, but tell us those that for you are the easiest to identify and remember. (For each of two or three of the elements listed in response to 4, the interviewer goes on to ask question 5.)

5 (a) Would you describe ———— to me? If you were taken there blindfolded, when the blindfold was taken off what clues would you use to positively identify where you were?

(b) Are there any particular emotional feelings that you have with regard to ———— ?

(c) Would you show me on your map where ———— is? (and, if appropriate:) where are the boundaries?

6 Would you show me on your map the direction of north?

7 The interview is over now, but it would help if we could just have a few minutes of free discussion. (Remainder of questions are inserted informally.)

(a) What do you think we were trying to find out?

(b) What importance is orientation and the recognition of city elements to people?

(c) Do you feel any pleasure from knowing where you are or where you are going? Or displeasure in the reverse?

(d) Do you find Boston an easy city to find your way in, or to identify its parts?

(e) What cities of your acquaintance have good orientation? Why?

Second, the interviewees were shown a stack of photographs of the city and asked to identify them and lay them out on a large map of the city.

Finally, some of the interviewees were taken out into the city streets with an interviewer to trace out the routes mentioned in the reply to question 3. Their comments were recorded on tape. If all respondents mentioned a particular route, this road scored 100 per cent and was shaded according. If only a quarter of respondents mention an edge, then a score of 25 per cent is recorded. The generalised maps produced thus reflected the strength of response.

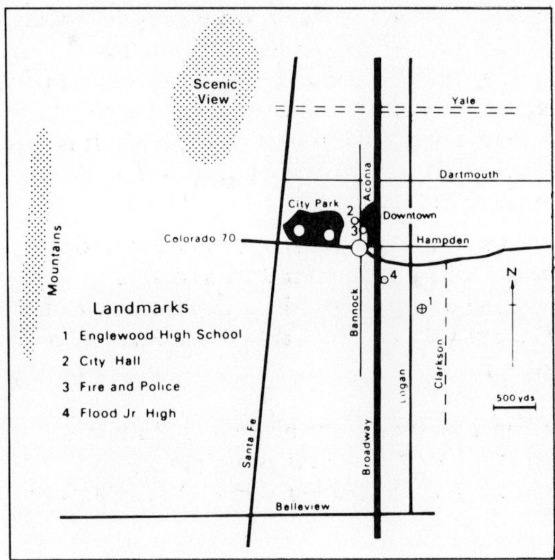

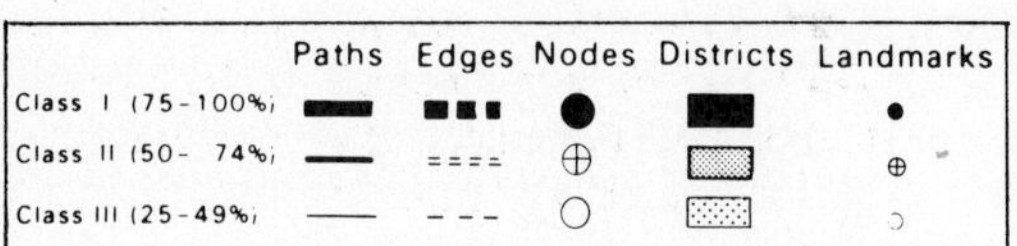

Figure 11A Citizens' image of Englewood, Denver, Colorado
Source: Harrison and Howard, 1972

Lynch's methodology has been widely used. Figure 11A is just one of many exercises repeating the method. The difficulties involved in measuring environmental knowledge have been summarised by the psychologist, Terence Lee (1976).

References

Harrison, J.D. and Howard, W.A. (1972), The role of meaning in the urban image, *Environment and Behaviour,* 4, 389-411.

Lee, T.R. (1976), Cities in the Mind, In Herbert, D.T. and Johnston, R.J. (eds), Social Areas in Cities Vol. 2: *Spatial Perspectives on Problems and Policies,* Wiley, Chichester, Sussex.

Lynch, K. (1960), *The Image of The City,* MIT Press, Cambridge, Mass.

BEHAVIOUR AND ENVIRONMENT

The development of the behavioural approach in geography, by which we mean the explicit focus on perception and decision-making, can be traced back to the work of the British geographer William Kirk. Professor Kirk argued that for too long geographers had drawn too simple a distinction between people and environment as in Figure 11B. The important distinction he went on to suggest should be drawn between the phenomenal environment, which is the external world of physical reality, and the perceived environment in which phenomenal facts are organised and evaluated (Figure 11C). It is the behavioural environment, argued Kirk, in which rational human behaviour takes place.

Figure 11B

Figure 11C

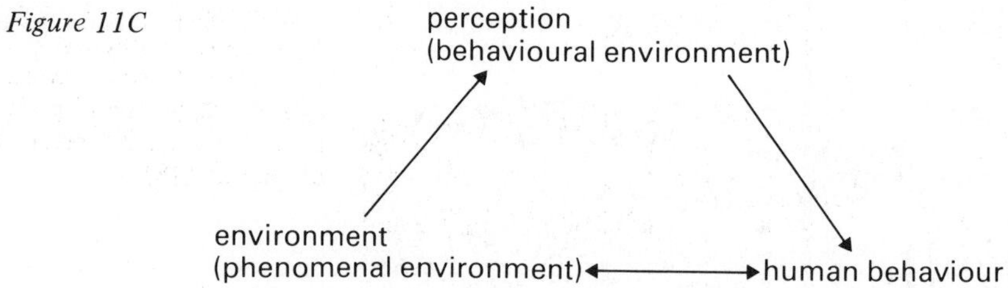

The American geographer, Professor Lowenthal, suggested that the phenomenal environment was refracted through the filters of culture and the lens of personal experience and imagination to produce the behavioural environment in which occurs individual behaviour. Superimposed on the accepted world shaped by one culture group there was also the slightly different personal viewpoints which were formed by unique individual experience, imaginations and memory. To understand fully human behaviour we need to look at the world of everyday experience. The geographer David Ley had argued, 'To understand the social process one must encounter the situation of the decision-maker, which includes incomplete and inconsistent information, values and partisan attitudes, short-term motives and long range beliefs.'

References

Kirk, W. (1951), Historical geography and the concept of the behavioural environment, *Indian Geographical Journal, Silver Jubilee Volume*, 152-60.

Ley, D. (1977), Social geography and the taken-for-granted world, *Transactions of the Institute of British Geographers, New Series 2*, 498-512.

Lowenthal, D. (1961), Geography, experience and imagination: towards a geographical epistemology, *Annals of the Association of American Geographers*, 51, 241-60.

We evaluate areas of the city on a number of criteria. The criteria vary according to the purpose. When looking for a new dwelling, for example, we rank residential areas according to the quality of the environment as a place to live. In contrast, when we are travelling through the city say, late at night, we will evaluate the different areas in terms of personal safety. Some streets will be considered more dangerous than others and they are to be avoided. Figure 11.4a shows the perception and evaluation of a portion of Philadelphia by local residents. Notice how there are definite black spots and for those with good street knowledge these will be avoided (Figure 11.4b). Here is an example of experience shaping perception and evaluation, which in turn influence behaviour.

Institutional behaviour

It is not only individuals who respond to images of the urban environment. Institutional bodies also have mental maps which affect their decisions. We can consider three examples.

First, there is the case of lenders of mortgage finance. In the USA banks, savings and loans associations and certain federal agencies all allocate

Plates 47 and 48
City walls can become channels of communication. The messages range from the humorous comments in London (47), to an expression of religious and political affiliation in a Protestant area of Belfast (48)

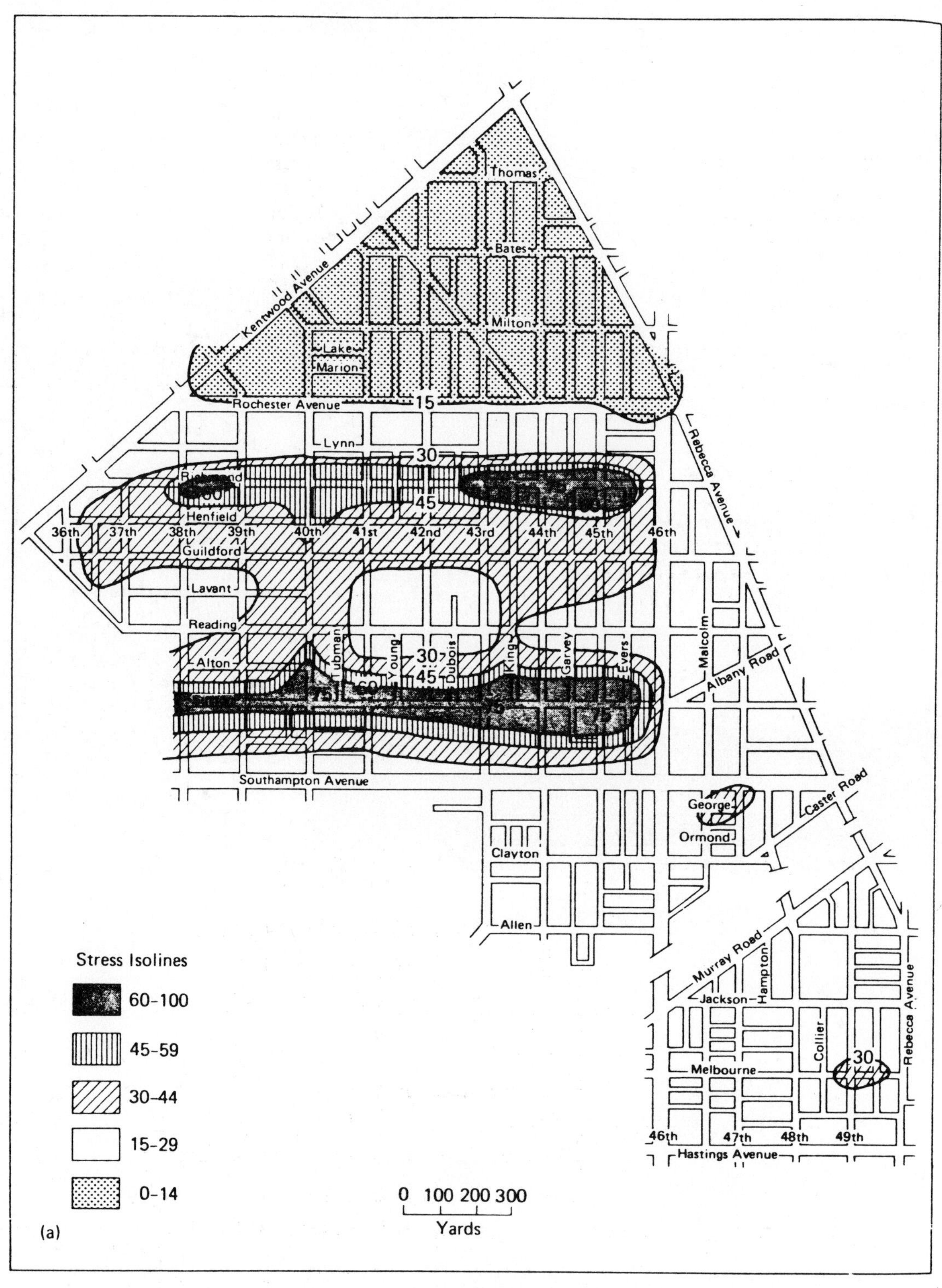

Figure 11.4 Stress surface and spatial behaviour in Philadelphia
Source: Ley, D. (1974), *The Black Inner City as Frontier Outpost,* Association of American Geographers, Monograph Series, No. 7

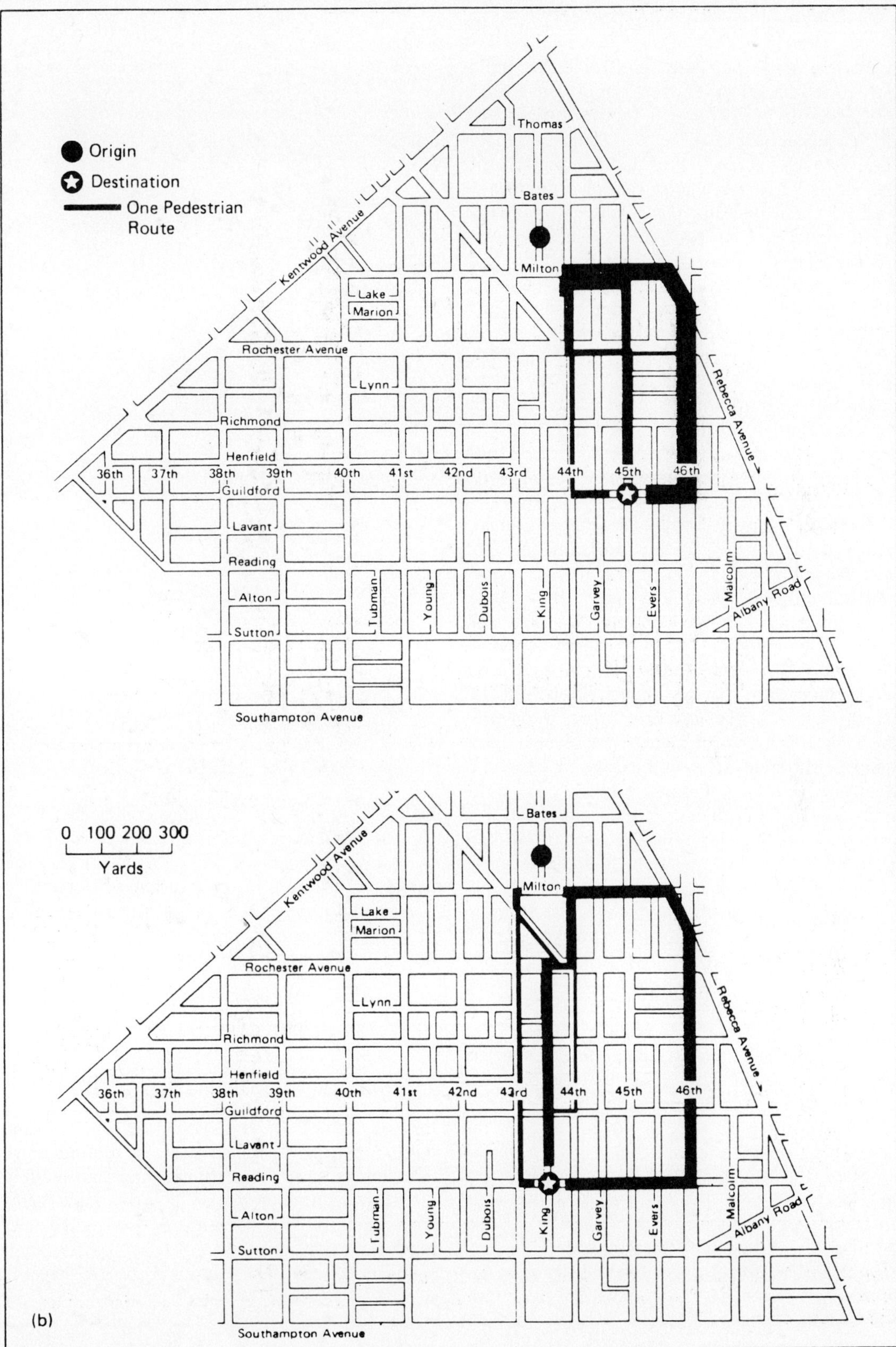

Figure 11.4 cont.

funds for house purchase. In Britain the building societies are the most important single institution. In both countries the institutions base their lending on the pattern of demand and on their corporate perception of the different residential areas. What has emerged from a number of studies on both sides of the Atlantic is that there are a number of inner-city areas which are considered high-risk areas. A policy of red-lining is pursued in those areas where very little mortgage finance is allocated. This policy can become a self-fulfilling prophecy as the lack of mortgage funds leads to further deterioration which provides further reasons for refusing funds. The shared image of a rundown neighbourhood held by mortgage-lending institutions is thus partly a reflection but also partly the cause of deterioration of inner-city housing in Britain and North America.

Second, employers and credit agencies evaluate people partly by their address. In many cases the area where you live is unimportant to your chance of getting a job or obtaining credit. However, in all major cities there are certain areas which have a very bad reputation and by common consensus are rated very poorly. People living in these areas are stigmatised as they are thought to be untrustworthy and unreliable. The urban economist Alan McGregor looked at patterns of unemployment in different areas of the city of Paisley in Scotland. One area, Ferguslie Park, had a notorious reputation in the city. McGregor found that even when holding everything else constant workers in Ferguslie Park had many more and longer spells of unemployment than workers in other parts of Paisley with similar employment characteristics. The evidence pointed to the operation of discriminatory hiring practices by employers in the Paisley area. Things may become so bad in stigmatised areas that either the name of the district has to be changed or the area is physically moved. The Pruitt Igoe public housing scheme in St Louis had gained such a bad reputation that people were refusing to live there. Eventually the authorities felt that nothing was left to do but to blow the whole place up.

Third, the headquarters of the major companies are located within the confines of a corporate image of the city. A high-rise block in a prestigious address is considered better for a corporation's image than a cheaper office block away from the favoured streets. Stockbroking companies try to locate in Wall Street, advertisers seek out addresses in Madison Avenue in New York and London banks try to locate in the area known as the City. The mental image which reflects the past decisions of companies guides the action of present-day decision makers.

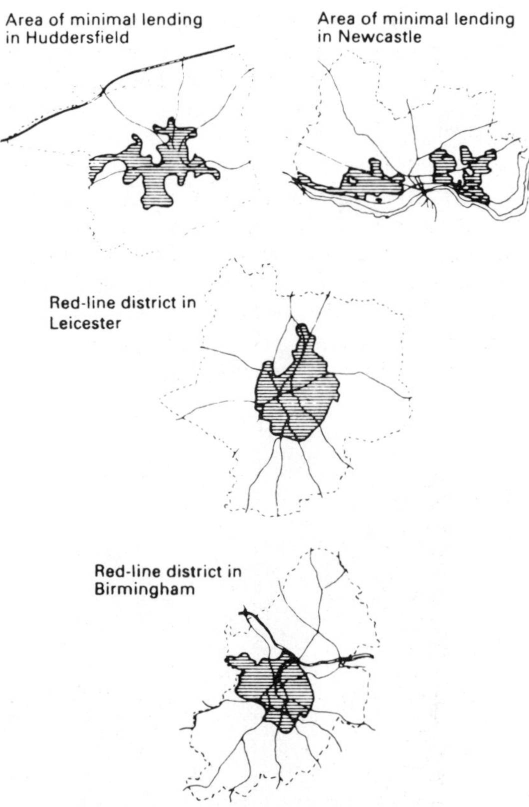

Figure 11.5 Red-line districts in British cities
Source: *Roof*, 1976

ACTIVITY IN THE CITY

Activity in time

Human activity in the city varies by time and space. We can distinguish between routine activities such as eating and sleeping and less frequent activities such as going on holiday or changing jobs. Here we will be primarily concerned with routine activity.

Since activity takes up time, people have to

organise their activities according to the constraints of time. The term *time budget* is used to refer to the study of the way households divide up their time. Two elements are important in the time budget. The first is the amount of time spent on different activities. Table 11.1 shows the results of a comparative study of time budgets in one day for households in the cities of four different countries. Notice two things - (a) the broad similarities: over half of all the time is taken up with working, eating and sleeping; (b) the specific differences in the exact amount of time spent on the different activities. In the USA they seem to spend more time in watching TV than in any other country. Although there are broad similarities, people in different countries vary in the amount of time they spend on different activities. The variation is not only restricted to international comparisons. People of different ages have different interests, different constraints and thus vary the amount of time they spend on different activities.

The second element in the time budget is the sequence of activities. Figure 11.6 shows the use of time chart drawn up by the BBC which indicates the timing of activities for two different

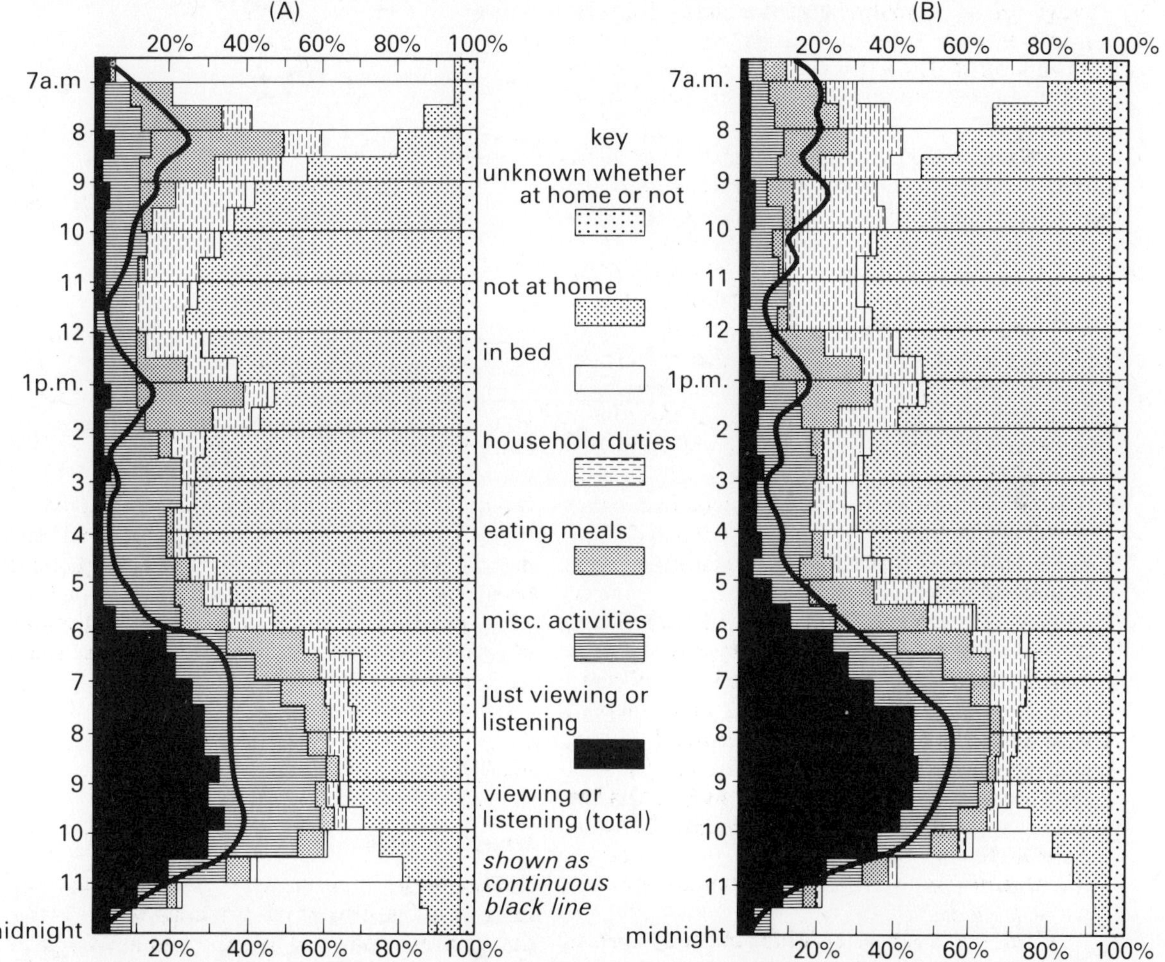

Figure 11.6 Time charts of two groups (a) high socio-economic status; (b) low socio-economic status
Source: BBC (1965), *What the People are doing, the People's Activities*, BBC Audience Research Dept., London

THE BEHAVIOURAL ENVIRONMENT

Much of classic location theory assumes that individual decision-making is made by 'economic men' who have perfect information and perfect ability to use this information in a completely rational manner. This abstraction of 'economic man' ignores variation between people, the existence of non-optional behaviour and the psychological reality of the limits to our knowledge as well as linguistically denying the economic role of women. The American geographer Allan Pred has suggested that we can incorporate the notions of imperfect knowledge and non-optimising behaviour in an alternative schema. He proposes the concept of the *behavioural matrix*. This is a matrix which allows us to plot the distribution of people with respect to their knowledge and ability to use it.

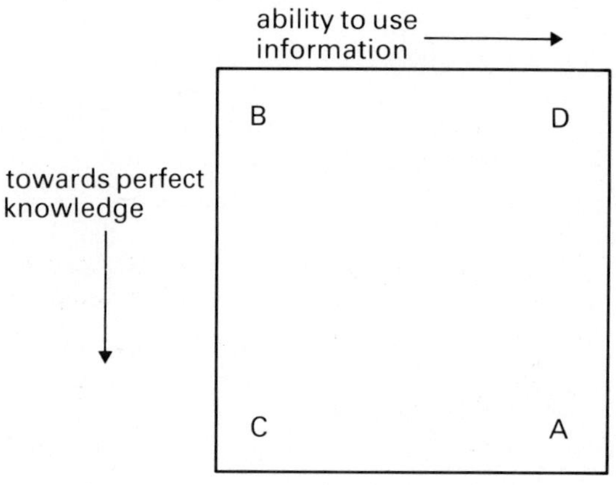

The behavioural matrix

Table 11.1 Time spent in primary activities (minutes*)

Activity	*Six cities in France*	*Lima Peru*	*44 US cities*	*Pskov, USSR*
Work	277	251	266	371
Housework	162	172	142	131
Household care	39	17	45	39
Child care	40	23	32	35
Personal needs (inc. eating, sleeping)	661	643	620	583
Non-work travel	31	52	50	55
Study-participation	19	42	28	46
Total mass media	91	87	134	113
Total leisure	121	152	123	67

socio-economic groups. Notice again how there are broad similarities; for example, most people are in bed at 7.0 a.m., are out of the house by 3.0 p.m. and they are back in the house by 8.0 p.m. There are, however, differences between the two samples. More blue-collar people watch TV or listen to radio for longer periods than the white-collar workers.

Activity in space-time

Activity takes place in space as well as time. The explicit consideration of space-time activity has been given special consideration by the geographer

* Because of rounding figures in each column may not add up to 1440.
Source: Szalai et al., 1972.

In this diagram A is the classic economic person, B has limited knowledge, and ability to use it, C has lots of information but lacks the wherewithal, while D makes the optimal choice on limited knowledge. The behavioural matrix allows the variability of individuals and the presence of sub-optimal behaviour to be explicitly incorporated.

Consider the case of the shopping patterns of B, and A.

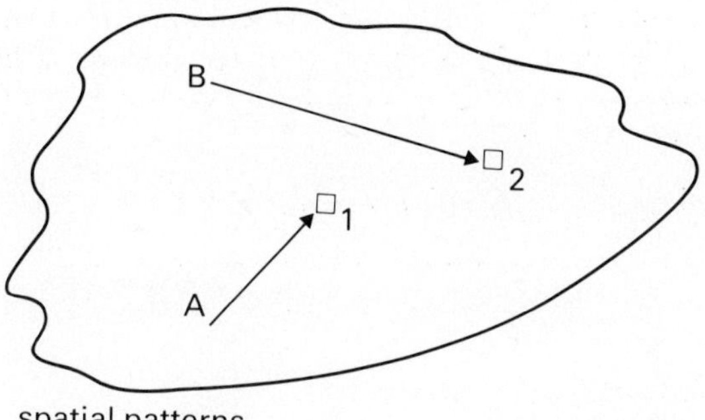

spatial patterns

A knows that shops 1 and 2 are exactly the same and since 1 is closer, A shops at 1. Person B, by contrast, isn't aware that the shops are the same and decides to shop at B. B's behaviour is sub-optimal.

In general most human action is sub-optimal.

Reference

Pred, A. (1967 and 1969), Behaviour and Location, *Lund Studies in Geography No. 27.*

Torsten Hagerstrand and his colleagues at the University of Lund in Sweden. They have suggested a way of representing space-time activity in diagrammatic form. Figure 11.7 shows how we can combine the elements of space and time in examining the space-time path of individuals. In Figure 11.7b the example shows a group of children 1, 2, 3 and 4 who travel to school and then return home. In this case there is a co-location in space and time. In Figure 11.7c there is a co-location in time. A typical example would be comparing the space-time path of individuals who have the same work hours. In Figure 11.7d there is a co-location in space, where in this case individuals buy at the same shop at different times. Figure 11.8 shows the space-time budget in one day of a Swedish family. In this case the father seems to have a relatively easy time of it as the mother is constantly scurrying backward and forward delivering and picking up children from school.

Much of our activity in the city revolves around those routine items of behaviour, termed *pegs*, which structure our day. Most of us have to work and therefore our place and time of work provides the main peg around which our activities are organised. The routine activities guide the cadence of our day. As Parkes and Thrift (1980, p. 218) have noted, 'when the day begins, its programme is already printed and the stage is set for another performance.'

Our everyday behaviour hangs around these pegs because there are constraints to our space-time paths. For any individual we can consider a *prism* which defines the accessible space available at a specific time period. Figure 11.9 shows two

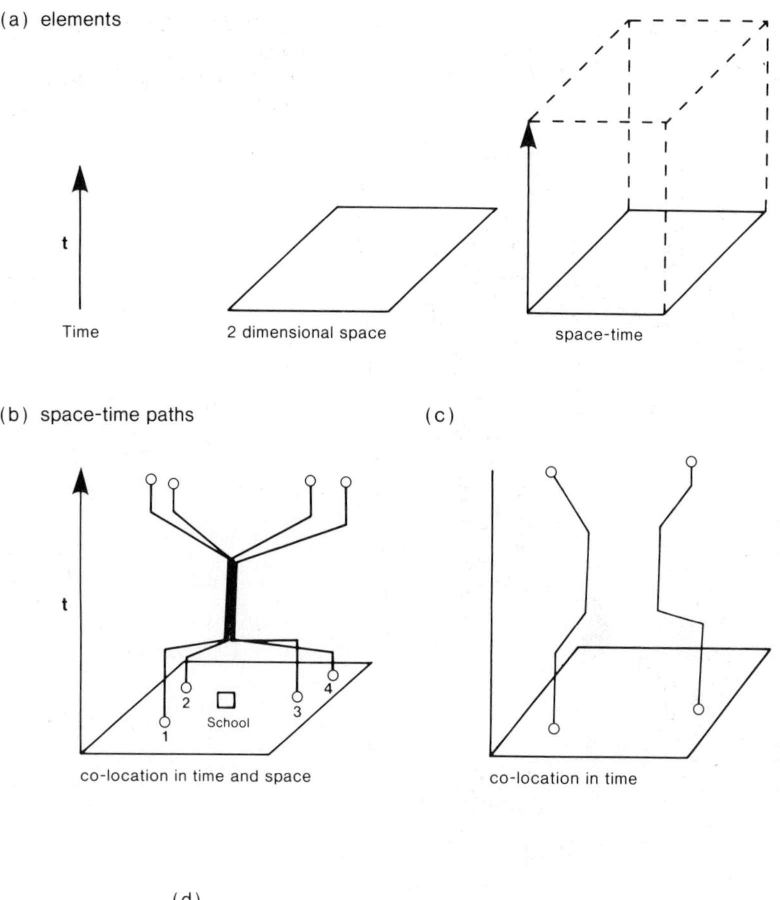

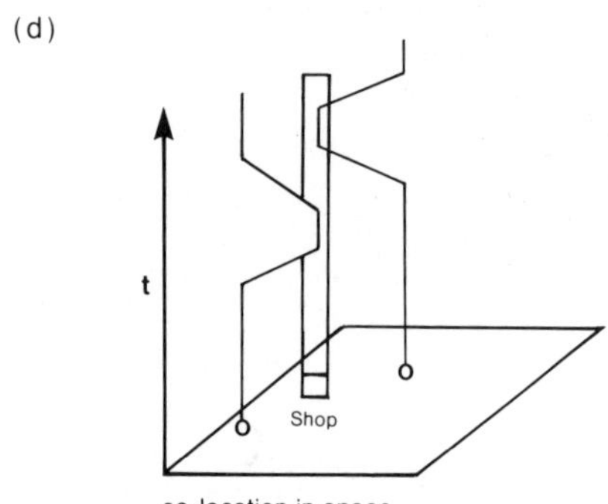

Figure 11.7 Space-time paths

contrasting prisms. In the case of A the individual is restricted to walking and the amount of space accessible at any particular time is thus limited because of the slow speed of travel. Individual B, by contrast, has access to a car and therefore can cover much larger distances over the same period of time. The prism is therefore much larger. We can conceive of space-time paths as a series of pegs when we are fixed in space and time, and prisms when there is some measure of individual choice

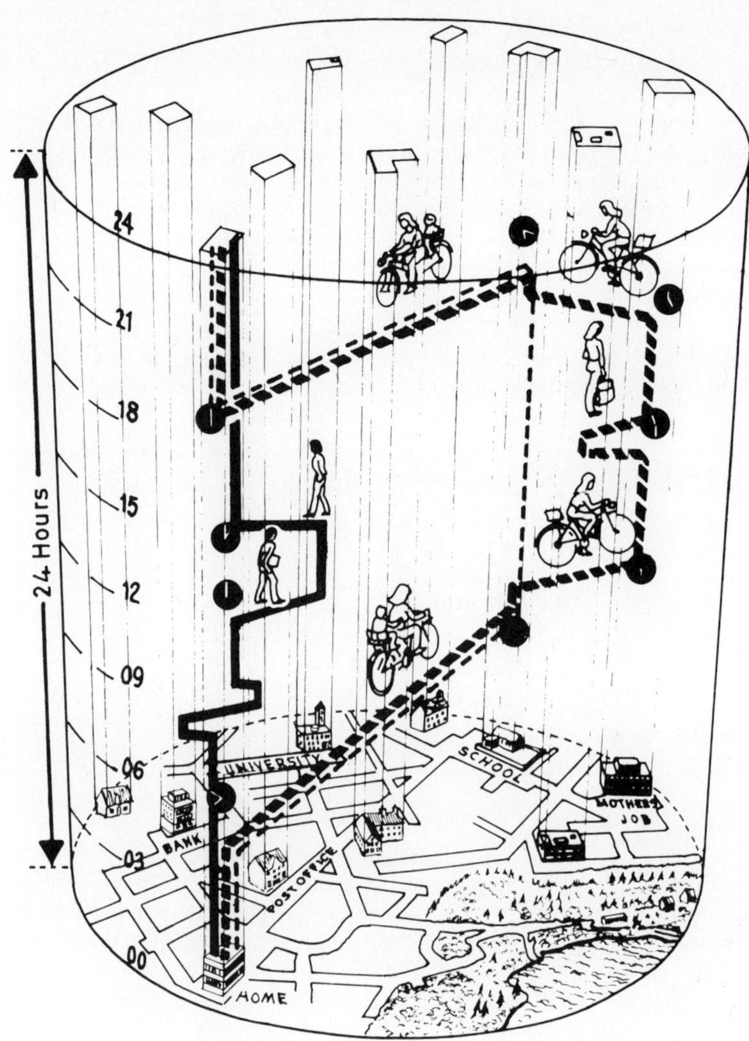

Figure 11.8 A space-time budget
Source: Parkes and Thrift, 1980

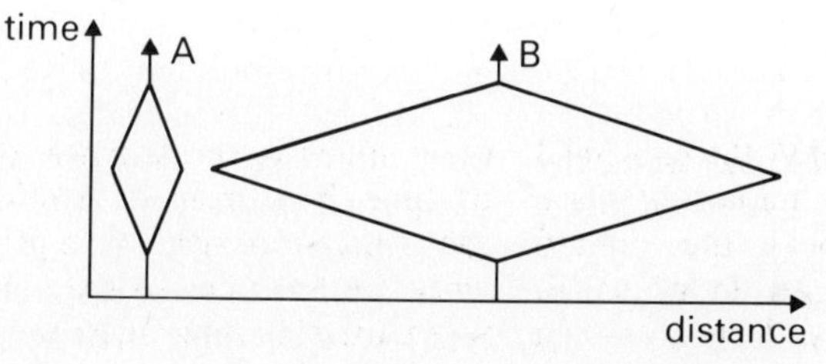

Figure 11.9 Prisms

SPACE-TIME DIARIES

Space-time paths are best recorded in a diary. The diary should record the starting time of an activity, its duration and frequency, and the sequential order of activities. Diaries are typically kept for one day. As an exercise get a one-day space-time diary constructed and get it filled in by different members of your class. Problems will emerge in the way different people name their activities. Try to obtain a standard set of terms which will aid comparison. Once you have ironed out this and any other problems, extend your sample. Plot the space-time paths of your different samples. What patterns do they trace?

A typical diary will have the following outline: leave the right-hand column blank so you can record standard activity terms and location identifiers.

Time	What did you do?	Time began	Time ended	Location	Leave blank
Midnight					
1 am					
2 am					
etc					

in the sequencing of activities. Figure 11.10 shows the idealised space-time path of an individual. This person, let's call him Joe, is in bed until 7.0 a.m. His work begins at 9.0 a.m. and he therefore has two hours in which there is some measure of choice; in the diagram the prism is relatively limited. From 9 to 1 Joe has to be at work, so he is fixed in both space and time. From 1 to 2, however, he has a lunch hour and therefore some measure of choice, but again the prism is limited in scope. He returns to work and does not finish till 5.0 p.m. Before he goes home to his meal at 7.0 p.m. he has another prism. His final fixed location is to be home in bed by 11.0 p.m. From the ending of his meal until he goes to bed he therefore has a degree of choice in where he can spend his time. Some evenings he may go to the cinema; others he may watch TV or do other activities in the home.

Prisms can be seen as areas of space-time choice. The degree of choice depends upon income and access to transport. Those with large incomes and ready access to automobiles have a much larger prism and hence greater choice than low-income households with poor transport facilities. The size of an individual's prism structures behaviour and circumscribes the area of choice in job and housing markets. Figure 11.11, for example, highlights the case of an individual whose space-time prism is relatively small. In this case it is a mother who has to drop off her child at 9 in the morning and pick the child up again in the afternoon. In the diagram A, B, and C are the times of the jobs available to the person. Notice how job C is entirely beyond the individual's prism and is therefore out of reach. Job A overlaps slightly but the individual can only take job B even although it may pay a lower salary. Some people are more constrained in space and time than others.

In a very real sense the urban population can be seen as space-time travellers. In our everyday

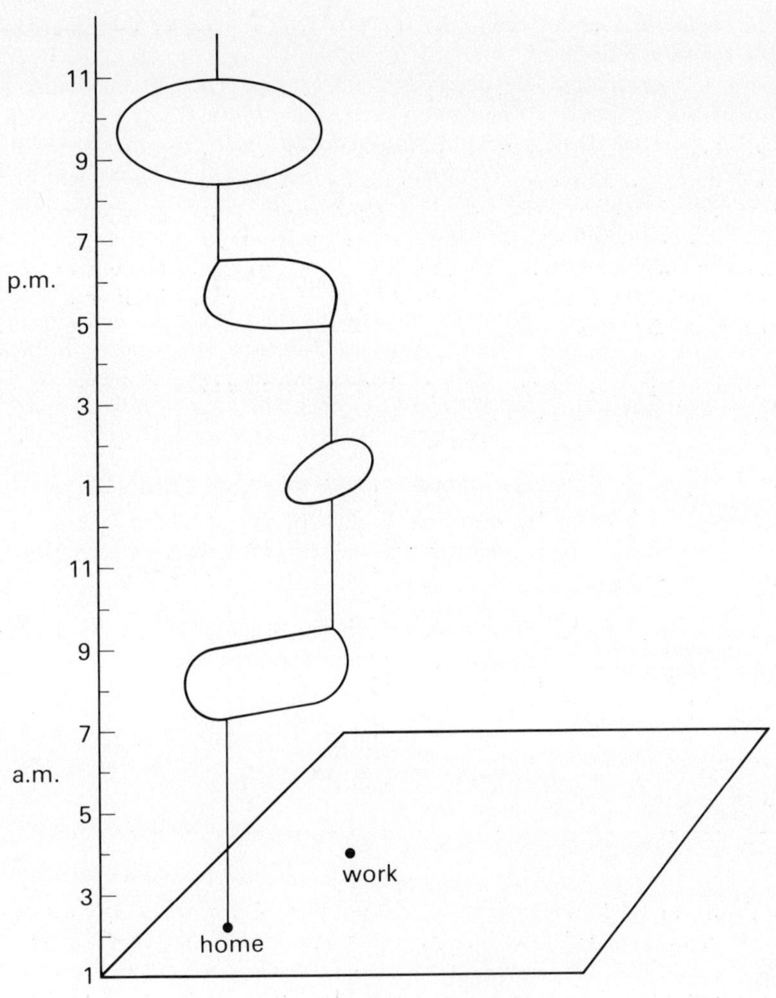

Figure 11.10 Pegs and prisms

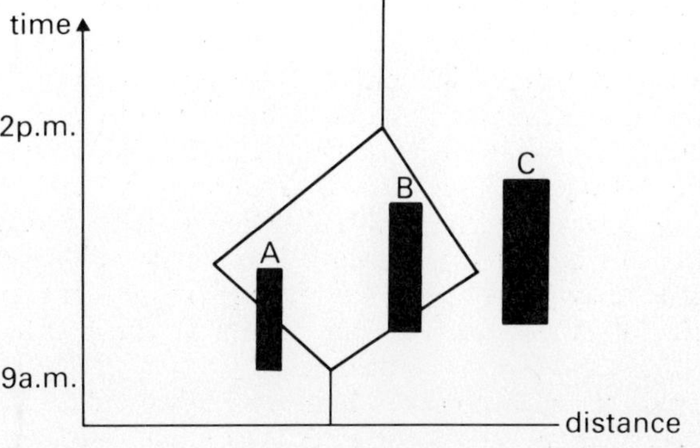

Figure 11.11 Prisms and job choice

activities we trace patterns through time and space. The physical structure of the city reflects and guides these space-time paths. Certain spaces are timed. The CBD operates during business hours. At nights and weekends it is deserted. The entertainment parts of the city only take on life in the evening and at the weekends. Different spaces of the city come into operation at different times. By our activities we time urban space.

GUIDE TO FURTHER READING

The classic work on urban environmental perception is:

Lynch, K. (1960), *The Image of The City*, MIT Press, Cambridge, Mass.

Subsequent work is reviewed in:

Gould, P. and White, R. (1974), *Mental Maps*, Penguin, Harmondsworth.

Pocock, D. and Hudson, R. (1978), *Images of The Urban Environment*, Macmillan, London.

Examples of individual and corporate behaviour include:

Adams, J.S. (1969), Directional bias in intra-urban mobility, *Economic Geography*, 45, 302-23.

McGregor, A. (1979), Area externalities and urban unemployment, In Jones, C. (ed.), *Urban Deprivation and The Inner City*, Croom Helm, London.

Weir, S. (1976), Red line districts, *Roof*, July, 109-14.

Time budgets are examined in:

BBC (1978), *The People's Activities and Use of Time*, Audience Research Department, British Broadcasting Corporation, London.

Szalai, A. et al. (1972), *The Uses of Time*, Mouton, The Hague, Netherlands.

The seminal work on space-time activity is:

Hagerstrand, T. (1970), What about people in regional science?, *Papers of the Regional Science Association*, 24, 7-21.

Since then there has been a large number of studies. For a general summary see:

Parkes, D.N. and Thrift, N.J. (1980), *Times, Spaces and Places*, Wiley, London.

12 The City as Ecological Unit

To see the city as an ecological unit is to consider the people/environment relationship. We can consider this relationship as a continuum. At one end are the people/ENVIRONMENT relationships, where people's lives are dominated by the environment. Neolithic settlments, for example, were always subject to severe environmental constraints and lived on the delicate balance between survival and catastrophe. In the PEOPLE/ENVIRONMENT relationship there is a measure of harmony. The environment is used but not irreparably damaged by human action. This state of affairs was more common in the past when there were limits on human action and it is the goal for many contemporary environmental activists. At the other end of the continuum is the PEOPLE/environment case where human actions, both planned and unforeseen consequences, dominate the ecological balance often with deleterious results. Two points need to be borne in mind. First, we have to be wary of the technological deterministic arguments which assume that technology itself causes the shift in people/environment relations. Technological sophistication can produce life-saving drugs as well as nuclear weapons of awesome destructive magnitude. It is not technology which is to blame but the way technology is used. Second, the PEOPLE/environment relationship does not imply the complete mastery of nature. In floods, storms, ecological breakdown, the environment strikes back.

The modern city is an example of the PEOPLE/environment relationship. The building of cities involves the creation of people-produced environments. Cities are attempts to escape from the tyranny of nature.

We can picture the city as a huge system which sucks in environmental inputs of energy, food and resources and produces a variety of environmental impacts. Let us examine some of these inputs and outputs.

ENVIRONMENTAL INPUTS

Energy

Human activity in the city uses up energy. When we leave heated dwellings to drive in cars to purchase goods and thow away cans, we use energy. The micro-climates we create by heating up places in cold climates and cooling them down in hot climates are energy-demanding. In seeking

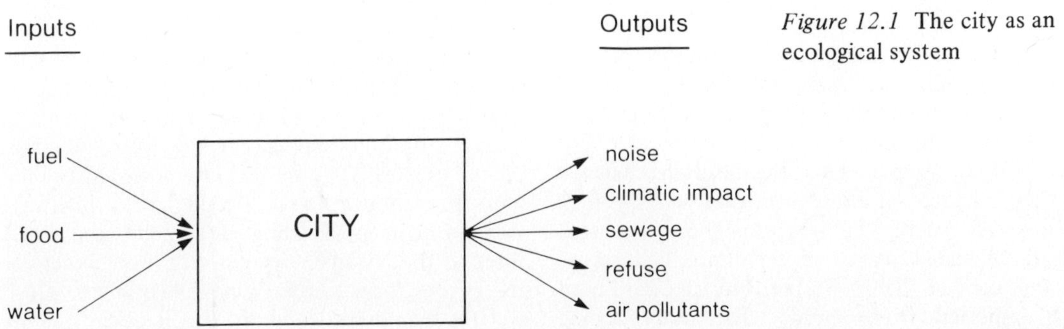

Figure 12.1 The city as an ecological system

Plate 49
The environment can strike back: a dust storm in Cairo

to overthrow the tyranny of nature we use up energy.

Two aspects of energy use are important. First, in the long term the use of energy has been growing. The increase reflects continued economic growth and rising real incomes. A typical US city of one million population now uses up 9,500 tons of fuel each and every day. There is an uneven distribution of use. The USA with 5 per cent of the world's population has over 30 per cent of the world's energy consumption. India, by contrast, has 15 per cent of the world's population but uses only 1.5 per cent of the world's energy consumption. The USA is a profligate user of energy even in comparison with the richer countries of Western Europe. Estimates suggest that 63 per cent of all energy used in the US is wasted. Houses are over-heated in winter, over-cooled in summer and automobiles are wasteful of gas.

Second, there is a great reliance on non-renewable fossil fuels. Over a third of all energy used in the world comes from oil, and this reliance has been steadily increasing. In 1900 9 per cent of the energy used in the United States came from oil. By 1950 this had increased to 40 per cent and by 1977 to 49 per cent. The result has been a greater reliance on those countries where oil is found. As energy consumption has increased, greater reliance is placed on the oil-producing areas of the world. In 1978, 43 per cent of US oil used was imported from abroad. The oil-producing nations have a powerful hand in price bargaining with the oil-consuming nations. The oil-producing countries of OPEC used this power to devastating effect in 1973 when the price of a barrel of oil was quadrupled. Paradoxically, the biggest user of oil, the United States, shielded its consumers from large energy price increases. Thus in 1979 while US drivers were paying one dollar a gallon, European drivers were paying two dollars for a gallon of petrol. The biggest sufferers of the OPEC oil increases were the poor third-world countries who had to pay more for the basic necessity of oil.

The era of relatively cheap fuel is over. At present we are like the giant, warm-blooded dinosaurs whose physiology was unable to adapt to the chilly conditions of the first Ice Age. We have felt the first cold blasts of a new energy era; can we adapt in time? To some extent there have already been some changes. Energy conservation is given a much higher priority, as is the search for alternative energy supplies. Whether we can find enough alternative energy at a reasonable price to maintain present-day activities is an important question.

In the medium to long term the changing energy situation may affect the form of cities. Cities, especially those of the core, with their sprawling suburbs tied together with highways along which gas-guzzling cars move, are really cities of the cheap energy era. In a more expensive energy era formal cities may change. Mass-transit systems may have to be developed since they use

THE LIMITS TO GROWTH

The title of a book published in 1972 summarised the more reactionary wing of the environmental argument. The book, *The Limits of Growth*, was written by a number of ecologists. Their aim was to investigate the global implications of accelerating industrialisation, rapid population growth, widespread malnutrition, depletion of non-renewable resources and pollution. They constructed a systems analysis type model and found that if present trends continued on this exponential growth curve then limits to growth would be experienced in just over a 100 years. Their model painted a picture of world collapse as resources are depleted and food *per capita* dwindles. They 'ran' this model with a number of assumptions, and their overall conclusion was that a global equilibrium could only be reached if population and industrial growth was stabilised, more emphasis was placed on soil management and ecologically conscious systems of agriculture and rates of resource depletion were reduced.

The limits to growth argument was very influential. The original book spawned a whole new area of literature. There were also many critics. Some highlighted empirical errors in the calculations, while others pointed out that reactionary policies were being disguised as inevitable, even desirable responses to the global predicament. The general response, however, was favourable. Although the predictions on specific timing now seem irrelevant, the general thrust of the argument now seems to be internalised into a conceptual understanding of the world. Most people accept that there are limits to growth.

References

Freeman, C. and Jahoda, M. (eds) (1978), *World Futures: The Great Debate*, Martin Robertson, London.

Meadows, D. et al. (1972), *The Limits to Growth*, Earth Island, London.

less energy and urban planners may seek to create more self-contained living areas where shops, industries and homes are located nearby in order to reduce the high energy costs of overcoming the home-workplace-shop separation. Some people are already voting with their feet. On the one hand, there is the move back to the central city by some middle-income groups, and on the other there is a move to small towns where activity centres are more concentrated. In both the central city and the small towns aggregate travel distances are reduced. Suburbs may become a thing of the (cheap energy) past. Future cities may be more concentrated, less dispersed and more energy-conscious.

Energy considerations will also be important in shaping the future growth of urban systems. Cities in energy-rich regions will be more attractive for firms than cities in energy-deficient regions. The decline of the frostbelt and the growth of the sunbelt in the United States, is an example of industry and the economic centre of gravity shifting from energy-deficit regions to energy-rich regions of the country. As energy costs increase, the energy considerations will become an important factor in industrial location strategies and in urban system growth and decline.

Food

Food is the basic necessity of life. The increase in world population, and especially the urban population, has increased the demand for more food. As people have left the countryside and moved to the cities, the immediate link between people and production of food has been broken. Urban populations rely on others to produce their food.

At the world scale two sets of problems are

encountered. The first is associated with the lack of nutrition. Statistics are scanty, but as a rough guide we can say that almost a third of the world's population go hungry. Actual estimates vary from 500 million (18 per cent of the world's population) to 1,600 million (40 per cent) people classified as underfed. The reasons for this are many. It is only rarely that there is not enough food. In most cases the problems of lack of distribution, too-low incomes, and what the Oxford-based economist Amartya Sen (1981) calls the collapse of the entitlement system mean that the links are broken between the supply of food and the urgent demand.

The second problem is associated with the form of agriculture. Recent years have seen tremendous improvement in agricultural production, especially in the core as output per agricultural worker has increased. The growth of agri-business and agri-corporations has seen increases in productivity. But this increase has been purchased by the use of mechanisation, growing use of fertilisers and pesticides, all of which are heavy energy users as well as containing the possibility of being ecologically damaging in the long run. The use of DDT, for example, while killing off unwanted pests, can also damage human health and disrupt the gauze-like sensitivity of the local ecological system with deleterious results. A National Academy of Sciences study of pesticides suggest that 25 per cent of them may cause cancer.

Increases in agricultural productivity necessary to feed the expanding urban population may be purchased at the expense of the workings of the ecosystem and human welfare.

Water

Water is a vital resource. It is one of those essential ingredients of life that people in the richer countries with readily available supplies take for granted. Water is used for: irrigation to grow food, industrial uses, and domestic and commercial use. The breakdown of uses in the USA is shown in Table 12.1. Notice in this table the difference between the average daily *per capita* use in the United States and the world figures shown in brackets. The USA uses more water on average than the rest of the world. There is a clear relationship between wealth of country and water use.

The main problem with fresh water supply is its limited supply and uneven distribution. There are definite limits to the supply of water. As water use increases and the limit is being reached, the price of water will rise and the carefree attitude to water may then become a thing of the past. The demand/supply equation varies across the globe and within countries. Across the world, while Norway is rich in water, the Middle East has had to install expensive desalination plants, in order to turn salt water to fresh water. Even within countries there are variations in water availability. Figure 12.2 shows the disparity between water and population distribution in the United Kingdom. The disparity involves the construction of costly pipelines to transport water to people. This will be one of the main future ecological constraints on the growth of some of the sunbelt cities of the United States.

Table 12.1 Water use in the USA 1975

	Total withdrawal (trillion gallons)	*Average daily* per capita *use (gallons)**
Irrigation	52	666(460)
Industrial use	61	784(38)
Domestic and commercial use	11	145(28)

* World average figures shown in brackets.

The supply of fresh water is being further reduced by pollution. Estimates suggest that 2 per cent of the world's fresh water supply is being polluted each year. The problem is greatest in the poor third-world cities lacking proper sanitation and sewerage infrastructure. The majority of the urban population in the periphery drinks contaminated water. The results are marked. Water-borne intestinal diseases affect 30 per cent of the world's population, 10 million people die from them and on average 27,000 people die each day due to diseases from contaminated water. Diseases such as schisposomiasis, which affects 300 million people, almost all in the periphery are spread through contaminated water. The use of polluted water not only transmits diseases, but debilitates the population, making them more susceptible to other diseases and illness. In the periphery the

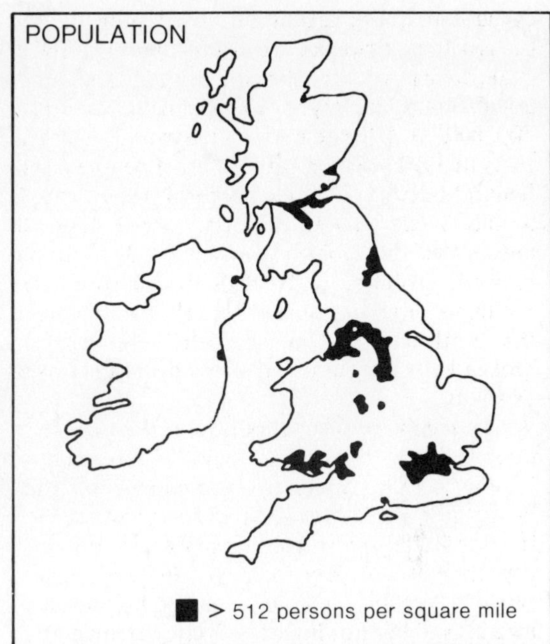

Figure 12.2 Water and population distribution

quality of water is, like the quality of life, very poor.

URBAN IMPACTS

Climatic change

Cities modify climates in a number of ways. The most important is through the warming of the surrounding area to produce an *urban heat island*. This area of warmer air around cities is caused by the large amount of heat produced in the city by human action and the heat absorption of the urban fabric of tarmac and concrete. Heat is absorbed by the manmade surfaces during the day, stored, and released by night. The net result is for the air around cities to be warmer than the surrounding rural areas.

The effect is to reduce the need for heat in cities in colder climates but to increase the need for air conditioning in hotter cities. The heat island in winter London means you can turn down the central heating, while in summer Los

Table 12.2 Climatic change caused by cities

Element	*Parameter*	*Urban compared with rural (– less; + more)*
Temperature	annual mean	+0.7°c
	winter maximum	+1.5°c
	length of freeze-free season	+2 to 3 weeks
Wind speed (short buildings)	annual mean	–20 to 30%
	extreme gusts	–10 to 20%
	frequency of calms	+5 to 20%
(tall buildings)	annual mean	+10 to 20%
	extreme gusts	+10 to 20%
Cloudiness	cloud frequency	+5 to 10%
	fogs	+100% in winter/+30% summer
Precipitation	amounts	+5 to 10%
	days	+10%
	snow days	–14%

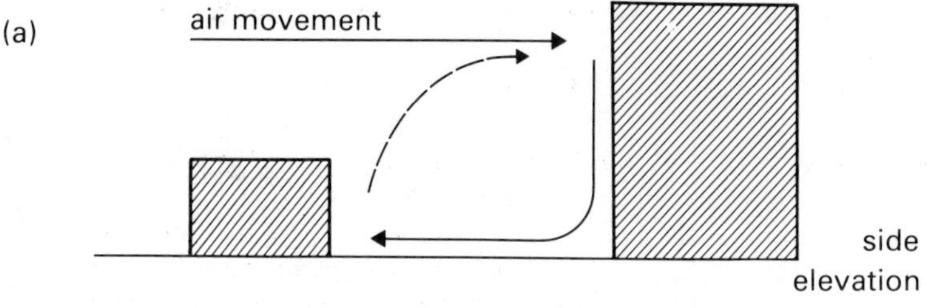

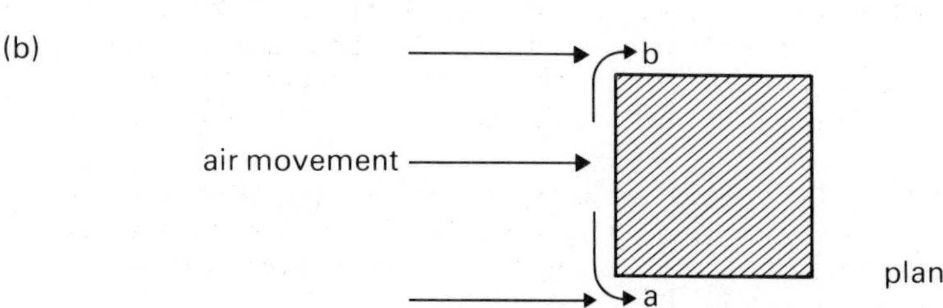

Figure 12.3 Buildings and air movement

Angeles you have to turn the air conditioning up.

Other climatic effects include increased precipitation because of thermally induced upward movement of air and the increase in cloud and raindrop nuclei generated by urban dust. Cities are thus cloudier, more thundery and slightly wetter than surrounding areas.

The buildings in cities also affect wind patterns. When the buildings are relatively small the overall effect of ciites is to reduce wind speed. The city becomes a sheltered micro-climate. However, as buildings increase in size the effect changes. Large isolated buildings obstruct air movement. Some wind is deflected downward creating winds on the ground going away from the building. A vortex can be created causing blustery conditions. The wind is also deflected around corners. If we take a plan view of a tall building as in Figure 12.3b we can see that the wind is deflected either over the top of the building or around the sides. The pedestrians at a and b will feel the effects of increased wind. The taller the building the greater the wind. Around the huge cavern-like structures of New York, for example, the force of the wind can be felt on the body.

Air pollution

Human activity in the modern city pollutes the atmosphere. Industrial processes, combustion of fuel and automobile engines all emit a variety of pollutants to the atmosphere. Fuel combustion is the biggest single source of air pollution; the car is a major air polluter. Air pollution occurs throughout the world in rural as well as urban areas. But the concentration of pollution is highest in urban areas as there are more sources of pollution in a small area. The air around cities is more polluted than air in rural areas and the larger the city the greater the pollution.

Over the long term and across the world air pollution has been increasing. The combined effects of industrialisation and urbanisation have led to greater fuel combustion, more industrial plants, and bigger cities generating more traffic.

The effects of air pollution are many. The

Table 12.3 The urban heat island

City	*Annual mean urban-rural temperature difference, +°c*
Chicago	0.6
Washington, D.C.	0.6
Los Angeles	0.7
Paris	0.7
Moscow	1.0
New York	1.1
London	1.3

MAKING THE POLLUTERS PAY

Industry is an important source of pollution. Factories belch out smoke, dump effluents and produce noice. Industrial processes can be dirty, smelly processes.

The main benefits of industry accrue to the shareholders and employers. The costs of their pollution-producing processes, however, are borne by the local community who may have their air polluted, their peace disrupted and their water contaminated. The problems in introducing pollution-control measures are twofold. First, the industrial corporations will fight against measures which involve them in high costs and a reduction in profit. The political scientist M.A. Crenson has shown with regard to air-pollution control in US cities how large corporations can suppress the pollution issue. Even if the measures are passed, the corporations will seek to influence the form of the legislation in order to minimise any cost of introducing pollution-control measures.

Second, if pollution is accepted as a problem, how can the costs and benefits be measured in order to assess pollution taxes or make compensatory payments? *Cost-benefit analysis* measures the price for environmental resources and the consequences of pollution-generating developments. Items included in a cost-benefit analysis are

direct costs: e.g. in air-pollution areas households have extra laundry, painting and repair, etc.

indirect costs: e.g. in air-pollution areas such costs include (a) reduction in house prices, (b) deteriorating health of local inhabitants.

The difficulty with cost-benefit analysis is that it becomes almost impossible to put a monetary value on some indirect costs. How much does a good pair of lungs cost?

References

Crenson, M.A. (1971), *The Un-Politics of Air Pollution: A Study of Non-Decision-Making in The Cities*, Johns Hopkins University Press, Baltimore.

Steck, H.J. (1975), Private influence on environmental policy, *Environmental Law*, 241-81.

Williams, A. (1972), Cost-benefit analysis: bastard science and/or insidious poison in the body politic, *Journal of Public Economics*, 1, 199-225.

greatest is to the health of urban dwellers, as there is a relationship between levels of air pollution and injury to the human respiratory system. There is a steady deterioration in the respiratory system of long-term urban dwellers and urban living is a major health hazard to young children, especially airborne lead pollution. In the Middle Ages when cities were islands of freedom in the sea of feudalism there was a saying in Europe which went 'city air makes people free.' Today most city air makes people ill.

The longer-term effects of air pollution are more difficult to predict. However, two hypotheses have been suggested. The first is the existence of the so-called *greenhouse* effect. It has been argued that the continual build-up of carbon dioxide (CO^2) in the atmosphere leads to a warming effect with three possible consequences:

(a) Warming of the ice caps leading to severe flooding.

(b) Increase in the areas of desert.

(c) Extension of the growing season in the cereal-producing regions of the world.

The second hypothesis relates to the ozone layer which acts to filter out harmful ultraviolet radiation from the sun. Some scientists have suggested that the chemicals in aerosol emissions combine with the oxygen in the ozone to destroy the filtering properties of the layer. The ultimate

Table 12.4 Major air pollutants

Pollutant	*Source*	*Effect*
Carbon oxides	Smoke, car fumes	Aggravates heart and respiratory diseases; can cause death at high concentrations.
Sulphur oxides	Burning of oil and coal	Aggravates respiratory diseases; cause of 'acid rain'.
Nitrogen oxides	Lighting, combustion in motor vehicles and industrial plants	Aggravates respiratory diseases; acid rain; causes photochemical smoke.
Hydrocarbons (methane, butane, benxene)	Incomplete combustion of fossil fuels	Injures respiratory system; photochemical smog.
Particulates (Solid particles suspended in air)		
Dust/soot	Coal burning, combustion	Injures respiratory system; causes cancer.
asbestos	damage to fireproofing; deterioration in brake linings	
Metals		
E.g. lead	Automobile exhausts	Respiratory diseases; cancer; nervous disorders.

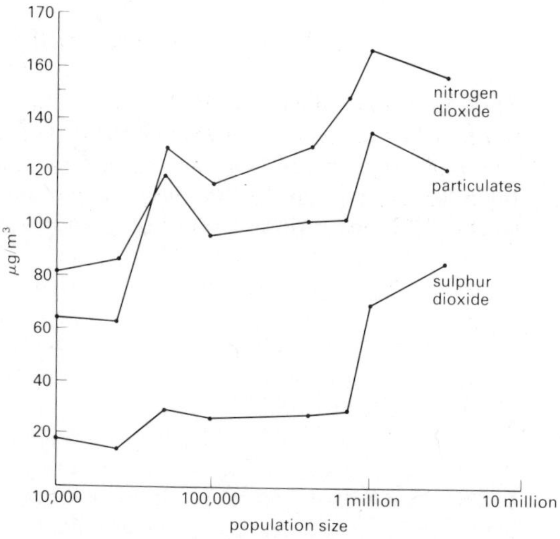

Figure 12.4 Air pollution and city size
Source: after Berry and Horton, 1974

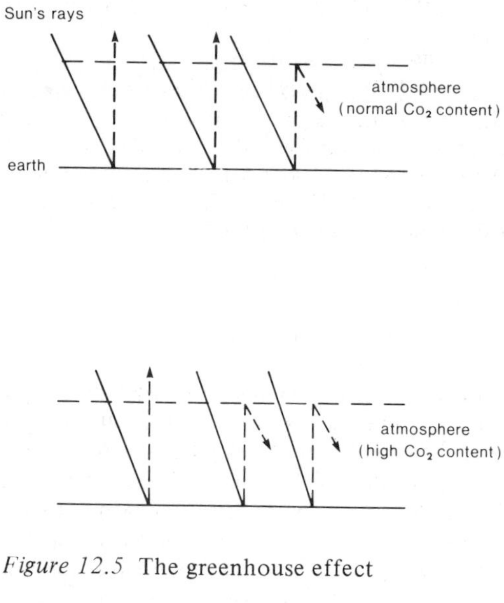

Figure 12.5 The greenhouse effect

THE ENVIRONMENTAL MOVEMENT

The late 1960s and early 1970s saw an important development in the political scene, especially in the richer countries. The era saw the rise of the environmental movement. Interest in the environment increased, and this can be seen in the greater coverage of environmental issues in the newspapers (Figure 12A), the growth of environmental-orientated interests groups (Figure 12B) and a whole variety of governmental regulations.

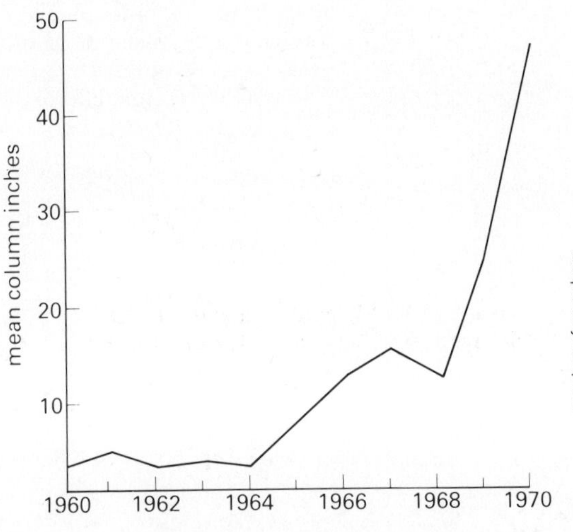

Figure 12A Environmental interest: the case of the *New York Times*
Source: after Munton, D. and Brody, L. (1970), American public opinion and environmental pollution, Ohio State University Department of Political Science Technical Report

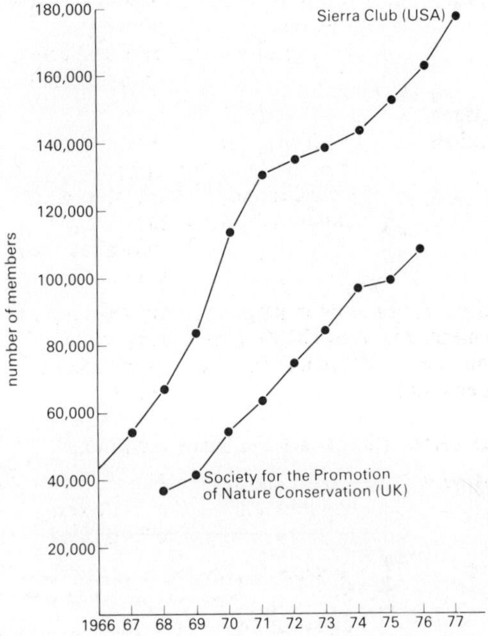

Figure 12B Growth of environmental groups

Environmental awareness had been provoked by a whole series of books, perhaps the first being Rachel Carson's *Silent Spring*, published in 1962. The tenor of the literature, which can be seen from the titles; 'Only One Earth' 'Spaceship Earth' etc., pointed to the delicate ecological balance, the limits to growth and the long-term costs of pollution and environmental degradation. The environmental movement was further stimulated by the rapid industrial growth of the 1960s and early 1970s, which did have deleterious effects on the environment.

The late 1970s and early 1980s have seen the environmental issue moving into the background of the political stage. To some extent the environmental movement has been successful in so far as environmental issues are considered as important; they are now an integral part of the intelligent person's view of the world. However, the waning of interest (see Figure 12C)

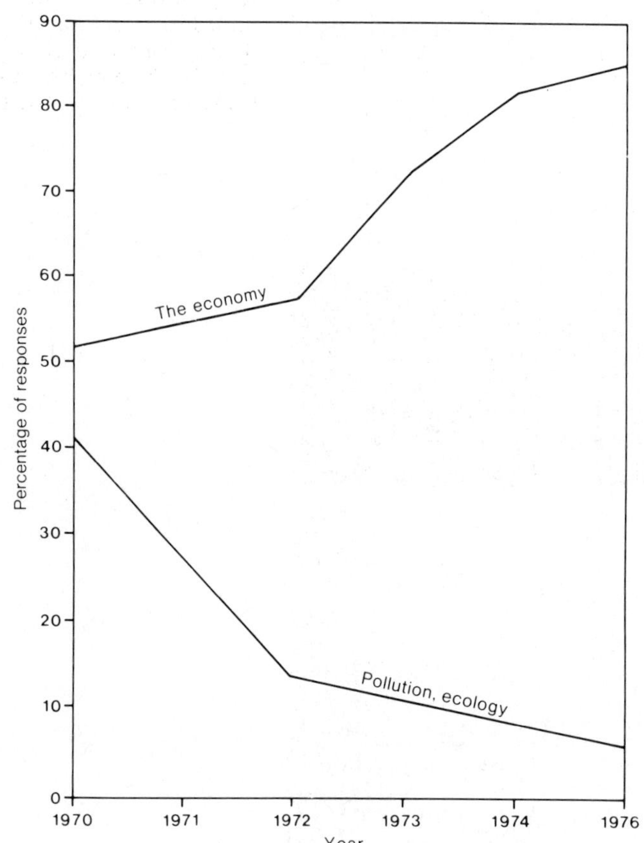

Figure 12C Biggest problems facing people
Harris Survey question: 'What are the two or three biggest problems facing people like yourself which you would like to see the next President (Congress) do something about? (Problems omitted are welfare reform, older people, foreign policy, racial discrimination and housing.)
*No data were available for 1971

reflects other issues elbowing their way into the centre of the stage. Since the mid 1970s public concern, in the USA as elsewhere, has been with employment, inflation and all those things which we associate with the term 'the economy'.

Reference

A useful discussion of the environmental movement is:

Sandbach, F. (1980), *Environment, Ideology and Policy*, Blackwell, Oxford.

Plates 50 and 51
Air pollution: (50) the view of Los Angeles from this Beverly Hills location is entirely obscured by smog; (51) smog cover in Athens

effect will be that more harmful ultraviolet rays will reach the earth. Both of these hypotheses are possibilities, not accurate predictions. But even this lack of predictability is in itself frightening. We simply do not know the full repercussions of human action on the long-term stability of our fragile ecosystem.

Smog

The most visible form of urban air pollution are the palls of smog which hang over many cities. We can distinguish between two major types of smog.

Industrial smog (sometimes called grey air) occurs in cities with cold, wet climates. It is composed of particulates and sulphur oxides. The smog is produced by the burning of coal and oil which produces sulphur which in turn reacts with the oxygen in the atmosphere to produce sulphur dioxide. Eventually the sulphur dioxide is converted to sulphur trioxide which reacts with water in the atmosphere to produce sulphuric acid. When washed out on to the earth this is termed acid rain, and it is dangerous to public health as well as corroding metals and other materials. Some of the sulphuric acid combines with ammonia to produce ammonium sulphate, a substance very hazardous to health. Industrial smog is eventually washed away by rain or wafted away by the winds. When the rain doesn't come and the winds don't blow, however, industrial smog builds up and those with respiratory diseases become more affected. This was the case in London in 1952 when almost 4,000 people died and in New York in 1965 when 400 people died.

Photochemical smog (sometimes called brown air) occurs above cities with warm dry climates. The main source of photochemical smog is the internal combustion engine. Car exhausts produce nitric oxide which combines with the oxygen in the air to produce the yellow-brown gas of nitrogen dioxide. Some of this combines with hydrogen in the atmosphere to produce nitric acid, the acid rain of warm dry climates.

Over the long term and worldwide air pollution has been increasing. There is now a growing realisation that it is hazardous to health. The richer countries have already begun to introduce anti-pollution measures; in the USA lead content in petrol has been reduced and in Britain the 1956 Clean Air Act enforced better standards of air pollution control. The result has been a reduction in smoke emissions, the amount of sulphur dioxide and the number of fog days. Pollution control works, but it is expensive. In the giant third-world cities pollution measures have yet to be formulated, let alone implemented. While the richer countries can afford pollution control measures and have the political power to enforce them, the states in the periphery have neither the concern nor the money to improve the quality of the environment for the mass of urban dwellers. A new type of inequality is appearing at the world level, a disparity in the quality of the urban environment.

Hydrological effects and water pollution

Cities have a number of effects on the hydrological system. The general trend is for a greater reliance on water resources as urbanisation increases, and there is a growing danger of overloading the hydrological system. Overloading occurs when more water is used than is replaced and/or the level of pollution is greater than the absorption capacity of the hydrological system. A river can absorb pollution given time. But if the rate of pollution is too high, the absorption capacity of the hydrological system is overloaded and the river becomes completely polluted.

The two most general urban impacts are using too much water and creating too much pollution. Since we have already dealt with water resources in a previous section of this chapter, this section will concentrate on outlining the level and character of water pollution. One of the single most important forms of pollution is the reduction of oxygen caused by the dumping of domestic sewage and industrial waste into rivers. These wastes impose an oxygen demand – termed Biochemical Oxygen Demand (BOD) – on the river and if the BOD is too great the river cannot reduce the wastes to inoffensive compounds. Without the presence of oxygen the wastes rot and the river becomes sterile. Around cities the greatest pollution comes from domestic sewage and industrial wastes. In the New York metropolitan area alone 6.8 billion litres of sewage per

Table 12.5 Major water pollutants

Pollutant	*Source*	*Effect*
Oxygen-reducing wastes	Domestic sewage; industrial wastes	'Kill' rivers
Disease-carrying agents (bacteria and viruses)	Domestic sewage	Waterborne diseases (typhoid, cholera, etc.)
Inorganic material (acids, salts, toxic metals)	Industrial waste	Hazardous to health; at extreme concentrations can kill
Organic chemicals (pesticides, detergents)	Domestic and industrial waste	Hazardous to health; kill fish
Radioactive substances	Natural sources, nuclear power plants	Causes cancer

day are shoved into the Hudson and East Rivers. With increasing urbanisation, water pollution has been increasing. Changes in the domestic economy have also made pollution worse. The phosphate level in rivers has been on the rise because the use of detergents (which contain phosphate) has been increasing.

Pollution control can be effective and, while the general worldwide trend has been for increasing pollution, there are local success stories. The Thames running through London is a case in point. Throughout the last 500 years it has been one of the most polluted rivers in the world. However, since the 1950s public investments to the tune of £100 million and the enforcement of new reduced levels of discharge for Thameside industry has halted the ecological deterioration. Despite increasing population, the Thames is now a cleaner river than it was a hundred years ago.

Pollution control is expensive. It also implies political will. Pollution has been an important topic of public discourse in the core since the 1960s but in the periphery there seems to be less popular support for pollution control. Perhaps this reflects the hierarchy of needs. When you are well fed and decently housed you can worry about the general quality of life and the state of the environment. But if you are struggling to get enough food, environmental concerns seem less pressing. In the long term, however, they are of vital concern for everyone.

Waste and garbage

The typical US city of 1 million gets through 2,000 tons of refuse a day. For all intents and purposes most cities are garbage-producing systems. They use up non-renewable resources and they dirty the environment. The deleterious effects of the production of waste and garbage are not only restricted to environmental concerns. It can be a costly business. In 1975 US local government spent $4 billion in collecting and disposing of urban solid wastes. The amount of waste produced is not an inevitable part of urban life. It reflects society's and individuals' attitudes. The huge amount of wasteful packaging reflects the throw-away approach, a mentality which says resources are infinite. Such attitudes are dangerous . . . and expensive.

Noise pollution

Cities are noisy places. The typical urban street produces a noise level of between 80 and 90 decibels.

The more noise and the greater the exposure the greater the effect. Households who inhabit busy urban streets for more than 15 years are on average likely to experience a 50 per cent reduction in the hearing capacity. After work conditions, urban noise is the biggest source of noise pollution. The effects of noise pollution vary from

Plate 52
The Klong which flows through Bangkok is very polluted. Notice the rotting rubbish on the surface of the river in the right of the picture

FROM PEOPLE/environment TO PEOPLE/ENVIRONMENT

The trend towards a PEOPLE/environment relationship is reversible. There are those in communes and small, self-contained societies who have turned their back on contemporary technology in order to seek a smaller-scale closer relationship with each other and the environment. The change can also occur by harnessing technology in the proper manner, e.g. the use of an urban recovery plan which uses modern technology to reclaim waste in order to heat homes. It is too simplistic to condemn all technology. When combined with an ideology which is aware of the delicate nature of our environmental context, then technology carefully handled and democratically controlled can be used to create a harmonious people/environment relationship.

annoyance – almost 50 per cent of US households interviewed in 1974 thought that their neighbourhoods were too noisy – through to deterioration of the aural mechanisms. Almost 16 million US citizens suffer from acute hearing loss and 30 million have significant hearing loss. Noise pollution in cities is incessant and continual. It is just one of the elements which make living in cities that much more stressful.

CONCLUSIONS

If we can stand back and cast a quick glance over human history we would see that with the growth of industrialisation and urbanisation the people/environment relationship has changed. The move has been from a people/ENVIRONMENT relationship towards a PEOPLE/environment relationship. Contemporary cities use much of the world's non-renewable resources and through the production of heat, dirt, noise, waste and garbage they have a deleterious impact on the environment. The effects on human health and long-term ecological balance are obvious. More recently, there has been a growing awareness, in the richer countries at least, that things must change. Resources extraction and environmental degradation cannot continue indefinitely without serious effects on our long-term tenure of the earth. Pollution control, the reduction of waste and the search for renewable resources are all trends in the right direction. However, in the periphery pollution control is well down the list of governments' agendas. An emerging division between rich and poor is the division between the better-cared-for, and the poorly maintained environments.

GUIDE TO FURTHER READING

There are a number of very good general textbooks on people/environment relationships. See:

Ehrlich, P.R., Ehrlich, A.M. and Holdren, J.P. (1977), *Ecoscience: population, resources, environment*, Freeman, San Francisco.

Goudie, A. (1981), *The Human Impact. Man's Role in Environmental Change*, Basil Blackwell, Oxford.

Miller, G.T. (1979), *Living in The Environment*, Wadsworth, Belmont, California.

Thomas, W.L. (ed.) (1956), *Man's Role in Changing the Face of the Earth,* University of Chicago Press.

On the basic issue of food see:

Sen, A. (1981), *Poverty and Famines: An Essay on Entitlement and Deprivation*, Clarendon Press, Oxford.

Specific works on people/environment relationships in cities include:

Berry, B.J.L. and Horton, F.E. (1974), *Urban Environmental Management*, Prentice Hall, Englewood Cliffs, N.J.

Douglas, I. (1981), The city as an ecosystem, *Progress in Physical Geography*, 5, 315-67.

Wolman, M.G. (1965), The metabolism of cities, *Scientific American*, 213, 179-90.

The urban impact on the atmosphere is discussed in:

Chandler, T.J. (1965), *The Climate of London*, Hutchinson, London.

Ferrar, T.A. (ed.) (1976), *The Urban Costs of Climate Modification*, Wiley, New York.

Thompson, R. (1978), *Atmosphere contamination*, Geographical Paper 68, University of Reading, England.

The hydrological impact is covered by:

McCaull, J. and Crossland, J. (1974), *Water Pollution*, Harcourt Brace Jovanovich, New York.

The problems of waste are treated by:

National Academy of Sciences (1975), *Resource Recovery From Municipal Solid Wastes*, National Academy of Sciences, Washington D.C.

Small, W.E. (1971), *Third Pollution: The National Problem of Solid Waste Disposal*, Praeger, New York.

The sources and effects of noise pollution are discussed in:

Environmental Protection Agency (1974), *Noise Pollution: Now Hear This*, EPA, Washington D.C.

Index